AF538967

The Birth of Indian Liberalism

Praise for *The Birth of Indian Liberalism*

"*The Birth of Indian Liberalism* is a remarkable achievement. It restores agency and cognitive autonomy to a group of thinkers and political actors who have been scorned or forgotten."
– John Dunn, University of Cambridge

"Parmanand's *Letters*, introduced with characteristic erudition by Rahul Sagar, open a fascinating new vista onto the vigour and creativity of modern Indian liberalism."
– Cécile Laborde, University of Oxford

"In restoring this forgotten argument, Rahul Sagar revolutionises the history of South Asia's political thinking."
– Jon Wilson, Nanyang Technological University

The Birth of Indian Liberalism

Mama Parmanand's *Letters to an Indian Raja*

Rahul Sagar

JUGGERNAUT BOOKS
C-I-128, First Floor, Sangam Vihar, Near Holi Chowk,
New Delhi 110080, India

Published in the United Kingdom by Manchester University Press 2026
First published in India by Juggernaut Books 2026

10 9 8 7 6 5 4 3 2 1

P-ISBN: 9789353453619
E-ISBN: 9789353456047

Typeset in Sabon Lt Std by New Best-set Typesetters Ltd

Printed at Thomson Press India Private Limited

Dedicated to
Dennis F. Thompson
teacher, advisor, liberal

Contents

Illustrations

Tables

Preface

For more than a decade now, I have immersed myself in the archives, seeking to understand how Indians liberated themselves from themselves. The least known part of this history, I have come to realize, is the contribution made by Maharajas and their *dewans* (ministers). This neglect is not accidental. Not a few tomes have been written on the Meiji, the Kaisers, and the Qing, describing these monarchies as the makers of modern Japan, Germany, and China. But the Maharajas of India have been viewed very differently. Because they submitted to British paramountcy and retreated into their *mahals* (palaces), they have been cast aside as irrelevant and decadent – as big landlords with small minds and weak hearts. The archives reveal that this depiction is deeply mistaken. Hardship is always the nurse of reflection – and so it was in nineteenth-century India. The abrupt ascent of British power and European ideas compelled Maharajas and their *dewans* to grapple with new concepts and sentiments. The results were varied, for the Native States were not a single entity. Many rulers lapsed into despondency or self-indulgence, but others set about vigorously reforming their kingdoms. The latter came to popularly be termed progressive Maharajas. They deserved the title then and they deserve to be studied now.

It was during such study, when I was scrutinizing the reading lists that tutors had prescribed to their wards in the Native States, that I came across a curiously titled entry, *Letters to an Indian Raja from a Political Recluse* (1891). When I tracked down this volume, of which only a handful of copies survive, I discovered that it was an artful presentation on the reasons why Maharajas ought to transform their regimes into constitutional monarchies. Appearing in an era in which intellectuals invariably wrote essays or gave speeches criticizing colonial rule, *Letters* stood out as a text that actually *proposed* a regime. This made it, in effect, the first work of political theory to be published in modern India. The discovery was thrilling – but there were pressing questions still to answer. Who was "A Political Recluse"? Why had he taken the trouble to write *Letters*? As I cast about for answers, I came upon a second edition of *Letters* that had been published in 1919.

The erudite preface to this edition, written by N. G. Chandavarkar, the former president of the Indian National Congress, revealed that the author was a little-remembered intellectual by the name of Narayan Mahadev Parmanand. This reclusive figure had published *Letters*, Chandavarkar shared, in the hope that Maharajas would outpace British India in freeing individuals from their shackles. Chandavarkar's tantalizing but brief remarks only stoked my curiosity: What had led Parmanand to have such high hopes of the Native States and why had his ambitious work disappeared from the shelves?

So began a search to shed light on a figure who had made it a point to live in the shadows. As I followed clues and assembled pieces, a hidden world revealed itself. I came to understand why Parmanand's contemporaries revered him as a political *rishi* (sage). Whether it was helping the Maharaja of Kutch outwit the Viceroy or exposing British officers guilty of corruption, or whether it was urging the Maharaja of Baroda to patronize Jyotirao Phule or crafting memorials that shook the Bombay authorities – his fingerprints were everywhere, and his name was nowhere. Impressed by Parmanand's selfless endeavors and his remarkable ideas, I made it my mission to bring them to wider notice. I have summarized what I have learned in the introductory essay that opens this volume. It is my humble tribute to the *saptarishi*s (seven sages) of Elphinstone who allowed me to inhabit their world and savor the feeling that Machiavelli describes in his famous letter detailing his days:

> When evening has come, I return to my house and go into my study … I enter the ancient courts of ancient men, where, received by them with affection, I feed on that food which only is mine and which I was born for, where I am not ashamed to speak with them and to ask them the reason for their actions; and they in their kindness answer me; and for four hours of time I do not feel boredom, I forget every trouble, I do not dread poverty, I am not frightened by death; entirely I give myself over to them.

Constitution Day, November 26, 2025

Acknowledgements

This book is a product of the generous research funding that NYU Abu Dhabi provides my *Ideas of India* initiative, which has allowed me to comb archives for long-lost works of Indian political thought. I am indebted to Dean Paula England and Associate Dean Janet Kelly for supporting this research, and I am grateful as ever to the administrators that manage my grants: Diana Pangan, Emily Del Monte, Nicoleta Nichifor, and Lily Moinette. I am also much obliged to the NYUAD Grant for Publication Program whose support made it possible for me to publish the map and photographs in this volume, and to Blaine Robbins and the Government and Public Policy cluster and Jeffrey Jensen and the Global Dynamics cluster for supporting travel to workshops where I presented early versions of this manuscript.

I completed this manuscript during my time as the Laurance S. Rockefeller Visiting Professor at the University Center for Human Values (UCHV) at Princeton University. I cannot express enough how thankful I am for this valuable opportunity. The theorists at Princeton have long been role models and I will always be indebted to them for their intellectual and personal generosity: Stephen Macedo, Alan Patten, Jan-Werner Müller, Chuck Beitz, Melissa Lane, Philip Pettit, Annie Stilz, Gregory Conti, and Pratap Bhanu Mehta. My thanks also to Derek Balcom, Tammy Hojeibane, Dawn Disette, and Gayle Brodsky for making my time at Princeton so comfortable.

I was fortunate to be able to present this manuscript before audiences at the Center for the Advanced Study of India (CASI) at the University of Pennsylvania, the Edmond & Lily Safra Center for Ethics at Harvard University, the Political Theory Workshop at George Washington University, the Association for Global Political Thought (AGPT) at American University, the UCHV Fellows Seminar at Princeton University, the South Asian Intellectual History (SAIH) Seminar at the University of Oxford, and the Global Intellectual History (GIH) Seminar at the University of Cambridge. At these venues I benefitted greatly from questions and comments from Tariq Thachil, Juliana Di Giustini, Lisa Mitchell, Nikhil Anand, Kiran Kumbhar, and Matt

Barlow; Eric Beerbohm, Arthur Applbaum, and Tim Scanlon; Lucia Rafanelli, Avia Pasternak, and Prithviraj Datta; Hansong Li, Andrew Hurrell, and Yin Shoufu; Roger Maioli, Anne Gray Fischer, Daniel Wodak, Pratap Bhanu Mehta, Wojciech Sadurski, Robert Tsai, Edward Baring, Gregory Conti, Stephen Macedo, Elena Yi-Jia Zeng, and David Owen; Faisal Devji, Bhadrajee Hewage, Zaki Rehman, Bilal Moin, and Ross Moncrieff; Shruti Kapila, Jessica Patterson, John Dunn, and my beloved teacher and advisor, Richard Tuck. Additionally, I also benefitted from discussions with Rohan Mukherjee, Anit Mukherjee, Janak Nabar, Dinyar Patel, Vikram Visana, Richard Bellamy, Christine Dunn Henderson, Chandran Kukathas, Keshava Guha, Karthik Muralidharan, Shivaji Sondhi, Onar Ulas Ince, and Kanti Bajpai.

An investigative enterprise of the sort hazarded here would not have been possible without research assistance. I am much obliged to Jonah Elsey, Navmee Goregaonkar, and Dipak Patekar for helping me dig through archives in London, Mumbai, and Pune, and I am grateful to Sravya Darbhamulla, Dipak Patekar, and especially Nikhil Bellarykar for translating numerous Marathi-language texts. For the preparation of this manuscript, I owe thanks to Khushi Singh Rathore and Sanchi Rai who typed up the original materials, and I am utterly indebted to Nidhi Shukla for her patient, diligent, and cheerful help even as I peppered her with endless queries, requests, and drafts. Needless to say, I am solely responsible for any errors in this volume and for the views expressed therein.

It is an honor to have this volume published by Juggernaut. I am utterly indebted to Chiki Sarkar and Parth Mehrotra for supporting my proposal and for their unwavering support and wise advice over the years. I am also grateful to Nishtha Kapil and Yash Daiv for guiding the manuscript through the production process, and to Gavin Morris for once again designing a stunning cover. I also want to express my deep gratitude to Christie's, and to Nishad Avari and Amélie D'Arenberg in particular, for allowing me to use Horace Van Ruith's gorgeous painting, "An Indian Man Reading the Newspaper in the Bazaar".

Finally, on a personal note, this volume is dedicated to Dennis Thompson, who mentored me at Harvard. He was a *rishi*: gentle and humorous in person, wise and moderate in politics, and visionary and patient in building institutions. I will always regret that this volume was published too late for him to see it in person, and I can only hope to repay his kindness by helping others as selfl essly as he helped me. I also want to take this chance to express my love and admiration for my parents, Prema and Jyoti Sagar. They have been exemplars of liberalism from the very start by being open-minded and big-hearted in every way. I must end, as always, with an expression of reverence for my daughters, Mia and Sophie, whose virtues I cherish. I often say, only half-jokingly, that I hope that I grow up to be as intelligent, courageous, energetic, and good-natured as they are. They are the greatest blessings I can ever have, and I thank God every day for entrusting them to me.

Glossary

abhang	verse poem composed by saints in Maharashtra
angrez sarkar	the Government of India
bahadur	honorific accorded to high officials; literally, the term means brave
bhakti	medieval-era religious movements characterized by devotional practices
bhayad	clansmen or feudatories; literally, the term means brothers
darbar	royal court
darbari	courtier
deshmukh	ruler; literally, head (*mukh*) of the country (*desh*)
dewan	prime minister
dharmshala	rest house; literally, a religious sanctuary
gaddi	throne; literally, the cushion on which the ruler would be seated
Gaekwar	the dynastic title of the rulers of Baroda; the corrected modern spelling is Gaekwad; literally, protector of cows (*gai*)
guru	teacher, guide
Jam Sahib	the customary title of the ruler in Jamnagar
karbhari	principal administrator
kazi	a judge responsible for administering Muslim civil law
Khan Bahadur	honorific awarded in British India for meritorious public service by Muslims
khangi	department for the royal household; the ruler's private purse
khas daftar	private secretariat
khatpat	colloquial term for bribery to obtain a favorable outcome
khazanchi	treasurer
lakh	hundred thousand
mahajan	term used interchangeably for trader, merchant, and moneylender

mahal palace; revenue district
Maharaja king or monarch
maharishi great sage
mahatma great-souled person
mamlatdar revenue official
mandir temple
math monastery
meherban kind; an honorific awarded to high officials in native principalities
mofussil countryside; rural areas
naib dewan deputy minister
nyayadhisha chief magistrate; chief justice
panchayat village council
pandit Sanskrit scholar
pantoji village schoolmaster
pattawala a uniformed peon
peshwa the prime minister in the Maratha Empire
prayaschitta penance performed to atone for violating traditional norms
purdah the practice of secluding women from public view
Raj kingdom; state
raj dharma a ruler's duty
Rao the customary title of the ruler in Kutch
Rao Bahadur honorific awarded in British India for meritorious public service by Hindus
rishi sage
ryot tenant cultivator
ryotwari revenue system wherein land tax is assessed and collected directly by the state and not by landlords or revenue farmers
sadhu monk
sahib master; sir
sanyasi wandering ascetic
sardar nobleman or minor chieftain
sarkar government
sar subah revenue commissioner; literally, head of the divisions or districts
sati self-immolation by widows
shastra classical treatise
subah civil and revenue administrator at the divisional or district level
swami religious teacher

swaraj	liberty; freedom
taluk	subdivision of a *zilla* (revenue district or administrative region)
talukdar	major landlord
tehsildar	revenue collector and inspector
vakil	lawyer; pleader; negotiator
Varisht Adalat	High Court
vilayat	abroad; overseas
zamindar	landlord; revenue farmer
zenana	quarters of the royal household in which women were secluded

Principal events

1838 Parmanand is born in Sawantwadi
1850 Enters the Central English School in Bombay
1855 Enrols in Elphinstone and joins the Paramhansa Mandali
1861 Appointed an Assistant Master in the Central English School
1862 Appointed the First Assistant Master of the English High School in Hyderabad
1863 Appointed co-editor of *Indu Prakash*
1864 Appointed editor of *Native Opinion*; introduced to Swami Anandashram
1867 Co-founds the Prarthana Samaj and serves as Treasurer
1868 Publishes *English and Native Rule in India*
1868 Appointed *naib dewan* of Kutch; Liberals come to power in Britain
1869 Resigns from Kutch; *The Stories of Birbal and Badshah* published in Bombay
1869 Appointed Assistant Registrar in the High Court
1870 Anandashram and J. P. Hughlings pass away; Parmanand receives the Dakshina Prize
1870 Appointed to the Revenue Department
1871 Parmanand drafts the memorials of the Ratepayers' Association
1873 Appointed editor of *Subodh Patrika* and a Justice of the Peace
1874 Declines invitation to serve under Dadabhai Naoroji in Baroda
1875 Malhar Rao deposed and Sayaji Rao selected as Gaekwad
1881 Sayaji Rao becomes Maharaja of Baroda
1883 Parmanand diagnosed with Parkinson's
1884 "The National Anthem Incident" in Poona
1886 Retires from the Revenue Department; Conservatives come to power in Britain
1887 The "Crawford scandal" commences
1889 Lepel Griffin publishes "The Native Princes of India"
1889 "Letters to an Indian Raja" begins appearing in the *Indian Spectator*

1890 Sayaji Rao commissions a Marathi edition of Machiavelli's *The Prince*
1891 *Letters to an Indian Raja* published
1893 Parmanand passes away in Bombay

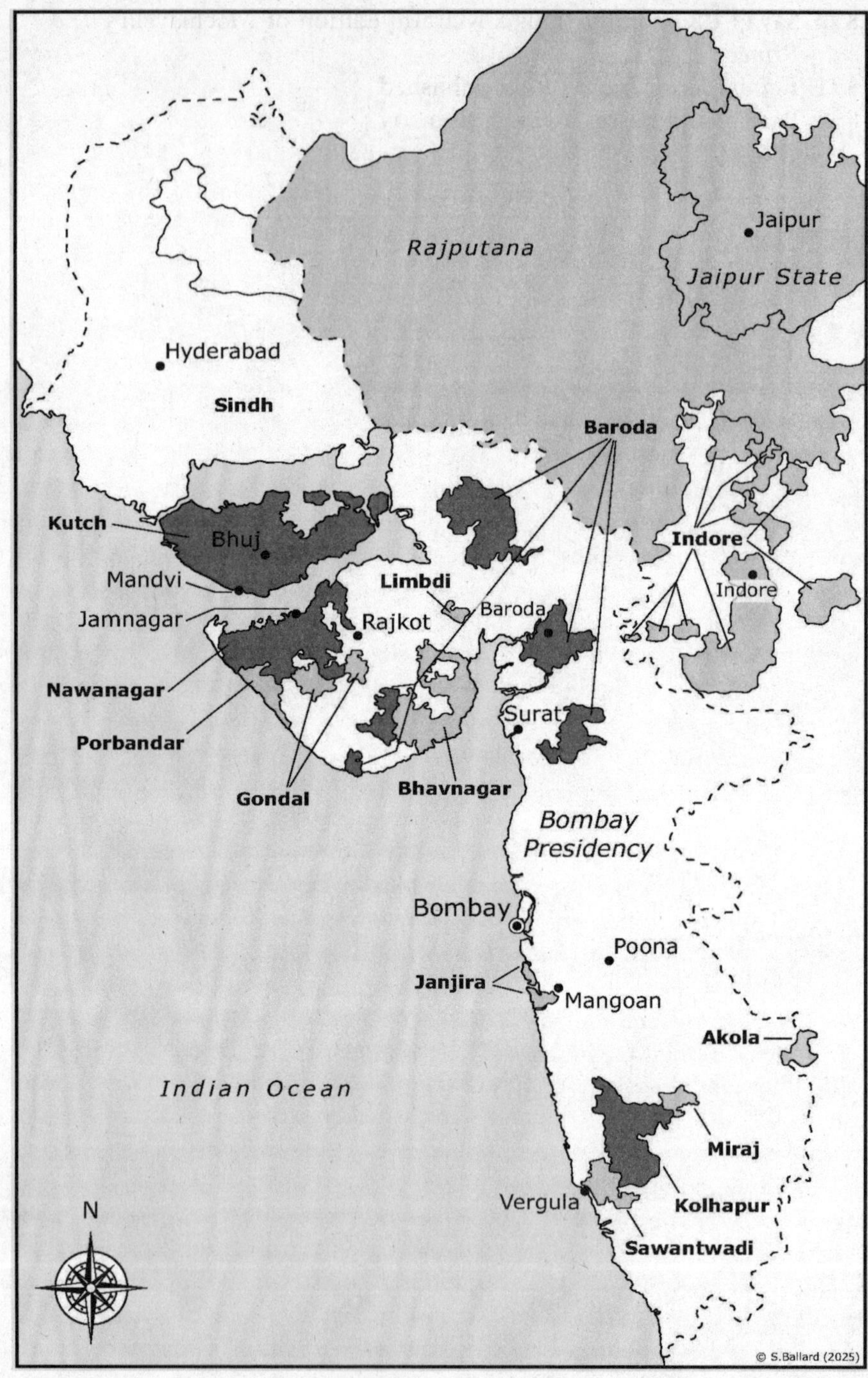

Western India in 1890. Map by Sebastian Ballard

Introduction: The Birth of Indian Liberalism

Letters to an Indian Raja (1891) is the first work of political theory to have been published in modern India in the English language. Its genesis lay in a public debate over which was more conducive to happiness – colonial or native rule. The most thoughtful answer to this question had come in a series of unsigned essays in the Bombay newspaper *Native Opinion*. These essays, which were republished as *English and Native Rule in India* (1868), argued that both regimes had their advantages and disadvantages. In British India administration was orderly, but it was operated by foreigners and therefore worked to the detriment of the governed. By contrast, in Indian India Maharajas cared more for their subjects, who were their kindred, but they governed erratically. The upshot was that the happiness of Indians depended on either the "popularization" of British rule or the "systematization" of native rule.[1] Since the imperial nature of British rule militated against it becoming more popular, the essays called for native rule to become more orderly. But what would such a regime look like? The answer came two decades later when the same author, writing under the name "A Political Recluse", published another series of essays in the Bombay newspaper *Indian Spectator*, detailing the reforms that would transform Native States into constitutional monarchies. Avidly followed across the country, these essays were then republished in 1891 as *Letters to an Indian Raja*.

More than a century has passed since *Letters* appeared. The Maharajas it addresses are no more and the British have long departed India. So why should we read it? It remains acutely relevant because it challenges two widely held beliefs about Indian politics. The first relates to *where* liberal thought emerged and flourished in India. Thus far, every notable account of Indian liberalism, above all C. A. Bayly's *Recovering Liberties*, has focused on how liberal ideas emerged and were employed in British India.[2] Though invaluable, these studies barely glance in the direction of Indian India where principalities such as Travancore, Baroda, Mysore, Gondal, Bhavnagar, and Kolhapur spearheaded liberal reforms – often in advance of British India. This is a serious oversight. *Letters* reveals that Indian liberals, especially in

Western India, originally laid their hopes in Indian India. In fact they hoped that, by taking the lead on reform, Indian India would pressure British India into liberalizing *its* rule.

A second belief that *Letters* challenges relates to the *content* of liberal thought in India. It has been argued, by Ramachandra Guha for instance, that "Indian liberalism is a sensibility rather than a theory".[3] *Letters* reveals that Indian liberalism *did* originally have a theory behind it. In common with every nineteenth-century form of liberalism, its objective was to uphold the interests of individuals. But, unlike liberals in Europe, who worried about how mass democracy, mass industrialization, and mass media were making the individual ever more subject to impersonal forces, Indian liberals focused on freeing the individual from bondage to an intimate force – the community. They saw communities as uniquely threatening because of how early their influence began, affecting the individual from the cradle on, and how deeply their norms impressed themselves upon the individual, shaping everything from tastes to fears. As a consequence, the means that Indian liberals proposed to safeguard the individual were different from those advocated by their contemporaries in Europe. They did not emphasize individuals' rights because they doubted that, corrupted by their upbringing and cowed by communal sanctions, their compatriots would dare to challenge inherited norms and identities. Instead, they sought help from enlightened monarchs who could paternalistically direct the religious and social transformation needed to foster individuality.

These claims about the significance of *Letters* may lead one to wonder why it has been ignored for so long. There are two factors to bear in mind. Most immediate are the peculiarities associated with the text and the author. Though the author was a celebrated writer, he had to dictate his thoughts to a notetaker as he was bedridden (or in the genteel language of the era, "at a disadvantage").[4] The resulting manuscript had several imperfections: overly long sentences, incompletely referenced quotes, and distracting typographical errors. The author's ill-health also meant that when the essays published in the *Indian Spectator* were republished as *Letters to an Indian Raja*, he was unable to write an introduction to guide the uninitiated reader. It did not help that he insisted on using a pen name, which meant that many would-be readers and reviewers were left unaware that the volume had been authored by a storied figure who had served in both British India and Indian India.

What affected the volume's reception still more was the political earthquake set off by the inauguration of the Indian National Congress in 1885. *Letters* encapsulated the decades-long effort that liberals had made to liberalize the Native States in the hope that this would then pressure British India to behave more liberally too. But, by the time *Letters* was published in 1891, the Congress had begun claiming that *it* represented the Indian nation, a claim it underscored by committing itself to the idea of popular representation. This meant that, almost overnight, works like *Letters* that looked to the Native States for political and moral leadership became quite irrelevant to audiences in British India. *Letters* had greater purchase in the Native States where it became a fixture on the syllabi of the schools and colleges set up to educate the nobility. But even there its appeal dimmed as it became evident that the Congress intended for India to become a republic. With Maharajas increasingly considered museum pieces, *Letters* disappeared from bookshelves, with only a handful of copies left in circulation by the middle of the twentieth century. And so, when a copy of the text became available online a decade ago, there was no one left to recall its significance.

Having outlined what *Letters* stands for, and why it deserves to be appreciated anew, let us examine it in detail. We will begin by studying in Part I the person responsible for writing it. Then, in Part II we will examine the political and intellectual context from which it emerged. Following this, in Part III we will analyze the ideas and institutions *Letters* recommends. In so doing, we will learn that liberals in India did not simply derive their ideas from Britain. To the contrary, they were the first to notice and address the challenge that multiculturalism poses for liberalism.

Part I: Who wrote *Letters to an Indian Raja*?

The reclusive figure responsible for *Letters to an Indian Raja* was Narayan Mahadev Parmanand (or Mama Parmanand[5] as he was affectionately termed). Though celebrated by his contemporaries as a "political *rishi*" (or sage), Parmanand is unknown in our time and his manifold contributions to nineteenth-century India lie forgotten.[6] His writings, which used to be carefully studied by rulers and ruled alike, have not been republished for a century. Even his name has all but disappeared, being recalled only in primers on "general knowledge", which note that he was a founder of the Prarthana Samaj (or Prayer Society). Mumbai, the metropolis that Parmanand did so much to shape, has done the bare minimum to commemorate him. Those intending to visit the restored Opera House in downtown Mumbai will find themselves asking for directions to Mama Parmanand Marg in Girgaon, but when they traverse that avenue, they will search in vain for a plaque explaining whom it is named after. The University of Bombay has done even less. In 1897, Parmanand's fellow graduates from Elphinstone College collected the then-handsome amount of six thousand rupees to establish a "Narayan Mahadev Parmanand Prize" to be awarded annually for the best essay in Marathi or Gujarati on the subject of reform.[7] The prize still exists but the award has not been revised to account for inflation, which means it stands at a now-inconsequential one thousand rupees. The Marathi press has done much better in the form of P. B. Kulkarni's 1963 biography *Mama Parmananda Ani Tyancha Kalkhanda* (*The Life and Times of Mama Parmanand*), which is based on Parmanand's now-lost correspondence.[8] This volume, which has never been translated into English and is now out of print, sheds invaluable light on his life and his relations with leading figures of his time. Unfortunately, it does not utilize archival materials, which are essential to contextualizing Parmanand's often allusive correspondence. We need, therefore, to start at the very start.

Early years

Parmanand was born in 1838 in the small principality of Sawantwadi in southern Maharashtra. This was two decades after the Bhonsles, the *deshmukh*s (rulers) of Sawantwadi, found themselves on the losing side of the Third Anglo-Maratha War (1817–18). The destruction and instability that accompanied that war impoverished merchants like Parmanand's father who owned a shop in the village of Mangaon.[9] As a result, Parmanand was born into poverty, which was only worsened by his father's death when he was two years old. To the family turmoil was added political tumult when the East India Company's extractive policies provoked scattered insurgencies that financed their operations through extortion, the victims of which included the family shop. Matters came to a head in 1845 when Sawantwadi was rocked by what the British described as a "small mutiny" after disgruntled members of the Bhonsle clan joined up with the insurgents.[10] It was during one such tense moment, while hiding in haystacks with Parmanand as clashes occurred in the distance, that his mother, Gangabai, formed the idea of sending the boy to Bombay, where his older sister, Nanubai, had made a home in the suburb of Girgaon following her recent marriage to a shopkeeper by the name of Krishnaseth Tivrekar.[11] Although reluctant to part with her only son, Gangabai was left with little choice after her brother, a *pantoji* (schoolmaster) who had been instructing Parmanand in Marathi, unexpectedly passed away in 1847, leaving the boy without any means of further education.

And so in 1848, when he was old enough to withstand the journey, off went Parmanand to Bombay. Though the idea was to have him assist in Krishnaseth's shop, the ten-year-old was soon doing more than "tying packets".[12] Discerning his abilities, his brother-in-law placed him under the supervision of Mahadev *pantoji*, a local teacher revered for the interest he took in his students.[13] For the next two years Parmanand received a sound education in Marathi and arithmetic. Despite being weighed down by chores in the house and the store, he was soon ready for more. Happily, his teacher

Narayan Mahadev Parmanand

was not the sort to dissuade his wards from taking advantage of the "new education" being offered in schools operated by the Native Education Society. [14] And so in 1850 Parmanand's family enrolled him in Bombay's premier middle school – the Central English School. There Parmanand's qualities of intellect and character became still more evident, and his keen interest in English and his gentle demeanor made him a favorite with his teachers and peers.[15] It greatly helped of course that he was surrounded by some of the brightest minds of his generation, several of whom, such as Ramakrishna Gopal Bhandarkar[16] and Bal Mangesh Wagle,[17] would go on to become lifelong friends.

The stimulating environment meant that by 1855 Parmanand was ready to sit the entrance examination for Elphinstone High School (or the "Junior" section of Elphinstone College as it came to be termed). His timing was near perfect. When he entered Elphinstone in 1855, the institution was in the midst of moving on from the humble ambition that Bombay officials had previously set for it, namely "the manufacture of teachers" for government schools.[18] This change was the result of the now-famous Wood's Despatch of 1854, a directive issued by the Company's then-President Charles Wood, which proposed to "raise the moral character" of the native populace by establishing public universities in India patterned after the University of London.[19] Consequently, over the next two years, while Company officers

Elphinstone College. British Library, Photo 937/(27)

scrambled to recruit sufficient faculty to make Elphinstone the nucleus of the University of Bombay, its students were given a "thorough foundation" in anticipation of the BA program.[20]

Parmanand relished his time in the Junior section.[21] Though he focused on mathematics, in which he earned laurels, his abilities in moral philosophy immediately attracted attention, with his lucid comments on John Locke's *Of the Conduct of the Understanding* among the "very gratifying" writing samples that were reprinted in Elphinstone's widely noticed inaugural report in 1856.[22] One of a handful to be singled out for public praise by the Director of Public Instruction, he was subsequently awarded a scholarship worth fifteen rupees per month, relieving him of his embarrassing dependence on his brother-in-law, who had a growing family of his own to care for.[23]

What happened outside the classroom during this time was equally important. Parmanand's circle of friends continued to expand. To the close companionship of Wagle and Bhandarkar were added two new entrants to the college, Vaman Aabaji Modak[24] and Mahadev Govind Ranade.[25] Alongside them, Parmanand dove into the leading student-run societies of the era: the Paramahansa Mandali (the Sacred Society) and the Students' Literary and Scientific Society. The former, which sought to reconcile religion and rationality, required its members to challenge the institution of caste and the ban on widow remarriage, while the latter served as a monthly forum for debate, where students "took turns delivering lectures" and had "warm discussions" on weighty matters such as the contrast between "the customs of Europe and Asia".[26] As a British observer put it, in these societies,

> released from the trammels and formalities of the classroom ... the young men were left to their own resources, and thrown on their wits at once, alike for information and for argument, and so acquired a self-reliance and independence and spirit of emulation, not otherwise to be looked for, and of the very greatest value in after life.[27]

The observation held entirely true in Parmanand's case. In the Students' Literary and Scientific Society he came to be known for writing carefully reasoned essays that ranged from the reflective ("On Emulation") to the practical ("The Mode of Passing Our Life"). One such essay, "The Needs of Our Students", which articulated the difficulties faced by Elphinstone's students, attracted an especially wide readership, giving him an early lesson on the growing power of the pen in metropolitan India.[28]

Elphinstone College

By May 1857 Parmanand was ready for the next step. While the Mutiny was underway in Upper India, he sat the matriculation examination for

Elphinstone's "Senior" section. A month later, he found his name second from the top of the list, a feat that gained him a "senior scholarship" that would pay him twenty-five rupees every month for the next two years.[29] And there was more good news to come. While Parmanand had been preparing to matriculate, Elphinstone had welcomed two promising graduates from Oxford, Sidney Owen and John Hughlings, who began teaching political economy and literature, respectively. Parmanand was immediately captivated by the latter of these figures, whom he promptly anointed his "Guruji" (or guide).[30] It was a telling choice because Hughlings embodied the ideal that British liberals were keener to profess than to practice, which was to tutor and befriend natives.

Born to a working-class family in Cheshire in 1831, Hughlings had become interested in teaching early in life. But he clearly wanted to be more than an ordinary schoolmaster because in 1850 he elected to attend Kneller Hall, a teacher training college whose graduates were expected to administer schools for the children of paupers.[31] Since his father, a druggist with a degree in medicine from Glasgow, could have afforded to educate him at the University of London, Hughlings' decision to attend Kneller Hall likely stemmed from a desire to help the less fortunate. At any rate, his stellar performance at Kneller Hall attracted the attention of the Master, Frederick Temple,[32] a prominent clergyman with a distinguished record at Oxford.[33] Convinced that Hughlings deserved a better education than Kneller Hall could provide, Temple "strongly recommended" him to Benjamin Jowett,[34] his "intimate friend" and former colleague at Balliol.[35] Concurring wholly in Temple's assessment, Jowett proceeded to help Hughlings into Pembroke in 1853.[36] And his patronage did not end there. Two years later, when the Company sought Jowett's recommendations for scholars they could appoint to British India's newly established universities, he told them he had just the man they needed – someone who had already evinced an interest in the downtrodden and was therefore likely to display "kindness and friendship to the natives".[37] And so, only a few months after graduating from Oxford in 1856, Hughlings found himself on a boat to India, with a monthly salary of six hundred rupees for company, an astonishing turn of events for a twenty-five-year-old who had been on the verge of entering the grim world of Victorian workhouses.[38]

Hughlings did not have an easy start in Bombay. When he arrived in January 1857, his "plebian" background and his bookishness stood out in an environment populated by unhurried "gentlemen" who typically owed their positions to family connections. As one such figure who briefly shared accommodation with him in Bombay sneeringly wrote home,

> I kept house with Hughlings, a young professor of literature and history at Elphinstone College, who was about as industrious a man as I had ever met.

> Ill-made, splay-footed, short in stature, endowed by nature with irregular and unhandsome features, he asserted himself among gentlemen by great erudition and an enormous capacity for hard work. When he was not lecturing, he sat at home reading Sanskrit and correcting the lecture books of the pupils who studied under him.[39]

The mocking tone did not last. Within months of Hughlings' start, the Mutiny broke out. The upheaval ended Company rule, and when the Crown took charge in 1858, the freewheeling "old civil service" gave way to a more fastidious Indian Civil Service chosen by examination. In the renovated bureaucracy that emerged, Hughlings' "single-minded labors for the higher culture of the natives of India" were more appreciated.[40] But there were new problems to contend with: His "simple and unobtrusive" personality made it difficult to break into the increasingly clubby atmosphere dominated by "covenanted" officers who had passed through public schools like Harrow and Rugby.[41] As an editorial in the Bombay press would later mourn after Hughlings was turned down for the principalship of Elphinstone:

> The truth is that notwithstanding his rare merits in many ways, Mr. Hughlings had one defect that stood in his way when it was a question of "getting on". Mr. Hughlings was always shy and somewhat reserved; the first years of his residence in Bombay almost painfully so. To the public he was little known and less understood, and big officials were in the same position. He was only well known to a few; but to those few he was thoroughly endeared, by his kindly affectionate nature, nice delicate feeling, fine intelligence, and exquisite sense of fun and humour.[42]

The backbiting in Anglo-Indian society had no discernible effect within Elphinstone where Hughlings came to be adored. To his students, he was the embodiment of virtues – past and present. Like the Hindu sages in their epics, he lived to serve higher causes; a man who could have spent his weekends hobnobbing at whites-only clubhouses chose to spend them teaching his dark-skinned students the art of essay-writing. At the same time, like the Victorian sages in their textbooks, he did not live apart from the world. This is because, having heard Jowett constantly remind his disciples that "we pedagogues lose influence by not doing our part sufficiently in the world and in society", Hughlings devoted his spare time to the public sphere, writing essays in *The Times of India* and later serving as the editor of the *Calcutta Review*, the most important Anglo-Indian periodical of the era.[43] He did not only model a public life, he swept his students along too, setting up a reading room for them and then paying out of his own pocket the hefty subscription fees for English newspapers and periodicals like *The Times*, the *Quarterly Review*, and *The Economist*, in the hope that watching "movements in society" and understanding the "questions of the day" would cultivate in them the "spirit of citizenship".[44]

All this meant that, though he was only seven years older than Parmanand, Hughlings came to have an extraordinary influence upon his student. Parmanand had already come to love literature and to partake in public discussion before Hughlings arrived at Elphinstone. What his Guruji provided was a visible example of how to combine intellect and activity in the service of society – of how words could remake worlds. To this quintessentially Victorian lesson was added Hughlings' inclination to work behind the scenes. This distinctive conduct may have stemmed from Hughlings' introverted nature, but Parmanand discerned a deeper moral in his Guruji's willingness to quietly serve larger causes. He came to see self-effacement, a quality typically associated with Hindu *sanyasi*s (ascetics), as essential to progress. This is because in the modern era improvement depended on public deliberation, which was not likely to be fair or rational when disputants were motivated by the prospect of gaining a public victory (or avoiding a loss of face).[45] Therefore, as Parmanand saw it, by disentangling ideas from personalities, the practice of self-effacement could help both the individual and society focus on facts and reasons rather than honor and identity.

Surrounded by such wholesome influences, Parmanand continued to flourish at Elphinstone, becoming one of the twenty-two students to matriculate into the BA program when it was launched in 1859.[46] But, by this point, there were other challenges looming – he was running out of time and money. He was now twenty-one years old and under pressure to display "manly self-reliance" by taking up a career.[47] There was also the question of marriage. In an era when boys were expected to marry in their early teens (and girls before they turned ten), Parmanand stood out for being unmarried. With the help of his liberal-minded sister and brother-in-law, he had been able to fend off his mother's pleas on the grounds that he needed to complete his education. But now Gangabai would wait no longer as Parmanand was becoming ineligible on the marriage market. Since he absolutely refused to marry a prepubescent girl, after much searching a thirteen-year-old by the name of Janaki, bluntly described by the matchmakers as "short in height, dark in complexion, ordinary in appearance, and lacking a dowry", was located in distant Vergula.[48] What mattered to Parmanand was that she was gentle and sociable – and willing to be educated. His principal requirements met, he agreed to marry in 1860, bringing his student days to a close.

The school master

Having become a householder, Parmanand did the responsible thing by taking up the role of a part-time Assistant Master in his *alma mater*, the

Central English School. The monthly salary of fifty-five rupees was a welcome step up, but the heavy workload began eating into his time for study. It did not help that Elphinstone was, during this time, descending into "perfect chaos".[49] Operating on the premise that students ought to be willing to pay for "useful" learning, the Company had long declined to spend much on education. In the early 1850s, the entire annual budget for education in Bombay Presidency, with a population of eleven million, had been a mere £25,000.[50] The Company's miserliness meant that Elphinstone was unprepared for the surge in enrollment after the Wood's Despatch made education a prerequisite for public employment.[51] As a result, during Parmanand's time, it was not unknown for a dozen students to have to share the library's copy of a textbook.[52] The hastily constructed classrooms, located in a "squalid bungalow", were deemed by the professors as "not worthy the name of a college".[53] Worse still, as teaching positions remained "grievously underpaid", a sufficient number of faculty could not be recruited from Britain, which meant that existing professors were overstretched ("the disproportion of teaching power to the number of students" was, one report declared, "almost ludicrous").[54] Some faculty members were "more than diligent" in meeting the shortfall, volunteering to teach outside their timetabled hours. Hughlings, for instance, came in every Saturday.[55] But others were less inclined to charity. They went on leave or resigned, leaving public-spirited figures like Hughlings even more overburdened.

Eventually, the combination of teaching too much and being taught too little exacted a toll. In May 1861, by which time Parmanand had already been at Elphinstone for four years, he was still not ready to sit the BA examination (nor, for that matter, was the college even in a position to hold the examination). Instead, he found himself sitting for the FA (First Examination in the Arts) alongside several noticeably younger batchmates. As a result, though one of only seven students to pass the "severe" FA examination (the "seven stars of Elphinstone"[56] as this pioneering group came to be called by their admirers in the native press), he decided he could not wait another year for the BA.[57] He therefore elected to leave Elphinstone, making him the only one in his circle who had to settle for an FA.[58]

Parmanand's sadness at having to quit his studies earlier than he would have liked was lessened by the sense that he had found his calling in life – to become a teacher, like his Guruji. In June 1861 he was promoted to full-time Assistant Master at the Central English School, a "highly regarded" position that paid ninety rupees per month.[59] Since he had already impressed his colleagues with his "thorough mastery" of the syllabus, Parmanand was now tasked with preparing students for Elphinstone's matriculation examination.[60] He performed well, sending record numbers on to his *alma mater*. He also followed in Hughlings' footsteps by modeling liberality, opening his home to students that needed additional tutoring, timely advice, or even a meal. The intimate setting allowed his quiet charm full play. His students soon came to see him as a "revered and sage guide", and many of them, Kashinath Trimbak Telang[61] in particular, formed a "deep attachment" to him that "lasted through life".[62]

Parmanand's position at the Central English School was not destined to last, however. The prevailing view in the Educational Department was that instruction in English ought to be "under the immediate direction of European professors" and that "native teachers" were better employed in less attractive towns in the Presidency where British officers were unwilling to live.[63] Thus, in October 1861, Parmanand was told that he was going to be appointed the First Assistant Master at the recently established English High School in Hyderabad.[64] The news came as a shock because Sindh was, the Director of Public Instruction candidly acknowledged, a "semi-barbarous" place where "superior education" was "quite incipient".[65] Still, given his limited means, Parmanand had no choice but to comply with the order to relocate to what a famous travelogue at the time ominously described as "the Unhappy Valley".[66] And so, leaving Janaki behind to care for his ailing mother and sister, in November 1862 he sailed from Bombay to Karachi, and then traveled by rail and ferry on to Hyderabad.

Though he found Sindh an intriguing place, Parmanand's fears about his prospects in Hyderabad were fully realized. The "small, unpretending" high school that he had been assigned to had less than a hundred students on the rolls and lacked sufficient room and basic equipment (it was, school inspectors from Bombay muttered under their breath, "really" a middle school).[67] The unfamiliarity of the surroundings was compounded by the need to learn Sindhi as most students and parents understood neither English nor Marathi.[68] The Educational Department knew the assignment was challenging and tried to bolster morale by promising that the difficulties would be transitory. "It was in circumstances such as these", the Director of Public Instruction exhorted his subordinates, "that Charlemagne and Alfred began in the dark ages".[69] But Parmanand was not inclined to wait for the Enlightenment to arrive in Sind. A mere five months in, he declared that the "weather did not suit him".[70] The climate in Sind, with its freezing winters and blazing summers, certainly was very different from tropical Bombay. But homesickness was the operative factor. Neither the relatively handsome salary of 125 rupees per month nor the prospect of being made headmaster in the near future was compensation enough for losing the stimulation that metropolitan Bombay provided, much less for putting up with "imperfect communication" with his family.[71] With no prospect of a transfer to more salubrious climes, Parmanand resigned in April 1863 and wended his way back to Bombay.[72]

Native Opinion

Parmanand's sudden departure from Sindh surprised his patrons in the Educational Department, but there was more to it than met the eye. His decision was also motivated by the appearance of a career prospect that had not existed when he had decided to become a teacher. In the same month that he had moved to Hyderabad, his friend Ranade had accepted the inaugural editorship of the English section of *Indu Prakash* (*Moonlight*), an Anglo-Marathi weekly that aimed to be a "just and moderate interpreter between the rulers and the ruled".[73] *Indu Prakash* was soon making waves in Western India, gaining a circulation of over a thousand copies a month. But then in March 1863, a month before Parmanand quit his post in Sindh, Ranade decided to step down as editor after Elphinstone offered him a plum position that would allow him to focus on his graduate education – and reduce the overwork that was damaging his eyesight. Into this open slot at *Indu Prakash* went Parmanand shortly after his return to Bombay, to the great delight of Hughlings who had always urged him to take up newspaper writing. And with this began a new phase of Parmanand's life.

The next eight months were a whirlwind as Parmanand came to grips with the "newspaper trade".[74] Alongside Vishnu Shastri Pandit,[75] who handled the *Indu Prakash*'s Marathi section, he churned out editorials on social reforms such as the maltreatment of widows or the education of mill hands that were being discussed in the societies and associations in Bombay of which he was an active member. But he also began taking on political subjects with carefully argued pieces, some of them discussed beforehand with Hughlings, on pan-Indian concerns such as the Government of India's proposal for an income tax. By the end of 1863, these editorials were being read and admired at some distance. The *Indian Mirror*, a leading English-language newspaper in Calcutta, was one such follower. It proclaimed Parmanand's style as "ingenuous, liberal, and truthful" and proposed that henceforth Bombay and Bengal ought to "work together" to address "all measures affecting our common country".[76]

These examples of reasoned deliberation in *Indu Prakash* were well and good but what made Anglo-Indians truly sit up were hard-hitting exposes, such as its report on A. J. Richardson, a judge in Ahmednagar, who had made himself infamous by maltreating natives employed under him.[77] At least some of these stories, which Parmanand typically sourced from Elphinstonians working in the *mofussil* (countryside), bore fruit. Richardson, for instance, received a public "reproof" for his poor conduct.[78] From results such as these, Parmanand's associates drew the vital lesson that a "well-conducted" English-language newspaper could bring local grievances to wider attention, and thereby make it harder for British officials in the *mofussil* to brazen their way through maladministration. And so, in January 1864, with the backing of Vishwanath Narayan Mandlik,[79] a prominent Elphinstonian with a lucrative law practice and growing political ambition, there appeared, for the first time in Bombay, "a wholly English native journal" – a weekly, with the pointed title *Native Opinion*, and with Parmanand as its editor.[80]

Native Opinion met with immediate success. It started out with five hundred subscribers paying fifteen rupees annually, making it one of the highest circulating newspapers in Bombay.[81] Because of its narrower scope, it could not vie with a bilingual newspaper like *Indu Prakash* in terms of reach. But precisely because it was entirely in English and more focused on public affairs, *Native Opinion* was read carefully by administrators, including the Governor, Henry Bartle Frere, who paid it the highest compliment by becoming a subscriber.[82] The attention only grew when *Native Opinion* began claiming British scalps, the first of which was G. Russell, "a certificated schoolmaster" whom the Educational Department had imported from England at great cost and placed over the Ratnagiri High School. Tipped off by Elphinstonians toiling under Russell, Parmanand accused the headmaster of routinely bunking school, leaving the once-flourishing institution "thoroughly disorganized".[83] The reports embarrassed the Educational Department, leading its director, Alexander Grant,[84] a baronet who had briefly taught Parmanand at Elphinstone, to sharply question his former student.[85] When Parmanand held his ground, Grant ordered an investigation that confirmed that Russell was indeed "quite incompetent for his novel duties".[86] Russell was promptly put on a boat back to England and Ratnagiri High School was given over to a native – Parmanand's beloved friend and classmate, Bhandarkar.

It was not only British India that *Native Opinion* drew a bead upon. By the middle of the 1860s, Elphinstonians had begun making forays into the Native States, the semi-autonomous principalities that dotted British India (with the bulk of them being in Western India). They had pragmatic reasons for doing so. Public employment, which was greatly desired because of the stability and income it provided, was hard to come by in British India. So-called "covenanted" (or tenured) positions were effectively closed to natives and uncovenanted positions involved putting up with the "inordinate self-conceit of *sahibs* (masters)" who were prone to hogging credit and shifting blame.[87] The Native States, whose rulers were keen to appoint Elphinstonians as tutors and translators, provided a welcome escape from this quandary. But it was not merely a share of the "official loaves and fish" that Elphinstonians wanted.[88] Many of them viewed the Native States in a patriotic light. At a time when democratic ideals were still incipient, the remnants of the Maratha Empire were to them more than mere signposts of the past. As Ranade evocatively observed of the Maratha nobility in a widely read editorial in *Indu Prakash*:

> Their fathers fell in glory on the battlefield. Their noble descendants are fighting the battle for their country on a more peaceful stage. It is such princely houses as these who link in their person the past and the present, who are the themes of our infant songs, and the heroes of our youthful dreams of the future. It is these houses whose memory we have to adore.[89]

The future of the Native States became a more concrete issue when in late 1864 *Native Opinion* began receiving intelligence from Jamnagar, a "first class principality" in Kathiawar with an annual revenue of fifteen lakhs.[90] It came in the form of letters, written in perfect English, exposing "grievous errors" in the administration of the Jam Sahib (the title of the ruler of Jamnagar).[91] Not used to receiving communications from "so remote a quarter", Vinayak Narayan Bhagwat, the day-to-day manager of *Native Opinion*, sought to ascertain the contributor's antecedents. The letters, he learnt to his surprise, originated with a "strange and rare character, a *sanyasin* or ascetic, an English-educated native of Bengal, who styled himself Anandashram Swami".[92] Struck by the sudden appearance of this "singular character" in the far reaches of Western India, Parmanand stepped in to make further enquiries. And with this began a new chapter in his life, as he steadily came under the influence of yet another reclusive figure who, like Hughlings, was graced with an "enlarged intelligence and enlightened sense of duty that made him anxious to serve God and to be instrumental in doing good to his fellow creatures".[93]

Anandashram, Parmanand learned, descended from a Kulin[94] Brahmin family in Calcutta whose "mercantile" interests had given them "easy circumstances".[95] After receiving a "sound" English education at a "mission school",[96] Anandashram elected to renounce his inheritance and devote himself to the "amelioration of India".[97] Viewing the garb and peripatetic life of a *sanyasi* to be the best means of realizing this objective, in the latter part of the 1850s he joined a *math* (monastery) in Kashi whose initiates were expected to undertake a twelve-year pilgrimage. He then proceeded to spend about half a dozen years in the Himalayas before working his way down to Rajputana in the early 1860s where his unique persona – an intelligent, cultivated, traveled, solidly built *sanyasi* fluent in four languages – attracted the favorable attention of that great appraiser of men, Ram Singh, the Maharaja of Jaipur.[98] It was a vital time in Jaipur. The Maharaja was reeling from the death of his *dewan* (prime minister) and former tutor, Shivdin Singh. With the aid of this minister, who had studied medicine at Agra College, Ram Singh had begun modernizing his kingdom, investing in modern education and medicine, public works, and communication channels.[99] Unable to find a suitable replacement for Shivdin within the confines of Jaipur, Ram Singh had recently imported Hari Mohan Sen, an accomplished graduate of Hindu College and former *khazanchi* (treasurer) of the Bank of Bengal, who had been given charge of the Maharaja's *khas daftar* (private secretariat).[100] Impressed by all that the Maharaja was doing for the "good of the people", Anandashram employed his authority as a *sanyasi* to urge commoners as well as obdurate members of the nobility to support vital reforms, especially Sen's proposal for a Royal Council that promised to introduce a semblance of "constitutional government" in Jaipur (which in fact came into being in 1867).[101]

Persuaded by this experience in Jaipur that "princes were the best agents for influencing the destinies and welfare of millions of fellow-beings", Anandashram subsequently turned his attention in the direction of Western India where "radically conservative" Rajput clans ruled over several "benighted" principalities.[102] Thus it was that he appeared in Jamnagar in 1864, from whence he began sending letters to the *Native Opinion* reporting on the state of affairs in the region. The Rajputs of this principality proved less hospitable than those in Jaipur, however. When copies of the "severe articles" in *Native Opinion* reached the ruler, Vibhaji Ranmalji, he ordered his spies to locate the writer.[103] It did not take them long to figure out that the recent English-speaking arrival was the likely offender. Anandashram was then brought before the furious Jam Sahib (as the ruler was traditionally titled) who demanded that he cease and repent, to which the *sanyasi* coolly replied: "I journey through the country examining into and exposing all that is false, cruel, and unjust, and giving my support to whatever is good wherever I find it; and this I shall continue to do."[104] Unimpressed, Vibhaji threatened to toss Anandashram into prison. With a laugh, the *sanyasi* reminded the Jam that he had renounced worldly pleasures, and so "jail to him was as good a place of residence as any other".[105] This exhibition of self-abnegation – or, more likely, the prospect of continued censure in the Bombay press – produced a change in the Jam.[106] Suddenly awakened to his "sense of duty", he offered the *sanyasi* the role of a *karbhari* (principal administrator) in his *darbar* (court).[107] Anandashram had no interest in the offer, which was likely meant to test his morals. Instead, he put Vibhaji on the spot by arguing that if the Jam truly wanted to reform his principality, then he would help him procure "a competent man" from Bombay.[108] And so there appeared, a few months later, an advertisement in *Native Opinion* seeking an "English Secretary" for the Jam on the handsome salary of five hundred rupees per month. The terms were eye-catching because the norm in the Native States was "a small regular salary to be supplemented by fifty times the amount of covert and unlawful gains".[109] What impressed

Ram Singh II, Maharaja of Jaipur. Royal Collection Trust, RCIN 2701827

Parmanand's circle more was the hand behind the advertisement. Wanting to support Anandashram's astonishing initiative, Bhagwat, a gifted translator who had earned laurels at Elphinstone before joining *Native Opinion*, decided to apply for the post in Jamnagar. He was promptly chosen – and with this remarkable turn of events, *Native Opinion*'s interest in Kathiawar only deepened.

Over the next eighteen months Anandashram and Bhagwat learnt some hard lessons, which *Native Opinion* broadcast to the wider world. They were able to make notable progress on some fronts, establishing a medical dispensary operating on modern lines, a primary school that taught English, and a scholarship that would send students from Kathiawar to the University of Bombay.[110] Of particular "satisfaction to the people" was the establishment of a judicial department headed by Bhagwat, who became the *nyayadhisha* (chief magistrate). Full of zeal, Bhagwat immediately began passing orders "irrespective of frowns or favors from persons in authority", leading to a ferocious counterattack from "vested interests".[111] The principal opposition came from Nagar Brahmins, a caste group that considered public office its "hereditary preserve" and hence viewed the arrival of a Deccani and a Bengali in the *darbar* as an "unwelcome intrusion".[112] Initially, the Nagar Brahmins' complaints were brushed aside. This was partly because the reforms were popular – and partly because the Jam was himself in a jam. Having failed to produce a son with any of his twelve Hindu wives, he had recently married Dhanbai, a "part-time Muslim prostitute", who had borne a son they both insisted was his, and he was now in the midst of petitioning the British to recognize this boy as his heir.[113] Given the delicate situation, Vibhaji wanted to avoid unfavorable press in Bombay, which is why he had been humoring Anandashram and Bhagwat. He changed his tune, however, when the duo, learning of his harebrained plan, warned him that it violated Hindu law and would cause an uproar in Rajputana.[114] Their criticism enraged Vibhaji, and provided their enemies with the opening they had been waiting for. They convinced the Jam that the interlopers would surely use their contacts in Bombay to defeat the planned succession, leading him to order "the prompt dismissal of the friends of reformation" in April 1867.[115]

The episode left Parmanand stunned. It was bad enough that the "foolish Jam" was prepared to leave the "people entrusted to his care" to such a dubiously procured heir (who would, fittingly enough, subsequently try to poison Vibhaji).[116] What affected Parmanand more was the "chicken-hearted" conduct of Colonel Richard Keatinge, the Political Agent (the British representative) responsible for overseeing Kathiawar.[117] This was the same man whom the Anglo-Indian press had recently celebrated for a memorandum he had written arguing that British India ought to help educate the princes of Kathiawar in order to lead them "out of their backwardness".[118] But instead of supporting Bhagwat in his contest with the "illiterate *karbharis*" of Jamnagar, Keatinge urged the Elphinstonian to move on to the post of Vice-Regent in the minor principality of Limbdi – and then proceeded to maneuver his own subordinate into Bhagwat's former post in Jamnagar.

The only conclusion that could be drawn from the entire affair, Parmanand wrote in *Native Opinion*, was that Political Agents did not want an "English-knowing man" in the *darbar* of a Native State because they dreaded the "logical and constitutional reply" that such a person would provide to any "vexatious pressure" they might want to apply on the hapless Jam. The "Politicals", he now realized, were no more friends of the "cause of good government" than the old *karbharis*.[119]

Still, Parmanand was not the sort to be despondent. This was even more so because, amid the intrigues in Jamnagar, Anandashram had come down to Bombay to meet with Parmanand's colleagues. The ensuing conversations had left them in no doubt that he was "a genuine *rishi*" – a man who "neither despised nor despaired this world but worked devotedly for it, even as he abjured its pleasures".[120] What particularly affected them was Anandashram's unceasing faith, and by the end of his visit they found themselves reciting the old proverb that the *sanyasi* so loved – "where there is life, there is hope".[121] And truly Anandashram did not stop persevering. For within weeks of being expelled from Jamnagar he was to be found in the *darbar* of the Rao of Kutch, having responded to that ruler's cry for help in dealing with a brewing crisis.

The Rao of Kutch

It had been a long time since Kutch had been in the news. Five decades prior, the East India Company became interested in the region for the usual reasons: trade and territory. It disliked the fact that Kutch's many harbors provided refuge for the pirates that preyed on its ships in the Arabian Sea. It also wanted "an opening into Sindh" as the rulers of that territory could not be trusted to side with the Company should Russia invade the subcontinent through Afghanistan.[122] With the Kachchhis enmeshed in internecine warfare, it did not take the Company long to gain a foothold in the country. At first it supported the Rao (the customary title of the ruler) against his chiefs or *bhayad* (brothers). But when Rao Bharmalji proved a little too keen to consolidate his power, and to thereby lessen his dependence on the Company, the British decided that he was of "unstable mind".[123] To wit, in October 1819 the *bhayad* were informed of the Company's desire to "re-establish the sovereignty of Kutch on a firm basis", and after the chiefs had assembled at the Residency (the official quarters of the British Resident or representative), they were taken on a brief excursion that ended with Bharmalji in prison, and his infant son, Deshalji, on the *gaddi* (throne).[124]

Since Deshalji was underage, a regency council, comprising leading chiefs, was established, with the British Resident as its "guiding spirit". This was, Company officers lamented, an "imperious necessity" owing to Kutch's "extremely helpless state", which they promised to rectify.[125] They soon learned that they had bitten off more than they could afford to chew. For in this one province alone were to be found the four great sins of the age – brigandage, slavery, *sati*,[126] and female infanticide – and very little by way of tribute. For about a decade, the Residents sent out to Kutch labored in the "cause of humanity", to little avail.[127] Once the Company realized that its nominal allies, the *bhayad*, were firmly committed to the "diabolical vices" it wanted to extirpate, it placed its hopes in Deshalji, who became the very first Maharaja to be placed under British tutelage. Initially, he was tutored by John Gray, the Company's storied chaplain in Bhuj who had previously led schools in Dumfries and Belfast, and was an essayist and poet of "no mean pretensions", and then by John Crofton, an "accomplished gentleman" and military officer.[128] Though Deshalji did not receive much more than a "good elementary education" from these instructors, the "strength and vigor" of his intellect made a great impression on them.[129] They were not the only ones to be moved. So pleased were contemporary travelers to find a ruler who "more resembles an English gentleman than an Indian Raja", that they promptly described the Rao as "perhaps the most interesting person in the East" (later visitors were more circumspect; finding the Rao more interested in English guns than Christian scripture, they complained that his education had ended too soon).[130] At any rate, as soon as the Rao came of age in 1834, he was placed in harness and asked to do what he could about the "ignorance, arrogance, and vice" of his clansmen, while the Company moved on to more profitable ventures like annexing neighboring Sindh.[131]

Over the next twenty-five years, Deshalji accomplished more than the Company anticipated, "quietly and discreetly" using his "influence and example" to promote "improvement".[132] In 1836 the slave trade was officially discountenanced; in 1852 the practice of *sati* was outlawed; and by the end of his reign in 1859 the Rao had inaugurated a census of births and deaths and a marriage fund for girls, which reduced the incentive for poor clansmen to commit female infanticide, leading to the proportion of females to males to rise from 1:8 to 1:3.[133] Deshalji himself became, Company officers noted with equal doses of horror and pride, the first Rao to ever "preserve a daughter".[134] Delighted by his "conspicuous attachment" to the cause of reform, and especially by his loyalty during the Mutiny, the British went on to declare him "the best of the princes in Bombay Presidency".[135]

This happy aspect began to change, however, when Deshalji's son, Pragmalji, ascended to the throne in 1860. Having been tutored by an Elphinstonian, the new Rao possessed "a fair knowledge of English", and was considered "an intelligent, hardworking, well-meaning man of a teachable disposition".[136] He differed from his father in one important respect, however. Deshalji had always been cautious about introducing "innovations" because, having seen

Deshalji II, Rao of Kutch. British Library, Add Or 1570

what had happened to *his* father, Bharmalji, he wanted to "avoid any struggle" with the *bhayad*.[137] Pragmalji, by contrast, "exhibited a constant desire to improve the administration of the province". A "great admirer of the English press", the new Rao subscribed to – and actually read – a wide array of newspapers and periodicals.[138] From them he came away with the idea that in the modern era it would no longer be "enough that a State should merely be administered in such a way as not to cause eruptions". Instead, it was essential that a Native State "show progress" in line with "districts under British management".[139]

The concern was not theoretical, as Kutch had begun losing a few thousand residents to British India every year. Given that its population amounted to only half a million, these losses were not insignificant. But the Rao's kindred, the *bhayad*, could not have cared less about the outward migration. They opposed change because they feared, quite rightly, that they would have to subsidize it. Back in 1819, the Company had rewarded the *bhayad* for their help in overthrowing Bharmalji by compelling Deshalji to sign a treaty that flatly "guaranteed their estates".[140] The result was that the *bhayad* henceforth refused to contribute a single *kori* (the lowest denomination in the local currency) toward the exchequer, even as they hampered trade and commerce by imposing transit charges and levying fines and punishments at will.[141] Consequently, by the time Deshalji stepped down, the *bhayad* effectively constituted – a prominent British missionary glumly reported – "187 independent states", each jealously opposed to any alteration of the status quo.[142]

It also meant that of Kutch's annual revenue of fifteen lakhs, only seven and a half lakhs actually belonged to the *darbar*, of which nearly two lakhs was taken by the British as tribute – and even the measly income that remained was highly variable because the utter reliance of Kutch's farmers on the rains made crop failures a common occurrence.[143] No wonder then that, shortly after Pragmalji had put several "works of public usefulness" into motion, and spent sizable amounts on famine relief without any help from the *bhayad*, he began squeezing his clansmen by resuming estates and enforcing more vigorously the orders of his *darbar*.[144]

The *bhayad* responded to these developments, sure enough, by demanding that the British intervene. They found a willing ear in Major Alexander Young Shortt, the Political Agent. Shortt had cut his teeth under George Le Grand Jacob,[145] one of a set of Bombay officers "whose distinctive feature was the extravagant length to which they carried the principle of protecting the subject from his sovereign".[146] Convinced that the Mutiny in 1857 had found no backers in Kutch only because its minor chieftains were content with their lot, Jacob had left behind strict instructions that extant arrangements were not to be disturbed. In keeping with these instructions, Shortt responded to the *bhayad*'s protests by brusquely ordering Pragmalji to refrain from making any "sudden changes".[147] The highhandedness did not go down well in the Kutch *darbar*. Considering his use of sovereign power to be legitimate, indeed commendable, Pragmalji reminded Shortt that the authoritative report on Kutch, written in 1830 by none other than John Malcolm,[148] the celebrated former Governor of Bombay, had directed British officers to support the Rao and seek "the diminution of that depraved, disobedient, and unmanageable class of petty chiefs, whose existence in their actual state is at variance with all plans of improvement and calculated to render unprofitable, if not to destroy, the alliance we have formed with this principality".[149] Irritated by this challenge to his authority, Shortt appealed to his superiors in Bombay for orders, all the while using his reports to depict the Rao as "more anxious for aggrandizement than his late father".[150]

By the middle of the 1860s the "Bhayad Affair", as it came to be known, had become a serious controversy, and reached the front pages of the national press. On one side, Pragmalji argued that he could neither extirpate social evils nor develop Kutch's trade and commerce if the *bhayad* were allowed "complete independence", and on the other, the *bhayad* represented, through Shortt, that the 1819 treaty "guaranteed them their independence in such a sense that it might not be interfered with in the cause of good government".[151] In private, high officials in Bombay rued having given the *bhayad* "too generous a guarantee", one that wholly shielded them from the "just resentments of their prince", and they recognized that Shortt was "biased

Pragmalji II, Rao of Kutch. Getty Research Institute, 2011.R.17

in favor of the feudatory chiefs".[152] Nonetheless, with the Mutiny still on their mind, the last thing they wanted was unrest, Shortt having persuaded them that the *bhayad* "may at any time rebel".[153] In the event, Bombay pushed the Rao to maintain the status quo, warning that he might be ordered to abdicate "in case he failed to comply".[154]

It was at this moment, with Bombay fuming away at the apparently "deplorable" changes in Kutch, that Pragmalji reached out to Anandashram for advice.[155] The English press was beginning to report adversely on Kutch, egged on by Bombay officials that wanted to see the Rao taken down a few pegs. A particular target was Pragmalji's recent decision to replace the ancestral palace of the Raos, the eccentric Aina Mahal, with "a really handsome palace".[156] Designed in a part-Gothic, part-Italian style by a British engineer from Bombay, the upcoming Prag Mahal was meant to symbolize the arrival of modernity in Kutch. The intention was no doubt noble, but the "lordly" structure, which would go on to cost an eye-watering twenty lakhs, allowed Bombay officials to depict Pragmalji as a man of "costly tastes" whose "idea of his power and prerogative" far outstripped the meagre resources of his "petty State".[157]

The adverse reports swirling in the press left the Rao vexed. How could he, an intelligent and well-meaning reformer, be treated so poorly by the very people who claimed to care about the advance of civilization? To this quandary Anandashram had a deceptively simple answer: If the Rao wanted good press, he would have to earn it. Pragmalji ought not to "yield a jot of his just rights", the *sanyasi* observed, but to disable his British critics he needed to show that he considered reform his "prime duty".[158] His investments in public works, which amounted to about half of his annual revenue (or about thirty-two lakhs over his fifteen-year reign), were wholly praiseworthy, but they were not the ultimate example of "regeneration".[159] To prove that Kutch had truly entered the modern age the Rao needed to show that his principality was no despotism. There were plenty of native rulers willing to spend money on ports, roads, bridges, hospitals, and schools, but almost none were prepared to curb their absolute power by introducing a constitutional form of government – and Kutch was no exception. As a widely read report by Shortt's predecessor had pointedly observed, "without his Highness' order, not even a horseman is dispatched from the stables in Kutch".[160] The inevitable consequence of such concentration of power was corruption. Since no ruler could actually monitor daily administration, Pragmalji was forced to rely on retainers to carry out his orders. There was little to prevent these subordinates from abusing the discretion delegated to them, which meant that his critics were never short of ammunition, with Shortt routinely describing the native officials of Kutch as "universally corrupt".[161]

Pragmalji was not insensible to the problem, which is why soon after coming to power he had proclaimed, to the astonishment of his *darbar*, that bribery, which was practically a custom in the Native States of Western India, would henceforth be considered a punishable offense.[162] But the threat had little effect because his subjects were hesitant to complain; they could not be certain that a complaint would receive due attention, much less that they would be shielded from recriminations. Nor did it help that Kutch lacked a written code of law, which meant that the bounds of public authority were hazy and therefore easily abused. Given this, the need of the hour, Anandashram advised the Rao, was to organize his administration into departments that would follow written rules and to place them under educated officials familiar with British Indian procedure. Pragmalji had already made some progress in this direction, having imported a few Elphinstonians into Kutch, but they were too low in the hierarchy to change the character of the *darbar*, which was dominated, as in Jamnagar, by conservative Nagar Brahmins.[163] What the Rao required, the *sanyasi* stressed, was a *dewan* able to both enact administrative reform and hold his own against the Political Agent. And he knew exactly who fit this description – Kazi Shahabuddin Ibrahim.[164]

A rising star in Bombay Presidency, Shahabuddin was then the deputy collector of Surat. But it was his backstory that made him the ideal appointment. He had been born in Sawantwadi in 1832 to a family of limited means but "high respectability", its members having held the hereditary office of *kazi*[165] for generations.[166] His performance in the local school had "arrested the attention" of the local Political Agent – none other than George Le Grand Jacob.[167] With his keen eye for talent, Jacob arranged for Shahabuddin to be admitted to Poona College (better known to history as Deccan College) and then, in view of his ability in mathematics, to the Poona Engineering College. Though the latter institution would have led Shahabuddin to a comfortable position in the Public Works Department, Jacob had higher hopes for his protégé. Thus, upon being appointed Political Agent to Kutch, he recruited Shahabuddin to serve as his secretary and subsequently helped him enter the Bombay Revenue Department. Never one to waste an opportunity, Shahabuddin shot up the ladder "by sheer force of his talents and persevering industry", becoming a *tehsildar*,[168] magistrate, deputy collector, and a Khan Bahadur[169] – all before he was thirty-five.[170]

These varied experiences meant that Shahabuddin had a clear sense of the pros and cons of colonial and native rule. He had witnessed firsthand the abuse of power in Bombay Presidency, where revenue and judicial functions were vested in the same officer, thus allowing a British collector to serve as both witness and magistrate in cases brought against the *ryot* (cultivators).[171] But, from his earlier stint under Jacob in the Kutch Political Agency, he knew that similar abuses were even more common in Kutch, where both functions were performed by *zamindar*s (revenue farmers), a class not known to care very much about due process. Thus, when he arrived in the capital Bhuj in mid-1867, he and Anandashram quickly agreed that by taking the lead on separating revenue and judicial functions, Pragmalji could become an exemplar of liberal reform.[172] Together, the unusual pair – a British-educated *kazi* and a missionary-educated *sanyasi* – prevailed on Pragmalji to trial a new system in Mandvi, the largest district in Kutch, where a court, operated by an independent Judicial Department, was to dispense impartial justice. Though the local *zamindar* was not happy to be stripped of his judicial authority, the people of Mandvi welcomed the change, leading Shortt to grudgingly report of a "marked improvement" in Kutch and to voice the hope that the Mandvi experiment would soon be "introduced into other *mahals* [districts]".[173] But in order to accomplish this ambitious reform, the overstretched *dewan* needed a trustworthy *naib dewan* (deputy minister) to help him formulate a law code and select individuals competent to serve as judges. As it happened, Anandashram knew someone who fit this description perfectly – Parmanand.

The Naib Dewan

Parmanand was in a difficult spot when Anandashram reached out seeking his services. In March 1867 he had stepped down as editor of *Native Opinion* when his three-year contract with Mandlik came to an end. There were multiple factors behind the decision. Principal was his "dread" at how Anglo-Indians had begun to respond to the exposés being published in *Native Opinion*.[174] His objective had been "to help the government by providing information that will only be known to natives".[175] But British India did not want so much help. In official circles, native editors were starting to be described as "professional traitors" dedicated to "seditious writing".[176] As British officialdom closed ranks, *Native Opinion*'s reports began to have declining impact. One galling example was the Bombay government's decision to renew Arthur Crawford, the municipal commissioner, even after the *Native Opinion* exposed his mismanagement of local finances.[177] Even more galling was the reaction to a report exposing negligence on the part of Thomas Brown Kirkham, the Principal of Elphinstone High School. Instead of reprimanding the errant official, the Director of Public Instruction – none other than Parmanand's former teacher, Alexander Grant – blasted the report as a "calumnious attack" and angrily cancelled his subscription to *Native Opinion*.[178] This was the same man who had, only a few years prior, given Parmanand a letter of recommendation that read: "Modest, truthful, and with a strong sense of duty, he would be sure to give his employer satisfaction."[179]

Then there was the hostility (or "John Bullism" as Parmanand put it) of the Anglo-Indian press.[180] Accustomed to having its pronouncements go unchallenged, it had come to loathe the upstart *Native Opinion*. There were plenty of observers who understood what was happening – that Anglo-Indians were consumed by "arrogant jealousy" at "self-assertion" by educated natives.[181] But this did not lessen the dismay that Parmanand felt when influential publications like the *Times of India* and *Bombay Gazette* routinely claimed that the English columns in *Native Opinion* were written by disgruntled Englishmen "dressed up as natives for the occasion", or that the columns merely voiced the "chronic hostility" of educated Maratha Brahmins.[182] There was little hope of rebutting such smears when a publication like the *Times of India* had a national circulation six times larger than *Native Opinion* (and a monthly edition, which went to London, that had a circulation a hundred times larger).[183]

It had also not been clear to Parmanand how much longer the *Native Opinion* would remain in circulation. The still-limited number of natives able to read English meant that the newspaper could not easily grow its subscriber base, and its unwillingness to tone down its editorials meant it could not attract advertisers (in contrast to outlets like the *Times of India*, which benefitted handsomely from official patronage). By the time Parmanand decided to resign, the enterprise was over twelve thousand rupees in the red and becoming more trouble than it was worth for Mandlik, who had to bear the brunt of the common misperception (which exists to this day) that he was the "sole contributor" to *Native Opinion* and therefore personally responsible for every barb it aimed at Anglo-Indian officialdom.[184]

After departing *Native Opinion*, Parmanand devoted several months to the cause of social reform. He played a central role in establishing and raising funds for the Prarthana Samaj (Prayer Society), an organization devoted to advancing the theistic ideals originally espoused by the Brahmo Samaj in Calcutta. But there were other responsibilities to live up to. Having become a father twice over, he had a family to care for, and so in June 1867 he took up employ in Graham & Co., a long-established Bombay mercantile firm. But the lure of the pen was too strong to resist and before he knew it, he was drawn into one of the most important debates of the era. The context was this: In the early part of 1867, two successive Secretaries of State for India, Stafford Northcote and Robert Cecil (or the Marquess of Salisbury), had overruled the Government of India and announced that the principality of Mysore was to be "restored" to its erstwhile rulers, the Wadiyars, who had been deposed by the Company in 1832 on account of "misrule".[185] In a subsequent debate in the House of Commons, Salisbury had defended the decision with the observation that the system of government in Native States had "a fitness and congeniality" that it was "impossible for us adequately to realize".[186] This was borne out, Salisbury added, by what he had heard from George Clerk, the former Governor of Bombay, who told him that in Kathiawar,

> Natives ... were continually in the habit of migrating from the English into the Native jurisdiction; but that he never heard of an instance of a Native leaving his own to go into the English jurisdiction. This may be very bad taste on the part of the Natives; but you have to consider what promotes their happiness, suits their tastes, and tends to their moral development in their own way.[187]

Seething at this challenge to its mandate, Calcutta fought back in the usual way – by taking advantage of its presence on the ground. In July 1867, the Viceroy, John Lawrence, sent out a circular to his Residents and Political Agents in the Native States canvassing their views on the "comparative merits" of colonial and native rule. Lest there be any doubt, Lawrence prefaced the circular with the observation that he was of the opinion that "the masses of the people are incontestably more prosperous and – *sua si bona norint*[188] – far more happy in British territory than they are under Native rulers".[189] Unsurprisingly, his subordinates rushed to confirm the Viceroy's assessment by contrasting the many "defects" of native administration with the many "excellences" of colonial administration, which ultimately led them to the happy conclusion that only "great jackasses" could prefer the former to the latter.[190]

These self-congratulatory missives, which were compiled and published by the Government of India in December 1867, left the normally unflappable Parmanand fuming. Not only had the Viceroy not cared to ask "a single native" what they thought, his officers had conveniently ignored the "real question" that Salisbury had posed, which was whether the natives were "very much happier" under colonial rule.[191] They ignored, for instance, Salisbury's acute criticism of the 1861 Orissa Famine, which had claimed more than a million lives (which Calcutta had gallingly blamed on the "fatalistic apathy" of the natives rather than their own miserly investments in irrigation and relief works).[192] With Anandashram's reports on the progress being made by Jaipur and Kutch still fresh in his mind, Parmanand decided to "supplement" the official record. Free from his editorial responsibilities, he now had time to develop a sustained argument. Thus, in January 1868 he published in *Native Opinion* a series of unsigned essays that examined the pros and cons of *both* colonial and native rule. The Native States were, he conceded, "wretchedly bungled tracts" where constraints on power, as authorized by the *shastra*s and by precedent, had fallen into disuse. But the Native States remained popular with subjects or at least tolerable places to live in, he noted, because "indigenous" rule had the virtue of being "flexible" and "sympathetic".[193] British India, by contrast, was certainly better administered, but its rule was disliked by subjects because it involved "a most costly administration, vexatious, uncertain and dearly purchased justice, caste exclusivism of the ruling race, and a closed and highhanded official bureaucracy".[194] What this meant, in sum, was that the happiness of Indians – that is, their economic and moral development – depended on either the "systematization" of rule in Native States or the "popularization" of rule in British India.[195] But, at least for the moment, neither path seemed open, because the imperial nature of British rule militated against concessions to its subjects in British India and also inhibited it from supporting potentially disruptive reforms in principalities like Jamnagar and Kutch.

The essays in *Native Opinion* were an immediate hit. So great was public interest that the press reissued them as a "brochure" with the title *English and Native Rule in India*, making it one of the very first English-language pamphlets to circulate the country. Though the publication was unsigned, Parmanand's authorship was known to those in positions of power. He fully expected that there would be adverse consequences, gloomily declaring in one of the essays that "nothing is supposed to be so acceptable to a European official as the genuine opinion and wishes of the native on every subject that may concern them both or the public at large, and yet when that opinion happens to be disagreeable or opposed to that of the inquirer ... their fate is unenviable".[196] Parmanand did not have to wait long to see his assertion validated. In February 1868, only a few weeks after Parmanand's essays were published, Bombay sanctioned the long-discussed post of "Reporter on Native Newspapers", which involved summarizing and evaluating relevant reports in native publications in the Presidency.[197] Still hoping to play the role of a fair-minded intermediary between ruler and ruled, Parmanand applied for the position, which was to be supervised by Grant, his former teacher at Elphinstone. For a month or two, his name was all over town, with numerous publications advocating on his behalf. But in the wake of *English and Native Rule in India*, which challenged the Viceroy by name, his supporters in the Anglo-Indian community began to peel away. Though he had previously indicated that he considered Parmanand well-qualified for the position, Grant suddenly ceased all communication with him and proceeded to silently award the post to Krishna Shastri Chiplunkar,[198] Parmanand's older associate.[199] Thankfully, not every teacher from Elphinstone was as narrow-minded as Grant. Ever on Parmanand's side, Hughlings immediately supplied a letter of recommendation that his disciple could use to apply for other positions:

> I have been acquainted with Mr. Narayan Mahadev Parmanand since I entered the country in 1857. For four or five years he was one of my pupils in Elphinstone College, for other one or two years he was employed in the Educational Dept;

> since which he has been conducting, as Editor, a newspaper of character and ability, *Native Opinion*. In all these different situations and functions I have seen a good deal of him and have always found him to be the same. He is exceedingly industrious, careful and accurate, modest and candid in disposition, and pleasing in manners. As a student he was extremely punctual and laborious and attained to considerable skill in English composition. In the various and responsible employments he has had since, I have never heard of one fault being objected to in him and they always have been employments which imply work and responsibility. He has always seemed to me to be a thoroughly sound man in respect of mind and character.[200]

Parmanand handled the setback with equanimity. To agitated missives from friends and well-wishers, he simply replied with his favorite *shloka* (or verse) from the Gita: *sukha duhkhe same krtva*.[201] But as the news that he had been snubbed got around, other takers for his talents appeared – the Native States, where his *English and Native Rule in India* had made a mark. A flood of offers followed, the most ardent of which came from the Kutch *darbar*. Initially, Parmanand rejected these propositions; it had never been his intention to parley his writing into a post. Besides, he had sensed – correctly it would turn out – that his temperament was not suited to administering a Native State. Nevertheless, his associates leaned on him to heed Pragmalji's call. Mandlik, who had served as Le Grand Jacob's secretary before Shahabuddin took over that role, only had good words for the current *dewan* of Kutch, as did Anandashram.[202] And there was a favorable wind blowing through Bombay at this time. A number of Elphinstonians had plunged (or were about to plunge) into the Native States, led by Ranade who had taken up the post of *nyayadhisha* (chief magistrate) in Kolhapur, the storied Maratha principality from which he originated.[203]

After much urging, in April 1868 Parmanand tentatively opened negotiations with Shahabuddin. The *dewan* was characteristically warm and accommodating. In short order it was agreed that Parmanand would receive 350 rupees a month (a sizable raise from the two hundred rupees a month he had been paid at *Native Opinion*) and that the contract would initially be for two years (which he had the right to exit early).[204] By the end of the month, the news was in the press, which lauded Kutch for appointing a "patriot" who had labored for his countrymen "at great sacrifice to self".[205] Parmanand himself was less sure the *darbar* had made the right choice, especially as Shahabuddin had made it clear that Parmanand was effectively being trialed to replace him – as and when his own deputation from Surat ended. Sensing Parmanand's unease, the *dewan* reassured him that, though the role would "seem quite hard and novel at first glance", both he and Pragmalji were "expecting very great things from you".[206] But Parmanand could not shake off the sense of dread. Bhagwat's experience in Jamnagar weighed heavily on him, as he too was going to serve as *nyayadhisha*, a post that was guaranteed to bring him into conflict with vested interests. The practical advice he received from Anandashram, close to the time of departure, did not help, with the simply dressed *sanyasi* telling his simply dressed disciple that,

> people in these parts will judge you based on your external appearance, rather than your precious internal qualities. So to make an impression on the people here and to keep them in awe, it is important to pay attention to external ostentation. Unlike Mumbai where simplicity is considered a virtue, there is nothing of the sort here. The people here are of a type to be swayed by externals. As the *naib dewan*, your attire and overall pomp should be one to do credit to the position.[207]

By June 1868 Parmanand was in Kutch, having sent in advance a photograph – the only one ever taken of him – so that the *dewan* could spot the *naib dewan* when he disembarked. The two men hit it off immediately and wasted no time in getting down to work. Over the next few months, a number of "salutary reforms" were launched.[208] A law code, the first of its kind in the region, was drafted, and Pragmalji was persuaded to sanction a costly but sorely needed census that would make it easier to "ascertain the actual number of persons leaving and entering" his principality.[209] He was also persuaded to establish a high school that would prepare Kachchhis for matriculation examinations at Elphinstone College and Poona College and thereby create, in due course, a talent pool for the *darbar* to draw upon.[210] There was also, of course, the much-awaited inauguration of the judicial department. Its impartial operation quickly earned Shortt's praise and, as news spread in the *mofussil* that the *dewan* and *naib dewan* would spare no one, there was a "marked decrease in crime".[211]

But it was not long before Parmanand encountered the very same challenge that his former colleague Bhagwat had faced in Jamnagar. A few months into his tenure, a case came before him involving a wealthy gentleman as the plaintiff, and a woman of ordinary means as the defendant. After hearing both sides, Parmanand ruled in favor of the defendant. Two months later, the defendant reappeared to complain that the court's order had not been complied with. When he enquired into the matter, Parmanand discovered that:

> There was an able and experienced courtier of the old school, a native of the place, who had filled the highest posts in the State, but who, though not in the service any longer (in fact he had been debarred from office for some misbehaviour at the instance of the British Government), because of his knowledge of State affairs and his large following possessed influence with the *darbar* and in consequence was resorted to by all disappointed suitors to gain their ends. The party dissatisfied with the decision in the case referred to, obtained through his influence secret instructions to the district official to suspend execution of the judicial order. When this interference with the course of justice was resented by the highest judicial officer, the old gentleman remarked

> in all sincerity that, if all things were to be managed straight in Native as in British territory, what should constitute a Rajvada or a Native Court?[212]

Taken aback by this challenge to his authority, Parmanand sought Shahabuddin's intervention. The *dewan* commiserated with his deputy but declared that he was powerless. "I have become fully aware of the extremely difficult circumstances you are having to struggle against, and work in," he wrote back, "but you know that in such matters, I too, cannot do anything." Though he had raised the matter with Pragmalji, "requisite steps" were not likely to be taken in the near future. Hence, Parmanand ought to "be prepared to get on as best as you can under these difficulties".[213] Parmanand was not offended by the blunt advice, which was reiterated by Anandashram the following day. It was, after all, the very thing Parmanand himself had said to Bhagwat when the latter was serving as *nyayadhisha* in Jamnagar, telling him to "tolerate abuses for a time in order to ensure safety to all their plans".[214] But now, standing the breach, Parmanand saw the matter differently: He was being tested by the "old interests" and to compromise now would "make a mockery of his sacred office".[215] What was the point of being a *nyayadhisha* whose judgements could be rudely "trampled underfoot"?

Parmanand understood full well why the Rao, who had spared no expense in obtaining his services, was unwilling to support him in this pivotal contest. Pragmalji's priority was to prevail over the *bhayad*, and so he was leery of alienating powerful constituencies in his own territory. And unfortunately, his contest with the *bhayad* was only intensifying. Even as Shahabuddin and Parmanand were setting up a system of independent courts, Shortt convinced Bombay to authorize the creation of a separate court to deal with questions of law and order in the *bhayad*'s domains. This institution, which Shortt termed the Jadeja Court,[216] was to comprise four members of the *bhayad* and the *naib dewan*, who were to decide on cases collectively, with final appeal to the Political Agent.[217] Not only did this proposal weaken Pragmalji's authority, but it was also quite unworkable because the *bhayad* were simply too fractured and ignorant to perform a judicial role. In fact, at the very moment that Shortt was projecting the *bhayad* as an "ancient restraint" on the "despotic Rao", these petty chiefs were being mocked in British India for their refusal to allow teachers and vaccinators into their domains.[218] At any rate, by the end of 1868 Pragmalji was at the end of his tether. He bluntly refused to cooperate with the proposed Jadeja Court, and informed Bombay that he would rather abdicate than give way.[219] As he angrily replied to Bombay's missives,

> while it is everywhere admitted as a condition indispensable to advancement that judicial administration should be under a central control, with a properly

> organized system, why is it proposed in Kutch to break up the supreme authority, and entrust judicial power, without system or control, into the hands of numerous, incompetent *zamindars*?[220]

This "really grave" development prompted Parmanand and Anandashram to come up with a daring plan.[221] Since Pragmalji was unlikely to support substantive reforms until the *bhayad* had been soundly defeated, they had to help him find a way to get London to discipline the Bombay officers that were backing the *bhayad*. The impending victory of the Liberal Party, under the crusading leadership of William Gladstone, gave them reason to hope that their plea on behalf of progress would be welcomed. The recent example of Mysore was before them, where the concerted efforts of English publicists, most notably Thomas Evans Bell,[222] had helped convince Parliament to overrule the Viceroy and restore the kingdom to the Wadiyars, the ruling clan that had been deposed by the Company. Hoping for similar success, they reached out to Dadabhai Naoroji, the renowned publicist who had recently established the East India Association in London and Bombay, of which Parmanand was a member.[223] They soon tasted blood. Having examined the materials sent by the Kutch *darbar*, Naoroji submitted a memorandum in November 1868 to the authorities in London, urging them to introduce a new "imperial policy" for the more progressive among the Native States. In characteristic fashion, he put the point acutely:

> The question is, whether the administration of the Native States is to be made sufficiently vigorous under central and able executives duly restricted by the paramount power and constitutional checks of spontaneous development, so as with larger resources to become capable of providing efficient machinery for governing the people and of developing the resources of the territory to the best advantage, or whether the power and resources of each state should be broken up into weak parts, powerless for any good either to the people or to the paramount power.[224]

The memorandum had some effect on George Campbell, who assumed the office of Secretary of State for India the following month. Persuaded that the Rao, who "so worthily" governed Kutch, may not have been given the "fullest and fairest hearing", he agreed to Pragmalji making his case anew.[225] But Campbell insisted that "no good object" could be served by the Rao sending an "agent" to England and urged him to submit fresh arguments to Bombay direct.[226] The *darbar* ignored the advice. Kutch's view, they were certain, had to be put forward by someone familiar with its complicated political and judicial arrangements – and sympathetic to the Rao.

There was only one person who had both the experience and stature to win over London – and that was Shahabuddin. Anandashram and Parmanand knew that the *dewan* had a soft spot for Pragmalji; in private he was wont to say that "there was not a Native Prince on this side of India so amiable, intelligent and considerate towards his servants as his Highness the Rao".[227] But Shahabuddin was in an "embarrassing position". He disagreed entirely with Shortt's policy, but as a "servant on loan" from the Bombay Revenue Department he could also not openly oppose the Political Agent.[228] More than once, he had considered writing an anonymous article exposing Shortt's imbecility, only to conclude that discretion was the better part of valor because, as he confided in Parmanand, "should anyone suspect that I am writing on the side of an Indian ruler, all the hopes I have entertained of advancement in the political line would be dashed".[229] Knowing that he would not be of much use in Kutch while the Rao was consumed by the *bhayad* business, Shahabuddin had recently voiced the desire to return to his position in Surat.[230] Fortunately, the "earnest solicitations" of his colleagues now convinced the *dewan* to do the unthinkable, which was to resign his appointment as deputy collector in Surat, and to prepare to depart for England with a view to presenting the Rao's case in person before the Secretary of State for India.[231] The audacious gambit, which sought to break

Bombay Government Secretariat. Victoria and Albert Museum, E.208:440-1994

British India's stranglehold over how Kutch was represented in London, left Calcutta aghast, with the Viceroy declaring it "a cause of some surprise" that one of his officers should have "apparently espoused the cause of the Rao".[232]

Once events were in motion, Parmanand decided it was time for him to depart Kutch. There was no telling if Shahabuddin would succeed, and Parmanand was not the type to while away time. Besides, there were great events underway in Bombay that he did not want to miss. The long-defunct Bombay Association, the pioneering political association in the metropolis, was in the midst of being "resuscitated", with Parmanand's friends taking the lead in making it "an exponent of the feelings and sentiments of the native community".[233] There were also family pressures: Though his mother and sister had passed away in the intervening years, he ached to be with his wife and children, whom he had left behind in Bombay. Of course he could not let Anandashram down, and so Parmanand made sure to identify a suitable person to take over the post of *nyayadhisha*. He fixed on Bhoghilal Pranvallabhdas, a well-regarded Elphinstonian, then serving as the Principal of the English School at Rajkot. Bhoghilal was fluent in Gujarati and familiar with Kutch, as Shahabuddin had previously invited him to inspect its schools.[234] Once Bhoghilal had agreed to replace him, Parmanand went before Pragmalji in late December 1868 to tender his resignation. It was a tragic moment. On the one side, the Rao, well-meaning but hemmed in by circumstance, on the other, his *naib dewan*, well-meaning but unable to bear the shame of compromise. "Parmanand! So then you're leaving!" was all that the disconsolate Rao could bring himself to say, his eyes red with emotion.[235] Choking up, Parmanand folded his hands and bowed deeply. And that was that.

The Bombay Government

Though his career as a *naib dewan* had been short-lived, it made Parmanand realize that he had some aptitude for judicial business. Thus, upon returning to Bombay he reached out to William Wedderburn, then the officiating Registrar of the Bombay High Court. The two had known each other for more than half a decade, having been introduced by Mandlik when *Native Opinion* was launched. Back then, Wedderburn was still making a name for himself as an official who cared deeply for the well-being of natives under his authority (a trait considered all the more remarkable seeing as his elder brother had perished in the 1857 Mutiny). After learning more about Wedderburn, Parmanand joined the ranks of those complimenting his "unostentatious laboring" on behalf of the native population.[236] Wedderburn, in turn, went on to become one of the few British officials that remained friendly toward Parmanand even after *English and Native Rule in India* was published. Wedderburn was aware of what Parmanand had tried to do as *nyayadhisha* in Kutch, as he had during that time been serving as an undersecretary in the Bombay Judicial Department. He therefore went out of his way to help Parmanand find employment in the Bombay High Court. There being no vacancy, he initially had to recruit Parmanand as a deputy bench clerk, which was quite the come down from being a *naib dewan*. Some

William Wedderburn. National Portrait Gallery, x35530

months later, in December 1869, Wedderburn's deputy put in for furlough, allowing him to appoint Parmanand as officiating Assistant Registrar.[237] This was a slightly more fitting post, but it would only last a few months. The only upside to the lack of steady employment was that it gave Parmanand time to write and reflect. To wit, in 1869 he published *Birbalva Badshaha Yanchia Goshti, or the Oriental Bertholde*,[238] a short account in the Marathi language of the wit and wisdom of Birbal, the famed Hindu courtier to the Mughal *badshah* (or emperor) Akbar.[239] Presumably inspired by Parmanand's time in Kutch, this now-lost booklet attracted critical attention and went on to win the prestigious Dakshina Prize in 1870.[240]

All said and done, this was one of the most trying periods in Parmanand's life. To the professional uncertainty was added immense personal loss. On New Year's Day in 1870, he learned that Anandashram had passed away two days prior. The Swami had been ailing for some time but, with Shahabuddin and Parmanand gone, he felt he could not leave Kutch to seek medical advice, and thus became a "victim to his goodness".[241] Consequently, the next two months were taken up in organizing "a suitable tribute" for the Swami, which was to be an English-medium school in Mandvi, funded by his many devotees in Kathiawar.[242] Barely had Parmanand come to terms with losing one guiding light than another went out. In March 1870, Hughlings suffered a month-long bout of dysentery that left him enervated. Hoping to "shake off" the illness, he followed his doctor's advice to undertake an extended sea-voyage – to distant Australia.[243] The grueling expedition only worsened Hughlings' health, leading to his death shortly after he arrived in Australia. And so, in July Parmanand found himself on another memorial committee, this time to raise subscriptions for a commemorative portrait that was to be placed in Elphinstone.[244]

The sudden loss of both his *guru*s, both of whom were still in the prime of their lives, left Parmanand disconsolate. He yearned to live up to their examples by devoting himself more fully to the service of others. Still, with a family to care for, he had no choice but to continue searching for stable employment. Into the breach stepped Wedderburn once again. Having been appointed Secretary in the Judicial Department in the interim, he elected to take Parmanand along with him, appointing him Acting Assistant Secretary in April 1870.[245] Though this appointment too was only temporary – to replace a British officer on a three-month furlough – it was the first time that this important post had been occupied by a member of "Young Bombay".[246] The timely development brought Parmanand renewed public attention as a "worthy" character and became the basis for a permanent appointment as Superintendent in the General and Land Revenue Department in August 1870.[247]

This is the post Parmanand would occupy for the next decade and a half. It was much less than he deserved – indeed he often despaired the endless "slog" that left him with little time to read and write.[248] His contemporaries blamed the lack of upward movement on his "innate modesty and retiring disposition, which was leading him to do much injustice to himself".[249] But, the fact of the matter was that higher appointments were not likely to come his way as British officials grew increasingly wary of Indians connected with the native press. Still, the post of Superintendent had one great virtue, which was that it gave him a bird's eye view of the functioning of important departments and thus helped him better comprehend the strengths and weaknesses of colonial administration. What he learned in the Secretariat, he parleyed into writing and action – when a vital principle was at stake. An early contribution in this regard were his "silent labours" on behalf of the Bombay Ratepayers' Association, the pioneering civic association in the metropolis.[250] So vital was his role that it deserves to be recounted.

The Ratepayers' Association was founded in November 1870 in response to the "extravagance" and "irresponsibility" of Arthur Crawford, the Municipal Commissioner under whom the municipal government had continually racked up budget deficits (which *Native Opinion* had long criticized to little avail).[251] The ratepayers were particularly incensed when the Justices of the Peace, who were appointed by the government to oversee the municipal government, tamely allowed Crawford to meet recurrent budgetary shortfalls by raising cesses, taking out loans, and licensing alcohol dens. Over the next two years, the association peppered the government with memorials demanding an "alteration in the constitution of the municipality to secure effective control over the executive and greater efficiency and economy in administration".[252] "Nearly all" of these memorials, which would later be cited as milestones in the quest for local self-government, were drafted by Parmanand.[253] Happily, the memorials, and the loud demonstrations that accompanied them, had impact. Though the Ratepayers' Association did not get all it wanted, in 1872 the Legislative Council passed the Bombay Municipal Act, creating two representative bodies, a Corporation and a Town Council, the majority of whose members were chosen by ratepayers. Crucially, the municipality's finances were brought under the control of the Town Council – in anticipation of which Crawford resigned his post and "fled" to England.[254] His successor would be, as *Native Opinion* had long urged, a Bombay native – a recent graduate of Lincoln's Inn by the name of Pherozeshah Mehta.[255]

Even at the time, Parmanand's "yeoman's service" to Bombay was "hardly known except to a few".[256] He had to be especially discreet because there were plenty of British officers in the Secretariat who, recalling the exposés he had published in *Indu Prakash* and *Native Opinion*, were spoiling for a fight. Any overt involvement in a native association whose "monster meetings" were causing a sensation in Western India would have given them more ammunition to use against him.[257] Subsequent events would bear out his caution: A much-anticipated promotion to the post of Assistant Secretary was snuffed out by the malice of a British officer who blamed Crawford's troubles on Parmanand's editorials in *Native Opinion* (whereas ironically Crawford himself would retrospectively praise the newspaper as "fair and temperate").[258]

Parmanand's associates bemoaned the constraints that employment in the civil service imposed upon his participation in public affairs, deeming it a "clog on him".[259] But there were no viable alternatives, especially once he foreswore returning to the Native States where, he was now convinced, the weight of tradition would make reform slow and grinding for the foreseeable future. With no "independent non-official career" as a doctor, lawyer, or merchant open to him – the paths by which his contemporaries had successfully "emancipated themselves" from immediate dependence on the Bombay government – he had no choice but to live within the constraints associated with public employment, and take comfort in the fact that he had colleagues that admired his "good qualities of head and heart".[260] The stature that came with being a senior civil servant was not to be scoffed at either. It contributed, for instance, to his being appointed a Justice of the Peace alongside the crème de la crème of the city.[261]

The upside to these constraints on political participation was that Parmanand had more time for his other great passion – social reform. The subject had animated him since his days in Elphinstone, where his membership in the secretive Paramahansa Mandali had brought him under the influence of Atmaram Pandurang,[262] Bhau Daji Lad,[263] and Ram Balkrishna Jayakar,[264] the pioneering Hindu reformers of the preceding generation. Like them, he became a strong votary of female education, caste reform, and widow remarriage.[265] Having witnessed up close the "mental torture" a woman had to endure after being widowed, the last of these causes was especially dear to him.[266] In 1865, shortly before his mother passed away, he had become one of the first members of the Bombay Widow Remarriage Association, and in June 1869 he had been one of the leading "native gentlemen" to attend the first Brahmin remarriage to be publicly celebrated in Bombay.[267] These actions were not costless. The association was fiercely opposed by the orthodox element in the city, whose adherents turned up at the wedding, leading to a confrontation in which Parmanand, among others, seized the list of attendees that the protestors were compiling to intimidate the guests.[268] This led the offended party to press charges against the reformers, Parmanand included. Though the public prosecutor refused to take up the case for "want of sufficient evidence", the orthodox proceeded to excommunicate the reformers, the consequences of which included their being ostracized at dinners, marriages, and funerals.[269] None of this had deterred Parmanand. He went on to create a "small colony" in his neighborhood for families of remarried widows, an arrangement that allowed them to give each other succor, and to associate freely with Parmanand and Janaki and their many influential friends.[270]

The episode summarized what would go on to distinguish Parmanand from his associates, namely his utter unwillingness to compromise on declared principles (a stance that was, admittedly, made easier by the fact that he was not a Brahmin). Having sworn to refrain from child marriage, he refused to marry a prepubescent girl, no matter how much his mother wailed; and having promised to advance women's education, he carried through by using Tukaram's[271] *abhang*s (devotional poems) to teach Janaki to read and write Marathi no matter how busy he was.[272] His friends were, unfortunately, not always able to summon the requisite courage, much to his annoyance. The only time in his life when he was cross with Telang, for instance, was when the latter elected to marry his underage daughter to appease his ailing wife ("I have fulfilled the lower duty and neglected the higher", a remorseful Telang wrote to Parmanand, who was unmoved by the excuse).[273]

The "lack of backbone" among his fellow Elphinstonians was especially apparent on matters relating to caste.[274] Nearly every one of them had been members of the Paramhansa Mandali, whose initiation ceremony required them to prove their "sincerity" by "eating a piece of bread baked by a Christian and drinking some milk tasted by the others".[275] They had also engaged in intercaste dining on a regular basis, but only in "strictest secrecy", as they feared "the wrath of the orthodox", who were on the lookout for the "set of bastards" at Elphinstone that were rumored to have violated caste rules.[276] And so, when an errant member stole the membership book in 1860, the Mandali effectively "ceased to exist", as few were prepared to openly associate with it and suffer the "caste persecution" that would follow.[277] This pusillanimity reappeared many times over the following decade. One embarrassing example, reported in newspapers as far away as New York and Sydney, came in 1870 when Alexander Grant invited the leading representatives of "Young Bombay" to meet with Norman Macleod, a visiting clergyman from Scotland. Not realizing that these "singularly pleasing and intelligent gentlemen" were meeting with him "on the sly", Macleod wrote a column in the British press commending them for having "renounced caste", cheerily adding that they "ate and drank with us".[278] When news of the column reached Bombay, it caused fury in orthodox circles. In short order, the co-convener of the dinner, Krishna Shastri Chiplunkar (the person Grant had chosen to be Reporter on the Native Press) had to appear before the leading authorities of his caste in Poona to publicly "beg forgiveness" for having "partaken a little fruit, ice-cream, and preserved ginger" with foreigners and to pay a substantial fine as *prayaschitta* (penance).[279]

Episodes such as this, which revealed that his fellow Elphinstonians were "not very sturdy Hindus", led Parmanand to the important conclusion that social reform depended ultimately on religious reform.[280] Therefore, once he had settled into the post of Superintendent, he devoted his free time to building up the Prarthana Samaj, which comprised those members of the now-defunct Paramahansa Mandali who considered spiritual upliftment their "main duty".[281] As usual, his efforts were "quiet, persistent and indefatigable", and before long his home, steered by the ever-supportive Janaki, began serving as the Samaj's de facto headquarters.[282] As the "soul of the Samaj" during this period, Parmanand pushed forward on two fronts.[283] As a practical matter, he sought to develop the Samaj into a means of defense against threats of ostracism. The only way for reformers to protect themselves from the "inconveniences" attendant on the "loss of caste", he wrote to his co-founders, was to "form themselves into a community of their own and bring about social intercourse and intermarriages among themselves".[284] To this end, in his capacity as Treasurer, he raised funds – from the Rao of Kutch in particular – for a *mandir* (or temple) where the families of Samaj members could congregate, and thereby develop a sense of community.[285] By the end of 1873, Upasana Mandir, built at a cost of twelve thousand rupees, was complete, giving the Samaj a much-desired focal point for its activities.[286]

The other part of Parmanand's involvement in the Prarthana Samaj was his role as the editor of the English section of its weekly newspaper, *Subodh Patrika*.[287] Originally launched in May 1873, the *Patrika* had previously been published only in Marathi, with a view to propagating and defending the theistic principles the Samaj had inherited from the Paramhansa Mandali (which had, in turn, inherited them from the pioneering Hindu reform organization, the Manav Dharma Sabha).[288] These principles, which called for revealed religions to be set aside in favor of a rational and universal faith, were deeply radical for the time, and *Subodh Patrika* had its hands full responding to ferocious criticism from the orthodox camp. The heated debate, and a low price of one paisa, meant that the *Patrika* soon had the largest circulation in Bombay Presidency, with some sixteen hundred weekly subscribers.[289]

The English section of the *Patrika*, which commenced in December 1877, ranged broadly. Rather than discuss the "dry abstractions" that occupied Brahmin theologians in the Marathi press, Parmanand wrote extensively on "practical religion", urging his audience, for instance, to see the importance of daily prayer, to treat the prospect of death with equanimity, and to realize that God did not reside in temples alone.[290] His objective in all these cases was to address the "prevailing indifference to religious questions" among the English-educated denizens of Western India.[291] Even so, the bulk of his editorials still focused on the moral aspect of the political and social questions of the day: whether it was fair for a budget to be passed without discussion in the legislature; why there were so few natives willing and able to serve in the military; how the government could prevent the use of torture by police officers; and so on.[292] The common thread running through these editorials was that they all pushed, in one way or another, for the British authorities to be more responsive to native interests and sentiments – the same principle that Parmanand had championed at *Native Opinion* and in his *English and Native Rule in India*.

As he had done with *Native Opinion*, Parmanand took advantage of his "masterful English" to gain a wider hearing for his views. On religious matters, he brought *Subodh Patrika* into conversation with Keshab Chandra Sen's *Indian Mirror*, which was the mouthpiece of the ascendant wing of the Brahmo Samaj. More impactful still were his efforts to forge a link between political actors in Bombay and Calcutta. He frequently made common cause with Motilal Ghosh, whose *Amrita Bazaar Patrika*, had the highest circulation in Bengal Presidency. As was his wont, Parmanand helped Ghosh by contributing unsigned essays that helped Bengalis understand ideas and movements in Western India, and more importantly, by using his networks to "pump out" information that would help *Amrita Bazaar Patrika* embarrass his perennial target – British officials that failed to live up to their "sacred duty" to India.[293]

Part II: Why write *Letters to an Indian Raja*?

Up to this point we have examined the events and personalities that shaped Parmanand's intellect and career. The crucial point to absorb is that he was one of the very few in his generation who had the chance to participate in public administration and high politics in both British India and Indian India. This unique vantage point allowed him to carefully study the strengths and weaknesses of these very different systems. His experience in Kutch, we have seen, left him uneasy about the prospect of progressive reform in the Native States. So why then did he elect to write *Letters to an Indian Raja*? The section below begins by outlining the personal tragedy that, ironically, freed Parmanand to write, and then moves on to consider the political developments that revived his hopes for the Native States.

The final decade

In October 1883, Parmanand's life changed – suddenly and irrevocably. One morning, while waiting for his daily train from Charni Station to

Victoria Terminus, he had a severe attack of vertigo and tremors that made him fall to the platform floor. After being revived, he was escorted to his office, where another bout of dizziness caused him to collapse at his desk. The doctor who was rushed to the Secretariat diagnosed the problem as overwork and advised an extended period of rest. Parmanand was therefore sent home and placed on sick leave. But within a few months it became apparent that he was suffering from a progressive disease (now termed Parkinson's).[294] The vertigo and tremors only worsened. His muscular system began stiffening up as well, causing acute discomfort when he sat or wrote for more than a few minutes. His voice lost strength too, compelling him to speak in a whisper tone. Though his mind remained clear and sharp, he was, for all intents and purposes, bedridden.

When it became clear that there was no hope of recovery, the Revenue Department gave Parmanand permission to work from home. This was, really, an act of compassion, meant to allow him, the sole breadwinner in his family, with his children still in school, the chance to complete the period of service needed to become eligible for a government pension. Embarrassed but helpless, Parmanand went along with the scheme, aided by his "saintly wife" and a "small congregation" of friends who served as notetakers and couriers.[295] In March 1886, he was finally able to put in for an "invalid pension".[296] Though he was still three months short of the "qualifying service" of fifteen years, he was now able to supply an authoritative letter, from an eminent physician in London that Wedderburn had consulted on his behalf, recommending convalescence at a "seaside residence".[297] Glad to bring the stopgap arrangement to an end, the Revenue Department readily supported Parmanand's application. The following month it announced that it "really approved" his past services and awarded him an "invalid gratuity" of 133 rupees per month for the remainder of his days.[298]

Freed from the "drudgery" of office work, Parmanand was now able to devote his energies, declining though they were, to the cause of reform.[299] While unable to participate in public events, he had other means to keep abreast of developments. Visitors continued to stream to his home, carrying intelligence and seeking his advice, making his bedroom "a sort of club for the discussion of public questions".[300] There was also a steady flow of correspondence to and from his many friends and admirers across the Presidency, which included Mandlik, Ranade, and Telang, who were on the Bombay Legislative Council. Newspapers were read out to him daily and he continued to edit the *Subodh Patrika*, which remained a leading English-language outlet in Western India. He also began to contribute regularly to an upcoming publication, *Indian Spectator*, which was closely followed by British officials. All this meant that Parmanand could, even from the confines of his bed, still influence outcomes and opinion in Bombay.[301]

A pivotal example was his role in bringing down his long-time foe, Arthur Crawford, who had in the intervening years returned to India and been appointed to a series of important positions culminating in the office of Revenue Commissioner of the Central Division of Bombay.[302] In 1886, Crawford, whose weakness for lavish parties and women meant that he constantly lived beyond his means, authorized the sale of some farm buildings at a "throwaway price" to a native merchant to whom he owed money.[303] When the Director of the Agriculture Section of the Revenue Department questioned the transaction, Crawford shot back by questioning the integrity of the individual who had alerted the Director to the suspicious transaction. The individual in question was the Director's assistant, Bhimbhai Kriparam, an officer of "high reputation and character" who had recently been awarded the title of Rao Bahadur.[304] Shocked by Crawford's wild accusation, Kriparam turned for advice to his former mentor in the Revenue Department – none other than Parmanand.

During his time as Superintendent, Parmanand had kept an eye on the rackets that Crawford had set up since his return to India. But he had not been able to build an open-and-shut case because Crawford shrewdly employed native agents to do his dirty work for him. The transaction that Bhimbhai had come across, however, had Crawford's fingerprints on it, and Parmanand therefore urged his former colleague to seize the chance to bring the corrupt Commissioner to book. He supplied Bhimbhai with additional examples of malfeasance by Crawford that he had uncovered during his own time in the Secretariat and pointed him to others that could supply similar information. With the help of these informants, Bhimbhai put together an "excruciatingly detailed" memorandum that he submitted in April 1887 to John Nugent, the Secretary of the Revenue Department.[305] Upon reviewing the "irrefutable evidence", Nugent ordered a secret investigation that confirmed that Crawford was responsible for corrupt practices of the "Mughal type", namely the sale of favors and public offices.[306] Having gotten wind of the enquiry, Crawford then tried to flee the country – disguised as a tramp – only to be intercepted and arrested in Bombay. A formal enquiry, known as the Crawford Commission, followed. To the public's shock, the commissioners, all of whom were British officials, went on to acquit Crawford, declaring that the *mamlatdar*s (native revenue officials) that testified to having given bribes to obtain their posts were part of a "conspiracy" to "discredit British authority" – even though the accusations had been verified by British police officers.[307] The Commission's "faulty method" was not enough to save Crawford, however. [308] In the course of the investigation and trial, he had confessed to borrowing money from natives residing in his jurisdiction, a violation of civil service rules that allowed Bombay's liberal-minded Governor, Donald

Mackay (or Lord Reay), to secure his dismissal and expulsion from India in 1888.[309]

Bhimbhai's role in exposing the "most notorious case of corruption in Victorian India" became well known to the public.[310] Parmanand's involvement remained, as always, out of sight. But how important his role was can be seen from a letter that Bhimbhai subsequently wrote to Parmanand's sons, saying that he "worshipped Mama as a superhuman being" and "always remembered his name for my salvation and kept his image before my eyes to guide me".[311] Nor was Bhimbhai the only channel that Parmanand employed in this case. Once the Crawford Commission had been formed, he used the *Subodh Patrika* to make the Bombay authorities aware of what natives knew about Crawford's underhand dealings.[312] Reay evidently deemed the articles published in the *Patrika* "so important and helpful" that he would every week "send a horseman and buy a few copies of the *Patrika* from its office", which he would then have his subordinates examine for clues.[313]

Though such victories gave Parmanand some satisfaction, they did not stop him from growing pessimistic about the prospect for reform in British India. There were too many warning signs to ignore. In Britain, the Conservatives had swept to power in 1886, ending the era of liberal reform so deeply associated with William Gladstone. With the Liberal Party having split over the question of allowing the Irish to rule themselves, it became clear that the Conservatives would be the dominant force in Parliament for the foreseeable future. What mattered to the Conservatives was securing Britain's empire, which involved protecting India from advances by Russia in the west and the French in the east. This meant that, going forward, Viceroys would be far less interested in undertaking or supporting domestic reform and public welfare and more interested in matters of defense and diplomacy. Indeed, this was already proving to be the case with Frederick Temple (or Lord Dufferin), who began his term in office by spending large sums on intervening in Afghanistan and annexing Upper Burma. These events brought back painful memories of the last time Conservatives had ruled the roost in British India under Robert Lytton (or Lord Lytton) who had spent his days meddling in Afghanistan even as the Great Famine carried away millions in the Deccan.

And it was not as if the Viceroy that Gladstone had appointed in the interim had given Parmanand grounds for optimism either. The tragic career of the recently departed George Robinson (or the Marquess of Ripon) was there for all to see. Though Ripon did much to support liberal ideals, for instance by repealing the Vernacular Press Act (which had severely cramped the right of the native press to criticize policies and officials), the ultimate effect of his reign was to highlight how deep the divide between ruler and ruled really was in British India. The breaking point came when Ripon tried to see through the Ilbert Bill, which, in its original form, permitted Indians to judge cases involving British defendants. The Bill led to a "storm of unequalled fury", as Anglo-Indians refused, on explicitly racial grounds, to be subject to such "indignity".[314] The rancor brought Ripon's time in India to a premature end in 1884 and made amply clear that "John Bullism" was growing rather than receding.[315]

This diagnosis was only confirmed by the animus that Anglo-Indians were expressing toward the Congress, which had emerged in 1885. It was bad enough that prominent liberals such as Dinshaw Edulji Wacha[316] (whose widely-reported speeches criticizing Dufferin for excessive military expenditure relied on Parmanand's expertise in revenue matters) were being denounced as troublemakers.[317] But the fact that even British officers that supported the Congress were being openly rebuked suggested that the British were not going to support "responsible self-government" any time soon.[318] The point was driven home when Wedderburn, who had been present at the inaugural meeting of the Congress, was penalized for being a "sympathizer".[319] It came about this way: In 1886, a vacancy opened up in the Bombay High Court. By seniority, Wedderburn was next in line. But, with the Conservatives now in charge in London, the appointment of this "political incendiary" was held up.[320] Reay, a remnant from the Gladstone era, tried to placate Wedderburn by appointing him Acting Chief Secretary, but once it became clear that London would not budge, feeling "badly slighted" Wedderburn retired prematurely in May 1887 and departed India.[321]

That no one in Bombay could escape the change in mood was made clearest by the coda to the Crawford scandal. Reay's decision to dismiss Crawford had already led to his being "assailed by invective" for undermining the "honor" of a "high British official".[322] The lesson the native press rightly drew from this was that the British "cared not for the existence of corruption" but for "the shame of its exposure".[323] From there it only got worse. To secure the testimony of *mamlatdar*s against Crawford, Reay had promised them immunity. This promise the Conservatives in Parliament subsequently declared a "grave administrative scandal", insisting that *mamlatdar*s that had admitted to acquiring their posts through bribery – that is, by giving in to Crawford's extortion – should be dismissed.[324] Unwilling to break his word, Reay offered to resign, but was instead ordered to enact a "sorry compromise" whereby the *mamlatdar*s in question were dismissed but granted financial compensation.[325] The outcome left Bombay liberals deeply embarrassed. It showed that when the stakes were sufficiently high, the British were fully capable of "playing fast and loose" with the truth.[326] The maltreatment of the *mamlatdar*s greatly strengthened the hand of those who doubted the "moral superiority" of the British and their vaunted "lawfulness".[327] It became the subject of Bal Gangadhar Tilak's[328] inaugural public speech, in which the Maratha leader mocked the ease with which the British had violated their "plighted honor".[329] The "crowded and enthusiastic" meetings that he addressed "throughout the Deccan" signaled that anti-British sentiments that prioritized *swaraj* (liberty) over *swabhav* (self-improvement) were becoming dominant in the Presidency.[330]

It was also becoming clear to Parmanand that the cause of religious reform was losing "strength and direction".[331] In decades past, it had seemed certain that the spread of English education would encourage "liberality", but now, contrary to his expectation, "a strong current of reaction" was setting in amongst the "new educated youth", many of whom came to meet and debate with him in person.[332] The "obstinacy" of the rising generation was manifest in the failure of the Prarthana Samaj to attract followers. By the early 1880s, its membership barely exceeded a hundred persons, of which not one was female or lower-caste or even non-Hindu.[333] This was not for lack of trying; the Samaj set up schools, reading rooms, and orphanages, organized prayer meetings, and even dispatched members to preach in the *mofussil*.[334] But it was all to little avail; the Samaj's membership remained confined "to a few English-educated, high-caste Hindus" in Bombay and Poona – in other words, "an elite within an elite".[335] The problem, in a nutshell, was that theism simply did not appeal widely. In spite of the efforts of Ranade and Bhandarkar to elaborate a form of theism that spoke to the "earnest religious wants of mankind", the Samaj's sparse bullet-pointed theology contrasted unfavorably with the mystical and emotional aspects of popular religion, not to mention the "numbers and organized strength" of "established religions".[336] The usual response Parmanand received from his interlocutors when he tried to propagate theism was "we have got our religion and we are satisfied with it".[337]

The conduct of leading theists did not help either. A decade prior, when visits from the leading Brahmos of Bengal – Keshab Chandra Sen,[338] Pratap Chunder Mozoomdar,[339] and Sivanath Sastri[340] – had fired the founders of the Prarthana Samaj with zeal, they had dared to dream of establishing "a Theistic faith throughout the country", leading them to tour India in search of allies.[341] But Sen's outsize personality and erratic behavior soon "jeopardized" the cause.[342] By espousing Christian terminology and praising British rule as providential, Sen caused an uproar in Bengal that led to a split in the Brahmo Samaj. Then, by marrying his fourteen-year-old daughter to the Maharaja of Cooch-Behar in a traditional Hindu ceremony, he embarrassed the few theists that had remained on good terms with him.[343] This list included Parmanand, who publicly castigated Sen in the *Patrika*.[344] By the time Sen died in 1884, having in the interim further galled public opinion by reinventing himself as a "*maharishi*" (great sage), the Brahmo Samaj was being described as "a failure", with a membership that did not amount to more than a thousand persons.[345] As Motilal Ghose cuttingly put it in a letter to Parmanand: In Calcutta "Brahmo is now a term of reproach".[346]

The Prarthana Samaj tried to mitigate the damage by differentiating itself from its turbulent cousin in Bengal. It stressed its desire to "remain within the mainstream" of Hinduism, citing the *bhakti* (devotional) tradition – and Tukaram in particular – as its inspiration.[347] This approach did not succeed in Maharashtra where conservatives, led by Tilak, pointed to claims, such as Bhandarkar's public declaration that the Samaj wished to do away with "mechanical modes" of worship and to learn from "foreign *rishi*s", as evidence of theists being opposed to Hinduism as practiced by common folk.[348] Nor was the Samaj's approach finding takers outside Maharashtra. The only other prominent pan-Indian reform movement during this era that also opposed child marriage, idolatry, and caste was the Arya Samaj. However, since it held the Vedas to be true religion, the Arya Samaj viewed the Prarthana Samaj's religious eclecticism with disdain.[349] The sharp critiques issued by its charismatic leader, Dayanand Saraswati,[350] caused angst within the Prarthana Samaj.[351] The Samaj was also unable to gain the support of the newly emergent Congress, whose multi-religious leadership quickly decided that it was "not fitted to deal with the social affairs of the multitudinous divisions of India".[352] Those clamoring for social and religious reform were shunted off into a National Social Conference.[353] Not wanting to compel change through British-enacted penal law, the National Social Conference tried to bring various religious authorities to agree on important social reforms – only to be frustrated by the "very unwieldy structure" of Indian society.[354] As a widely cited editorial observed,

> Customs which are sanctioned in Bengal are discarded in Madras. What is held moral in the Punjab is thought the reverse in Bombay. Under the circumstances, we have little hope for good results of such Social Conferences.[355]

It was not all grim news, however. Even though British India was becoming less conducive to reform, Parmanand could take solace in signs that the Native States were, finally, entering a phase of earnest improvement. The principal stimulus was the spread of modern education, which had previously been restricted to a handful of rulers, the most notable of whom in Western India were Ram Singh of Jaipur and Pragmalji of Kutch (which was precisely what had drawn Anandashram to them). The landscape had begun to change in the latter part of the 1860s when the British came to see the education of Maharajas as the most durable means to help the Native States "keep pace with the ever advancing spirit of the age".[356] By the end of that decade, British officers, drawn from the civil service or the military, had started fanning out to serve as tutors and guardians to the princes of Mysore, Patiala, and Cooch Behar, and to staff the "Wards' Colleges" and "Chiefs'

Colleges" that were being established to educate the future rulers of smaller principalities.[357] Bombay, where more than half of the Native States were located, felt the change most acutely. Several of the principalities within its bounds had already tried employing Elphinstonians as tutors, but the results had been mixed. Because these instructors depended on the goodwill of the *darbar* and the cooperation of the *zenana* (women's quarters), they had struggled to discipline and educate their wards. All this began to change, however, when Richard Keatinge, the Political Agent who had so disappointed Parmanand by his unwillingness to support Anandashram and Bhagwat in Jamnagar, was able to convince the nobility of Kathiawar to fund the establishment of Rajkumar College at Rajkot. Launched in December 1870, this boarding school brought the princes of the region under the spell of its remarkable Cambridge-educated principal, Chester Macnaghten. It was closely followed by Mayo College, which was established in Ajmer in 1872, and Daly College in Indore in 1876.[358]

These developments meant that by the early 1880s many of the leading princes of Western and Central India were being schooled in "high thoughts and noble aims", the most notable of which was that the purpose of the "princely life was to live for others, and not for ourselves".[359] Macnaghten personally supervised the education of over 150 "young chiefs and nobles", nearly every one of whom "signalised their accession to power by spreading schools, dispensaries, and useful public works throughout their states".[360] His orations, which had a tremendous effect on his students, were masterpieces of theism that encouraged listeners and readers, more effectively than the Prarthana Samaj ever did, to abide by "a worldwide religion in sympathy, which binds us to one another, and binds us to the good".[361] Among the most successful graduates were the future rulers of Gondal and Bhavnagar who, within a decade of leaving Rajkumar College, had so revolutionized their principalities that the English press ran out of words of praise, with the latter, for instance, being described by the *Encyclopedia Britannica* as the "model ruler of a model state".[362] Thus it was that Keatinge could proudly declare two decades after the founding of Rajkumar College that "the contrast between the chief of today and the chief of 1850" was simply "astonishing".[363] This was not a subjective assessment: The Maharaja of Gondal, for example, spent one million pounds on public works in the opening decades of his reign. The consequences were dramatic, with the number of schools, for instance, going from one to eighty.[364]

It wasn't just the internal conditions of the Native States that were becoming favorable for political and social reform; the external environment was also increasingly promising. The return of the Conservatives to power in Britain may have boded ill for liberals in British India, but not for the Maharajas in Indian India. This was because, under the influence of Benjamin Disraeli, the Conservatives had come to see the Native States as bulwarks against any Russian advance on British India and were therefore starting to treat them more thoughtfully.[365] Viceroy Richard Bourke (or Lord Mayo)[366] had underlined the change in perspective at a momentous gathering in Ajmer in 1870, where he declared before the nobility of Rajputana,

> If we wished you to remain weak, we would say: Be poor and ignorant and disorderly. It is because we wish you to be strong that we desire to see you rich, instructed, and well-governed.[367]

This change in how the Native States were to be treated had been closely supported by Disraeli's colleague and successor, the Marquess of Salisbury. During his tenures as Secretary of State for India in 1867–68 and 1874–78, Salisbury had thought carefully about how Britain might encourage the Native States to modernize without alienating them from their traditions. The answer was to promote a particular kind of upper-class education that would both reform the Indian aristocracy and draw it closer to its British counterpart. The emergence of the Congress only increased the appeal of this approach. Feeling nothing but disdain for the "cackling" of the *babus*[368] that wanted them to spend more on public welfare and less on Britain's imperial projects, the Conservatives began to view the Indian nobility as more suitable representatives of the Indian people, deeming them "pillars of the British Empire" that would readily supply men and material in times of need.[369] Salisbury's ascension to Prime Minister in 1886 gave hope that, going forward, Britain would subject loyal and well-educated Maharajas to "the lightest possible form of control".[370]

Parmanand had been watching these developments closely. Though the breakdown of his health had brought his visits to the Native States to an end, he had never ceased to think about how they might be regenerated. The unexpected death of Anandashram, which was followed soon after by the equally unexpected demise of Pragmalji of Kutch, had deprived him of his dearest allies and left him dejected for a time. But then, as his comrades once again began taking up important posts in the Native States, his hopes lifted. He himself was approached many times by rulers hoping to tempt him back to Indian India. Though he declined the overtures, he maintained close contact with his friends serving in the Native States. The list of correspondents was a long one: the most notable being Kazi Shahabuddin and Vinayak Janardan Kirtane, then serving as the *dewan*s of the kingdoms of Baroda and Indore, respectively; Krishnaji Lakshman Nulkar,[371] who had been *dewan* of Kutch under Pragmalji's successor and was now on the Bombay Legislative Council; and Madhava Narayan Shirgaonkar,[372] Shankar Pandurang Pandit, and Vinayak Narayan Bhagwat, who had been or were currently serving as regents in the principalities of Kolhapur, Miraj, Porbandar,

Akola, Janjira, and Limbdi.[373] Regular exchanges with such figures afforded Parmanand great insight into the changes underway in the Native States and gave him hope that Indian India might take up the business of advancing moral and material well-being at the very moment when these liberal ideals were falling out of favor in British India.

The appeal of Baroda

The Native State that most occupied Parmanand's attention was Baroda, the second-largest and wealthiest of the kingdoms to emerge out of the Maratha Empire. Previously, during the reign of Khande Rao, which stretched from 1856 to 1870, Baroda had been in the news for all the wrong reasons. This was the period immediately following the Mutiny when, in the interest of stability, the British gave the Native States a wide berth so long as they displayed loyalty. A few Native States, led by Travancore and Cochin, took advantage of the relative calm to modernize themselves. Baroda did not. It became, instead, an embodiment of Oriental despotism, with the Gaekwad[374] coming to be known for extravagances such as the Baroda Carpet (made from more than a million pearls) and for cruelty (such as when he had convicts trampled by elephants).[375] The movement of men and ideas across the borders of British India and Indian India meant that Baroda's shortcomings did not escape wider notice during this time, with Parmanand's *English and Native Rule in India* being among those to underline its reputation as "one of the worst governed among its sort".[376] Though the mandarins in London were shocked by Khande Rao's "barbarous" conduct, he was able to evade consequences by promising to be less "careless", and then by dying in 1870.[377]

Khande Rao's death, which brought his brother, Malhar Rao, to the *gaddi*, did not help. From its previous dealing with Malhar Rao, Calcutta had already learnt that he was susceptible to "bad advice" – and, sure enough, the new Gaekwad plunged almost immediately "into a career of misrule, extravagance, and folly". [378] But the times were changing. By this point Parliament had come into the hands of the Liberals led by Gladstone. Well aware that this dispensation was unimpressed by the *laissez faire* policy that had been followed since the Mutiny, which had permitted only "niggling interference" in the Native States, the Anglo-Indian press fell upon the Gaekwad, exposing depravities – the poisoning of opponents, the abduction of women, the seizure of property – that shocked public opinion.[379] These reports troubled the Viceroy too; the principalities of Central and Western India were, Mayo rued, "going back" in time.[380] Accordingly, he had, from the start of his tenure, warned Maharajas that when "we support you in your power, we expect in return good government".[381] As fate would have it, Mayo was assassinated before he could transform this principle into a criteria that could be used to evaluate a kingdom as large and important as Baroda. Nonetheless, the general idea he had articulated was one that was already gaining ground in London – and so the reckoning for Baroda was not long coming.

With Mayo gone, Gladstone was able to make his first viceregal appointment. This was Thomas Baring (or Lord Northbrook), who arrived in India in the summer of 1872. Now events began to speed up, thanks to the "active horror" of the Resident, Robert Phayre, whom Northbrook dispatched to Baroda in March 1873.[382] Phayre's high-pitched reports on the "immoralities and inequities" of the *darbar* compelled the Viceroy to authorize a formal investigation.[383] When the investigation concluded that many of the charges levelled were "substantially true", Malhar Rao was given a "solemn warning" in November 1873 to undertake "thorough and lasting reform", starting with the dismissal of *darbari*s (courtiers) of "evil repute".[384] The Gaekwad responded by choosing to appoint as his new *dewan* none other than Dadabhai Naoroji.[385] This decision owed much to what Naoroji had been able to do to help the Rao of Kutch. That pivotal episode in modern Indian history is so little known that it needs be recounted in some detail.

Recall that, per the plan crafted by Parmanand and Anandashram, Shahabuddin was to travel to Britain to present the Rao's case before the Secretary of State for India. Correspondingly, in July 1869 Shahabuddin came down to Bombay to meet with Naoroji, who was visiting the city. The two men took a liking to each other and proceeded to travel together to London.[386] Upon arriving in London, Shahabuddin became a regular at the East India Association, which allowed him to cultivate the "old Indians"[387] that flocked to its meetings.[388] At the head of the list was Bartle Frere, the former Governor of Bombay – and former subscriber to *Native Opinion* – who considered Kutch the "most orderly" Native State in Western India.[389] Frere was on the Council of India, the body that advised the Secretary of State for India, and was almost certainly the route by which Shahabuddin came into possession of an explosive memo that Shortt, the officious Political Agent in Kutch, had kept from the Rao.[390] The memo, entitled "The Rao of Kutch and His Bhayad", had been prepared in 1867 by John Wyllie, the recently deceased former Undersecretary in the Foreign Department in Calcutta, who had been a darling in Liberal circles. A blistering attack on Shortt's policy, the memo declared that the "advantages secured to the Kutch *bhayad* by the Treaty of 1819 were absolutely unjust" and that the Government of India ought to "strengthen the hands of the Rao over all Kutch".[391] Frere, who was "well versed in the techniques of influencing public opinion", was likely also the reason why *The Globe*, a leading London paper, suddenly decided to take an interest in distant Kutch. Its editorials now chided the

Secretary of State for the "inexcusable delay" in meeting with Shahabuddin and urged the Council of India to review Wyllie's memo, which would "convince anyone that the Rao is in the right".[392]

These developments in London, which came at the same time as Mayo had begun expressing the view that his officers ought to support "well-disposed chiefs" against their "insubordinate petty barons", unnerved Shortt.[393] Sensing that his policy would soon be "superseded", Shortt went on leave from Kutch, never to return.[394] So grateful was Pragmalji for the forum that Naoroji had provided his *dewan* that he proceeded to endow the East India Association with £5,000 in October 1871, "with a view to secure its permanent establishment in the interest of the natives of India".[395] But there was more to come; the value of the East India Association as a place to shape views and make deals soon became even clearer.

Frere had not taken interest in Kutch out of mere goodwill. When Shahabuddin arrived in London in the autumn of 1869, the Foreign Office had come into the hands of Liberals keen to eradicate the slave trade in East Africa, which was centered in Zanzibar. Frere was at the forefront of these efforts, which gained new momentum following reports from British officers and missionaries in East Africa that Indian merchants, who dominated commerce in the region, were the source of funds and provisions for the Arab slavers that ran the trade.[396] Seeing as nearly all of these merchants were from Kutch, Frere used Shahabuddin's contacts to obtain intelligence on the operation of the slave trade in the region.[397] Based on this information, the Foreign Office directed the British consul to warn Kachchhis to refrain from getting "mixed up" with the slave trade.[398] But then a problem arose. The Sultan of Zanzibar denied that the British consul had jurisdiction over Kachchhis, as they were not British subjects, while the Rao, whose subjects they actually were, had no means to control what Kachchhis did on the African coast.[399] Eventually, in August 1872 the Foreign Office decided to send a mission, headed by Frere, to pressure the Sultan to outlaw the slave trade and to compel Kachchhis to obey the British consul. Seeing as Shahabuddin had "considerable influence with all classes" on account of being both the *dewan* of Kutch and a *kazi*, Frere asked him to join the mission.[400] Shahabuddin did more than that. At his urging, Pragmalji issued a proclamation to his subjects in Zanzibar and Muscat demanding "immediate abandonment of the [slave] trade under penalty of the confiscation of all their property in Kutch".[401] The Rao also publicly tasked Shahabuddin to collect, during his time in Zanzibar, the "names and castes" of Kachchhis that failed to comply with this proclamation.[402] These orders, which gave the Frere mission teeth, earned Pragmalji laurels in Britain.[403] They also ensured that, prior to his departure for Zanzibar in November 1872, Shahabuddin was given a "fair hearing" by the Foreign Office, which let out that it was "favorably impressed" by his character and address.[404] By the time Shahabuddin arrived back in Kutch in April 1873, his labors in London were already starting to have effect. There was a noticeable softening in the tone that Bombay took with Kutch, and it would only be a matter of time before it would publicly renounce Shortt's policy, warning the *bhayad* that henceforth they would need to "bear their share in the general expense of the country, and cooperate with the *darbar*".[405]

Having carefully observed these proceedings, the Maharajas of Western and Central, each with their own tale of woe, now began flocking to Naoroji for aid and advice. Thus it was that Malhar Rao of Baroda reached out to Naoroji in December 1873. Unfortunately, little went well in this case. The Gaekwad wanted Naoroji to pull another rabbit out of the same hat; he wanted him to use his "influence with high European Officers" to persuade Calcutta to remove Phayre, the obnoxious Resident who was roiling Baroda.[406] Meanwhile, given how Naoroji had helped Pragmalji outmaneuver Shortt, there were not a few civil servants in Bombay, Phayre included, that considered him a "political adventurer" and "artful intriguer", and were convinced that he intended to reenact Kutch.[407] Why else, Phayre muttered, would the Gaekwad have hired Naoroji as *dewan* when he lacked "administrative training"?[408]

The Gaekwad and the Resident were both mistaken. Naoroji was only too aware that Baroda was unlike Kutch. It had genuine problems and so even the most well-crafted pleas to Calcutta or London would accomplish little until its deficiencies were addressed. Thus, to the disbelief of the Gaekwad and the Resident, Naoroji set about recruiting the leading members of the Bombay branch of the East India Association to serve alongside him.[409] At the head of the list was Shahabuddin, who quit Kutch to take up the post of *sar subah* (revenue minister), and Parmanand's dear friend Wagle, who was appointed Chief Justice of the Varisht Adalat (High Court). Parmanand too was "summoned" to take up a "high post" and "serve the cause".[410] The salaries on offer were impressive: Wagle, for instance, was to be paid two thousand rupees per month.[411] Even so, Parmanand declined the offer. Though he was a "friend and well-wisher" of Naoroji, he was still smarting from the experience in Kutch and was not keen to step away from his hard-won post in the Bombay Secretariat.[412]

It turned out to be the right decision. Naoroji quickly found himself in a position very similar to what Bhagwat had experienced in Jamnagar and Parmanand had experienced in Kutch. He was squeezed between the *darbari*s, who reviled the "Parsi Minister" for diminishing their stature, and the "imperious and unconciliatory" Resident, who considered it his duty to maintain a "tight grip" on the "venomous snake" ruling Baroda.[413] This was not a moment where Malhar Rao could afford to lose allies and so he chose to placate his *darbari*s, appointing them to a parallel government that retained effectual power.[414] Thus, for instance, Wagle was paid his hefty salary but not allowed to actually sign judicial decrees and had to suffer the ignominy of seeing *darbari*s he convicted being pardoned within hours.[415] The situation was unsustainable, and it became all the more so when Phayre accused the Gaekwad of trying to poison him. Exhausted, in December 1874 Naoroji and his officers resigned en masse. Shortly after this, the Viceroy "suspended" Malhar Rao's sovereignty while a "public enquiry", comprising three British officials and three Indian nobles, examined whether the Gaekwad had in fact authorized an attempt on Phayre's life.[416] When the commissioners split down the middle, with the British officials finding Malhar Rao guilty and the Indian nobles acquitting him, London resolved the deadlock in April 1875 by deposing him on grounds of "gross misgovernment" and deporting him to Madras.[417]

The proceedings in Baroda were generally condemned in the Indian press.[418] Few had sympathy for Malhar Rao, but the arbitrary manner in which a Maharaja had been treated by a Resident and then unseated by a Viceroy known to be a trusted colleague of the great Gladstone left observers stunned – Parmanand included. The angst dissipated, however, as it became clear that the Viceroy intended to make amends. He would live up to the claim that Mayo had previously made at Ajmer, namely that Britain wanted to strengthen the Native States. To wit, Northbrook placed Baroda's administration in the hands of Sir Madhava Rao, the statesman celebrated for making Travancore a "model state", who was engaged as the *dewan*, and Philip Melvill, an officer praised for his intelligence and courteousness, who was appointed Resident. At the same time, the Viceroy steered Gopal Rao, a twelve-year old from a distant branch of the Gaekwad clan, on to the *gaddi*, and placed his education in the care of Frederick Elliot, an Oxford-educated civil servant of "extraordinary charm", who had previously served as Director of Public Instruction in Berar.[419] These remarkable moves, which won Northbrook plaudits across the country, raised the hope that the future Maharaja of Baroda, now retitled Sayaji Rao, would grow up to be a "model prince" able to lead the decrepit remnants of the Maratha Empire into the modern era.

The next decade went about as well as it could. By the time Parmanand retired in 1886, Baroda had entered on "a perfectly new course".[420] Under Madhava Rao's "energetic administration", its public finances, previously on the verge of bankruptcy, were flourishing; its environs, which had been infamous for their filthiness, were now sanitary and beautified; its people, who had long lacked basic amenities, now had schools, libraries, hospitals, gardens, bridges, roads and railways; and its *darbar*, which had been characterized by corruption and dominated by favorites for as long as anyone could remember, was now winning honors for its efficiency and impartiality.[421] The Maharaja of Baroda was equally transformed. When Sayaji Rao, hitherto a cowherd, had arrived in Baroda in 1875, he knew "neither letters nor numbers".[422] He was, however, "industrious, thoughtful, and anxious to get on".[423] These favorable aspects of his character allowed his tutor to address his lack of education and grooming on a war footing. Consequently, by the time Sayaji Rao ascended to the throne in 1882, he had a handle on English, Marathi, Gujarati, and Hindustani, and was at least acquainted with the basics of history and geography, and the sciences and political economy.[424] Most importantly, there was every reason to expect continued improvement because the Maharaja was "addicted to reading English books in his leisure hours".[425] And that was not all. Prior to taking charge of Baroda, Sayaji Rao also received from his principal officers a "special education" on the principles of public administration.[426] This instruction, which extended over nine months, took the form of lectures and tutorials that imparted the insights that the Maharaja's senior-most administrators had gleaned over the course of their distinguished careers. Thus it was that Elliot, the Gaekwad's tutor, could proudly announce in his summary report on Baroda: "The past history of the Baroda state is a dark and miserable one: its future is full of hope and vigor."[427]

The opening years of Sayaji Rao's reign gave reason to believe that Elliot's assessment was correct. Having declared at the time of his investiture that "the primary and paramount aim of my life will be to preserve and promote the welfare of my beloved subjects", the Maharaja proceeded to devote great energy to building upon the foundations laid by Madhava Rao.[428] He toured his kingdom, inaugurated waterworks that ensured his capital would have an "abundance of wholesome drinking water", established a cotton mill to encourage manufacturing, and built a substantial hospital that would soon rank among the "premier institutions of its kind in India".[429] Little wonder, then, that when the Viceroy visited Baroda in 1886, he could praise Sayaji Rao as one of those "conscientious rulers whose life is a blessing to their people", declaring with genuine admiration on behalf of his delegation after it had toured Baroda, "I do not think it has ever fallen to me or to any of us in a single day to see so many sights which have occasioned us such real or such legitimate pleasure".[430] Dufferin was far from alone in feeling this way. Mandlik, well known for being stiff, had an equally warm assessment. In a private letter, written after he had interviewed the Gaekwad, he praised Elliot for making Sayaji Rao "erudite, discerning, good-natured and alert", and held Baroda's future to be "very promising".[431]

Still, as time passed, two difficulties began to make themselves felt. The first was the Gaekwad's proclivity for personal rather than constitutional rule. Before Sayaji Rao assumed power, his *dewan*, Madhava Rao, had tried to convince the Gaekwad that the surest path to happiness, for himself and his people, lay in adopting a constitutional form of rule. To wit, he advised the Maharaja to devolve power to a council comprising his principal officials, and to then limit himself to overseeing this council.[432] The *dewan*'s proposal responded to wider concerns that had been building up for some time about the political experiment that the Conservatives had launched. Salisbury and Mayo had assumed that the Native States had always been, and would always be, characterized by absolute rule.[433] Given this, the way forward, they concluded, was to make Maharajas "cultivated and polished gentlemen" who would employ their unchecked powers responsibly.[434] But as the Maharajas that had been taught "good manners" began to come of age, professional administrators such as Madhava Rao, that had to work alongside them in the Native States, started to worry that the temptations held out by absolute rule were "so overpowering as to wash off the varnish of education in a few years".[435] A number of Parmanand's closest friends were persuaded that Madhava Rao was right. To wit, in January 1880 Ranade published in the *Quarterly Journal of the Poona Sarvajanik Sabha*, the preeminent forum for debate in Western India, an essay entitled "A Constitution for Native States", which laid out the "settled principles" that Native States ought to enact, with Baroda receiving particular attention.[436] This was followed up in September 1881 by a formal address from the Sabha to the Gaekwad. Presented by Nulkar, who had previously served as the *dewan* of Kutch, the address entreated Sayaji Rao to consolidate "a constitution containing within itself all the good that is to be found in indigenous institutions, improved and corrected from time to time, in consonance with the notions of a civilized government".[437]

These pleas on behalf of constitutional rule did not go unopposed; they were ferociously countered by traditionalists led by Tukoji Holkar, the Maharaja of Indore, and Maratha nationalists led by Tilak. Both objected to what was disparagingly termed "Dewanism" or the notion that administration in the Native States ought to be entrusted to professional administrators invariably drawn from British India.[438] To traditionalists, administrators that had cut their teeth in British India were prone to "servile imitation" of Anglo-Indian statesmen; their admiration of the routines and rules of British India ruined precisely what was distinctive and valuable in a Native State, which was the informal and discretionary rule of a Maharaja.[439] The Maratha nationalists, meanwhile, were certain that administrators emanating from British India would be "tools in the hands of the British", with Tilak using his columns in *Kesari* and *Mahratta*, as well as anonymous pamphlets, to savage Madhava Rao for attempting to reduce Baroda to a "mere *zamindari*".[440] These criticisms had deep impact on the Gaekwad because they were supported by his tutor Elliot who, to the shock of many in British India, declared that he wanted to see his ward first "strengthen his government" and only then "gradually to establish a constitution".[441]

The debate was settled when Sayaji Rao came to power. Madhava Rao was hounded out and the Gaekwad began ruling personally, with Elliot by his side. The consequence, in terms of administration, was less than ideal, with the Maharaja involving himself in everything from purchasing door handles to renegotiating complicated land tenures.[442] Worse still, whether due to insecurity or his "restless" nature, the Gaekwad was overly "inquisitive" about even routine matters.[443] He would literally bring his officers to tears by questioning them incessantly about cases and holding up decisions until

Sayaji Rao III, Maharaja of Baroda. National Portrait Gallery, Ax28670

he had personally viewed files – which had to be sent to him even when he was abroad.[444] Cracks soon appeared. By 1887, Shahabuddin, who had taken over as *dewan* from Rao, had thrown in the towel. So too had Kirtane, the *naib dewan*, whom Parmanand had known since their days at Elphinstone, and Pestonji Jehangir, Parmanand's former colleague in the Bombay Revenue Department, who had been serving as Settlement Officer in Baroda.

Parmanand had a good sense of the problem because nearly everyone in the upper echelons of the Baroda *darbar* was personally known to him. Lakshman Jagannath Vaidya, who succeeded Shahabuddin as *sar subah* in 1883 and then as *dewan* in 1886, had been one of Parmanand's dear students at the Central English School. Another important official, Ramachandra Rao Dhamnaskar, the *subah* of Baroda (who would eventually rise to become *dewan*) was also in "unceasing" contact with Parmanand during this time.[445] Dhamnaskar had been a favorite student of Bhandarkar's, and owed his position in the *darbar* to Parmanand, who had recommended him to Shahabuddin.[446] Aside from reports from these figures, Parmanand experienced the growing dysfunction firsthand when he appealed to the Gaekwad to provide a grant for Jyotirao Phule, the fiery advocate of the downtrodden castes, who was bedridden following a stroke. Sayaji Rao had previously been introduced to Phule by Dhamnaskar. Educated to have "broad sympathies", the Gaekwad had "heartily" patronized Phule, even inviting him to address the Baroda *darbar*.[447] But since that time, Sayaji Rao had been compelled to maintain a diplomatic distance as Phule's stringent criticism of "the annuities paid to idle Brahmins" out of taxes collected from "hard-working peasants" made the latter deeply unpopular with the Gaekwad's upper-caste Maratha supporters in Poona.[448] To remedy matters, Parmanand sent in a petition rebutting Phule's critics and outlining all that this colossus had done for the "emancipation of the Maratha mind", a list that included setting up schools for children from the lower castes, penning an array of literary works against the caste system, and setting up organizations such as the Satyashodhak Samaj (Society of Truth Seekers), which, patterned after the Paramhansa Mandali, advocated for the interests of the dispossessed.[449] Unfortunately, by the time Sayaji Rao got around to addressing the petition, Phule had already passed away, and though the resulting grant from the Gaekwad did save Phule's family from penury, the experience underscored that the Baroda *darbar* was slipping back into the "old Rajwada style"[450] where serious matters of public welfare depended on a courtier – in this case Dhamnaskar – being able to take advantage of an "opportune moment" when the Maharaja was in good spirits.[451]

The second difficulty that began to make itself felt in Baroda was the Gaekwad's spirited nature. Before Sayaji Rao assumed office, Madhava Rao counseled him to do what he could to strengthen Baroda, but only within the bounds of the limited sovereignty that British India afforded the Native

States. This was because the vicelike grip of the British over the Native States, and the tacit support they enjoyed from the populace in British India, made them an "irresistible" force.[452] It was therefore preferable, the *dewan* argued, to work around British India than to confront them, in preparation for a better day.

This piece of advice did not go down well either. The Gaekwad was, as the young tend to be, hotheaded. He was deeply affected by the rising tide of Maratha nationalism, which was centered in Poona and advocated by newspapers like *Kesari* and *Mahratta*. This line of thought pictured the Maratha kingdoms as precious islands of self-rule and therefore urged them to cling to every vestige of sovereignty, and to use their sizable resources to help their brothers in British India free themselves from foreign domination. This invigorating vision had plenty of support in Baroda, especially among the Maharaja's family and friends, who looked to him to spearhead a broader Maratha revival. Remarkably, this bold idea also had the support of Elliot who, to the horror of his colleagues in the Indian civil service, took the liberty of introducing his ward to Niccolò Machiavelli's *The Prince*.[453] So impressed was the Maharaja by this bracing work of political theory that he went on to commission a pioneering Marathi translation, to which he appended a preface in which he declared the condition of India akin to that of Italy as described by Machiavelli in the "last portions of the book" (a not-so-subtle reference to the chapter entitled "An Exhortation to Liberate Italy from the Barbarians").[454]

By the time Parmanand came up to his retirement, the Gaekwad's sentiments were starting to have effect. Calcutta was watching closely, with some of its highest officers now describing the Maharaja as "very independent and aggressive", and Baroda as a seat of "discontent and disorder".[455] A series of diplomatic clashes ensued as the British made it a point to disillusion the Gaekwad of his "assumption of equality between his state and the British Empire".[456] One of the earliest of these clashes imposed a heavy toll on Parmanand's associates. It came to pass in this way: An important figure in the Prarthana Samaj during this time was Shankar Pandurang Pandit, a renowned Elphinstonian whose Sanskrit scholarship had led to his being appointed to the distinguished post of Oriental Translator. In October 1884, Pandit and other leading members of the Poona branch of the Samaj, including Ranade, Bhandarkar, and Modak, set in motion a "High School for Native Girls" to provide the girls of the city with an advanced education in English. Poona being the bastion of social orthodoxy, this move aroused significant controversy.[457] With all eyes on the venture, Pandit, who was the Secretary of the school, invited the Gaekwad to be the chief guest at its inaugural prize distribution ceremony. This would, he hoped, mark out the Gaekwad as a supporter of the Samaj's efforts to advance female education.

But then arose an awkward question of etiquette. It was becoming customary around this time to sing at public occasions in British India the "national anthem" – in effect a rendition of "God Save the Queen" in the appropriate regional language. As there was not yet an acknowledged Marathi version of this anthem, the organizers of public functions in Poona had been using another composition, "Devi Shri Victoria", as a stand-in. Composed by the Poona Gayan Samaj, this piece of music was not entirely popular, with critics describing it as a "long, meaningless rigmarole, full of grammatical mistakes".[458] There was also a great deal of confusion about whether audiences ought to sit or stand when it was sung, seeing as it was not in fact the national anthem, and went on for nearly ten minutes.[459] At another public event, a few days prior to the prize distribution ceremony, the Gaekwad had declined to stand when this song was sung. This was, the Poona press speculated, not without foundation, because he considered it "derogatory to his sovereignty".[460] Hoping to avoid unpleasantness, Pandit elected to skip over the part of the program that called for the singing of "Devi Shri Victoria". Unfortunately for him, he had also been compelled, out of courtesy, to invite to the ceremony William Lee-Warner, a notoriously "meddlesome" civil servant then serving as Director of Public Instruction. Lee-Warner, who had also been present at the previous event where the Gaekwad had refused to rise, now "smelt disloyalty". He demanded that the so-called "national anthem" be sung as originally scheduled, and when Pandit objected on the ground that it would cause "confusion" as to who should sit or stand, Lee-Warner threatened him with "serious consequences".[461] In the end, the "shabby song" was sung, and the Gaekwad was compelled to stand.[462]

There was worse to come. Not satisfied with having had his way, Lee-Warner proceeded to file an official complaint against Pandit, turning the brouhaha into a national controversy that came to be termed "The National Anthem Incident". With the Anglo-Indian press coming down heavily on the "disloyal pride" of the "stupid young educational reformers" in Poona, the Bombay authorities were compelled to make "an example" of Pandit.[463] Initially, they censured him and, when that was deemed too light a punishment, they removed him – a scholar that Max Müller considered the equal of the best scholars in Europe – from his prized post of Oriental Translator.[464] Known for his proud bearing (his favorite motto was "I may break, but I will not bend"),[465] Pandit refused to take up the lower-rung position he had been transferred to, electing to instead go on an extended leave of absence.[466] Though he was eventually rehabilitated, after his fellow Samajists prevailed on the Governor to show clemency, Pandit's official career never recovered from the blow, and he ended his days in half-exile as the *dewan* of the small principality of Porbandar.[467] The wider lesson that Parmanand's circle drew from the painful episode was that, with the Maharaja "dancing on a razor's edge", seeking to rally the Maratha nation without falling foul of the British demand for loyalty, Baroda's prospects were less certain than they had originally anticipated.[468]

The political recluse

This then was the troubling context in which Parmanand decided to enunciate the principles that he hoped the Natives States, and Baroda in particular, might follow. What prompted him to put his thoughts down on paper was his coming into direct contact with Sayaji Rao. Up to 1884, the Gaekwad only knew Parmanand by reputation – as a notable Elphinstonian, as the celebrated editor of *Subodh Patrika*, and as a friend to the leading figures in the Baroda *darbar*. But as officials like Vaidya and Dhamnaskar – men the Gaekwad had handpicked – moved into his innermost circle, he began to hear about Parmanand regularly. And the more he heard, the more interested he became in corresponding with this unusual character. Initially, the contact was indirect, with Dhamnaskar asked to obtain Parmanand's views on matters of policy. But when Parmanand's condition began to decline, the Maharaja wrote to him personally, offering in March 1889 to employ his younger son, Ramkrishna, who had completed a medical degree and intended to practice as a surgeon. Though he declined the offer, Parmanand did not pass up the chance to press his thoughts upon the Gaekwad, whose prolonged travels overseas were turning him into an "absentee Maharaja", to the dissatisfaction of his subjects as well as his ministers.[469] The time may have come, Parmanand quietly noted in his letter to the young Maharaja, "to put confidence and responsibility on others", adding that "this sort of supervision or rule is, I think, a duty". He concluded with a promise to elaborate when he had the chance, saying:

> I do indeed wish your Highness all health, happiness and success, and feel much concerned whenever anything happens to your disadvantage in any particulars; but this concern is not quite disinterested, because it is due to the consideration that your Highness's welfare is tantamount to the happiness directly of lakhs of fellow creatures and indirectly of many more. I will not explain myself further just now. If God grants me health, I hope to do it on some future day.[470]

That day came sooner than anyone expected. The immediate stimulus was the publication in June 1889 of the newly retired Anglo-Indian civil servant Lepel Griffin's essay, "The Native Princes of India and Their Relations with the British Government", which boldly declared that in the Native States "maladministration is phenomenal, and tyranny and extortion are the rule, while the officials, from the highest to the lowest, are hopelessly corrupt".[471] Having previously served as the British representative to various principalities in Central and Western India, he had, Griffin modestly informed his audience at the Royal Colonial Institute in London, "as intimate a knowledge" of the Native States "as any Englishmen can hope to obtain". His vast experience apparently revealed to him that "the art of government" had never "been developed in India, or indeed in any part of Asia".[472] And it would always be so, he declared, because regardless of the education and advice that might be provided, "the young prince, surrounded by fiddlers, and parasites, and courtesans, cannot hear the voice of duty for the rhymical music of the bangles of the women, and the fantastic tingle of the Indian lute calling him to love and wine".[473]

These "cocksure" remarks did not go unchallenged. In London, a number of retired officers let loose on the "prancing proconsul", who was, they ventured, venting his "disappointment" at having been denied the post of Lieutenant Governor of the Punjab.[474] The East India Association, for instance, provided a forum for the more experienced and successful diplomat, Richard Meade,[475] to underline that a number of Maharajas, especially those of Mysore and Baroda, deserved the "greatest respect" for being so "well-disposed" and "painstaking".[476] But Griffin's view had support in high places. His view more or less echoed what his mentor, James Fitzjames Stephen, had surmised during his tour of duty in India, namely that education "cannot make silk purses out of sows' ears".[477] Little wonder then that Meade was promptly silenced by the higher-ranked John Strachey,[478] who insisted that, though one could "find Native chiefs who deserve and obtain the respect and affection of their people", the chances were that "the progress made by worthy rulers will be swept away by the vice and caprice of their successors".[479] This counter, from a sitting member of the Council of India, to whom Fitzjames Stephen had dedicated his *Liberty, Equality, Fraternity* (1874), allowed influential British periodicals like *Spectator* to gladly conclude that "with all our defects, we are juster and more enlightened than any native rulers".[480]

In India, Griffin's "vaingloriousness" caused a furor. There were dozens of editorials condemning his "contempt for everything native".[481] Parmanand too was irritated, but his response was more measured. There was in Griffin's remarks, he quietly noted, "a substratum of truth which even Native States will do well to ponder over".[482] But how to bring this "substratum" to light? The entire episode revived memory of Viceroy John Lawrence's self-congratulatory epistle that had provoked Parmanand to write *English and Native Rule in India* two decades prior. Back then Parmanand could only point in the general direction that the Native States might proceed to improve the lives and prospects of their subjects. But now, given the strides the Native

States had made in the intervening period, he could do more; he could show them, and the Gaekwad in particular, how to *durably* advance moral and material well-being.

Happily, the helping hand Parmanand needed to accomplish this task was available. Over the summer, he was able to secure the assistance of Narayan Ganesh Chandavarkar. This was no ordinary amanuensis. After a glittering career at Elphinstone, Chandavarkar had been appointed editor of *Indu Prakash* in 1878 and had concurrently become a successful pleader in the High Court in 1881.[483] Devoted to Parmanand, whom he met through the Prarthana Samaj, and whom he considered "a modern *sadhu*", Chandavarkar had long frequented his house to participate in the engrossing discussions that occurred there.[484] The admiration was mutual and Parmanand had already played a pivotal role in shaping Chandavarkar's public career. It was on Parmanand's advice, at a meeting in his home in Girgaon, that Chandavarkar was selected to represent Bombay on the historic delegation that the leading political associations in India sent to England in 1885 to make the newly expanded electorate there aware of the concerns of Britian's colonial subjects.[485] The widely reported mission made Chandavarkar a household name in India and set the stage for his rapid ascent in the Congress (which he would go on to preside over in 1900).

With Chandavarkar sitting at the foot of his bed, Parmanand would have a draft read out, which the two would then discuss and modify. A number of the drafts were also shared with and commented upon by Ranade and Bhandarkar, making them, in effect, a statement of their collective worldview. Once Parmanand and Chandavarkar were in agreement over the precise wording, the revised piece would be dispatched to Behramji Malabari,[486] the editor and proprietor of the *Indian Spectator*, one of the few Bombay papers with a readership that spanned India and England.[487] Malabari was eager to publish the letters, partly because Parmanand was one of his most valued writers, but also because he originated from Baroda, where his father had been a clerk in the service of Khande Rao.[488] A severe critic of Malhar Rao's "career of crime", Malabari had celebrated the removal of that "atrocious idiot", and then reported in his best-selling travelogue, *Gujarat and the Gujaratis*, on the reforms underway in Baroda under Sayaji Rao, which would, he hoped, prove a "lasting memorial" to Northbrook's "wisdom and justice".[489]

Parmanand's first letter appeared on November 17, 1889. The very same day Parmanand sent a copy of the letter to Dhamnaskar, excitedly instructing him:

> If you happen to see the Great Man at Baroda, you may, if he does not seem aware already of the appearance of the letters, ask him to see them himself, that is without the aid of any of his senior officers, for the latter may not like

N. G. Chandavarkar. British Library, 10606.de.16

the tone of some of the remarks and are likely to be prejudicial against the subject, although all the remarks are intended to be general and are neither suggested by nor intended to apply to any individuals anywhere.[490]

The remaining letters followed thereafter, usually every Sunday (or every other Sunday when Parmanand's health delayed the proofreading). They immediately caused a stir in the Native States, and the mail that poured into the offices of the *Indian Spectator* indicated that they were being read far and wide.[491] The pseudonym "A Political Recluse" provoked curiosity as well, leading to speculation about the identity of the author. But it also meant that, unfortunately, only a small set of readers was aware that the writer had served in both British India and the Native States, and previously authored *English and Native Rule in India*. Regardless, Parmanand absolutely refused to publicly acknowledge authorship of the letters. For instance, when Sorabji Jehangir, a celebrated photographer and senior functionary in the Baroda *darbar*, kept insisting on including him in an upcoming album, Parmanand replied somewhat sharply:

> While thanking you for your high opinion about my poor worth, I must ask you to be so good as not to include me in the book you are preparing on "Some Bombay Worthies Past and Present". I have taken no very prominent past in any important sphere or field. I have produced no literary work nor even opened my mouth at any public meeting except once on a trifling occasion. Further, my public service has been short and all in a subordinate capacity. I am aware that an intimate friend of mine has suggested my name in this connection and he must have done so because he has seen some good points in me; but I do not think that is sufficient reason; for every man however humble, has some good points which are known to his associates. I hope these reasons will suffice to justify my refusal of your request. But if they do not, let me add that the proposal is so personally detestable to my nature that I trust that you will not insist on it.[492]

Parmanand did care, however, about how the letters were received by those to whom they were addressed. A month into the series, Dhamnaskar wrote to say that the Gaekwad had read the opening letters "with attention" and, upon realizing that they were directed at him, had begun to await them "with eagerness".[493] Consequently, when the letters in the *Indian Spectator* stopped appearing in February and then again in April 1890, Sayaji Rao asked Dhamnaskar to enquire as to the cause of the delay. Upon learning that the cause was Parmanand's ill-health, the Gaekwad offered to support Parmanand's medical care and voiced the hope that the series would still be completed and then published as a book that he could "keep close to him".[494]

This was a very welcome compliment. Parmanand had, from the start, envisioned compiling the letters into a book – but only if his audience deemed them "useful".[495] Since this was proving to be the case, he now agreed to publish them, as Chandavarkar and Malabari had been pressing him to do. Unfortunately, he was also, during this time, becoming too ill to proceed with the series. Malabari therefore intervened with a proposal to take advantage of the unanticipated delay. As he would be touring England over the summer, he could procure from a respectable Anglo-Indian with knowledge of the Native States, a laudatory preface to the volume, that would increase its visibility and appeal in England. After much agonizing the decision was made, on Malabari's insistence, to approach the former civil servant W. W. Hunter,[496] whose influential weekly column on Indian affairs in *The Times* had made him a celebrity. It was not the wisest decision though, as Hunter was pressed for time and he only grudgingly agreed to write a preface for an author he had not met.

In the meantime, Parmanand's health only worsened. He was now struggling even to speak, with assistants having to put their ears to his lips to make out what he wanted to say. As a result, the series slowed to a crawl, with months-long pauses between some of the installments. As the gaps between the letters grew, it became harder for readers to follow the thread of the argument, dulling the reception of the final parts of the series. Only in December 1890 was the series finally completed, more than a year after it had begun. The complete set was immediately dispatched to Hunter and by April 1891 his preface was ready. It was not as laudatory as Malabari had hoped (*The Times* would correctly describe it as "favorable though guarded").[497] To make matters worse, by this point Parmanand's ability to wield a pen was nearly gone – he was reduced to jotting with a pencil for a few minutes at a time. As a result, the process of revision went slowly.

In the end, *Letters to an Indian Raja* was only published in November 1891. This was two long years after the first letter in the series had appeared. The delay meant that the novelty of the exercise had been lost. Worse still, because it was seen as a "reprint" of letters that had already appeared in the *Indian Spectator*, the volume was not reviewed as widely as Malabari had hoped.[498] Nor did it help that the literary periodicals of the era were in the hands of Anglo-Indians who acknowledged the appearance of the volume but declined to review it as their audiences preferred reading "for pleasure than for instruction", especially when the instructor was a native.[499] All this mattered not one bit to Parmanand. He was delighted to hear from Dhamnaskar that the two copies with "beautiful binding" that he had sent to Sayaji Rao had been well received:

> I yesterday communicated your suggestions to him each and all and he expressed great thanks for your kindness and for the interest you take, adding that he would act and follow your advice to the best of his abilities. He also told me he liked the book very much and said, you were a very intelligent and powerful writer, and that if you had been in good health, he would have secured your services.[500]

Following the publication of *Letters*, there was a steady flow of enquiries from the Gaekwad, who began acquiring the books it cited. Then came a more substantial testament to Parmanand's efforts. In March 1892, at the launch of the long-awaited Ajwa Sarovar, the dam that would henceforth supply cholera-prone Baroda with fresh water, the Gaekwad delivered one of the most important speeches of his career, in which he laid out his vision for his kingdom. Though he did not cite Parmanand by name, the proposals he put forward in his speech were precisely those that "A Political Recluse" had advocated. In the Gaekwad's own words:

> As for the machinery of government, I own that in some fear and trembling I am attempting to decentralise and at the same time to supervise ... The bench system for civil and criminal cases, the separation of the judicial from the executive branch, and the *panchayat*[501] system are among the efforts I am making to improve and simplify our administration.[502]

There were other aspects of Parmanand's advice that could not be discussed publicly or even in writing. By this time Sayaji Rao was routinely locking horns with the Residents that Calcutta was sending out to Baroda, all of whom were being instructed to keep a close watch on him. And so, in April Dhamnaskar wrote to say that the Gaekwad wanted to meet with Parmanand to discuss a sensitive matter in person:

> You made the recommendation in your letter that in matters of the government of princely states, Political Agents ought to be held responsible like the rulers are. That does not seem practicable to His Highness. He wanted to deliberate the matter with you.[503]

Unfortunately, as Sayaji Rao had anticipated, Parmanand was in no position to travel up to Lonavala, which is where the Gaekwad had retreated to avoid the irksome Resident in Baroda, E. V. Reynolds, who was objecting to the Gaekwad traveling to Europe – unless he and his wife were taken along as well.[504] Nor was Parmanand willing to impose on the Maharaja. Sayaji Rao should not, he insisted, take the trouble to come down to Girgaon to see him, for he was "not worthy" of such a visit.[505] The modesty was characteristic, but the deeper issue was one of protocol. There was no way for Parmanand, with his limited resources and unpredictable ailment, to host the Gaekwad, whose "four-horse carriage before the house of a small man like me would draw a crowd of people on the road".[506] And with this, the chance to meet slipped away forever. A month later, Sayaji Rao left for the Swiss Alps. By the time he returned in January 1893, Parmanand was in the final stages of decline, drifting in and out of consciousness. The Gaekwad had his own problems, the most pressing of which was the arrival of a cantankerous new Resident, John Biddulph. In the event, the correspondence between them slowed to a trickle, leaving an important element of *Letters* undiscussed.

The end came in September 1893. Surrounded by family and friends, Parmanand slipped away as quietly as he had lived. A suitably private and dignified cremation, ministered by Bhandarkar, the oldest of his friends, followed. Within days, letters of condolence began pouring in, every one of them attesting to Chandavarkar's memorable description of Parmanand – that "to know him was to love him".[507] Then followed obituaries in newspapers around the country, most written by the select few that had been privy to his activities behind the scenes. He was, they informed their bewildered audiences, a "*mahatma*", a "model Hindu", a "genuine patriot", and "our Nestor".[508] The simplest and most widely read appraisal came in *The Times of India*. Parmanand had been, it gently declared, "amongst the wisest, if the most unobtrusive, of councilors" to have graced the era.[509]

Afterlife

A month after Parmanand passed, some of the greatest names in Bombay, led by Ranade and Pandurang, formed a committee to "perpetuate his memory".[510] Over the following year, six thousand rupees were raised from across Bombay Presidency. Initially, it was proposed to combine these funds with other donations made to the Prarthana Samaj to establish a "Narayan Mahadev Parmanand Girls' School". Eventually, after some debate, the majority of the committee voted to invest the money in a bond in the name of the University of Bombay, which created the "Narayan Mahadev Parmanand Prize" for the best essay in Marathi or Gujarati on any the topics that most occupied him: social reform, religion, philosophy, and economics.[511]

By the turn of the century, the prize had come into being, but memory of the figure it was named after was fading rapidly. There were multiple, intersecting reasons for this. A common theme in the obituaries written for Parmanand was anxiety at the rapid depletion in "the ranks of the intellectual Hindus" in Bombay.[512] The normal course of generational change does indeed seem to have accelerated during this time, with medical knowledge not able to keep up with the stresses and strains of urban life. Strikingly, nearly every figure in the "small circle of thinkers" that had emerged out of Elphinstone would pass away at a relatively early age, with only a lucky few, such as Bhandarkar and Wacha, living long enough to see "a thousand full moons".[513] The consequence was that the ideals that Parmanand's generation had championed were left without proponents at the very moment when the revolutionary ideal of *swaraj* was sweeping across British India.

Going forward, the only figures in Bombay that recalled Parmanand were his fellow travelers in the Prarthana Samaj, especially Bhandarkar and Chandavarkar. But the influence and relevance of these figures declined precipitously as the national mood, now shaped by charismatic figures like Aurobindo Ghosh, became combative. Within the Congress, meanwhile, the notion that well-educated and well-meaning "representative men" could instruct individuals about their "true interests" was scuttled by the rise of "mass leaders" such as Tilak. The latter, who represented group interests, had no reason or desire to foster individuality; to the contrary, they sought to mobilize and entrench identities rooted in region, caste, language, and religion – precisely as Parmanand had feared.

Shunted aside by the so-called "extremists" in the Congress, the following generation of liberals, led by Gopal Krishna Gokhale[514] and Tej Bahadur Sapru,[515] focused their energies on pushing for constitutional reform in British India. They did obtain concessions from the British in the form of the expansion of the legislative councils, starting with the Indian Councils Act of 1909 (the so-called Minto-Morley Reforms) and subsequently the Government of India Act of 1919 (the so-called Montagu-Chelmsford Reforms). But this proved a pyrrhic victory, as liberals were then saddled with figuring out how to organize and manage popular representation, a process that led them to incorporate rather than resist group identities and interests. This development marked a reluctant but complete abandonment of the ideals that Parmanand's generation had stood for. That earlier crop of liberals had sought to make use of civil associations and the public sphere to *transcend* religious and social divisions in the citizen body. But, to the generation that followed them, this path no longer seemed viable, especially once the Congress came under the sway of that great mobilizer, Mohandas Gandhi. As one of the old hands, C. Sankaran Nair,[516] memorably complained in his *Gandhi and Anarchy* (1922), "there is scarcely any item in the Gandhi program which is not a complete violation of everything preached by the foremost sons of India till 1919", but his fellow "so-called moderates only whispered their protests against his policy so as not to be heard beyond a few feet", because they knew very well that "Mr. Gandhi's emotional outbursts, fastings, penances, *sanyasi* waist cloth, have carried away the emotional masses, women and students".[517] In the decade that followed, liberals came to play a very attenuated role in politics in British India, where they principally served as mediators between the British and their more radical counterparts in the Congress.

Throughout this time of rapid change in British India, *Letters to an Indian Raja* remained in print and continued to make regular appearances in the press in relation to Indian India.[518] The stimulus was the growing worry that, a few obvious examples aside, most of the rulers in the Native States were not in fact moving out of their old groove.[519] They remained, observers and visitors bemoaned, "absolutely idle creatures" whose administrations continued to be "in a lamentable condition".[520] Part of the blame was placed on the functioning of the so-called "Chiefs' Colleges". No longer headed by men with the stature and abilities of Macnaghten, the founding Principal of Rajkumar College, they were coming to be characterized by declining standards and diminishing attendance.[521] At least equal blame was placed on the conservatism and apathy of the *darbar*s in Native States. These institutions were filled to the brim with what the press described as the "Old India" party – men who hoped, "by attaching themselves to the past, to retard the march of time and the disquieting elements that it brings".[522] It was in response to this inertial character of the Native States that *Letters* was frequently cited in the press, particularly its counsel on the necessity of educating princes.[523] This advice was not much followed, however. This was, in substantial measure, because following the turn of the century, British India began encouraging the nobility, especially in Western India, to enter military careers. With this, the incentive to study, much less obey, the demanding counsel contained in *Letters* only declined. It was games like polo and tennis, not moral development, that the Maharajas busied themselves with, leaving their private tutors to do their homework for them.[524]

At the time of Parmanand's passing, the hope had been, as the influential Anglo-Gujarati newspaper *Kaiser-i-Hind* put it, that the "younger lions" who sat at the feet of this accomplished *guru* would take up his mantle and serve the Native States.[525] It turned out otherwise. Precisely because they were capable and moderate, these "younger lions" were invariably drafted into high offices in British India. For instance, Chandavarkar, the most eminent of Parmanand's protégés, went on to preside over the Congress in 1900, but had to withdraw from politics after he was chosen to replace Ranade on the Bombay High Court in 1901 and then appointed Vice-Chancellor of Bombay University in 1909.[526] By the time Chandavarkar retired from official life in 1913, the liberal ideals he represented had almost completely fallen out of favor in British India where the Congress was coming under the sway of Gandhi, a figure whose ideas of moral and material progress were diametrically opposed to those of the "Political Recluse". And so, like his mentor, Chandavarkar tried to see if the Native States might serve as a refuge for liberal ideals. He soon learned otherwise.

In 1913 Chandavarkar was invited to take up the post of *dewan* in Indore, the second-largest Maratha kingdom in Central India. The Holkars of Indore had never been amenable to genuine reform. A few eminent statesmen, including Madhava Rao, his brother Raghunath Rao, and his protégé, Vinayak Janardhan Kirtane, had tried their hand, only to give up in exasperation.[527] Still, with Parmanand's example before him, Chandavarkar acceded to the Maharaja's fervent pleas, hoping that Tukoji Rao Holkar, who had ascended to the *gaddi* in 1911 at the age of twenty-one, was being honest when he said that he wanted the distinguished jurist and educator to "make a model ruler" of him.[528] He was not. Upon arriving in Indore, Chandavarkar found the Maharaja about to depart for Europe. When Holkar eventually returned six months later, he claimed to be appreciative of all that Chandavarkar had done in the interim, but made it clear that henceforth he, not his *dewan*, would have the final say on all important matters. One of these was whether he would take on a second wife, an act of bigamy that deeply embarrassed Chandavarkar, who was a staunch proponent of social reform and concurrently serving as the president of the Prarthana Samaj.

In less than a year it was all over. Having learned that patience would not gain him the Maharaja's compliance, Chandavarkar quit Indore in 1914. There was a wider lesson to be drawn from the experience. It was becoming clear to observers that, shaken by the emergence of violent opposition in British India in the opening decade of the twentieth century, the Raj was prepared to give the Native States a much longer leash so long as they promised to weed out "sedition".[529] With the pressure to undertake constitutional reform having been lifted, the Maharajas were now freer to exercise personal rule (indeed the British would soon begin using the term Princely States, to emphasize that in their eyes sovereignty lay in Maharajas personally). Having witnessed this change firsthand, when the Viceroy tamely allowed Holkar to take a second wife, Chandavarkar published in 1919 a second edition of *Letters to an Indian Raja*, hoping that it might spur other laggard Maharajas to do better. He was far from alone in this hope. With "the tide of democracy rising" in the wake of the Great War, several observers tried to rouse the Maharajas.[530] The list included D. V. Gundappa, whose carefully reasoned *The Problems of Indian Native States* (1917) urged the increasingly backward principalities of Rajputana to introduce representative government, and Madhava Rao's sons, who in 1921 published their father's hitherto confidential memos in favor of constitutional government in the Native States.[531]

None of these works had any discernible impact on the Native States. That the day had grown much too old was made clear by a bestseller published the same year as Chandavarkar's edition of *Letters to an Indian Raja*. This was Lala Lajpat Rai's *Political Future of India* (1919), which declared that most Maharajas were "parasitical" creatures who, "protected by British bayonets", had no incentive to reform, and would have to be made to "fall in line". This day, he promised, would soon come, because "the age of despotism is gone".[532] What made these statements especially striking was the fact that Rai was a leading figure in the Arya Samaj, whose founder, Dayanand Saraswati, had once hoped that Maharajas would champion India's revival, which is why he traveled from *darbar* to *darbar*, urging them to live up to the duties that the *shastra*s imposed on them.

Rai's condemnation revealed that, even in the most supportive quarters, patience with the Maharajas had run out.

The increasingly "anomalous" character of the Native States was brought into focus by the passage of the Government of India Act in 1919. By introducing representative government in British India, it raised questions about the relationship between elected legislatures in the Presidencies and the Native States, where "personal rule" was still the norm. The Maharajas responded by insisting that they were "sovereign" and proposed various forms of "federation" with a renovated British India that would safeguard their "independence".[533] Liberals such as V. S. Srinivasa Sastri and K. M. Pannikar supported these pleas – on the ground that "certain" of the Native States had "done well" and that "if they have the elements of adaptability, to give them a chance of continued usefulness in the future".[534] The claim that there were well-performing Native States was sound. The majority of the Maharajas *were* "a decent bunch" and they *did* provide their subjects with greater access to public goods than British India did – this much is borne out by statistics.[535] Even so, public opinion hardened against the Maharajas, as "Congress ideals" spread rapidly.[536] Per this view, the "barren dynasticism", "reckless extravagance", and "loyalty to the Crown" displayed by even the more "advanced" of the Maharajas were deemed impediments to "progressive nationalism".[537] And so, by the end of the decade the Native States were being uniformly deprecated as "the last stand of despotism in Asia", with two very widely read books, Alexander Powell's *Last Home of Mystery* (1929) and P. L. Chudgar's *The Indian Princes under British Protection* (1929) underlining that Maharajas had never surrendered their right to ignore the law at their "sweet will".[538]

The Maharajas were well aware that the ground was moving beneath their feet. Some begged the British to "protect them from the Congress". Others, such as Mysore, Travancore, and Aundh, recognized that it was "now impossible to fight the Congress", and responded by drafting constitutions (the last of these becoming a famous, if miniscule, exemplar of Gandhian democracy).[539] But it was all too little too late. In the wider public sphere, the conclusion had already been drawn that constitutionalism would never really succeed in the Native States because autocrats inevitably had a self-indulgent "mentality".[540] Few lacerated the Maharajas more deeply than K. L. Gauba, whose *The Pathology of Princes* (1930), which went into ten editions, made much of their "license". His target was abysmal rulers, like the Maharaja of Patiala with his 350 concubines, of whom Gauba famously wrote that "while the Englishman starts his day on bacon and eggs, the German on sausages, the American on cornflakes, His Highness prefers a virgin".[541] But, as was becoming common at the time, Gauba did not hesitate to tar *all* the Maharajas with the same brush, declaring that the public wanted to know not how they "spend their days" but rather how they "spend their nights".[542] The remarkable change in tone from 1901, when Naoroji could publicly extol the "splendid prospect" held out by "good administration" in the Native States, could not have been more marked.[543] An era had ended – and with it went the audience for *Letters to an Indian Raja*.

Part III: Why read *Letters to an Indian Raja*?

Now that we have examined the context in which *Letters to an Indian Raja* was produced, we are better positioned to understand what it teaches. We will proceed in three steps. The first section analyzes the advice that *Letters* contains. Parmanand, we will see, recommends that Maharajas completely revamp their households, their diplomacy, and their administrations. The second section explains how Parmanand's recommendations transform our understanding of Indian liberalism. It argues that *Letters* rebuts the notion that Indian liberalism lacked a clear program and devolved into a vague defense of privilege. The concluding section then discusses what *Letters* contributes to liberal theory. It contends that *Letters* offers a prescient critique of multiculturalism, helping liberals see when and why they ought to paternalistically reform, rather than tolerate, social norms and religious beliefs of an illiberal character.

What Letters *teaches*

Letters to an Indian Raja opens with the essay entitled "On Counsel", the purpose of which is to help the Maharajas of India understand why Parmanand has chosen to address them. Knowing that these readers are likely to be busy or inattentive, the essay immediately fixes on the epochal challenge confronting them. Both rulers and ruled in the Native States, it observes, were intimately familiar with the great drawback common to all monarchies – namely, that "an unbroken succession of capable princes" was the exception rather than the norm. But it had become clear to all concerned that this traditional weakness was now proving entirely fatal because of the emergence of a competitor unlike any the Maharajas had met before – the British. The sophisticated civil administration that the British had established in India had made them "irresistible", and since becoming the paramount power in the subcontinent, they had proven only too willing to set aside the Native States' "claims of right". In sum, what the Native States confronted was the prospect of extinction.

Having gotten the attention of his readers, Parmanand turns to explain why he – an English-educated native residing in British India – is on their side. The impending demise of the Native States would be a great tragedy, "On Counsel" argues, because they had a virtue that British India could never acquire. As an imperial power that was alien to the country, Britain was more interested in maintaining its rule than in fostering Indians' moral and material progress. It was therefore only too willing to patronize "reactionary" tendencies that hindered "the growth of citizenship". The Native States, by contrast, had no reason to fear "national progress" – it was entirely to their advantage, as it would strengthen them and also pressure the British to expend their energies on matching the improvements in the Native States rather than incessantly expanding their empire. It was this fundamental asymmetry – the fact that Maharajas had more to gain from "national progress" than the British did – that had prompted Parmanand to write *Letters*. To wit, the volume intended to offer Maharajas "a few suggestions" on how they might conduct themselves in future. If they followed his counsel, Parmanand promised, they would "have the means not only of marching alongside British India, but even going ahead of it in some important respects and furnishing an example to it".

The second essay, entitled "On Religion", brought home vividly this difference between British India and the Native States. In 1858 the Queen's Proclamation had declared that Britain would "abstain from all interference with religious belief".[544] But, in practice, Parmanand observed, it had done quite the opposite. By placing on the curriculum of schools and colleges the works of John Stuart Mill and Herbert Spencer, the British were teaching Indians "materialism, scepticism, or agnosticism". The "victims" of such an education, Parmanand argued, might become wealthy and clever, but they would be rendered "faithless".[545] This was a pernicious outcome because only belief in the divine could compel individuals to take up and persevere with demanding causes, making it a vital prerequisite to the arduous business of social and political reform. In the absence of such faith, there could only be paltry rationalism of the kind infamously modeled by Young Bengal, whose challenge to orthodoxy had amounted to little more than hedonism and meanness – such as drinking alcohol, dressing in suits, and lobbing beef into the houses of Brahmins. In Parmanand's words,

> Our young men are forced into the unhappy position of sceptics [and] the reorganization of society seem impossible under such circumstances [because] knowledge alone does not suffice for men, nor material prosperity, nor good government. The things of this life are fleeting, the life to come is eternal, and men and nations can only be happy in recognizing and acting righteously on this divine fact. Without faith, life is without an aim, death without hope, and there can be neither individual happiness, nor national greatness.[546]

The British had all along foreseen that introducing modern education, with its emphasis on scientific enquiry, would corrode popular Hinduism, whose rituals and scriptures had become obscure even to the priests responsible for administering and interpreting them. As Charles Trevelyan, the officer most responsible for persuading Company officials to inaugurate modern education, boldly declared in his *On the Education of People in India* (1838),

> Hinduism is not a religion which will bear examination. It is so entirely destitute of anything like evidence, and is identified with so many gross immoralities and physical absurdities, that it gives way at once before the light of European science. ... As this change advances, India will become quite another country.[547]

For decades, the British convinced themselves that encouraging Hindus to question the rationality of their inherited traditions and beliefs would aid the cause of Christianity. Typical was Herbert Edwardes' confident declaration in his *Prospect of Triumph of Christianity in India* (1866) that "while the Hindus are busy pulling down their own religion, the Christian Church is rising above the horizon".[548] What the British did not anticipate was that the skeptical gaze that educated Indians were directing at Hinduism would also be directed at Christianity – Indians who could read the Bible could also read, as Sayaji Rao had, what Machiavelli had to say about the Church. Little wonder then that, by the time *Letters* was published, it had become clear that Christianity was failing to obtain a hold on India for the same reason as it was losing its hold on England – to the empirically minded, the miracles that Christians celebrated were no more plausible than those of the heathens they ridiculed. And so, when British missionaries tallied up the numbers, they found that "scarcely a convert has been gained from the ranks of the infidel progeny of the education schemes" and that their doctrines had more takers among the "ignorant, superstitious *ryots*".[549]

These doubts about established religions did not mean, however, that educated Indians had to be agnostic or irreligious. A central purpose of "On Religion" was to show educated Maharajas that there *were* reasons to believe in God. These reasons had been articulated in eighteenth-century Europe under the banner of deism. According to this school of thought, God's existence could rationally be inferred from remarkable features of the external and internal worlds that humans inhabited. The awe-inspiring beauty and marvelous order of the natural world and the ever-present voice of conscience – these were some of the pieces of evidence, accessible to every human, that revealed to humankind the existence of a divine hand. This knowledge had immense consequences, deists noted; it had served to make humans aware of their smallness in the universe and compelled them to think about and act on higher purposes. Thus it was that Voltaire, whom Parmanand approvingly quotes, was led to declare that "if God did not exist, he would have to be invented".[550]

Why did Parmanand want to introduce Maharajas to the catalog of reasons for the existence of God? It was not because he wanted to instill in them the fear of God, the tactic that moralizers have employed throughout the ages to rein in monarchs. Rather, he wanted to highlight that Maharajas had a unique opportunity before them. If there was a God, then Indians had "a claim to something more than the mere secular good government" that British India was offering them. They were entitled to what the British enjoyed in Britain – a monarch that was "the head of the Church as well as of the State" and thus able to use the authority and resources at her disposal to shape the religion, and thereby the morality, of her subjects. Here then was an opportunity for Maharajas to do what the British could never do in India, which was to bring about "permanent good" by elevating the religious beliefs, and thereby the morals, of the populace. This did not mean, Parmanand stressed, that Maharajas ought to "coerce men's consciences". Rather, they ought to introduce "a system of religious instruction by means of books, lessons lectures, and discourses" that would bring "higher religious thought" into greater prominence and thus help sweep away what was "rude and irrational" in established religions.

There was a specific form of "higher religious thought" that Parmanand had mind: The theology championed by the Prarthana Samaj. Inaugurated by Rammohan Roy in the opening decade of the nineteenth century, this theology "maintained the existence of one sole God" and "required from its professors a mental rather than a corporeal worship".[551] Roy's objective in formulating this austere form of Hinduism – which he termed theism, and which Christians described as "Vedantic Deism" – was to provide an alternative to popular Hinduism whose "injurious rites" were, he argued, destroying "the texture of society".[552] "On Religion" makes clear that Parmanand hoped that the Maharajas of India might be converted to the cause of Hindu theism. It was an audacious gambit, but there was careful thought behind it. By the closing decade of the nineteenth century, it had become clear to the leaders of the Prarthana Samaj that they had failed to obtain "any practical influence over the people". True, they held great sway over the educated elite of Bombay, to the great frustration of Christians such as the prominent preacher Nehemiah Goreh, whose *Four Lectures to the Brahmos in Bombay and Poona* (1875) denounced theists for "daring to set up a new religion" that was leading their "enlightened" brethren away from "the blessings which Christianity alone imparts".[553] Still, the fact of the matter was that the Prarthana Samaj's flock was nowhere near large enough to achieve its ultimate objective, which was to engender "moral progress" – to root out the irrationality and parochialism that had hindered the "growth of citizenship". And so, the time had come to be bold. If the Prarthana Samaj could obtain a foothold in a Native State, especially a prominent one such as Baroda, it would have opportunity to showcase its ideals and thereby engender a wider religious and social transformation. Thus it was that *Letters* started by dwelling "at great length" on the question of religion; the aim was to get Maharajas to see that "if a State is to be elevated among nations, its first ambition ought to be to aim at its own moral elevation", which in turn depended on the cultivation of the kind of "higher religious thought" that would unite rather than divide subjects (as established religions did) and enliven rather than demoralize them (as agnosticism did).

The third essay, "On Education", examines how the Native States could address the great drawback of monarchy – namely, the uneven quality of heirs. The traditional method, long sanctioned by custom and now also advocated by the British, was to educate princes, so as to ensure that those who ascended to the throne were worthy of the responsibility. But there were deep flaws in how this education was being imparted in the Native States. One such flaw concerned the environment in which princes were being raised. Since most Maharajas had a "plurality of wives", their households were steeped in "intrigue" as various branches of the royal family sought to advance their "relative rights and claims". The end result was moral corruption: Education could accomplish little when the daily life of princes involved navigating "plots and counterplots" that fostered "bitterness and ill-will". The great preliminary to a true and moral education, then, was for Maharajas to shun polygamy in favor of monogamy. Even better, Parmanand boldly adds, would be for Maharajas to adopt a "successor based on the possession of mental and moral qualities rather than birth".

The other flaw in the education of princes concerned the institutions in which they were being trained. Until quite recently, princes and their companions had received little formal education, leaving many of them "ignorant and uneducated". With the advent of modern education in British India, some of the more forward-thinking Maharajas had procured tutors to educate their children. But it was a mistake, Parmanand observed, to have princes study "within their own homes" where "obsequious teachers" and "pandering parasites" tended to make them "wayward and capricious from early age". Instead, the Native States ought to follow the example being adopted by the monarchies of Western Europe, where princes were expected to display a "manly and vigorous prosecution of studies carried on in the classrooms of public schools and colleges, in competition with the intellect of the commonalty". The great object in having princes go up against the "sons of the middle classes" was that it would help them see that "they are no better than ordinary men". This painful realization would spur them to behave well, Parmanand reasoned, because it would leave them with the knowledge that the only way they could justify their rank in the modern era was by exhibiting noble conduct.

The fourth essay, "On Prudence", continues with the theme of education but the concern here is with the knowledge that Maharajas themselves must acquire. In particular, they should not make the mistake, Parmanand warns, of thinking that, having ascended to the throne, they no longer need to study – or that they have better uses for their time. In fact, this was precisely the moment, he argues, at which they most need to partake in reading and reflection. What particularly deserved their attention was "life-lore"; that is, they ought to study books that "open to view the springs of men's conduct in life", as this knowledge would be essential to performing their "first and foremost duty", which was to govern well.

So, who should their role models be? Tellingly, Parmanand advised Maharajas to eschew the "low statecraft and unscrupulous cunning" on display in Machiavelli's *The Prince* (which had, it should be recalled, become the Gaekwad's favorite text). Instead, it was essential that Maharajas study the lives of those who had displayed "constructive genius" – that is, rulers that had engaged in "far-seeing statesmanship". To wit, Parmanand advised Maharajas to study less the daring means by which Chhatrapati Shivaji[554] was able to found the Maratha Empire and more the "exalted wisdom" he displayed after he was anointed king, which is when he established a "civil government" (a point that would subsequently be pressed by Ranade's *Rise of the Maratha Power* (1900), which showed how deeply liberal in spirit were the laws and institutions of the Maratha Empire).[555]

Parmanand offered two reasons why Maharajas ought to focus on what it takes to build rather than acquire a state. The first was "the circumstances of the time": British dominance meant that, for the foreseeable future, Maharajas had little choice but to restrict themselves to "peaceful operations within their dominions". The second, and more important reason, was the "spirit of the times", namely, the changing norms of the era. The duty of the modern ruler was not to acquire more territory, Parmanand observed, but to govern well what they already possessed. The presence of the British made this duty all the more unavoidable because Maharajas' subjects, who were becoming ever more aware of the improvements being made in British India, would cry out for intervention if they felt they were being left behind. Hence, a Maharaja would be best served, Parmanand concluded, by studying those who had excelled in the art of governing rather than the art of war, for only the lessons imparted by the former could bring Maharajas peace and glory in the present age.

It was not enough, Parmanand knew from his experience in Kutch, for Maharajas to want to govern well. They also had to work their way around the imperious British, who were prepared to take advantage of any opposition provoked by even well-meaning reforms. Thus, the very next essay, "On Relations with British India", takes up the question of how Maharajas might manage this side of the equation. This was no ordinary diplomatic challenge. Because the Native States were in "subordinate alliance" with the British, the latter were entitled to check and criticize their "internal administration". Ignoring the "friendly advice" offered thereupon by a governor or viceroy never ended well for a Maharaja. A further complicating factor in this already humiliating arrangement was that official communication between Native States and British India had to be routed through the official representative, the Resident or Political Agent. Because this officer was "alien in race, language, religion, sentiment and habits of thought", it was not uncommon for his reports on the doings of a Maharaja to be "misled or warped" by his "personal opinions or prejudices" or "by the workings of adverse parties or cliques". As a consequence, the prospect of unwarranted or vexatious interference was never far from the minds of rulers and served to demoralize them. Maharajas faced, as Parmanand dryly puts it, the "not very easy task of keeping a distant arbiter of your fate pleased through his agents".

To this unhappy set of circumstances, "On Relations with British India" offers an innovative "constitutional remedy". It proposes to make Residents co-adjudicators with Maharajas so that they would be "responsible along with the Raja for the good government". It also proposes that, in the event of a serious disagreement between the parties, differences between the Maharaja and Resident be adjudicated by a "special tribunal" rather than the Foreign Department, which usually favored its agent, the Resident, regardless of the actual merits of the case.

Parmanand's proposal was not entirely unprecedented. A close analog, which he had reported on frequently during his time as editor of *Native Opinion*, could be seen in the principality of Bhavnagar where, during the minority of Maharaja, its celebrated *dewan*, Gaurishankar Udayshankar,[556] and the capable Resident, E. H. Percival, had worked wonders as co-administrators. This example notwithstanding, Parmanand knew his idea was "radical", not so much because it compelled Maharajas to share power with the Residents (which was, in effect, already happening), but because it would lessen the ability of the Foreign Department to ride roughshod over the Native States. Still, so pernicious were the effects of the routine "divergence" of views between Maharaja and Resident, he argues, that it had become necessary to place their relations on a sounder footing by incentivizing Residents to behave as partners rather than mere censors. It was only when a Resident was "able to realise the difficulties in the way of the prince better than he now can", Parmanand argued, that he would use his authority and influence to judiciously advance rather than retard the cause of good government.

Having discussed how Maharajas ought to reform their households (in Nos. II–IV) and defuse the diplomatic challenge before them (in No. V), Parmanand turns to examine how Maharajas ought to transform their administrations. This discussion, which begins with the essay "On Constitutional Rule", takes up nearly the remainder of the volume (Nos. VI–XI). The fact that Parmanand devotes far more attention to administration than to diplomacy is telling. It indicates that he was aware that the relationship between British India and the Native States would likely not be reconceptualized in the manner he had proposed. This was a pity, as having the Resident on the Maharaja's side would make reform "comparatively easy", but it was hardly fatal to progress. Even if Residents were to continue to busy themselves in "accumulating black marks against the ruler", there was much that Maharajas could still do to improve the lives of their people – and thereby preserve their sovereignty. As Parmanand put it, "the straightest, surest, wisest and worthiest course" that Maharajas could adopt was to "turn their principalities into states", as this would "create that identity of interests" between ruler and ruled that would allow the Native States to "fight with the British government for their rights and interests on equal ground".

With the goal set, Parmanand lists ten principles by which Maharajas ought to abide. The first two are taken up for discussion in "On Constitutional Rule" itself. Foremost among these is the requirement to strictly demarcate the *khangi* (or privy purse) from the treasury (or the public purse) so as "not to be forgetful of justice to the taxpayer". This change ought to be effected, Parmanand advises, by allocating to the *khangi* a fixed proportion of revenue, with the Maharaja legally barred from charging any additional sums to the public purse. This stricture leads to the second principle, which is the "supremacy of law over all individual will and power". Far from relying on self-restraint or goodwill, Parmanand demands that Maharajas "must not be above the law". A prerequisite for this, he warns, is that Native States replace hazy and contested customary law with a modern code of law, so that the rights and privileges of all persons, including the Maharaja, become clear and distinct.

The following essay, "On Public Administration", takes up the next four principles on Parmanand's list. These relate to how public offices should be organized. The first order of business, he advises, must be to delegate executive and judicial powers down a chain of command rather than leave them concentrated in a few hands in the *darbar*. This is because responsibility can only be enforced, Parmanand notes, when roles and duties are defined precisely. The practical implication for the Native States was that their characteristic "looseness" needed to be replaced with a clear "gradation of power and responsibility". As greater delegation increased the size of the public service, Parmanand observes, Maharajas would find themselves in the highly desirable position of being able to separate executive and judicial offices, which would reduce the ability of public servants to abuse their power. This was especially desirable in the upper rungs of the administration, Parmanand counseled, where officials had to deal with matters of relatively greater importance.

Of course, these changes – specialization and separation – would greatly increase the demands imposed on the senior officials in the *darbar*, who would now be required to formulate policy as well as oversee the lower rungs of the bureaucracy. These offices would therefore need to be filled by persons of merit and probity. Such persons, Parmanand warned, could not be secured or retained merely by promising generous salaries. Maharajas would also have to offer them "certainty of tenure" when in office as well as credible "provision for old age and infirmity". Otherwise, capable individuals would prefer to serve in British India, as the settled rules and guaranteed pensions on offer there were far preferable to the unpredictable favor of a monarch.

The final piece of the puzzle was to ensure financial accountability, a subject that caused Maharajas no small amount of anxiety. The worry was that, even if they could rely on senior officials to keep tabs on the bureaucracy below them, how could they be sure that the senior officials would behave faithfully? The traditional remedy was to employ spies, which only led to constant intrigue and a pervasive sense of dread. Far better, Parmanand counseled, was to follow the example set by British India, which kept its officers in line by routinely subjecting them to audits. By having auditors report directly to them, Maharajas would be able to identify cases of "peculation and misappropriation" – without needlessly demoralizing their officers down the line. And from this would emerge, Parmanand promised, a public administration where "public morality was combined with public spirit".

Having outlined how Maharajas could make their administrations more effective, Parmanand devotes the next two essays ("On District Administration" and "On the Village System") to identify a suitable check upon its operations. The former of these essays poses the problem thusly: There could be no doubt that the Native States ought to discard the Mughal model of farming out administrative functions, which was characterized by corruption and inefficiency, in favor of British India's "departmental system", which favored specialization and responsibility. But the "departmental system" had, Parmanand observes, an "inherent drawback", which was that it required district officers be entrusted with an immense amount of discretion. In British India, the "social gulf" between ruler and ruled had led to countless examples of such discretion being "misused". The British were not oblivious to the problem. They had sought to rein in their officers in two ways: They allowed natives to appeal to courts and to petition higher officers, and, more importantly, they required their civil servants to strictly abide by procedures and precedents that constrained how they used their discretion. These remedies were far from ideal, especially in view of the time and expense involved in appealing and petitioning, but they certainly were not trivial concessions. What could the Native States do to keep pace? Parmanand's worry was that a "departmental system" would lead to even more abuse in the Native States. Though the Native States had the advantage of "social solidarity" between ruler and ruled, the fact that subjects had become accustomed to living at the mercy of district officials meant, he worried, that they would not even consider opposing or contesting abuses of power, especially since officers in the Native States would now be backed by a powerful "centralized" authority. It would therefore be necessary, he stresses, to develop "local institutions" whose health and vitality would have a decisive impact on "the condition of its subjects".

Could the necessary counterbalance be found in the *panchayat* (village council), which was commonly described in this era as an early instance of a representative institution? Not in its extant form – of this Parmanand was certain. In "On the Village System", he directly contradicted prevailing opinion, including that of his friend and patron, Wedderburn, when he declared that the *panchayat* had been "overpraised and credited with virtues that did not belong to it".[557] It had in fact proven an "isolating influence" in two important respects. Because it had encouraged natives to be "indifferent and apathetic to all but their village affairs", it had hindered them from "combining on an extended scale". To make matters worse, as roles in the *panchayat* had come to be appropriated by particular castes, this institution had caused collective life in villages to be oriented toward guarding status rather than cooperating on common ends. The ultimate consequence was a narrowing of minds. With social and political life organized around group identities, the individual was subordinated, willingly or not, to the dictates of the group, to disobey which meant "civil death".[558]

The degradation of the "village system" did not mean, however, that it ought to be dispensed with. It could indeed prove a counterbalance to the Native State's newly empowered administration – *if* Maharajas made an effort to restore the moral basis of the *panchayat*. In its original form, Parmanand noted, the *panchayat* called for civic roles to be allocated according to "character and qualification more than mere birth or hereditary position". Were Maharajas to encourage these positions to once again be filled on this basis – by awarding them as honors and rewards – then the "honest and proper execution" of civic duties would become the norm. This would make municipal self-government viable, and thereby greatly lessen the need for Maharajas to send out to the districts all-powerful officials before whom his humble subjects might cower.

Parmanand was well aware that the functioning of the administrative structures he was proposing depended on more than the caliber of the bureaucrats and the checks imposed upon their conduct. It was at least as important that Maharajas refrain from uninformed interference with personnel and procedures. Hence, the next two essays in the series ("On the Council and Assembly" and "On Public Instruction") take up the questions of exercising and sharing sovereign power. In the former of these essays, Parmanand urges Maharajas to raise themselves "above the details of the administration" and to focus instead on providing "comprehensive supervision and an inspiring direction". In particular, they should vest the making of laws and regulations and oversight of the administration in a cabinet and a council, respectively, and correspondingly restrict their personal role to that of vetoing proposals and acting as the "highest court of appeal" in controversies. Such a "systematization of the administration" would, Parmanand insists, leave the Maharajas' sovereignty "untouched, except to a very small extent". In fact, it would, he promises, a little too earnestly, strengthen Maharajas, because it would lead their rule to be greeted with subjects' "unfeigned respect".

But then, having said this much, Parmanand raises a doubt as to how long this "unfeigned respect" is likely to endure. It is "very desirable", he observes, that the workings of the "central authority" be "supplemented" by a "popular element" in the form of "a consultative assembly composed of the leading representatives of all the different interests and classes" who must be permitted to make "well-grounded representations" on matters of public concern, especially relating to laws and taxes. Parmanand stresses that he is not calling for "self-government", because progress in that direction must be slow and halting "for a people disunited by race and caste, creed and tradition". At the same time, he notes that a Maharaja's subjects could subsequently "establish their fitness and evince their desire for it by a successful and satisfactory discharge of their local and municipal functions". Not only that, Parmanand goes on to underline that it is in fact the Maharaja's duty to awaken "the mental and moral capacities of your subjects by means of a general diffusion of knowledge and of culture" such that they come to shed their "sectional jealousies" and learn to combine and cooperate in "common causes" – developments that would inevitably increase pressure on the Maharaja to share or limit his sovereignty.

Why a Maharaja ought to foster general progress, even though it would make "autocracy" less viable, is made clear in the following essay, "On Public Instruction". In this essay, Parmanand traces the subjugation of the

Native States to the destructive consequences of their social order, and to the institution of caste in particular. On one side, this institution had condemned the multitude to live in ignorance and thus made it impossible for Native States to take advantage of the "talents and capacities" of their subjects. On the other, it had condoned occupations becoming hereditary, which had led to a loss of "communion or sympathy between the manufacturing and consuming classes" and thereby facilitated "foreign competition". The net result of these "twin evils" had been a decimation of finances, which was the "backbone of a state". Now, seeing as "social solidarity" was "essential for a successful development of national industries", Parmanand observes, Maharajas had no choice but to "provide for the enlightenment of their subjects". This required, in the first instance, "a compulsory system of primary education among the masses" to be offered "free of cost". This arrangement needed to be supplemented by establishing public institutions such as museums and libraries that would "exert an educative and inspiring influence on the mass of its people generally". The Native States would also need to invest in "original research and investigation into the physical and moral sciences" and offer prizes and patronage in order to innovate or to "set entirely new lines of business in motion". But not every social obstacle to economic prosperity could be overcome through "rewards and encouragement" alone. This was especially true regarding the condition of women. The fact that even educated men in British India were slow to change their thinking and behavior when it came to the opposite sex indicated that the cause of women's freedom required "a superior lead and example". This "want could be supplied only by princes and rulers", Parmanand underlined, because, unlike the governors of British India, who were "aliens", Maharajas could "directly lead Indian society and mould its sentiments".

No less important was what Maharajas could do to cultivate the "moral resources" of the population, which constituted "the real greatness of a people". Here there was much to be learned, Parmanand argues, from the Chinese, whose constitution "may well be regarded as liberal" because its institutions, and the imperial exam system in particular, created an "impersonal order" that rewarded merit and virtue without regard for "birth and position". Maharajas ought to follow this example, he counsels, by awarding "distinction within your own dominions for the public recognition of worth and the reward of merit among your own subjects". This would create, in effect, an "aristocracy of intellect", who could then "stand midway between a vast body of interested officials on the one hand, and the mass of the people on the other". Such a body would serve as a check on the exercise of sovereign power, but its operation would actually "strengthen and enhance" the Maharaja's "power and dignity", Parmanand insists, as he would be viewed as the "patron" of the beneficial change.

The final essay in the series, entitled "On Good Government", completes the discussion on what Maharajas should *personally* do to improve the condition of their principalities. In addition to encouraging religious and social reform (as discussed in Nos. II and XI, respectively), Parmanand now urges Maharajas to also keep in "complete touch with the country". They ought to undertake "periodic tours" and engage in "free intercourse" with their subjects in the *mofussil*, as this would keep them abreast of popular sentiment and provide them an opportunity to swiftly remedy "unmerited privation, hardship or suffering". When combined with "constitutionalized government", such "personal accessibility" and "continued ministrations" would create, Parmanand declares, "a felicitous combination" of the "poet's ideal of the king in the East with that of him in the West".

Having listed the most important of a Maharaja's duties, Parmanand concludes by addressing, more explicitly than in No. I, the question of why a Maharaja should be inclined to follow his advice "when an indolent continuance of the existing order of things is possible". He answers the question by listing three "motives" that should spur them to act. The first is humanity, wherein Parmanand observes that every "enlightened" person wishes "to leave the world better than he found it". The second motive is glory, with Parmanand reminding Maharajas that even in their own family histories, only those monarchs that had abided by the "dictates of right and wrong" were "esteemed" and "famous". The third, and much more amply discussed motive, is self-interest, with Parmanand warning Maharajas that despotism was far from "favorable to the steady fortunes of the state nor of the reigning dynasty" because "under such rule the state rises or falls both in reputation and prosperity according to the personal character of the ruler, and personal character is not only uncertain but more often than not falls short of the requisite standard". What made such fluctuations in talent and ability especially dangerous was that it allowed the British to encroach on the Maharajas' sovereignty. This threat was, he admitted, being dulled by circumstances: The British were increasingly unwilling to pressure the Native States, lest this provoke an insurrection and thereby make it easier for the Russians to advance on their "unwieldy" empire in India. But, far from making reform unnecessary, British tentativeness afforded Maharajas a rare opportunity to strengthen their principalities – on their own terms.

What Letters *means for Indian liberalism*

Now that we have mapped out Parmanand's vision for the Native States, it is time to examine what it reveals about the trajectory of Indian liberalism. Arguably, *Letters* transforms our understanding of *where* liberalism emerged in India and *what* it stood for. But its significance becomes clear only when we understand how modestly Indian liberalism has been portrayed over the past century, and so a brief overview is in order.

The earliest commentary on Indian liberalism emerged in the closing decade of the nineteenth century, when the ruling Conservatives in Britain were becoming anxious about the inexorable rise of the Indian National Congress. At this moment it suited both sides – hopeful Indians and remorseful Britons – to depict the Congress as a natural outcome of the permissive policies enacted by the colonial authorities over preceding decades. Pramatha Nath Bose spoke for many of his compatriots when he declared in *A History of Hindu Civilization during British Rule* (1896) that the Congress embodied liberal ideals of representation and deliberation that had "taken deep root in the Hindu mind" due to "the progress of English education", which had transplanted the "spirit" of John Milton, Edmund Burke, and John Stuart Mill.[559] Repeated enough times, this notion became a commonplace, appearing in widely read accounts such as Arminius Vambréy's *Western Culture in Eastern Lands* (1906), which proclaimed that the fact that "liberal ideas in so short a time have been able to take such hold of the Asiatic mind deserves to be acknowledged as the greatest triumph of British influence".[560] This narrative was subsequently reinforced by the Liberals in Britain when they returned to office in 1906. Unlike their Conservative counterparts, they saw the development as a happy one – and were keen to take credit for it. Perhaps the finest such example was provided by James Ramsay MacDonald's *The Awakening of India* (1910), in which the future British prime minister memorably declared liberal ideals to be "the only battery of guns which India has captured from us and condescends to use against us".[561]

These declarations about the paternity of Indian liberalism went unchallenged in the earliest scholarship on the topic. By the time this scholarship began appearing in the 1930s and 1940s, the political landscape had completely changed. Having lost control of the Congress in 1907, the liberals (or "moderates" as they were commonly termed) had formed the National Liberal Federation in 1916. But with radical ideologies, which depicted Indian liberals as "soft-headed and weak-kneed", on the ascendant, the National Liberal Federation was unable to make headway, and so by the 1930s liberals were living in "splendid isolation".[562] As a result, scholars in the 1930s and 1940s had little reason to investigate the finer points of doctrine – they were principally interested in understanding why liberal ideas had appealed to prior generations. Therefore, pioneering works such as Maganlal A. Buch's *Rise and Growth of Indian Liberalism* (1938), V. N. Naik's *Indian Liberalism: A Study* (1945), and K. M. Panikkar's *In Defence of Liberalism* (1962) did not examine whether Indian liberals really had derived their ideas from British liberals.[563] Instead, they focused on historical explanation, tracing the factors behind "the growth of the liberal spirit" in India, which included the expansion of modern education, the emergence of the press, and the growth of modern professions. They were also interested in evaluating the consequences of these developments, the most notable of which was the formation of voluntary associations that sought to reform social norms, religious practices, and political beliefs.[564] The general consensus was that while Indian liberals had met with limited success in their efforts to overturn oppressive social norms, especially those relating to caste and gender, they deserved credit for popularizing the concepts of deliberation and representation, and thereby setting in motion "the wheels of parliamentary democracy". The adoption of the Constitution in 1950, in particular, came to be regarded, as Ray Price movingly put it, "as much their memorial as other men's victory".[565]

It was not long before such positive assessments of Indian liberalism came under fire. Because the pioneering studies of Indian liberalism in the pre-Independence period had neglected to analyze its intellectual foundations, they left open the door for two kinds of critiques in the post-Independence period. These critiques decried Indian liberalism as neither Indian nor liberal. The former accusation came from postcolonialists fixated on the notion of authenticity, who castigated the lives and ideas of India's liberals as a "form of mimicry" that had served to undermine indigenous traditions and values.[566] The latter accusation came from Marxists fixated on the notion of class, who described Indian liberals as "self-seeking bourgeois individualists" who used concepts such as property rights to constrain and dominate those lower down the social and economic ladder.[567] Eventually, these streams merged under the rubric of "subaltern studies", which accused Indian liberals of being "elitists delivering a derivative discourse".[568] So calumnious was the denunciation that it needs to be cited more fully. This is what Ranajit Guha, the first among equals in the subaltern camp, had to say about Indian liberals in *Dominance without Hegemony* (1998):

> The indigenous bourgeoisie, spawned and nurtured by colonialism itself, adopted a role that was distinguished by its failure to measure up to the heroism of the European bourgeoisie in its period of ascendancy. Pliant and prone to compromise from their inception, they lived in a state of happy accommodation with imperialism ... and settled for pressure politics as their main tactical means in bargaining for power. Compromise and accommodation were equally characteristic of their attitude to the semi-feudal values and institutions entrenched in Indian society. The liberalism they professed was never strong enough to exceed the limitations of the half-hearted initiatives for reform which issued from the colonial administration. This mediocre liberalism, a caricature of the vigorous democratic culture of the epoch of the rise of the

> bourgeoisie in the West, operated throughout the colonial period in a symbiotic relationship with the still active and vigorous forces of the semifeudal culture of India.[569]

These sweeping claims about the apparently dismal character and conduct of Indian liberals appear rather less brilliant once we start considering the lives of the individuals in question. Over the past decade, valuable biographies have appeared describing how liberals – from Dadabhai Naoroji through to Gopal Krishna Gokhale and on to V. S. Srinivasa Sastri[570] – challenged imperial excess.[571] This introductory essay has joined this revisionary movement by detailing Parmanand's life, showing the ways in which he targeted errant British officials and shielded Native States against colonial encroachment even as he pushed Maharajas to reform tradition-bound administrations and societies. Understanding the fraught circumstances in which Indian liberals like Parmanand operated – the unglamorous risks they ran, the now-forgotten plots they executed, the unseen battles they fought – reveals how injudicious is the claim that they passed their days persuaded of "the desirability of their subjection".[572] There may have been effete *babu*s and corpulent *zamindar*s in Calcutta that did no more than deliver speeches and raise toasts, but outside hallowed Bengal there were not a few liberals who emerged from little and worked hard to support those who had even less. Parmanand, for instance, redirected the patronage that Sayaji Rao offered him in the direction of others such as Phule, and worked tirelessly for the upliftment of girls and widows, in spite of the public denunciations and social ostracism it provoked.[573] To take only one statistic: the night schools he helped establish for day laborers in Bombay had, within two decades of his passing, educated some twenty-six thousand individuals.[574]

Though biographical literature on India's liberals has provided a welcome corrective to the raving abstractions of the subaltern movement, it has not been able to fully articulate the theory underpinning Indian liberalism. Because India's preeminent liberals were politicians, whose lives revolved around action rather than theorizing, their biographers have been compelled to reconstruct their ideas by drawing on an array of disjointed sources: speeches and essays, private correspondence, petitions, and memoranda. The result has been rich intellectual histories that have clarified what Indian liberals fought for and described the context in which their beliefs were formed. But history is not theory. A history *explains* the career of an idea whereas a theory *justifies* an idea; a history *observes* how laws and institutions have operated whereas a theory *proposes* what laws and institutions ought to be established. To understand the *ism* in Indian liberalism, we want an account of the ideals that Indian liberals wanted to enact; what we have instead is a catalog of their grievances and their piecemeal proposals in response to crises in British India. Little wonder, then, that even sympathetic observers have been led to conclude that Indian liberalism is no more than a "sensibility" or a "manner of thought".[575]

This is not to suggest that the scattered writings of Indian liberals in British India contain *nothing* of theoretical significance. At least two insights can be gleaned from them. The first concerns the state. Because liberals in India viewed Britain as principally interested in "draining away" resources from her colonies, they deeply distrusted the Raj. At every session of the Congress, they demanded that it "do justice" to India by exhibiting fiscal discipline. They called on it to "retrench" the bureaucracy (by refraining from imperial ventures and employing fewer British personnel) and to "protect" domestic producers (by lowering taxes and raising tariffs).[576] The second insight concerns society. Because the British were "alien rulers" prone to sneering at Indian religions and customs, liberals sought to protect *samaj* (society) from the *sarkar* (government).[577] They demanded that communities be permitted to ascertain for themselves whether and how to reform their social norms and religious doctrines, and they called on the Raj to exhibit strict neutrality on this "sensitive" matter.

The foregoing means that if we only examine what was said and done in British India, we invariably come away with the sense that Indian liberalism was characterized by *vagueness* and *defensiveness*. But contrast this with what we find in *Letters*. It reveals that Indian liberals saw matters very differently when they addressed themselves to Maharajas who could "directly lead Indian society and mould its sentiments". In this setting, Indian liberals were in favor of using the state to transform religious beliefs, social norms, and political practices in order to promote freedom in the private sphere and collective action in the public sphere. Far from supporting group rights, they urged rulers to dissolve distinctions of caste, gender, and religion, and to promote equality of opportunity and of citizenship. Altogether then, *Letters* reveals that the demands that Indian liberals directed at the British Raj do not comprise the full extent of Indian liberalism – and certainly do not capture its original character. If we are interested in understanding what Indian liberals wanted *to do* – as opposed to what they wanted the British *not to do* – then we need to examine what these liberals said about the Native States, where they could imagine more freely.[578]

And what did their imaginations yield? *Letters* shows that liberals who engaged with the Native States came to espouse what political philosophers term *liberal perfectionism*. This is the idea that political authority should be employed to advance the good life. For these liberals, the good life amounted to human flourishing, which consisted of two virtues. The first was "self-realization". This virtue emerged when individuals were able to refine their intellect and cultivate their personality. The second was "moral progress". This virtue involved learning to care for the interests of others, which was a prerequisite to social cooperation. Since neither of these desirable traits could be developed when individuals were weighed down by traditional norms and identities, *Letters* wants the authorities to free individuals by providing them with the secular education and the spiritual training needed to become independent-minded and responsible persons. Its focus therefore is on detailing the mechanisms by which such "moral laws" could be enacted in the Native States. Principal among these, we have seen, is the creation of a professional bureaucracy and a nobility founded on merit. Together, these institutions would elevate the citizenry – the former by providing public services, the latter by exemplifying high-souled conduct. Parmanand believed these mechanisms were practical, as evidenced by the Chinese imperial system, which he held up as an exemplar of "impersonal" rule for Maharajas to study. But these ennobling institutions would only emerge if sovereigns willed them into existence – and Maharajas, Parmanand reasoned, had better reasons than the British to do so.

Letters reveals, then, that there *was* a form of liberalism in India that had a well-developed theory behind it. It addressed Indian India and concerned itself with promoting self-fulfillment and collective action; the former through the provision of resources and opportunities, the latter through social and religious reform. This form of liberalism predated, and unsuccessfully opposed, the "communitarian" liberalism that developed in British India following the launch of the Congress. This latter form of liberalism focused on political representation, which, being organized on the basis of group membership, ultimately came at the expense of both individuality and solidarity.

The claim that *Letters* reveals the original, now-forgotten form of Indian liberalism may be challenged in the following way: Can *Letters* really be considered emblematic of a wider intellectual phenomenon, the critic will ask. Is it not merely the *sui generis* production of a singular individual? The answer is an emphatic no. Recall here that Parmanand involved a number of his associates, including Ranade, Telang, Bhandarkar, and Chandavarkar, in the production of *Letters*. At the very least then, *Letters* can safely be said to represent the views of the Prarthana Samaj (which is one reason why Chandavarkar took the trouble to publish a second edition). This was no marginal group, comprising as it did judges, vice-chancellors, *dewan*s, editors, and even presidents of the Congress. But there is more to it than that. The fact that *Letters* originally appeared in the *Indian Spectator*, the preeminent liberal forum of the era, speaks to its still wider appeal. Malabari would not have expended precious goodwill to have Hunter draft the preface to *Letters* were it an eccentric production (nor for that matter would Hunter have lent his prestige to it, much less recommended the volume to "serious thinkers" in India and England).

And we can say still more. Parts I and II of this introduction have made clear that *Letters* grew out of a wider phenomenon, which involved thinking through how the Native States could develop into constitutional monarchies of the kind that could be found in nineteenth-century Europe. This intellectual phenomenon may have been limited in scope and duration – it was centered in Bombay Presidency, which is where the bulk of the Native States were to be found, and it faded away in the wake of the Great War, which brought democratic ideals to the fore. But that it existed, and that it involved a number of prominent figures who described themselves as liberals (or as moderates), cannot be doubted. Nor can there be any question that this cogitation on constitutional monarchy was followed carefully by Maharajas, especially those deemed to be "highly progressive".[579] In Western India, this ideal was pressed on them by the Poona Sarvajanik Sabha in particular.[580] But *Letters* played an important role too because it became a text of choice for royal tutors. The most important of these educators was Stuart Fraser, who served as the tutor to Shahu IV of Kolhapur, Bhavsinhji II of Bhavnagar, and Krishnaraja Wadiyar IV of Mysore between 1894 and 1902. A highly regarded Oxford-educated civil servant, who went on to serve as Resident in both Mysore and Hyderabad, Fraser made his wards study *Letters* carefully as part of their "special education".[581] Its impact is perhaps clearest in Shahu's public addresses, which advocated the dissolution of the caste system, fairer access to public services, and mass education as a path to self-government.[582] The Maharaja translated these ideals into decrees that, for instance, expanded the role of the "depressed castes" in the professions (in 1902), introduced free and compulsory primary education (in 1911), supported widow remarriage and intercaste marriage (in 1917), and lifted disabilities imposed on "untouchables" (in 1919).[583] Such legislation led to Shahu being described as "extremely radical" in his adherence to "liberal principles", and placed Kolhapur ahead of British India when it came to enacting social and religious reform, much to the delight of figures like Chandavarkar.[584] This is not to suggest that Shahu's actions can be solely attributed to *Letters* – he engaged with multiple intellectual traditions, including the doctrines of the Arya Samaj.[585] Rather, the point is that paternalistic liberalism of the kind advocated in *Letters* had a broad and consequential existence, at least until the close of the Great War.

What Letters *means for liberal theory*

Having seen how *Letters* transforms our understanding of Indian liberalism, what remains is to examine whether the theory it offers is distinctive. As

Shahu IV, Maharaja of Kolhapur. British Library, Photo 2_8(3)

noted earlier, until quite recently, Indian liberalism was viewed as the country cousin of British liberalism, with critics deriding it as an example of "mental colonization". Happily, such sweeping assertions about the supposed unoriginality of political thinking in the colonized world have begun to give way to more nuanced claims. As scholars have traced what Indians actually said and did at the time, it has become clearer that the intellectual "entanglements" provoked by colonialism in fact led to the "co-production" of concepts and ideas.[586] *Letters to an Indian Raja* is a prime example of such "creative political thinking", wherein Indians critiqued and revised ideals circulating in Britain.[587] To see why, we need to understand how it departs from Victorian liberalism.

The concept of liberalism has been defined in a "dizzying variety of ways".[588] One way to simplify the story is to see liberalism as "a history of opposition to assorted tyrannies" that threaten individual freedom.[589] What were the "assorted tyrannies" that concerned nineteenth-century Europe, the period in which the term liberalism first began to be used in the public sphere?[590] In the early part of the century, it was the excesses of the French Revolution that weighed most heavily on minds. The resulting anxiety about mobs and demagogues led figures like Francois Guizot and Alexis de Tocqueville to focus on representative government as a check on democracy. During this time, "to be a liberal meant, at a minimum, that one favored the rule of deliberative and representative assemblies, which protected individual rights and fostered discussion".[591] In the latter part of the century, a different concern came to the fore. Now it was the excesses of industrialization that seemed the most pressing threat to individual freedom. A sharp contrast was drawn between the privileges of the landed aristocracy and the "plight of the poor" and "distress of the working class".[592] This was the period in which liberals "began to say that people should be accorded not just freedom, but the *conditions of freedom*", and they termed this program "new liberalism".[593] Crucially, the "new" liberals, who were led by Thomas Hill Green, viewed the relationship between the individual and the state very differently from their predecessors. Unlike "classical" liberals, who saw legal constraints as the "negation of liberty", the "new" liberals regarded the law as the enabler of "progress".[594] They called upon the state to enact social and economic programs that would "secure sufficient personal freedom for citizens to act as rational moral agents".[595] Then, as the century came to a close, a third concern began to make itself felt. This was the worry about "sectionalism", or the sense that the social and economic reforms that "new" liberals had been championing were fostering an antagonistic politics centered around class interests. For a "socialist liberal" such as Leonard Hobhouse, the answer was not to retreat to the *laissez-faire* doctrines of "classical" liberalism, which was excoriated for its "hedonism", but to instead focus on the "collective interest" that members of society had in advancing each other's moral development. That is, liberals now sought to identify, as the famous slogan had it, "with the masses as against the classes".[596] They stressed in particular that the nation rather than the state was "indispensable to the development of moral character", and the pervasive sense that "industrial society" had weakened the "social tissue" meant that late Victorians came to be preoccupied with the "restoration of community".[597]

Compare the foregoing with what *Letters* has to say. It clearly shares the great concerns that animated liberals in nineteenth-century Europe – unruly mobs, debilitating vices, and selfish individualism – and incorporates the remedies they provide – representation rather than democracy, legislation to advance welfare, and a public morality centered on the common good. Among these influences, it is the impress of the "new" liberals that stands out, especially Green's conviction that "self-realization is the ultimate end of all mankind", and that it was therefore the business of the state to provide individuals the "possibilities to make the best of themselves".[598]

So where then is the novelty in *Letters*? It lies in the diagnosis of *where* the challenge to "self-realization" came from in the Indian context. In contrast to liberals in Europe, who worried about how recent developments – mass democracy, mass industrialization, and mass media – were subjecting individuals to vast and impersonal forces, *Letters* worries most about freeing the individual from bondage to the *community*. This focus may seem to have a parallel in the anxiety that John Stuart Mill had already expressed in *On Liberty* (1859) about the need to protect individuals from the "tyranny of prevailing opinion and feeling".[599] Is *Letters* then merely a rehash of a familiar complaint? Not at all. Mill was worried about "social tyranny" or the "tendency" of the *majority* to impose "its own ideas and practices on those who dissent from them" and to thereby "fetter the development of any individuality not in harmony with its ways".[600] Parmanand's generation in India, by contrast, worried about communities, especially those of a religious nature, which were seen as uniquely threatening because of how early their influence began, affecting the individual from the cradle onward; how deeply their norms impressed themselves upon the individual, shaping everything from tastes to fears; and how severe their penalties could be, including the ability to impose "civil death" by expulsion. This was an *intimate* and *lifelong* tyranny, effected by the joint family, the village council, and the local priest, any of whom could override the most private of an individual's choices, such as what they ate, whom they married or dined with, what occupations and activities they engaged in, and where they resided or even traveled.[601]

This fear of overpowerful communities helps explain why, unlike liberals in Europe, who spent the nineteenth century gnashing their teeth over whether to protect or curb rights because they wanted to promote welfare without sacrificing freedom, Indian liberals unapologetically stressed the paternalistic language of improving character rather than safeguarding rights. They did not emphasize individual rights because, based on the evidence before them, they doubted that, corrupted by their upbringing and cowed by communal sanctions, individuals would actually exercise these rights in the interests of their own moral development, much less in the interests of society. This did not mean that they were oblivious to the danger that rulers could trample on the interests of subjects – the concern that traditionally undergirded the concept of rights. How could they be unaware of this danger when they were confronted daily with instances of despotism in both British India and Indian India? The reason they had little to say on the subject of rights was because for them the most important safeguard against the abuse of power was – once again – character. Since there was no alternative but to have the state take the lead in reshaping communities, they demanded that rulers and bureaucrats, whether in British India or in Indian India, have high character. As the old Pali proverb, that Parmanand cites more than once, has it, *yata raja tata prajah* ("as the king is, so the subjects are").

The desire to thoroughly reform social norms and religious beliefs in turn helps explain why, unlike liberals in Europe, who were addressing themselves to their fellow citizens, *Letters* was addressed to a monarch. It was not as if Parmanand's circle did not try to reconcile flourishing with freedom by praising, as liberals in Britain did, the idea of "voluntary action" by "civil society".[602] This is why they founded the Prarthana Samaj, following in the footsteps of their heroes – Gladstone in the world of politics and Green in the world of ideas – who were trying, through oratory and print, to persuade an ever-increasing pool of English voters that the improvement of all was in the interests of all. But the Samajists soon learned that those on the receiving end of their sermons were usually loathe to be told what their "true" interests were, or to do what they were told was in the "common good". The utter unwillingness of the Congress to take up the unpopular business of social and religious reform proved an especially cruel blow. The grim conclusion Parmanand reached was that because mass politics in British India placed a premium on those who could mobilize large numbers, it would serve to entrench the leaders of communities, who would subsequently have an incentive to keep their flock together by stressing their exclusive identity and distinctive norms, whether rooted in region, caste, language, or religion. This dynamic would ultimately serve to perpetuate hierarchies and patterns of life that stymied the moral development of individuals and retarded collective action. This is why Parmanand decided to take the help of a monarch who could be enlightened through education and then given the task of directing the social and religious transformation needed to free the individual from the grip of the community, which would set the stage for the flowering of a responsible and wholesome individuality that would ultimately benefit the nation. To put it another way, *Letters* takes the view that in societies where communal norms dominate, a ruler can be made liberal by education, but a people can only be made liberal by authority.

The approach taken by *Letters* is not without its dangers. Principal among these is that, like the "new liberalism" it is so attracted to, it is a "positive" theory.[603] That is, *Letters* posits that there is a definite end or goal to human life, which is to flourish or develop by cultivating one's individuality and sociability. The problem is that, armed with such a theory, the authorities can then compel individuals to act in ways they intensely dislike, on the grounds that it will help them attain the "good life".[604] *Letters* is not oblivious to the danger. To its credit, it insists on maintaining countervailing power in society – an aristocracy of talent and virtue – that is meant to check the incursions of an energetic and well-meaning state. But, unfortunately, this is not a very satisfactory answer because it does not address the vital question of how disagreements between the Maharaja and his remade aristocracy ought to be resolved. Presumably, in the absence of any formal division of sovereign power, the Maharaja will have the final say in the event of a dispute with civil society. What then? There is always lurking in the background the idea articulated by English republicans such as John Milton and John Locke that Maharajas that misuse their prerogative will eventually see rebellion but, perhaps out of a desire to eschew confrontational language, *Letters* does not explicitly discuss this ultimate check on monarchical authority.

This is not the only weakness in the theory that *Letters* puts forth. Though it relies on Maharajas to be visionary reformers, and outlines the motives they have to engage in such perilous activity, it does not provide sufficient reason to believe that royal clans, which were infamous for being tradition-bound, would in fact educate their princes in the desired way – or that such an education would make these budding Maharajas prudent enough to follow the advice contained in *Letters*. Parmanand was hardly unaware of how awful Maharajas could be – Anandashram's experience in Jamnagar was never far from his mind. Even so, knowing that the rising generation in India was increasingly drawn to republican ideals, Parmanand should have devoted far more space and attention to explaining how philosophers were to become Maharajas or, more plausibly, how Maharajas were to be turned into philosophers. This silence is all the more troubling because disillusionment with monarchy was not some passing fad that could safely be ignored; it was becoming a global phenomenon. We are left to wonder how Parmanand would have reacted to the bloody end that the Qing met in 1911 – the monarchy that *Letters* encourages Maharajas to study.

So far we have argued that *Letters* reveals that the liberalism that emerged in Western India in the second half of the nineteenth century was "something more substantial than a dressing-up of conventional liberal concerns in the fancy dress of Indian particularity".[605] The theory it offers, and the intellectual tradition it represents, is distinctive because it expects paternalistic and enlightened Maharajas, rather than popular representatives, to advance liberal values. Here it may be objected that even if *Letters* is distinctive, it does not amount to a contribution to liberal theory because it does not reveal something of broader applicability. How could it, the skeptic may wonder, when it seems rooted in the particular circumstances that liberals confronted in nineteenth-century India? What can Bombay teach London?

Arguably, *Letters* constitutes an enduring contribution to liberal theory because the problem it addresses – the challenge that communal norms can pose to individuality – has become a much wider concern due to mass migration from the formerly colonized world. Now the whole world is India. Therefore, it makes sense for liberals in the West to reflect on what Indian liberals had to say about the challenge that *multiculturalism* poses to individuality. Liberals in the West write as if they were the first to encounter multiculturalism. But before there was Canada there was India. There may therefore be much to learn from its history. *Letters*, we have seen, teaches that where communities are overpowerful, paternalism may be necessary to advance individuality. To see why this lesson is discomfiting, we need to briefly see how it departs from contemporary liberalism.

As migrants from distant cultures, and especially from deeply observant Islamic societies, settle in the West, contemporary liberals have had to address the question of whether they should tolerate social norms and religious practices of an illiberal character. With examples of Islamic fundamentalism on the rise, public figures in the West have begun to demand that their societies exhibit a more "muscular liberalism" (in the words of a former prime minister of Britain).[606] But can contemporary liberalism be "muscular"? The basic premise of contemporary liberalism is that we disagree over what constitutes the good life. Its objective is to resolve this disagreement *fairly* by subjecting public questions to *egalitarian procedures* and by granting individuals *autonomy* to conduct their private lives as they see fit. This framework makes it extremely difficult to regulate religious beliefs and social norms. This is because respect for the equality of individuals seems to demand respect for the self-regarding choices they make, among the most sacred of which is the religion and community they identify with.[607] As a result, when Western liberals voice discomfort with illiberal norms and practices in migrant communities, such as veiling, they face accusations of "a dislike of cultural diversity".[608]

Flummoxed by the challenge posed by multiculturalism, contemporary liberals have limited themselves to debating what the "limits" to their toleration ought to be. The broad consensus is that liberal societies should display "benign neglect" or even "accommodate" cultural and religious groups that have illiberal norms and practices – so long as the members of those groups have *the right to exit*.[609] But how meaningful is this standard? How plausible is it for an individual – birthed, raised, educated, and ensconced in a community that has severe sanctions at its disposal – to truly exercise free choice about whether to abide by its strictures? Such a person would be, Ayaan Hirsi Ali writes, like a "caged bird" that stays inside even when the door is open because "it has internalized its imprisonment".[610] This worry about the "insufficiency of free choice" has led to calls, from feminists for instance, for "state intervention" in cultural practices that contain "norms of inequality".[611] But contemporary liberals cannot accommodate this demand because the practices in question, such as veiling, are invariably backed by religious injunctions, which they are loath to challenge. They maintain that, given pervasive disagreement on religious matters, interfering with religious norms or practices would be arbitrary and therefore illegitimate. The only defensible stance, per this view, is state neutrality, which leaves individuals free to believe or practice religion as they see fit.[612]

The liberalism on display in *Letters* is not hobbled in this way. Living alongside religious fanatics, who clung to their ways and were willing to kill those who questioned them, Parmanand's contemporaries were under no illusions that the authorities should be neutral on questions of faith. In this respect, they agreed with the criticism that James Fitzjames Stephen's *Liberty, Equality, Fraternity* (1873) directed at John Stuart Mill's *On Liberty* (1859). Drawing on his experience in India, Stephen challenged Mill's praise of religious liberty by showing how it can become necessary to interfere with religious belief or practice.[613] When men are "deeply stirred" by gospels or revelations, Stephen notes, they make it their business to "compel others" to accept them as "absolute truths".[614] In such instances, "real neutrality" is only possible when the number of zealots is so few "that their opinions can be regarded as unimportant by the rest".[615] But, should such zealots grow in number, he acerbically notes, we can be certain that "they will no more tolerate error for the sake of abstract principles about freedom than anyone of us tolerates a nest of wasps in his garden".[616]

Though Parmanand's circle agreed with Stephen that liberals could not afford to be neutral when it came to "religious dogmas", they had a very different idea about the standard that religions should be held up to. Stephen's claim, contra Mill, that there were instances where it may be legitimate for the authorities to interfere with religion, as when British India banned *sati*. In such cases, he argued, it was legitimate to use coercion to uphold a "well-regulated life" or "what we understand by civilization".[617] This statement is vulnerable to the criticism that it arbitrarily takes the norms of Victorian-era England to constitute "civilization". *Letters* does not make this mistake. It offers a different, distinctly cosmopolitan, standard. It argues that it is legitimate for the authorities to reform religious beliefs in order to make them compatible with, and supportive of, human flourishing. To contemporary liberals this statement may seem no better than Stephen's. What constitutes "human flourishing", they will argue, will invariably be disputed. But this objection misses the point. *Letters* emerges from a tradition that believed that it is in fact possible to overcome subjectivity. Comparing and contrasting religions would, the leaders of the Prarthana Samaj believed, help expose what was excessive or eccentric in each of them. Thus, for instance, if a survey of the great religious traditions revealed that an injunction, such as the caste system or indeed veiling, lacked wide support among them, then liberals would be entitled to deem it an arbitrary and therefore illegitimate constraint on human freedom.

We may balk at the notion that the state should involve itself in theological debate, but that a liberal state needed to craft and enforce a theology in order to foster a liberal society, of this Parmanand and his associates were certain. This is because where religious communities have the power to intimidate dissenters and critics, neutrality is no answer at all. It sidesteps rather than confronts the threat that religious norms and practices can pose to individuality. Thus it is that *Letters* teaches contemporary liberalism that human flourishing can come to depend on paternalism – and bequeaths us the challenge of formulating and enforcing a theology that can support individuality. This theology would have to founded, these pioneering liberals believed, on theistic lines because only a belief system that does not divide the world into believers and unbelievers leaves individuals free to flourish.

Notes

1 Narayan Mahadev Parmanand, *English and Native Rule in India* (Bombay: Native Opinion Press, 1868), 279 (British Library, Tr.958(n)).
2 C. A. Bayly, *Recovering Liberties: Indian Thought in the Age of Liberalism and Empire* (Cambridge: Cambridge University Press, 2011).
3 Ramachandra Guha, "The Absent Liberal: An Essay on Politics and Intellectual Life", *Economic and Political Weekly* Vol. 36, No. 50, 4663, 4665; C. A. Bayly, "Empires and Indian Liberals", in Catherine Hall and Keith McClelland, eds., *Race, Nation and Empire: Making Histories, 1750s to the Present* (Manchester: Manchester University Press, 2010), 74.
4 Narayan Mahadev Parmanand, *Letters to an Indian Raja from a Political Recluse* (Bombay: Tatva-Vivekachaka Press, 1891), 137.
5 This was what Parmanand was called by his much-adored nephew (*mama* being the term for maternal uncle). His friends at Elphinstone adopted the usage and eventually so did Bombay society.
6 "The Late Justice Telang", *Bombay Gazette*, October 5, 1898, 6; L. V. Kaikini, ed., *The Speeches & Writings of Sir Narayen C. Chandravarkar* (Bombay: Manoranjak Grantha Prasarak Mandali), 1911, 41.

7 "The Narayan M. Parmanand Memorial", *Times of India*, August 21, 1897, 3; "The Narayan Mahadev Parmanand Prize", *University of Bombay Calendar for the Year 1907–1908*, Vol. 1 (Bombay: Government Central Press, 1907), 583–84.
8 P. B. Kulkarni, *Mama Parmananda Ani Tyancha Kalkhanda* [*The Life and Times of Mama Parmanand*] (Mumbai: P. B. Kulkarni, 1963).
9 Kulkarni, *Mama Parmananda*, 16–17.
10 Isabel Burton, *The Life of Captain Sir Richard F. Burton*, Vol. 1 (New York: D. Appleton & Company, 1893), 143; "Major-General Sir George Le Grand Jacob, C. B., K. C. S. I.", *Journal of East India Association*, Vol. 13, 1880–81, 109–10.
11 Dwarakanath Govind Vaidya, *Prarthanasamajaca Itihasa* [*A History of Prarthana Samaj*] (Bombay: Prarthana Samaj, 1927), 23.
12 Kulkarni, *Mama Parmananda*, 23.
13 Chunilal Lalubhai Parekh, *Eminent Indians in Indian Politics with Sketches of Their Lives, Portraits and Speeches* (Bombay: Education Society's Steam Press, 1892), 250; Jyotis Chandra Dasgupta, *A National Biography for India* (Dacca: Jyotis Chandra Dasgupta, 1911), 43.
14 *The Sixth Report of the Proceedings of the Bombay Native Education Society, 1830* (Bombay: Native Education Society, 1831), 11.
15 *Annual Report of the Elphinstone Institution for the Year 1850* (Bombay: Education Society's Press, 1851), 294.
16 R. G. Bhandarkar (1837–1925) became a famed scholar and social reformer and later served as Vice-Chancellor of the University of Bombay.
17 B. M. Wagle (1839–88) went on to become a noted lawyer and Judge of the Small Causes Court in Bombay.
18 "Native Education in Western India", *Bombay Calendar and Almanac for 1856* (Bombay: Times Press, 1856), 190.
19 "Government Education in the Bombay Presidency", *Bombay Quarterly Review*, Vol. 4, No. 8, 1856, 326; Baman Das Basu, *History of Education in India Under the Rule of the East India Company* (Calcutta: Modern Review Office, 1922), 155–58.
20 *Report of the Director of Public Instruction, Bombay, for the Year 1858–59* (Bombay: Education Society's Press, 1860), 27–28; Naheed Ahmad, "A History of Elphinstone College 1827–1890: A Case Study in the Early Formation of an English-Educated Intelligentsia in Bombay", DPhil thesis, University of Oxford, 1982, 114.
21 *Bombay Gazette*, March 6, 1856, 226; *Bombay Gazette*, January 4, 1856, 14.
22 *Papers Relating to the Examinations held at the Elphinstone College in December 1855* (Bombay: Bombay Education Society's Press, 1856), 96–98.
23 *Papers Relating to the Examinations held at the Elphinstone College in December 1855*, 9, 249; *Report of the Director of Public Instruction, Bombay, for the Year 1857–58* (Bombay: Education Society's Press, 1859), 88.
24 V. A. Modak (1836–97) became a distinguished educator and in 1882 was appointed the first native principal of Elphinstone High School.

25 M. G. Ranade (1842–1901) went on to have a glittering career as a scholar, social reformer, administrator, and judge, eventually serving on the Bombay High Court.

26 Dinyar Patel, *Naoroji: Pioneer of Indian Nationalism* (Cambridge, MA: Harvard University Press, 2020), 34; *Times of India*, November 15, 1861, 3.

27 "Native Education in Western India", 194; Kulkarni, *Mama Parmananda*, 56.

28 *Proceedings of the Students' Literary and Scientific Society for the Years 1854–59* (Bombay: Gazette Press, 1856–60), 14–15; Vaidya, *Prarthanasamajaca Itihasa*, 24.

29 *Proceedings of the Bombay Educational Department*, Vol. 7, 1859 (Maharashtra State Archives, Comp. 229, 123–24); *Report of the Director of Public Instruction 1857–58*, 89; *Report of the Director of Public Instruction 1858–59*, 78; *Report of the Director of Public Instruction, Bombay, for the Year 1859–60* (Bombay: Education Society's Press, 1861), 184.

30 Kulkarni, *Mama Parmananda*, 25.

31 Andrea Geddes Poole, *Philanthropy and the Construction of Victorian Women's Citizenship: Lady Frederick Cavendish and Miss Emma Cons* (Toronto: University of Toronto Press, 2014), 162.

32 Frederick Temple (1821–1902) went on to become Headmaster of Rugby and then Bishop of Exeter.

33 "Certificates of Merit", *English Journal of Education*, Vol. X, 1852, 155.

34 Benjamin Jowett (1817–93), later the Master of Balliol and then Vice-Chancellor of the University of Oxford.

35 Evelyn Abbott and Lewis Campbell, *The Life and Letters of Benjamin Jewett*, Vol. 1 (New York: E. P. Dutton and Co., 1897), 195; "The Late Professor J. P. Hughlings", *Allen's Indian Mail*, Vol. 28, No. 928, July 26, 1870, 705.

36 Joseph Foster, "Hughlings, John Powell", in *Alumni Oronienses: The Members of the University of Oxford, 1715–1886* (London: Parker and Co., 1888), 710; Henry Moseley, *Report on the Kneller Hall Training School* (London: George E. Eyre and William Spottiswoode, 1855), 17.

37 Abbott and Campbell, *The Life and Letters of Benjamin Jewett*, 350.

38 *Indian News and Chronicle of Eastern Affairs*, July 17, 1856, 331.

39 Joseph Crowe, *Reminiscences of Thirty-Five Years of My Life* (London: John Murray, 1895), 248.

40 *Report of the Department of Public Instruction in the Bombay Presidency for the Year 1869–70* (Bombay: Education Society's Press, 1870), 61.

41 *Report of the Department of Public Instruction 1869–70*, 61.

42 "The Late Professor J. P. Hughlings", 705.

43 Abbott and Campbell, *The Life and Letters of Benjamin Jewett*, 351.

44 D. E. Wacha, *Shells from the Sands of Bombay: Being My Recollections and Reminiscences 1860–1875* (Bombay: K. T. Anklesaria, 1920), 675–76; Kulkarni, *Mama Parmananda*, 29.

45 Vaidya, *Prarthanasamajaca Itihasa*, 31.

46 *Report of the Director of Public Instruction 1858–59*, Appendix K, 4; "Examination of Candidates for Senior Scholarships", *Bombay Gazette*, February 16,

1860, 159; Balkrishna Nilaji Pitale, ed., *The Speeches and Addresses of Sir H. B. E. Frere* (Bombay: n.p., 1870), 107.

47 *Report of the Director of Public Instruction 1858–59*, Appendix K, 3.

48 Kulkarni, *Mama Parmananda*, 36–39.

49 Ahmad, *A History of Elphinstone College*, 154. Also see "The Elphinstone Institution", *Bombay Gazette*, January 4, 1856, 14.

50 "Native Education in Western India", 196.

51 Ahmad, *A History of Elphinstone College*, 96–98.

52 "Government Education in the Bombay Presidency", 375.

53 "Government Education in the Bombay Presidency", 332, 336; "Presentation of an Address to Sir Alexander Grant", *Times of India*, September 28, 1868, 3.

54 "Government Education in the Bombay Presidency", 338; Ahmad, *A History of Elphinstone College*, 42, 146, 153; *Papers Relating to Education in India* (London: House of Commons,1870), 391; "The Elphinstone Institution", *Bombay Gazette*, October 13, 1858.

55 *Allen's Indian Mail*, 705.

56 A playful reference to the *saptarishi*s (or seven sages) of Hindu mythology. The astronomers of ancient India named the seven stars that make up the Big Dipper constellation after these sages.

57 Pitale, *The Speeches and Addresses of Sir H. B. E. Frere*, 107; *Report of the Director of Public Instruction, Bombay, for the Year 1861–62* (Bombay: Education Society's Press, 1863), 57; L. V. Kaikini and K. Natarajan, eds., *The Speeches & Writings of Sir Narayen G. Chandavarkar* (Bombay: Manoranjak Grantha Prasarak Mandali, 1911), 414–15.

58 *Bombay University Calendar for 1886–87* (Bombay: Thacker & Co., 1886), 311.

59 Christine E. Dobbin, *Urban Leadership in Western India: Politics and Communities in Bombay City, 1840–1885* (Oxford: Oxford University Press, 1972), 40–41.

60 Kulkarni, *Mama Parmananda*, 48.

61 K. T. Telang (1850–92) went on to have a meteoric career as a scholar and administrator, becoming Vice-Chancellor of the University of Bombay, a member of the Legislative Council, and Judge of the Bombay High Court.

62 Jyotis Chandra Das Gupta, *A National Biography for India* (Dacca: B. C. Das, 1911), 43; Vasant Narayan Naik, *Kashinath Trimbak Telang: The Man and His Times* (Madras: G. A. Natesan & Co., 1895), 13; Kaikini and Natarajan, *The Speeches & Writings of Sir Narayen G. Chandavarkar*, 219.

63 *Papers Relating to the Examinations held at the Elphinstone College in December 1855*, 68; *Report of the Director of Public Instruction, Bombay, for the Year 1862–63* (Bombay: Education Society's Press, 1864), 145–46; "The Schools of the Bombay Presidency", *Times of India*, August 14, 1861, 3.

64 The former capital of Sindh. Conquered by the East India Company in 1843, the province of Sindh was incorporated into Bombay Presidency in 1847.

65 *Report of the Director of Public Instruction 1862–63*, 87; *Report of the Director of Public Instruction, Bombay, for the Year 1865–66* (Bombay: Education Society's Press, 1866), 21.

66 *Civil and Military Gazette*, May 7, 1896, 8; Richard Francis Burton, *Scinde; or, the Unhappy Valley* (London: Richard Bentley, 1851).

67 "Appointments: Narayen Mahadeo", *Proceedings of the Bombay Educational Department*, Vol. 2, Comp. 208, 1860 (Maharashtra State Archives); *Report of the Director of Public Instruction 1857–58*, 464; *Report of the Director of Public Instruction 1865–66*, 21.

68 *Report of the Director of Public Instruction 1865–66*, 71.

69 *Report of the Director of Public Instruction 1862–63*, 87.

70 Vaidya, *Prarthanasamajaca Itihasa*, 24.

71 Narayan Vishvanath Mandalik, ed., *Writings and Speeches of the Late Honourable Rao Saheb Vishvanath Narayan Mandalik* (Bombay: Native Opinion Press, 1896), 3.

72 *Report of the Director of Public Instruction 1861–62*, 54. Parmanand was not the only one to dislike Hyderabad. His successors in the post, none other than his friends Bhandarkar and Modak, would also plead, more successfully, for transfers, leaving the Educational Department to glumly conclude that Marathas sent out to Hyderabad clearly preferred "to better themselves elsewhere" (*Report of the Director of Public Instruction 1865–66*, 71).

73 G. A. Mankar, *A Sketch of the Life & Works of the Late Mr. Justice M. G. Ranade* (Bombay: Caxton Printing Works, 1902), 37.

74 *Times of India*, June 23, 1863, 4.

75 V. S. Pandit (1827–76) graduated from Poona College in 1856 before heading the English School in Dharwar. Inspired by Ishwar Chandra Vidyasagar, he founded the Bombay Widow Remarriage Association in 1861.

76 *Times of India*, June 11, 1863, 3.

77 *Times of India*, September 16, 1863, 2.

78 Bombay Judicial Department Proceedings, January 1864, No. 49, 10 (British Library, IOR/P/407/69); *Solicitor's Journal & Reporter*, Vol. 8, June 11, 1864, 629.

79 V. N. Mandlik (1833–89), an early graduate of Elphinstone College, served the British in Sindh, was called to the Bar in 1863, and went on to serve on the Bombay Municipal Corporation and Bombay Legislative Council.

80 "Native Opinion", *The Indian Spectator*, May 22, 1909, 405; *Public Opinion*, Vol. 9, No. 292, April 27, 1867, 472; Damodar Ganesh Padhye, "A Short Sketch of the Life of the Late Rao Sahib V. N. Mandlik", in Vishvanath Narayan Mandlik, ed., *Writings and Speeches of the Late Honourable Rao Saheb Vishvanath Narayan Mandlik* (Bombay: Native Opinion Press, 1896), 5.

81 Uma Das Gupta, "The Indian Press 1870–1880: A Small World of Journalism", *Modern Asian Studies*, Vol. 11, No. 2, 1977, 230.

82 Gupta, "The Indian Press 1870–1880", 231; Kulkarni, *Mama Parmananda*, 73, 259, fn. 1.

83 *Report of the Director of Public Instruction 1865–66*, 21.

84 Alexander Grant (1826–84) graduated from and taught at Oxford before coming to Bombay in 1861. He would go on to be Vice-Chancellor of the University of Bombay and then Principal of Edinburgh University.
85 Kulkarni, *Mama Parmananda*, 74.
86 *Report of the Director of Public Instruction 1865–66*, 21.
87 George Birdwood, "The Native Press of India", *Journal of the Society of Arts*, Vol. 25, No. 1270, March 23, 1877, 410–11; Parmanand, *English and Native Rule in India*, 277.
88 Birdwood, "The Native Press of India", 400.
89 *Times of India*, February 4, 1863, 3. Also see Richard P. Tucker, *Ranade and the Roots of Indian Nationalism* (Bombay: Popular Prakashan, 1977), 115.
90 "Nowanuggur's Succession", *Native Opinion*, Vol. 4, No. 50, December 15, 1867, 393.
91 "In Memoriam of a Sannyasi Political", *Native Opinion*, Vol. 7, No. 2, January 9, 1870, 10.
92 *Native Opinion*, Vol. 4, No. 24, June 16, 1867, 185–86.
93 *Native Opinion*, Vol. 4, No. 24, June 16, 1867, 185–86.
94 A sub-caste that claimed the highest status among Bengali Brahmins.
95 "Another Look at Free Religious Movements in India", *Index*, Vol. 1, No. 11, March 12, 1870, 7; "The Jayapur Royal Council", *Native Opinion*, Vol. 4, No. 41, October 13, 1867, 1.
96 This would have been either General Assembly's Institution or the Free Church Institution.
97 *Native Opinion*, Vol. 7, No. 2, January 1870, 14.
98 George Cupples, *Memoir of Mrs. Valentine, Jeypore* (London: James Nisbet, 1882), 107.
99 Jadunath Sakar, *A History of Jaipur, c. 1503–1918* (Hyderabad: Orient Longman, 1984), 353–64; Robert Stern, *The Cat and the Lion: Jaipur State in the British Raj* (Leiden: E. J. Brill, 1988), 120, 123–24.
100 On Shivdin, see *Allen's Indian Mail*, Vol. 22, No. 637, August 4, 1864, 614; Jwala Sahai, *The Loyal Rajputana* (Allahabad: Indian Press, 1902), 257–58. On Hari Mohan Sen, see Loknathe Ghosh, *The Modern History of the Indian Chiefs, Rajas, Zamindars & C.*, Part II (Calcutta: J. N. Ghose, 1881), 140–42; Nirmal Sinha, ed., *Freedom Movement in Bengal, 1818–1904* (Calcutta: Academic Publishers, 1968), 117–20.
101 "The Jayapur Royal Council", 1; Sinha, *Freedom Movement*, 117–20.
102 Robert Booth, *Life and Work in India: Embodying A Short Sketch of the History and Progress of Kathiawar from 1865 to 1899* (London: J. G. Hammond & Co., 1912), 80.
103 Norman Macleod, *Peeps at the Far East: A Familiar Account of a Visit to India* (London: Strahan & Co., 1871), 152.
104 Macleod, *Peeps at the Far East*, 153.
105 Macleod, *Peeps at the Far East*, 153.
106 Parmanand, *Letters to an Indian Raja*, 244.

107 Parmanand, *Letters to an Indian Raja*, 244–45; "In Memoriam of a Sannyasi Political", 10.
108 Parmanand, *Letters to an Indian Raja*, 244–45.
109 *Native Opinion*, Vol. 4, No. 24, June 16, 1867, 186.
110 *Native Opinion*, Vol. 4, No. 24, June 16, 1867, 186; "The Jam Shri Vibhaji Scholarship", *Bombay University Calendar* (Bombay: Thacker, Vining & Co., 1867), 124–25.
111 *Native Opinion*, Vol. 6, No. 13, March 28, 1869, 100.
112 *Native Opinion*, Vol. 4, No. 24, June 16, 1867, 186.
113 Alan Ross, *Ranji: Prince of Cricketers* (New York: Faber & Faber, 2012), 24–25.
114 "Nowanuggur's Succession", 393.
115 *Native Opinion*, Vol. 4, No. 17, April 28, 1867, 133–34.
116 "In Memoriam of a Sannyasi Political", 10; *Native Opinion*, Vol. 6, No. 3, January 17, 1869, 13.
117 *Native Opinion*, Vol. 4, No. 24, June 16, 1867, 186.
118 C. Wodehouse, "The Keatinge Rajkumar College, Kathiawar", *Calcutta Review*, Vol. 60, January 1875, 59–68.
119 *Native Opinion*, Vol. 4, No. 24, June 16, 1867, 186.
120 "Another Look at Free Religious Movements in India", 7.
121 "Another Look at Free Religious Movements in India", 7; Kulkarni, *Mama Parmananda*, 117.
122 W. J. S. Wyllie, *Essays on the External Policy of India* (London: Smith, Elder & Co., 1875), 263; "The Right Hon. Sir Henry Pottinger", *Dublin University Magazine*, Vol. 28, October 1846, 434.
123 S. N. Raikes, *Memoir and Brief Notes Relative to the Kutch State* (Bombay: Education Society's Press, 1855), 38, 40; George W. Forrest, ed., "Minute by the Hon. Mountstuart Elphinstone Dated January 26, 1821", in *Selections from the Minutes and Writings of the Honourable Mountstuart Elphinstone, Governor of Bombay* (London: Richard Bentley and Son, 1884), 564–66.
124 Raikes, *Memoir and Brief Notes Relative to the Kutch State*, 41–42.
125 Raikes, *Memoir and Brief Notes Relative to the Kutch State*, 43–44.
126 The practice of self-immolation by widows.
127 Alexander Walker and J. P. Willoughby, eds., *Measures Adopted for the Suppression of Female Infanticide in the Province of Kattywar* (Bombay: Bombay Education Society's Press, 1856), 359–60; "Correspondence Relative to Infanticide in India", *Accounts and Papers of the House of Commons*, Vol. 35, 1843, 215–16, 337.
128 "The Right Sir Henry Pottinger", *Dublin University Magazine*, Vol. 28, October 1846, 433; "Rev. James Gray", *Scottish Notes and Queries*, Vol. 2, Second Series, No. 5, November 1900, 69; "Gray, James, the Rev.", *The Popular Scottish Biography: Being Lives of Eminent Scotsmen* (Edinburgh: Edinburgh Printing and Publishing Co., 1841), 376.
129 *Asiatic Journal and Monthly Register*, Vol. 17, New Series, July 1835, 168.
130 "Mr. Gray, Chaplain in Kutch", *Oriental Christian Spectator*, Vol. 2, No. 5, May 1831, 158–59; "The Proper Government for Oude", *Spectator*, March

20, 1858, 315; "Mrs. Postan's Cutch; or Random Sketches of Western India", *Tait's Edinburgh Magazine*, Vol. 6, January 1839, 29–30; *Asiatic Journal and Monthly Register*, Vol. 28, 1839, 138.

131 "Correspondence Relative to Infanticide in India", *Accounts and Papers of the House of Commons*, Vol. 35, 1843, 207.

132 "Sir John Malcolm's Minute", *Gazetteer of the Bombay Presidency: Cutch, Palanpur and Mahi Kantha*, Vol. 5 (Bombay: Government Central Press, 1880), 270; "The State of Kutch", *Madras Mail*, September 21, 1869.

133 C. U. Aitchison, *A Collection of Treaties, Engagements, Sunnuds, Relating to India and Neighbouring Countries*, Vol. 6 (London: Longmans, Green, Reader and Dyre, 1864), 436–37; "Correspondence Relative to Infanticide in India", 212; Raikes, *Memoir and Brief Notes Relative to the Kutch State*, 64–67; William Henry Sykes, "Traits of Indian Character", *Journal of the Royal Asiatic Society of Great Britain and Ireland*, Vol. 17, 1860, 242.

134 *Accounts and Papers of the House of Commons*, Vol. 35, 1843, 206.

135 *Bombay Gazette*, August 7, 1860, 748; *Friend of India*, August 23, 1860, 801.

136 "The State of Kutch".

137 James Burnes, "From the Conclusion of the Treaty of 1816 to the Conclusion of the Treaty of 1819", in *A Sketch of the History of Cutch from its First Connexion with the British Government in India to the Conclusion of the Treaty of 1819* (Edinburgh: Robert Cadell, 1839), Postscript, 221–27.

138 *Times of India*, February 19, 1863, 3.

139 "The State of Kutch".

140 Aitchison, *A Collection of Treaties,* 438.

141 Wyllie, *Essays on the External Policy of India*, 304.

142 William Brown Keer, *Notes of a Mission Tour in Ceylon and South India, and in Kattywar and Cutch in the Bombay Presidency* (Bombay: Times of India Office, 1869), 17.

143 L. F. Rushbrook Williams, *The Black Hills: Kutch in History and Legend* (London: Weidenfeld and Nicolson, 1958), 243.

144 *Gazetteer of the Bombay Presidency*, 173.

145 George Le Grand Jacob (1805–81) was a decorated military officer and diplomat. His interest in Indian languages and antiquities and his keen eye for native talent had made him a leading figure in Bombay Presidency.

146 Wyllie, *Essays on the External Policy of India*, 279.

147 *Selections from Despatches Addressed to Various Government Councils between the 1st January and 31st December, 1865* (London: George Edward Eyre and William Spottiswoode, 1866), 147.

148 John Malcolm (1769–1833) was one of the great statesmen of the Company era. A soldier, historian, and diplomat, he served as Resident in Central India, as Ambassador to Persia, and retired as Governor of Bombay.

149 "Sir John Malcolm's Minute", 273–74; *Bombay Gazette*, March 12, 1870, 3.

150 *Selections from Despatches*, 147.

151 *Gazetteer of the Bombay Presidency*, 196–98.

152 "Sir John Malcolm's Minute", 271; *Gazetteer of the Bombay Presidency*, 202–3.

153 *Selections from Despatches*, 147.
154 "The Rao of Cutch", *Allen's Indian Mail*, Vol. 26, No. 839, November 11, 1868, 1116.
155 *Selections from Despatches*, 147.
156 "The State of Kutch", *Times of India*, December 22, 1870, 2.
157 *Gazetteer of the Bombay Presidency*, 172, 217.
158 "In Memoriam of a Sannyasi Political".
159 "In Memoriam of a Sannyasi Political".
160 Raikes, *Memoir and Brief Notes Relative to the Kutch State*, 68–69; Williams, *The Black Hills*, 244.
161 Wyllie, *Essays on the External Policy of India*, 319.
162 *Times of India*, February 19, 1863, 3.
163 Roper Lethbridge, *The Golden Book of India* (London: Macmillan and Co., 1893), 105–6.
164 Thomas Evans Bell, *Our Great Vassal Empire* (London: Trubner & Co., 1870), 28.
165 The term in Arabic for a judge responsible for administering Muslim civil law.
166 *Journal of the East India Association*, Vol. 6, 1872, 241–42.
167 *Journal of the East India Association*, Vol. 6, 1872, 241–42.
168 A revenue collector and inspector.
169 An honorific awarded by the Government of India to acknowledge meritorious public service by Muslims.
170 Sorabji Jehangir, *Representative Men of India* (London: W. H. Allen Co., 1889), 109.
171 *Report from the Select Committee [of the House of Commons] on East India Finance: Together with the Proceedings of the Committee, Minutes of Evidence, and Appendix* (London: H.M.S.O., 1871), 416–17.
172 *General Report on the Administration of the Bombay Presidency for the Year 1866–67* (Bombay: Government of India, 1868), 103–4 (British Library, IOR/V/10/280/2).
173 *General Report on the Administration of the Bombay Presidency for the Year 1867–68* (Bombay: Government of India, 1869), 98–99 (British Library, IOR/V/10/281/1).
174 Parmanand, *English and Native Rule in India*, 278.
175 G. R. Havaldar, *Rao Saheb V. N. Mandlik: A Biography in Two Volumes* (Bombay: G. R. Havaldar, 1927), 153.
176 Birdwood, "The Native Press of India", 399–400.
177 *Native Opinion*, Vol. 4, No. 49, December 8, 1867, 386; *Native Opinion*, Vol. 4, No. 44, November 3, 1867, 345–46; *Native Opinion*, Vol. 4, No. 32, August 11, 1867, 149–50; *Native Opinion*, Vol. 4, No. 22, June 2, 1867,170.
178 Kulkarni, *Mama Parmananda*, 98–99.
179 Kulkarni, *Mama Parmananda*, 100.
180 "Native and English Ideas of Loyalty", *Native Opinion*, Vol. 4, No. 25, June 23, 1867.
181 Birdwood, "The Native Press of India", 400.

182 Robert Knight, *Reply to a Letter Addressed to Malcolm Ross, Esq., President of the Manchester Chamber of Commerce, by John Dickenson, Jun., Esq., on the Subject of the Manchester Conference, January 24, 1866*, London: William John Johnson, 1866, 9–11; *Bombay Gazette*, August 11, 1868, 3.

183 Gupta, "The Indian Press 1870–1880", 233.

184 A good example here is Biman Behari Majumdar, *History of Indian Social and Political Ideas* (Calcutta: Firma, 1996), 338. Also see Havaldar, *Rao Saheb V. N. Mandlik*, 155; *Bombay Gazette*, August 11, 1868, 3.

185 John Clark Marshman, *History of India* (London: William Blackwood and Sons, 1876), 363, 529.

186 "Observations", in *Hansard*, Vol. 187, May 24 (London: UK Parliament, 1867), Col. 1074.

187 "Observations", Vol. 187, Col. 1074. Salisbury may have also been influenced, directly or indirectly, by a brochure that the India Reform Society had circulated in London prior to the Mutiny. Entitled *The State and Government of India Under its Native Rulers* (1853) it had challenged the annexationist doctrine put forward by Governor General James Broun-Ramsay (the Marquess of Dalhousie). The society wrote of the Native States that "they are neither so black, nor we so white, as we paint them and ourselves – that their government and institutions were neither so defective, nor ours so perfect, as we assert them to have been". The brochure was reprinted a half century later in Dadabhai Naoroji, *Poverty and Un-British Rule in India* (London: Swan Sonnenschein, 1901), 581–614. Also see C. S. Srinivasachari, "The India Reform Society and Its Impact on the Indian Administration in the Decade 1853–62", *Indian Journal of Political Science*, Vol. 8, No. 1, 1946, 651–52, fn. 5.

188 A famous Latin phrase, originally from Virgil's *Georgics II*, which means "if only they knew it".

189 *Correspondence Regarding the Comparative Merits of British and Native Administration in India* (Calcutta: Government of India, 1867), 2 (British Library, IOR/L/PS/20/H44).

190 Parmanand, *English and Native Rule in India*, 252, 280–81. Parmanand was citing here Patrick Smollett's caustic remarks in Parliament (see "Observations", in *Hansard*, Vol. 191, March 27 (London: UK Parliament, 1868), Col. 418).

191 Parmanand, *English and Native Rule in India*, 251.

192 *Times of India*, March 7, 1863, 3; Arthur Lukyn Williams, *Famines in India: Their Causes and Possible Prevention* (London: Henry S. King & Co., 1876), 63, 114.

193 Parmanand, *English and Native Rule in India*, 255, 281. Bayly is the only scholar to have noticed that *English and Native Rule in India* even exists, though he mistook Ramchandra A. Udas, the business manager of the Native Opinion Press, to be the author. This may be why he failed to realize that the pamphlet represented the considered view of the liberals of Western India (Bayly, *Recovering Liberties*, 167).

194 Parmanand, *English and Native Rule in India*, 281–82.

195 Parmanand, *English and Native Rule in India*, 279.

196 Parmanand, *English and Native Rule in India*, 277–78.
197 *Report of the Department of Public Instruction in the Bombay Presidency for the Year 1867–68* (Bombay: Education Society's Press, 1868), Appendix F, 37–38.
198 K. S. Chiplunkar (1824–78) was a pioneering Marathi writer and translator, and a *pandit* (scholar of Sanskrit). In the Education Department since 1847, he was at the time serving as the principal of the Poona Vernacular College.
199 Kulkarni, *Mama Parmananda*, 94, 100; *Report on Native Papers for the Week Ending 23rd May 1868* (London: India Office Library and Records, 1868), 8.
200 Cited in Kulkarni, *Mama Parmananda*, 36.
201 The verse contains a central lesson of the *Bhagavad Gita*, which is to persevere in duty unaffected by happiness or sorrow (Bibek Debroy, *The Bhagavad Gita* (New Delhi: Penguin Classics, 2005), 3.28). Kulkarni, *Mama Parmananda*, 101.
202 *Native Opinion*, Vol. 4, No. 10, March 10, 1867, 77.
203 Mankar, *A Sketch of the Life & Works of the Late Mr. Justice M. G. Ranade*, 40–41.
204 Narayan Mahadev Parmanand to Kazi Shahabuddin, April 24, 1868; Kazi Shahabuddin to Narayan Mahadev Parmanand, May 3, 1868 (reprinted in Kulkarni, *Mama Parmananda*, 103–4).
205 *Native Opinion*, Vol. 5, No. 20, May 17, 1868, 157.
206 Shahabuddin to Parmanand, May 3, 1868.
207 Swami Anandashram to Narayan Mahadev Parmanand, May 9, 1868 (reprinted in Kulkarni, *Mama Parmananda*, 105–6).
208 *Annual Report of the Administration of the Bombay Presidency for the Year 1868–69* (Bombay: Government of India, 1869), 108 (British Library, IOR/V/10/281/2).
209 *Annual Report of the Administration of the Bombay Presidency 1868–69*, 109.
210 *General Report of the Administration of the Bombay Presidency, 1869–70* (Bombay: Government of India, 1870), 131 (British Library, IOR/V/10/282/1); *Annual Report on the Administration of Kutch, 1870–1* (Bombay: Education Society's Press, 1871), 4 (British Library, IOR/V/10/1494).
211 *Annual Report of the Administration of the Bombay Presidency 1868–69*, 109.
212 Parmanand, *Letters to an Indian Raja*, 181–82; Kulkarni, *Mama Parmananda*, 113–14.
213 Cited in Kulkarni, *Mama Parmananda*, 114; "Rao of Kutch and His Bhyad", Foreign Department, Political-A, January 11, 1869, Vol. II, No. 119 (National Archives of India).
214 *Native Opinion*, Vol. 4, No. 24, June 16, 1867, 186.
215 Kulkarni, *Mama Parmananda*, 110–11.
216 The name of the tribe to which the Rao and his *bhayad* belonged.
217 "Draft Agreement Between H.H. the Rao and Government Re: Bhayads", March 29, 1868 (British Library, IOR/R/2/18A/A/29).
218 *Annual Report of the Administration of the Bombay Presidency 1868–69*, 108–9; *General Report of the Administration of the Bombay Presidency, 1869–70*, 130–31; Williams, *The Black Hills*, 239–40.

219 "Relations between the Rao of Kutch and his Bhyad", Foreign Department, Political-A, October 1868, No. 10, 2 (National Archives of India).
220 *The Globe*, November 9, 1870, 2.
221 Jehangir, *Representative Men of India*, 110.
222 Thomas Evans Bell (1825–87) was a retired Company officer and administrator. Opposed to annexation, he produced important essays detailing and defending the rights of Native States, especially Nagpur and Mysore.
223 Vikram Visana, *Uncivil Liberalism: Labour, Capital and Commercial Society in Dadabhai Naoroji's Political Thought* (Cambridge: Cambridge University Press, 2022), 135–37.
224 "Memo by Dadabhai Naoroji" in "Kutch: Further Papers Regarding Relations of the Rao with his Bhayad", No. 12, 466–75 (British Library, IOR/L/PS/6/560).
225 "Rao of Kutch and His Bhyad", Foreign Department, Political-A, April 1869, No. 31 (National Archives of India); "Relations of the Rao Kutch with his Bhyads", Foreign Department, Political-A, May 1869, No. 289 (National Archives of India).
226 "Relations of the Rao Kutch with his Bhyads", May 1869, No. 289.
227 Kulkarni, *Mama Parmananda*, 90.
228 Jehangir, *Representative Men of India*, 110.
229 Kulkarni, *Mama Parmananda*, 90.
230 "Rao of Kutch and His Bhyad", January 11, 1869, No. 119.
231 Jehangir, *Representative Men of India*, 110; *Gazetteer of the Bombay Presidency*, 199; "Rao of Kutch and His Bhyad", January 11, 1869, No. 119.
232 "Rao of Kutch and His Bhyad", Foreign Department, Political-A, January 11, 1869, No. 330 (National Archives of India); Bombay Political Department Proceedings, January 1869, No. 260, 14–15 (British Library, IOR/P/441/99).
233 *Minutes of Proceedings of the First Annual General Meeting of the Bombay Association* (Bombay: Duftur Ashkara Press, 1869), 5–6 (British Library, Tr. 512(K)).
234 *Native Opinion*, Vol. 6, No. 17, April 25, 1869, 133.
235 Kulkarni, *Mama Parmananda*, 116.
236 William Wedderburn, *Speeches and Writings* (Madras: G. A. Natesan, 1918), vi; *Report on Native Papers Published in the Bombay Presidency for the Week Ending 7th May 1887* (London: India Office Library and Records, 1887), 8.
237 Kulkarni, *Mama Parmananda*, 119–20; "List of Officers holding Judicial Appointments in the Bombay Presidency", Proceedings of the Bombay Judicial Department, Vol. 9, 1870 (Maharashtra State Archives).
238 The title translates to *The Stories of Birbal and Badshah*. It equates Birbal with Bertholde, an unsightly figure from a French fable who proves a sagacious advisor to the ruler of Lombardy ("Adventures of Bertholde", *London Magazine*, Vol. 22, June 1753, 272–77).
239 *Birbalva Badshaha Yanchia Goshti* [*The Stories of Birbal and Badshah*] (Mumbai: Native Opinion Press, 1869).
240 "Report of the Dakshina Prize Committee for 1870–71" in *Report of the Department of Public Instruction in the Bombay Presidency for the Year 1870–71* (Bombay: Education Society's Press, 1871), 392–93.

241 "In Memoriam of a Sannyasi Political".
242 *The Athenaeum*, February 19, 1870, No. 2208, 263.
243 *Illustrated London News*, August 6, 1870, 154.
244 *Pioneer*, July 14, 1870, 4; Wacha, *Shells from the Sands of Bombay*, 676.
245 *Bombay Gazette*, April 29, 1870, 2; "Index to the Abstract for May 1870", *Bombay Proceedings (Judicial)*, 1870 (British Library, IOR/P/442/4, v).
246 A phrase used to designate the pioneering generation of Elphinstonians who were conspicuous for their knowledge of English and for their advocacy of social and religious reform in Western India.
247 *Native Opinion*, Vol. 7, No. 19, May 8, 1870, 148; Kulkarni, *Mama Parmananda*, 120–22.
248 Kulkarni, *Mama Parmananda*, 122.
249 *Native Opinion*, Vol. 7, No. 1, January 2, 1870, 5.
250 N. G. Chandavarkar, "Preface" in *Letters to an Indian Raja from a Political Recluse* (Bombay: R. Tukaram, 1919) (reproduced here as Appendix III, 287–88); Kulkarni, *Mama Parmananda*, 132.
251 H. P. Mody, *Sir Pherozeshah Mehta: A Political Biography*, Vol. 1 (Bombay: Times Press, 1921), 56–80; *Bombay Gazette*, November 5, 1872, 59.
252 K. K. Chaudhuri, ed., *Maharashtra State Gazetteers: Greater Bombay District*, Vol. 3 (Bombay: Government of Maharashtra, 1986), 260–61.
253 Chandavarkar, "Preface to the 1919 Edition", Appendix III, 287–88; Kulkarni, *Mama Parmananda*, 132.
254 Michael D. Metelits, *The Arthur Crawford Scandal: Corruption, Governance, and Indian Victims* (Delhi: Oxford University Press, 2020), 210.
255 Pherozeshah Mehta (1845–1915) would go on to be a successful barrister, municipal administrator, and Congress leader, whose outsize persona would lead Mohandas Gandhi to deem him the "uncrowned king of Bombay".
256 Chandavarkar, "Preface to the 1919 Edition", Appendix III, 287–88; Vaidya, Prarthanasamajaca Itihasa, 31, fn.
257 *Bombay Gazette*, November 5, 1872, 3; Mody, *Sir Pherozeshah Mehta*, 61; Knut Aukland, "Connecting British and Indian, Elite and Subaltern: Arthur Crawford and Corruption in the Later Nineteenth Century Western India", *South Asian History and Culture*, Vol. 4, No. 3, 2013, 317.
258 Kulkarni, *Mama Parmananda*, 127–28; Arthur Travers Crawford, *Our Troubles in Poona and Deccan* (London: Archibald Constable, 1897), 77–78.
259 *Kaiser-i-Hind*, September 24, 1893, 3.
260 *Bombay Educational Record*, Vol. 29, No. 11, November 11, 1893, 32; Dobbin, *Urban Leadership in Western India*, 50.
261 *Bombay Civil List* (Bombay: Government Central Press, 1877), 226–27.
262 Atmaram Pandurang (1823–98) was amongst the earliest graduates of Grant Medical College, where he was later the Chair of Botany. He practiced as a physician and served as Sheriff of Bombay in 1879.
263 Ramachandra Vitthal Lad (1822–74), commonly known as Bhau Daji, was an early graduate of Grant Medical College. A prominent physician and benefactor of women's education, he served as Sheriff of Bombay from 1869 to 1871.

264 Ram Balkrishna Jayakar (1826–66) served as a teacher in Ratnagiri and Thane and then as *daftardar* (head clerk) in the Customs Department. Utterly opposed to caste, he co-founded the Paramhansa Mandali in 1848.

265 *Bombay Gazette*, January 19, 1860, 62; Kulkarni, *Mama Parmananda*, 63.

266 Pathare Reform Association, *Marriage of Hindu Widows* (Bombay: Indu-Prakash Press, 1869), Appendix A, i.

267 *Marriage of Hindu Widows*, Appendix I, xlviii; *Indu Prakash*, June 21, 1869.

268 "Native Reforms", *The Homeward Mail*, July 27, 1869, 96.

269 W. W. Kolhatkar, "A Plea for Widow Remarriage", in K. P. Karunakaran, ed., *Religion and Political Awakening* (Meerut: Meenakshi Prakashan, 1965), 210–11; "The Pundit Vishnu Shastri", *Journal of National Indian Association*, No. 68, August 1876, 242–43.

270 Kulkarni, *Mama Parmananda*, 43–44; Behramji M. Malabari, "The Position of Women in India", *The Times*, August 30, 1890, 13.

271 Tukaram (1608–50[?]) was a poet and ascetic whose devotional songs and poems espousing egalitarianism have had a profound influence on Maharashtrian culture and identity.

272 Kulkarni, *Mama Parmananda*, 41.

273 K. T. Telang to N. M. Parmanand, January 26, 1893 (reprinted in Kulkarni, *Mama Parmananda*, Correspondence); Narayan Bhosale, "Dialectics of Women Reforms in 19th Century Maharashtra", in Shraddha Kumbhojkar, ed., *19th Century Maharashtra: A Reassessment* (Newcastle upon Tyne: Cambridge Scholars Publishing, 2009), 39.

274 Macleod, *Peeps at the Far East*, 376.

275 J. V. Naik, "Early Anti-Caste Movement in Western India: The Paramahansa Sabha", *Journal of the Asiatic Society of Bombay*, Vols. 49–52, 1974–76, 148.

276 Hulas Singh, *Rise of Reason: Intellectual History of 19th Century Maharashtra* (New York: Routledge, 2016), 98; Naik, "Early Anti-Caste Movement in Western India", 155.

277 Singh, *Rise of Reason*, 98; Naik, "Early Anti-Caste Movement in Western India", 155; Rosalind O'Hanlon, *Caste, Conflict and Ideology: Mahatma Jotirao Phule and Low Caste Protest in Nineteenth-Century Western India* (Cambridge: Cambridge University Press, 2002), 101–2.

278 Macleod, *Peeps at the Far East*, 68.

279 Macleod, *Peeps at the Far East*, 375–76.

280 Macleod, *Peeps at the Far East*, 375. Also see *Bombay Gazette*, March 16, 1870, 3.

281 Kulkarni, *Mama Parmananda*, 168; Kenneth Jones, *Socio-Religious Reform Movements in British India* (Cambridge, Cambridge University Press, 1989), 138–40.

282 Sivanath Sastri, *History of the Brahmo Samaj*, Vol. 2 (Calcutta: R. Chatterjee, 1912), 415–16.

283 Sastri, *History of the Brahmo Samaj*, 416.

284 Vaidya, *Prarthanasamajaca Itihasa*, 43–44; Kulkarni, *Mama Parmananda*, 172–73.

285 *Pioneer*, December 18, 1872, 4; *Pioneer*, October 11, 1872, 4.
286 Sastri, *History of the Brahmo Samaj*, 417.
287 The title means clear or simple (*Subodh*) communication (*Patrika*).
288 Established in Surat in 1844 by Mehtaji Durgaram and Dadoba Pandurang Tarkhadkar, the Manav Dharma Sabha (Society of the Religion of Humanity) challenged superstitions they saw as corrupting and weakening Hinduism. R. L. Raval, "Social Environs and Reform Movement in 19th Century Gujarat: The Case of Durgaram Mehtaji", *Proceedings of the Indian History Congress*, Vol. 47, No. 1, 1986, 591–98.
289 Birdwood, "The Native Press of India", 400.
290 Kulkarni, *Mama Parmananda*, 181, 202.
291 *Bombay Gazette*, June 3, 1885, 3.
292 *Subodh Patrika*, March 23, 1884; *Subodh Patrika*, May 4, 1884; *Subodh Patrika*, October 26, 1884; *Subodh Patrika*, July 6, 1884.
293 Motilal Ghosh to Narayan Mahadev Parmanand, November 14, 1875 (reprinted in Kulkarni, *Mama Parmananda*, Correspondence); C. Hayavadana Rao, ed., *The Indian Biographical Dictionary (1915)* (Madras: Pillar & Co., 1915).
294 Kulkarni, *Mama Parmananda*, 437–39.
295 Kulkarni, *Mama Parmananda*, 439.
296 Bombay Proceedings (Financial), 1886, No. 278 (British Library, IOR/P/2876, 297-8).
297 Kulkarni, *Mama Parmananda*, 438.
298 Bombay Proceedings (Financial), 1886, No. 278 (British Library, IOR/P/2876, 297-8).
299 Kulkarni, *Mama Parmananda*, 436.
300 Chandavarkar, "Preface to the 1919 Edition", Appendix III, 287.
301 Vaidya, *Prarthanasamajaca Itihasa*, 26–27.
302 Metelits, *The Arthur Crawford Scandal*, 24.
303 Kulkarni, *Mama Parmananda*, 134; *The Proceedings of a Public Meeting of the Citizens of Poona Held on the 1st September 1889* (Bombay: Bombay Gazette Steam Press, 1889), 20–21.
304 Rao Bahadur was an honorific awarded by the Government of India to acknowledge meritorious public service by Hindus. *Correspondence Relating to the Case of Mr. Crawford, C. M. G, of the Bombay Civil Service* (London: Eyre and Spottiswoode, 1889), 200, 202–3; Metelits, *The Arthur Crawford Scandal*, 24.
305 Kulkarni, *Mama Parmananda*, 134; Metelits, *The Arthur Crawford Scandal*, 24–25.
306 Metelits, *The Arthur Crawford Scandal*, 20–21; Aukland, "Connecting British and Indian, Elite and Subaltern", 322. The reference here was to the practice of *nazarana*, or the collection of tribute.
307 A. Godley, *Copies of, or Extracts from Correspondence Relating to Memorials from Members of the Civil Service as to the Mamlatdars Incriminated in the Crawford Case*, Parliamentary Papers, Vol. 54 (London: Henry Hansard and Son, 1890), 5–8; *Correspondence Relating to the Case of Mr. Crawford*, 202–3.

308 Godley, *Copies of Correspondence Relating to Memorials*, 5–8; *Correspondence Relating to the Case of Mr. Crawford*, 202–3.
309 *Correspondence Relating to the Case of Mr. Crawford*, 200, 202; Metelits, *The Arthur Crawford Scandal*, 125–26, 211.
310 Aukland, "Connecting British and Indian, Elite and Subaltern", 314.
311 Kulkarni, *Mama Parmananda*, 135–36.
312 Aukland, "Connecting British and Indian, Elite and Subaltern", 325.
313 Baban Bapu Korgaonkar, "Some of My Memories Related to the Patrika" in Dwarkanath Govind Vaidya, ed., *Subodh Patrika Diamond Jubilee Special Number, 1873–1933* (Bombay: Subodh Patrika, 1933), 66; *Report on Native Papers Published in Bombay Presidency for the Week Ending September 1, 1888* (London: India Office Library and Records, 1888), 8; Vaidya, *Prarthanasamajaca Itihasa*, 31.
314 S. K. Ratcliffe, *Sir William Wedderburn and the Indian Reform Movement* (London: George Allen & Unwin, 1923), 55–56.
315 Ratcliffe, *Sir William Wedderburn*, 55–56; T. Koditschek, *Liberalism, Imperialism, and Historical Imagination: Nineteenth-Century Visions of a Greater Britain* (Cambridge: Cambridge University Press, 2011), 306.
316 D. E. Wacha (1844–1936) studied at Elphinstone College. A magnate and editor, he held key posts in the Bombay Municipal Corporation and the Bombay Presidency Association, and served as President of the Congress in 1901.
317 Kulkarni, *Mama Parmananda*, 163–64.
318 Wedderburn, *Speeches and Writings*, 2.
319 Ratcliffe, *Sir William Wedderburn*, 61.
320 E. C. Moulton, "William Wedderburn and Early Indian Nationalism, 1870–1917", in K. A. Ballhatchet and D. Taylor, eds., *Changing South Asia: Economy and Society* (London: SOAS, 1984), 38, 40.
321 Edward C. Moulton, "Wedderburn, Sir William", in *Oxford Dictionary of National Biography* (Oxford: Oxford University Press, 2012); *Report on Native Papers Published in the Bombay Presidency for the Week Ending 14th May 1887* (London: India Office Library and Records, 1887), 4–5.
322 James Bryce, "Lord Reay, 1839–1921", *Proceedings of the British Academy*, Vol. 10, 1921–23, 533–34; Metelits, *The Arthur Crawford Scandal*, 131; *Report on Native Papers Published in Bombay Presidency for the Week Ending 18th May 1889* (London: India Office Library and Records, 1889), 9.
323 *Report on Native Papers Published in the Bombay Presidency for the Week Ending October 5, 1889* (London: India Office Library and Records, 1889), 10.
324 Metelits, *The Arthur Crawford Scandal*, 101.
325 *Report on Native Papers Published in Bombay Presidency for the Week Ending 23rd November 1889* (London: India Office Library and Records, 1889), 10–11.
326 *Voice of India*, October 1, 1889, 505; *Report on Native Papers Published in the Bombay Presidency for the Week Ending October 5, 1889* (London: India Office Library and Records, 1889), 7, 11; *Report on Native Papers Published*

in Bombay Presidency for the Week Ending 2nd March 1889 (London: India Office Library and Records, 1889), 10–11; *Report on Native Papers Published in Bombay Presidency for the Week Ending 28th September 1889* (London: India Office Library and Records, 1889), 12–13.

327 Godley, *Copies of Correspondence Relating to Memorials*, 4–5; *The Proceedings of a Public Meeting of the Citizens of Poona Held on the 1st September 1889* (Bombay: Bombay Gazette Steam Press, 1889), 33–51.

328 B. G. Tilak (1856–1920) was educated at Deccan College. The editor of *Kesari* and *Maratha* and co-founder of Fergusson College, he dominated public life in Poona. He would go on to become a national icon for self-rule.

329 Aukland, "Connecting British and Indian, Elite and Subaltern", 326.

330 *Report on Native Papers Published in the Bombay Presidency for the Week Ending October 5, 1889* (London: India Office Library and Records, 1889), 14–15.

331 Jones, *Socio-Religious Reform Movements in British India*, 144.

332 Vaidya, *Prarthanasamajaca Itihasa*, 34, fn.

333 J. V. Naik, "Social Composition of the Prarthana Samaj: A Statistical Analysis", *Proceedings of the Indian History Congress*, Vol. 48, 1987, 504–9.

334 J. V. Naik, "The Prarthana Samaj", in S. P. Sen, ed., *Social Contents of Indian Religious Reform Movements* (Calcutta: Institute of Historical Studies, 1960), 308–12; Jones, *Socio-Religious Reform Movements in British India*, 144.

335 J. V. Naik, "Social Composition of the Prarthana Samaj: A Statistical Analysis", 504–9; J. Masselos, *Towards Nationalism: Group Affiliations and the Politics of Public Associations in the Nineteenth Century* (Bombay: Popular Prakashan, 1974), 85.

336 Sivanath Sastri, *History of the Brahmo Samaj*, Vol. 2 (Calcutta: R. Chatterjee, 1912), vii; M. G. Ranade, "A Theist's Confession of Faith", in M. B. Kolasker, ed., *Religious and Social Reforms: A Collection of Essays and Speeches* (Bombay: Gopal Narayen & Co., 1902), 250.

337 Motilal Ghosh to Narayan Mahadev Parmanand, May 21, 1885 (reprinted in Kulkarni, *Mama Parmananda*, Correspondence).

338 Keshab Chandra Sen (1838–84) was a central figure in the Brahmo Samaj. In 1866 he led a breakaway faction to create the Brahmo Samaj of India. A rump of this body later became the Church of the New Dispensation in 1881.

339 P. C. Mozoomdar (1840–1905) was a prominent Bengali theologian. A key lieutenant of Keshab Chandra Sen, he led the New Dispensation after Sen's demise.

340 Sivanath Sastri (1848–1919) joined the Brahmo Samaj of India in 1869. In 1878 he co-founded the Sadharan Brahmo Samaj in protest against Keshab Chandra Sen's conduct.

341 Sivanath Sastri, *History of the Brahmo Samaj*, viii; *Native Opinion*, Vol. 10, No. 2, January 12, 1873, 26.

342 Sastri, *History of the Brahmo Samaj*, vii.

343 Charles Heimsath, *Indian Nationalism and Hindu Social Reform* (Princeton, NJ: Princeton University Press, 1964), 96–97; Benoy Ghoshe, ed., *Selections from*

English Periodicals of 19th Century Bengal, Volume VII, 1878–80: Brahmo Public Opinion (Calcutta: Papyrus, 1959), 250–51.

344 Vaidya, *Prarthanasamajaca Itihasa*, 40.

345 Rev. Henry Bruce, "Female Education in India", *Independent and Weekly Review*, May 1, 1884, 9; Sophia Dobson Collet, "The Brahmo Somaj versus 'The New Dispensation'", *Contemporary Review*, Vol. 40, November 1881, 730; Koditschek, *Liberalism, Imperialism, and Historical Imagination*, 278.

346 Motilal Ghosh to Narayan Mahadev Parmanand, May 21, 1885 (reprinted in Kulkarni, *Mama Parmananda*, Correspondence).

347 Masselos, *Towards Nationalism*, 83–84; Anna C. Schultz, *Singing a Hindu Nation: Marathi Devotional Performance and Nationalism* (Oxford: Oxford University Press, 2013), 40; J. V. Naik, "Dharmavivechan: An Early 19th Century Rationalistic Reform Manifesto in Western India", in V. D. Divekar, ed., *Social Reform Movements in India* (Bombay: Popular Prakashan, 1991), 67; J. N. Farquhar, *Modern Religious Movements in India* (New York: Macmillan, 1915), 79.

348 R. G. Bhandarkar, "Basis of Theism, and Its Relation to the So-Called Revealed Religions", in Narayan Bapuji Utgilkar, ed., *Collected Works of Sir R. G. Bhandarkar*, Vol. 2 (Poona: Bhandarkar Oriental Research Institute, 1928), 615; Naik, "The Prarthana Samaj", 307–8, 315; Naik, "Dharmavivechan", 69–70. More generally, see Heimsath, *Indian Nationalism and Hindu Social Reform*, 221.

349 Farquhar, *Modern Religious Movements in India*, 76.

350 Dayanand Saraswati (1824–83) was a celebrated *sanyasi* and Vedantist. A pioneering social and religious reformer with a pan-Indian following, he founded the Arya Samaj in 1875. His birth name was Mula Sankara.

351 Har Bilas Sarda, *Life of Dayanand Saraswati World Teacher* (Ajmer: P. Bhagwan Swarup, 1946), 180.

352 Oday Pertap Singh, *Democracy Not Suited to India* (Allahabad: Pioneer Press, 1888), 90.

353 Heimsath, *Indian Nationalism and Hindu Social Reform*, 220–22.

354 C. Yajnesvara Chintamani, ed., *Indian Social Reform in Four Parts* (Madras: Thompson and Co., 1904), 315–18.

355 *Public Opinion: A Weekly Review of Current Thought and Activity*, Vol. 55, March 1, 1889, 261.

356 J. A. Mangan, "Eton in India: The Imperial Diffusion of a Victorian Educational Ethic", in Gary McCulloch, ed., *The RoutledgeFalmer Reader in History of Education* (New York: Routledge, 2005), 165; Caroline Keen, *Princely India and the British: Political Development and the Operation of Empire* (London: I.B. Tauris, 2012), 47–48.

357 Aya Ikegame, *Princely India Reimagined: A Historical Anthropology of Mysore from 1799 to the Present* (London: Routledge, 2013), 53–70; Satadru Sen, *Colonial Childhoods: The Juvenile Periphery of India, 1850–1945* (London: Anthem Press, 2005), 143–86.

358 H. H. Sir Bhavsinhji, *The Late Chester Macnaghten: Forty Years of the Rajkumar College, Rajkot, 1870–1910*, Vol. 1 (London: Hazel, Watson & Viney, 1911), 424–50.

359 Chester Macnaghten, *Common Thoughts on Serious Subjects: Being Addresses to the Elder Kumars of The Rajkumar College, Kathiawar* (London: John Murray, 1896), xx, xxviii.
360 Macnaghten, *Common Thoughts on Serious Subjects*, xviii.
361 Macnaghten, *Common Thoughts on Serious Subjects*, xxxvi–xxxvii.
362 "Takhtsingjee", *New Volumes of the Encyclopaedia Britannica*, Vol. 33 (New York: Adam and Charles Black, 1902), 170–71; "An Indian State-Ling", *Saturday Review of Politics, Literature, Science and Art*, Vol. 71, No. 1854, 1891, 570–71; "The Gondal State", *Indian Magazine and Review*, No. 287, 1894, 605–6. Also see Nasrullah Khan, *The Ruling Chiefs of Western India and the Rajkumar College* (Bombay: G. Claridge & Co., 1904), 54–59.
363 Macnaghten, *Common Thoughts on Serious Subjects*, xix; George Frederick Samuel Robinson, *The Native States of India: A Paper Read Before the Leeds Philosophical and Literary Society* (London: Kegan Paul, Trench & Co., 1886), 25.
364 Robert Booth, *Life and Work in India: Embodying A Short Sketch of the History and Progress of Kathiawar from 1865 to 1899* (London: J. G. Hammond & Co., 1912), 57; M. Griffith, *India's Princes: Short Life Sketches of the Native Rulers of India* (London: W. H. Allen & Co., 1894), 223–25.
365 "Extract from Earl Canning's Last Private Letter to General Sir Mark Cubbon, K. C. B., Commissioner of Mysore, Dated Nov. 24th 1860", in Evans Bell, *Retrospects and Prospects of Indian Policy* (London: Trubner & Co., 1868), 343.
366 Richard Bourke (1822–72) had served as Chief Secretary for Ireland and then as Viceroy from 1869 until he was assassinated in 1872. He was highly regarded by Indians, especially the aristocracy of the Native States.
367 William Wilson Hunter, *A Life of the Earl of Mayo, Fourth Viceroy of India*, Vol. 1 (London: Smith, Elder & Co., 1875), 207–8; Bhavsinhji, *The Late Chester Macnaghten*, 386–87.
368 A respectful term for a gentleman. Accorded to clerks in the Bengal Presidency that owed their positions to their literacy, the term eventually came to be used disparagingly, to refer to natives that mimicked English modes.
369 "The Congress in Britain", *India: A Journal for the Discussion of Indian Affairs*, June 6, 1890, 149; *Indian Mirror*, November 23, 1889; "Indian Affairs", *Times*, November 17, 1890, 6. See especially C. U. A. [Charles U. Aitchison], *The Native States of India: An Attempt to Elucidate a Few of the Principles Which Underlie Their Relations with the British Government* (Simla: Government Central Branch Press, 1875), 41. More generally, see "Utilisation of the Armies of Native States", *Voice of India*, Vol. 7, No. 1, January 1889, 12–21.
370 Hunter, *A Life of the Earl of Mayo*, 215. Also see Matthew Stubbings, "British Conservatism and the Indian Revolt", *Journal of British Studies*, Vol. 55, No. 4, October 2016, 747–49.
371 K. L. Nulkar ([?]–1893) began his career as a clerk to Le Grand Jacob and went on to hold important official posts in Bombay before leading the Poona Sarvajanik Sabha. He would later serve on the Viceroy's Legislative Council.

372 M. N. Shirgaonkar ([?]–[1889?]) served in the Education Department in Bombay before being appointed *karbhari* (senior administrator) of Janjira and then Joint Administrator of Miraj.
373 Kulkarni, *Mama Parmananda*, 355.
374 The customary title of the ruler of Baroda.
375 *Bombay Proceedings (Political)*, September 1866, No. 67, 7–8 (British Library, IOR/P/441/96).
376 Parmanand, *English and Native Rule in India*, 251, 257.
377 *Bombay Proceedings (Political)*, September 1866, No. 67, 7–8 (British Library, IOR/P/441/96); Ghose, *The Modern History of the Indian Chiefs*, 143.
378 *Bombay Proceedings (Political)*, April 1869, No. 181, 8 (British Library, IOR/P/441/99); Ghose, *The Modern History of the Indian Chiefs*, 143.
379 Hunter, *A Life of the Earl of Mayo*, 212; Dinshah Ardeshir Taleyarkhan, *Criticisms of the Indian Journals on A Review of Baroda Affairs* (Bombay: Oriental Steam Printing Press, 1872).
380 Hunter, *A Life of the Earl of Mayo*, 212.
381 Hunter, *A Life of the Earl of Mayo*, 208.
382 Dinshah Ardeshir Taleyarkhan, *The Revolution at Baroda, 1874–75* (Bombay: Education Society's Press, 1875), 13.
383 Taleyarkhan, *The Revolution at Baroda*, 13.
384 Thomas Henry Thornton, *General Sir Richard Meade and the Feudatory States of Central and Southern India* (London: Longmans, Green & Co., 1898), 166; F. A. H. Elliot, *Gazetteer of the Bombay Presidency*, Vol. 7 (Bombay: Government Central Press, 1883), 282.
385 Taleyarkhan, *The Revolution at Baroda*, Appendix II.
386 *Times of India*, July 28, 1869, 3.
387 An affectionate term for officers that had retired to Britain after a long civil or military career in India.
388 *Dadabhai Naoroji: A Sketch of his Life and Life-Work* (Madras: G. A. Natesan, 1920), 8–9.
389 John Martineau, *The Life and Correspondence of Sir Bartle Frere*, Vol. 2 (London: John Murray, 1895), 129.
390 *Bombay Proceedings (Political)*, March 1869, No. 222, 23 (British Library, IOR/P/441/99).
391 *Index to the Bombay Government Records for Cutch Vol. 2, 1858–82* (British Library, IOR/R/1/6/176, 31); Wyllie, *Essays on the External Policy of India*, 304, 309.
392 R. J. Gavin, "The Bartle Free Mission to Zanzibar, 1873", *Historical Journal*, Vol. 5, No. 2, June 1962, 138–39; *Globe*, November 9, 1870, 2. Shahabuddin was also carrying with him the carefully printed *Memorial from His Highness the Rao of Kutch to His Grace the Duke of Argyll* (Bombay: Education Society's Press, 1869).
393 Hunter, *A Life of the Earl of Mayo*, 226; *Times of India*, August 29, 1871, 2.
394 *Times of India*, February 9, 1872, 2.
395 *Illustrated London News*, Vol. 59, No. 1675, October 21, 1871, 375.

396 Samuel Wilberforce, *Essays Contributed to the "Quarterly Review"*, Vol. 2 (London: John Murray, 1874), 288–91; *The Globe*, October 22, 1872, 2; *Homeward Mail*, October 22, 1872, 1084; "Slave Trade in Zanzibar", Foreign Department, Political-A, Nos. 45–51, December 1868, 3–4 (National Archives of India).
397 Kazi Shahabuddin, "Memorandum on the Connexion of Indian Traders on the Eastern Coast of Africa with the Slave Trade", February 14, 1870, in *Slave-Dealing and Slave-Holding by Kutchees in Zanzibar* (British Library, IOR/L/PS/18/B90, 14–16).
398 Charles New, *Life, Wanderings and Labours in Eastern Africa* (London: Hodder and Stoughton, 1873), 36–37.
399 Shahabuddin, "Memorandum on the Connexion of Indian Traders", 16; "Slave Trade in Zanzibar", 5.
400 Chhaya R. Goswami, "The Slave Trade at Zanzibar and the Role of Kutchis", *Proceedings of the Indian History Congress*, Vol. 64, 2003, 1288; "The East African Slave Trade: A Meeting of Native Gentlemen", *Homeward Mail*, Vol. 19, No. 756, January 20, 1873, 54.
401 *Allen's Indian Mail*, March 10, 1873, 223; Goswami, "The Slave Trade at Zanzibar", 1288; "Papers Relative to the Proffered Co-Operation of the Rao of Kutch", Foreign Department (Political), 1873, No. 22, 336–41 (British Library, IOR/L/PS/6/106).
402 *Pall Mall Gazette*, March 3, 1873.
403 *Allen's Indian Mail*, March 10, 1873, 223. For an example of the effect, see India Proceedings (Foreign Department), February 1873, No. 339 (British Library, IOR/P/768).
404 Jehangir, *Representative Men of India*, 110; *Greenock Telegraph*, February 4, 1873, 2.
405 *The Kutch Bhayad Papers: Being a Compilation of the Official Correspondence Relating to the Status of Bhayads, and the Extent and Scope of the British Guarantee Held by Them* (Bombay: Education Society's Press, 1879), iii–iv.
406 *The Gaikwari Raj: Being a Reprint of the Notices Which Appeared in the "Hitechhu" of Ahmedabad* (Ahmedabad: Pitamberdas Tribhowandas Mehta, 1875), 115–16.
407 Dinyar Patel and S. R. Mehrotra, eds., *Dadabhai Naoroji: Selected Private Papers* (Delhi: Oxford University Press, 2016), xxiii.
408 Thornton, *General Sir Richard Meade*, 171–72.
409 Patel, *Naoroji*, 77–79.
410 Kulkarni, *Mama Parmananda*, 356; R. P. Masani, *Dadabhai Naoroji: The Grand Old Man of India* (London: George Allen and Unwin, 1939), 148.
411 *The Gaikwari Raj*, 76.
412 Kulkarni, *Mama Parmananda*, 356.
413 H. P. St. George Tucker, *Baroda Complications and Press Etiquette with a Few Words in Defence of Colonel Phayre and the Bombay Government* (London: W. Ridgway, 1875), 11, 13. For excellent overviews of the period, see Patel, *Naoroji*, 78–81; Masani, *Dadabhai Naoroji*, 145. Also see Dadabhai Naoroji,

"The Baroda Administration in 1874", in Chunilal Lallubhai Parekh, ed., *Essays, Speeches, Addresses and Writings (on Indian Politics) of the Honorable Dadabhai Naoroji* (Bombay: Caxton Printing Works, 1887), 382; Bartle Frere to Dadabhai Naoroji, November 7, 1873, in *Baroda Administration in 1874: A Statement in Reply to Remarks in the Baroda Blue Book of 1875* (London: Vincent Brooks, Day and Son, 1879), 23–24.

414 *The Gaikwari Raj*, 76–77, 112.

415 *The Gaikwari Raj*, 76–77, 107.

416 "The Viceroy's Proclamation", *London Evening Standard*, May 15, 1875, 5.

417 W. W. Hunter, *Imperial Gazetteer of India*, Vol. 2 (London: Trubner & Co., 1885), 164.

418 *London Evening Standard*, May 15, 1875, 5.

419 Henry Butler to Thomas Baring, September 17, 1875, in *Papers of the Earl of Northbrook* (British Library, Mss. Eur. C144/23).

420 Hunter, *Imperial Gazetteer of India*, 168, Elliot, *Gazetteer of the Bombay Presidency*, Vol. 7, Preface.

421 Hunter, *Imperial Gazetteer of India*, Vol. 2, 168; Elliot, *Gazetteer of the Bombay Presidency*, Vol. 7, 286; Govindbhai Hathibhai Desai and Arthur Beaumaurice Clarke, *Gazetteer of the Baroda State*, Vol. 1 (Bombay: Times Press, 1923), 605–7.

422 Govind S. Sardesai, *Shri Sayajirao Gaekwad Yanche Sahavasat* (Pune: S. Jagannath & Co., 1956), 14.

423 India Proceedings (Foreign Department), 1881, No. 51 (British Library, IOR/P/1742); Philip W. Sergeant, *The Ruler of Baroda* (London: John Murray, 1928), 32–33.

424 Sergeant, *The Ruler of Baroda*, 35–37.

425 India Proceedings (Foreign Department), 1881, No. 51 (British Library, IOR/P/1742).

426 Rahul Sagar, *The Progressive Maharaja: Sir Madhava Rao's Hints on the Art and Science of Government* (New York: Oxford University Press, 2022).

427 Elliot, *Gazetteer of the Bombay Presidency*, Vol. 7, 286.

428 Alban G. Widgery, ed., *Speeches and Addresses of Sayaji Rao III Maharaja Baroda, Vol. 1, 1877–1910* (Cambridge: Cambridge University Press, 1927), 22.

429 Widgery, *Speeches and Addresses of His Highness Sayaji Rao III*, 23; Fatehsinghrao Gaekwad, *Sayajirao of Baroda: The Prince and the Man* (Bombay: Popular Prakashan, 1989), 110.

430 Widgery, *Speeches and Addresses of His Highness Sayaji Rao III*, 24–27.

431 Havaldar, *Rao Saheb V. N. Mandlik*, 651.

432 "Suggestions from the Poona Sarvajanik Sabha", Political Department, Section No. 34, Daftar No. 835, File No. 51, 1881, 13–14 (Baroda Records Room); *Homeward Mail*, May 13, 1889, 578.

433 C. U. A., "The Native States of India", 40.

434 [Mahadev Govind Ranade,] "A Constitution for Native States", *Quarterly Journal of the Poona Sarvajanik Sabha*, Vol. 2, No. 3, January 1880, 2.

435 [Ranade,] "A Constitution for Native States", 2.
436 [Ranade,] "A Constitution for Native States"; Mahadev Govind Ranade, "The Rulers of Baroda", in *The Miscellaneous Writings of the Late Hon'ble Mr. Justice M. G. Ranade* (New Delhi: Sahitya Akademi, 1915), 64–65.
437 "Suggestions to H.H. the Gaikwar of Baroda Regarding the Future Constitution", *The Quarterly Journal of the Poona Sarvajanik Sabha*, Vol. 4, No. 3, 1882, 24–26.
438 H. M. Hyndman, *The Bankruptcy of India: An Enquiry into the Administration of India under the Crown* (London: Swan Sonnenschein, Lowery & Co., 1866), 123.
439 Behramji M. Malabari, *Gujarat and the Gujaratis: Pictures of Men and Manners Taken from Life* (London: W. H. Allen & Co., 1882), 78–79. Also see Govind Talwalkar, *Virata Jnani Nyayamurti Ranade* (Poona: Prestija Prakasana, 1989), 53–54.
440 *The Groans of Baroda or An Appeal on Behalf of Distressed Humanity*, Baroda, 1881, 1, 8 (British Library, Tr. 506(n)); Trimbak Vishnu Parvate, *Bal Gangadhar Tilak: A Narrative and Interpretative Review of His Life, Career and Contemporary Events* (Ahmedabad: Navajivan Publishing House, 1958), 30; *Report on Native Papers Published in the Bombay Presidency and Berar for the Week Ending 21st January 1892* (London: India Office Library and Records, 1892), 12–13; Gaekwad, *Sayajirao of Baroda*, 62–63.
441 "Suggestions to H.H. the Gaikwar of Baroda Regarding the Future Constitution", 29.
442 Gaekwad, *Sayajirao of Baroda*, 89–90.
443 Sardesai, *Shri Sayajirao Gaekwad*, 16–17.
444 Gaekwad, *Sayajirao of Baroda*, 93, 118.
445 Kulkarni, *Mama Parmananda*, 359–62.
446 Dhananjay Keer, *Mahatma Jotirao Phooley: Father of Indian Social Revolution* (Bombay: Popular Prakashan, 1944), 212.
447 Keer, *Mahatma Jotirao Phooley*, 181–82; Jotirao Phule, "A Letter to Mr. Laxman Jagannath, the Diwan of Baroda", in P. G. Patil, ed., *Collected Works of Mahatma Jotirao Phule*, Vol. 2 (Bombay: Education Department, 1991), 83.
448 Jotirao Phule, "A Letter to Shrimant Maharaj Sayajirao Gaikwad, Baroda State", in Patil, ed., *Collected Works of Mahatma Jotirao Phule*, Vol. 2, 81–82.
449 Keer, *Mahatma Jotirao Phooley*, 268–70; Pandurang Balaji Kavde, *Mahatma Jyotirao Phule Yanche Charitra* [*The Biography of Mahatma Jyotirao Phule*] (Nasik: Pandurang Balaji Kavde, 1968), 191. A valuable short biography for Phule can be found in Rohini Mokashi-Punekar, "Phule in His Times: A Brief Note on His Life and Works", in *The Third Eye and Other Works: Mahatma Phule's Writings on Education* (Hyderabad: Orient Blackswan, 2023), 1–13.
450 A reference to the courtly culture of the late Maratha Empire, where ceremony and pomp reigned.
451 Kulkarni, *Mama Parmananda*, 272, 363, fn. 2; Gaekwad, *Sayajirao of Baroda*, 91; Keer, *Mahatma Jotirao Phooley*, 275.
452 Gaekwad, *Sayajirao of Baroda*, 81–82.

453 "Col. Biddulph's Note on Baroda Affairs", Foreign Department, Confidential-B, Internal Branch, Section-A, 1895, 20–24 (British Library, IOR/R/1/1/1040).
454 "Col. Biddulph's Note on Baroda Affairs", 20–24. The translation was Govind S. Sardesai, *Rajadharma* (Baroda: Vatasal Press, 1890), 2–4.
455 "Removal of British Troops from Baroda", Foreign Department, Internal-A, Nos. 65–81, June 1885, 14–16 (British Library, IOI/R/1/1/699).
456 "Memorandum by Oliver St. John, September 28, 1888", Foreign Department, Confidential-B, Internal Branch, Section-A, 1895, 73–74 (British Library, IOR/R/1/1/1040).
457 Ganesh L. Chandavarkar, *A Wrestling Soul: Story of the Life of Sir Narayan Chandavarkar* (Bombay: Popular Press, 1955), 42–43.
458 "The National Anthem Incident at Poona", *Bombay Gazette*, October 31, 1885, 3.
459 "The National Anthem Incident at Poona", 3; *Civil and Military Gazette*, November 28, 1885, 4.
460 *Report on Native Papers Published in Bombay Presidency and Berar for the Week Ending 31st October 1885* (London: India Office Library and Records, 1885), 12.
461 J. R. B. Jeejeebhoy, "An Account of Some Unfortunate Officials of the Bombay Government", *Proceedings of the Indian History Congress*, Vol. 10, 1947, 495; Shrinivas Narayan Karnataki, *Rao Bahadur Shankar Pandurang Pandit Yanche Charitra* [*Biography of Rao Bahadur Shankar Pandurang Pandit*] (Mumbai: V. Prabha and Co., 1935), 90–92; *Times of India*, October 5, 1885, 6.
462 *Bombay Gazette*, November 2, 1885, 4; *Civil and Military Gazette*, November 5, 1885, 4.
463 *Times of India*, October 3, 1885, 4.
464 F. Max Müller, *Essays Chiefly on the Science of Religion* (London: Longmans, Green & Co., 1880), 352.
465 A translation of the well-known Marathi proverb "*moden pan vaknar nahi*".
466 Kulkarni, *Mama Parmananda*, 210.
467 *Indu Prakash*, March 26, 1894, 3; Karnataki, *Shankar Pandurang Pandit*, 94–95.
468 Sardesai, *Shri Sayajirao Gaekwad*, 16.
469 Gaekwad, *Sayajirao of Baroda*, 132.
470 Narayan Mahadev Parmanand to Sayaji Rao Gaekwad, March 16, 1889 (reprinted in Kulkarni, *Mama Parmananda*, 363–64).
471 Lepel H. Griffin, "The Native Princes of India and Their Relations with the British Government", *Proceedings of the Royal Colonial Institute*, Vol. 20, 1888–89, 373.
472 Griffin, "The Native Princes of India", 374.
473 Griffin, "The Native Princes of India", 374.
474 *Western Daily Mercury*, June 20, 1889, 4; "The Native States of India", *Journal of the East India Association*, Vol. 21, August 1889, 148; *Homeward Mail*, July 13, 1889, 871; *Civil & Military Gazette*, July 15, 1889, 3; G. R. Elsmie, *Thirty-Five Years in the Punjab 1858–1893* (Edinburgh: David Douglas, 1908), 333.

475 Richard Meade (1821–94) was a celebrated soldier and diplomat. Esteemed by every Viceroy, he served successively as the British representative to the Native States of Gwalior, Indore, Mysore, Baroda, and Hyderabad.

476 "The Native States of India", *Journal of the East India Association*, Vol. 21, August 1889, 134–35; *Madras Weekly Mail*, July 27, 1889, 78.

477 James Stephen, *Liberty, Equality, Fraternity* (Indianapolis: Liberty Fund, 1874), 89–90.

478 John Strachey (1823–1907) had previously served as Lieutenant Governor of the North West Provinces and as Finance Minister (or Member) on the Viceregal Council. He had entered the Council of India in 1885.

479 John Strachey, *India* (London: Kegan Paul, Trench and Co., 1888), 308–9, 319–20.

480 "Sir John Strachey's *India*", *Spectator*, January 12, 1889, 57.

481 *Voice of India*, August 1, 1889, 384–91. Also see Mehdi Ali, "The Attack on the Native States of India", *Nineteenth Century*, Vol. 26, No. 152, October 1889, 545–60.

482 *Native Opinion*, July 11, 1889 (reprinted in *Voice of India*, August 1, 1889, 386).

483 Jyotis Chandra Das Gupta, *A National Biography for India*, Vol. 3 (Dacca: Gandaria Press, 1911), 209–11.

484 D. S. Apte, *Sir Narayan Ganesh Chandravarkar Yanchi Vyakhyane* (Bombay: Damodar Savlaram Aani Mandali, 1914), 130–31; Kulkarni, *Mama Parmananda*, 257.

485 Kulkarni, *Mama Parmananda*, 248.

486 Behramji Merwanji Malabari (1853–1912) was a prominent Bombay litterateur and social activist. A Parsi by adoption, he attracted controversy by urging the British to intervene in Hindu society to protect the rights of women.

487 Dayaram Gidumal, *The Life and Life-Work of Behramji M. Malabari* (Bombay: Education Society's Press, 1888), lxxi.

488 Gidumal, *The Life and Life-Work of Behramji M. Malabari*, iii, lxiv–lxv.

489 Behramji M. Malabari, *The Indian Muse in English Garb* (Bombay: Reporters' Press, 1876), 60–69; Malabari, *Gujarat and the Gujaratis*, 52.

490 Kulkarni, *Mama Parmananda*, 366, fn. 1.

491 Kulkarni, *Mama Parmananda*, 367.

492 Narayan Mahadev Parmanand to Sorabji Jehangir, November 16, 1892 (reprinted in Kulkarni, *Mama Parmananda*, 2, fn. 1).

493 Kulkarni, *Mama Parmananda*, 367.

494 Kulkarni, *Mama Parmananda*, 367.

495 Kulkarni, *Mama Parmananda*, 366.

496 W. W. Hunter (1840–1900) was a highly regarded civil servant, scholar of history, and compiler of statistics. He is best known for supervising the exhaustive fourteen-volume *The Imperial Gazetteer of India*.

497 *The Times*, February 11, 1892, 3.

498 *Reports on Publications Issued and Registered in the Several Provinces of British India during the Year 1891* (Calcutta: Home Department, 1892).

499 *Pioneer*, November 19, 1891; *Madras Weekly Mail*, December 29, 1892.
500 Kulkarni, *Mama Parmananda*, 370, fn. 1.
501 A council that evolved to manage civil disputes within a village. It commonly adjudicated disagreements relating to caste and property. Literally, the term means a commission of five (from the Sanskrit *panca* or five).
502 Widgery, *Speeches and Addresses of His Highness Sayaji Rao III*, 34.
503 Kulkarni, *Mama Parmananda*, 378.
504 Gaekwad, *Sayajirao of Baroda*, 143.
505 Kulkarni, *Mama Parmananda*, 379.
506 Anant Kanekar, "Acknowledgement", in Kulkarni, *Mama Parmananda*, 12.
507 Kaikini and Natarajan, *The Speeches & Writings of Sir Narayen G. Chandavarkar*, 568.
508 "The Late Mr. Narayan M. Parmanand", *Indu Prakash*, September 13, 1893, 4; *Madras Weekly Mail*, September 21, 1893, 263; *Kaiser-i-Hind*, September 24, 1893; *Amrita Bazar Patrika*, October 1, 1893, 4; *The Colonies and India*, October 7, 1893; *Bombay Educational Record*, Vol. 29, No. 11, 1893, 249–50.
509 *The Tribune*, September 23, 1893.
510 *Amrita Bazar Patrika*, October 8, 1893, 9.
511 "The Narayan M. Parmanand Memorial", *Times of India*, August 21, 1897, 3; "The Narayan Mahadev Parmanand Prize", *University of Bombay Calendar for the Year 1907–1908*, Vol. 1 (Bombay: Government Central Press, 1907), 583–84.
512 *The Kaiser-i-Hind*, September 24, 1893.
513 *The Tribune*, September 23, 1893.
514 Gopal Krishna Gokhale (1866–1915) studied at Elphinstone and became a prominent editor, teacher, and activist in Pune. Famed for his intellect and moderation, he served on the Imperial Legislative Council from 1902 to 1915.
515 Tej Bahadur Sapru (1875–1949) practiced law, served on the United Provinces Legislative Council and Imperial Legislative Council, led the National Liberal Federation, and frequently acted as a political mediator.
516 C. Sankaran Nair (1857–1934) studied law at Presidency College in Madras. He served as President of the Congress in 1897, was appointed to the High Court in 1908, and then to the Viceregal Council in 1915.
517 C. Sankaran Nair, *Gandhi and Anarchy* (Madras: Tagore & Co.,1922), xi–xiii. Also see C. F. Andrews, "Sir Tej Bahadur Sapru", in L. F. Rushbrook Williams, ed., *Great Men of India* (Bombay: Home Library Club, 1939), 399.
518 Govinda Das, "Feudatory India", *Indian Review*, Vol. 11, No. 8, August 1910, 577–80; *Voice of India*, November 16, 1901, 362; *Voice of India*, January 25, 1902, 62; G. R. Abhyanker, *Native States and Post-War Reforms* (Poona: Arya Bhushan Press, 1917), 20.
519 For instance, see Maharajah of Bobbili, *Advice to the Indian Aristocracy* (Madras: Addison & Co., 1905); "The Constitution of Native States: An Important Memorandum of the Late Rajah Sir T. Madhava Rao", *Indian Review*, Vol. 7, No. 11, 1906, 422–31.

520 Joseph Chailley, *The Administrative Problems of India*, trans. William Meyer (London: Macmillan and Co., 1910), 227–28.

521 Keen, *Princely India and the British*, 84–86; *Report on Native Papers Published in the Bombay Presidency and Berar for the Week Ending 16th June 1883* (London: India Office Library and Records, 1883), 14; Khan, *The Ruling Chiefs of Western India and the Rajkumar College*, 18–23; "The Education of Indian Princes: An Indian", *Indian Review*, Vol. 15, No. 8, August 1914.

522 Chailley, *The Administrative Problems of India*, 235.

523 "The Education of the Indian Aristocracy", *Civil & Military Gazette*, December 4, 1903, 4; J. E. Scott, *In Famine Land* (New York: Harper & Brothers, 1904), 71–72.

524 Chailley, *The Administrative Problems of India*, 223.

525 *The Kaiser-i-Hind*, September 24, 1893.

526 Chandavarkar, *A Wrestling Soul*, 112.

527 V. N. Bhatye, *Indore Affairs* (Bombay: Bombay New Press, 1896) (British Library, Tr.768(b)).

528 Chandavarkar, *A Wrestling Soul*, 139.

529 "Measures for Combating the Spread of Sedition into Native States", Foreign Department, Confidential-B, Internal Branch, Section-A, 1911, No. 3 (National Archives of India, IOR/R/1/1/1088); Ian Copland, "The Maharaja of Kolhapur and the Non-Brahmin Movement 1902–10", *Modern Asian Studies*, Vol. 7, No. 2, 1973, 211–13.

530 Alexander E. Powell, *The Last Home of Mystery* (New York: Garden City, 1929), 90, 94, 96.

531 Madhava T. Rao, "The Education of the Ruling Princes", *Feudatory and Zemindari India*, Vol. 1, No. 2, September 1921; D. V. Gundappa, *The Problems of Indian Native States* (Madras: Home Rule League, 1917); M. W. Burway, *An Open Letter to Young Prince* (Indore: M. W. Burway, 1923); T. Madhava Row, "Administration of Indian States", *Feudatory and Zemindari India*, Vol. 6, No. 5, 1927, 829–32; Jadunath Mozoomdar, *An Epistle to the Princes of India* (Jessore: J. Mozoomdar, 1930).

532 Lala Lajpat Rai, *The Political Future of India* (New York: B. W. Huebsch, 1919), 98–109.

533 P. L. Chudgar, *Indian Princes under British Protection: A Study of Their Personal Rule, Their Constitutional Position and Their Future* (London: Williams & Norgate, 1929), 148.

534 Chudgar, *Indian Princes under British Protection*, 203, 208–9.

535 Ian Copland, *The Princes of India in the Endgame of Empire, 1917–1947* (Cambridge: Cambridge University Press, 1997), 6–7; Lakshmi Iyer, "Direct versus Indirect Colonial Rule in India: Long-Term Consequences", *Review of Economics and Statistics*, Vol. 92, No. 4, 2010, 693.

536 Basudev Chatterji, ed., *Towards Freedom: Documents on the Movement for Independence in India, 1938*, Vol. 3 (New Delhi: Oxford University Press, 1999), 3092–95.

537 K. M. Panikkar, *Indian States and the Government of India* (London: Martin Hopkinson, 1932), 175; Chudgar, *Indian Princes under British Protection*, 213–15.

538 Powell, *The Last Home of Mystery*, 95–97; Chudgar, *Indian Princes under British Protection*, 92–99, 145–47. Another widely read publication was the *Indian States' Committee Report and Public Opinion Thereon* (Poona: Aryabhusan Press, 1929), 6–7, 11–12.

539 *Constitutional Developments in Mysore: Report of the Committee Appointed to Work Out the Details of the Scheme* (Bangalore: Government Press, 1923); "Mysore Reforms", *Feudatory and Zemindari India*, Vol. 2, Nos. 10–11, 1923; Mushirul Hassan, ed., *Towards Freedom: Documents on the Movement for Independence in India 1939*, Vol. 1 (New Delhi: Oxford University Press, 2008), 770–75. An important recent study is Tejas Parasher, *Radical Democracy in Modern Indian Political Thought* (Cambridge: Cambridge University Press, 2023), 31–59, 93–120.

540 Chudgar, *Indian Princes under British Protection*, 212–16.

541 K. L. Gauba, *H. H. or The Pathology of Princes* (Lahore: Times Press, 1930), 190. Gauba would later confess that his book featured "some exaggeration" (K. L. Gauba, *Friends and Foes: An Autobiography* (New Delhi: Indian Book Company, 1974), 95).

542 Gauba, *H. H. or The Pathology of Princes*, 298–99.

543 Dadabhai Naoroji, "Some Further Opinions on the Subject of Native Rulers and British Rule", in *Poverty and Un-British Rule in India*, 623.

544 *Proclamation of the Queen to the Princes, Chiefs, and People of India, Allahabad, November 1, 1858* (London: House of Commons, 1908), 2.

545 "The Cry of Young Bombay", *Missionary Herald*, Vol. 61, No. 11, 1865, 365.

546 "The Cry of Young Bombay", 366.

547 Charles E. Trevelyan, *On the Education of People in India* (London: Longman, Orme, Brown, Green, & Longmans, 1838), 202–3.

548 H. E. B. Edwards, *Prospect of Triumph of Christianity in India* (London: Church Missionary House, 1866), 14.

549 "Does Deism Tend to Belief or Unbelief?", *Benares Magazine*, Vol. 3, No. 3, 1850, 178, 181.

550 James Parton, *The Life of Voltaire*, Vol. 2 (Boston: Houghton, Mifflin, and Co., 1889), 554. The original line is: *si dieu n'existait pas, il faudrait l'inventer*.

551 Rammohan Roy, *The Precepts of Jesus, the Guide to Peace and Happiness* (Boston: Christian Register Office, 1828), v.

552 Roy, *The Precepts of Jesus*, vi.

553 Nehemiah Goreh, *Four Lectures Delivered in Substance to the Brahmos in Bombay and Poona* (Bombay: Education Society's Press, 1875), 3, 63, 91.

554 Shivaji I (1630–80) founded the Maratha Empire in 1674. In contrast to despotic Deccan Sultanates and the Mughal Empire, he governed collegially and tolerantly.

555 Govind Rande, *Rise of the Maratha Power* (Bombay: Punalekar & Co., 1900), Ch. 7.

556 Gaurishankar Udayshankar (1805–92) was *dewan* of Bhavnagar from 1847 to 1879, during which time he modernized its finances, launched public works, and helped establish Rajkumar College. He was knighted in 1877.

557 William Wedderburn, "The Panchayat: Conciliation as a Remedy for Agrarian Disorders in India", *Journal of East India Association*, Vol. 11, 1878, 131–32.

558 For an earlier critique, see "The Punchayet, or Hindu Form of Arbitration", *Asiatic Journal*, Vol. 21, 1826, 481.

559 Pramatha Nath Bose, *A History of Hindu Civilisation during British Rule, Vol. III: Intellectual Condition* (Calcutta: W. Newman & Co., 1896), 58.

560 Arminius Vambery, *Western Culture in Eastern Lands* (London: John Murray, 1906), 211.

561 J. Ramsay Macdonald, *The Awakening of India* (London: Hodder and Stoughton, 1910), 196.

562 Ranganathan, "The Nature of Indian Liberalism", 51; B. R. Nanda, *The Moderate Era in Indian Politics* (Delhi: Oxford University Press, 1984), 5; Shruti Kapila, "Self, Spencer and Swaraj: Nationalist Thought and Critiques of Liberalism, 1890–1920", in Shruti Kapila, ed., *An Intellectual History for India* (Cambridge: Cambridge University Press, 2010), 105, 110.

563 Bimanbehari Majumdar, *History of Political Thought: From Rammohun to Dayananda*, Vol. 1 (Calcutta: University of Calcutta, 1934); Maganlal A. Buch, *Rise and Growth of Indian Liberalism from Ram Mohun Roy to Gokhale* (Baroda: University of London, 1938); Beni Prasad, "Influence of Modern Thought on India", *The Annals of the American Academy of Political and Social Science*, Vol. 233, May 1944, 49–50; V. N. Naik, *Indian Liberalism: A Study* (Bombay: Padma Publications, 1945); M. V. Krishna Rao, *The Growth of Indian Liberalism in the Nineteenth Century* (Mysore: H. Venkataramiah, 1951); D. B. Shukla, *A History of Liberal Party* (Allahabad: Indian Press, 1960); K. M. Panikkar, *In Defence of Liberalism* (Bombay: Asia Publishing House, 1962), 7–10; A. Ranganathan, "The Nature of Indian Liberalism", *Civilisations*, Vol. 14, No. 12, 1964.

564 Krishna Rao, *The Growth of Indian Liberalism in the Nineteenth Century*, i.

565 For an overview, see Ray T. Smith, "The Role of India's 'Liberals' in the Nationalist Movement, 1915–1947", *Asian Survey*, Vol. 8, No. 7, July 1968, 607–24.

566 Bayly, *Recovering Liberties*, 343.

567 Bayly, *Recovering Liberties*, 144. Also see Barun De, "A Biographical Perspective on the Political and Economic Ideas of Rammohun Roy", in V. C. Joshi, ed., *Rammohun Roy and the Modernization in India* (Delhi: Vikas Publishing House, 1975), 147–48. A more recent critique along these lines is Nazmul Sultan, *Waiting for the People: The Idea of Democracy in Indian Anticolonial Thought* (Cambridge: Belknap Press, 2024), 91.

568 Bayly, *Recovering Liberties*, 343.

569 Ranajit Guha, *Dominance without Hegemony: History and Power in Colonial India* (Cambridge, MA: Harvard University Press, 1998), 5, 165–76.

570 V. S. Srinivasa Sastri (1869–1946) served on the Madras Legislative Council and the Imperial Legislative Council before founding the National Liberal

Federation in 1922. He went on to be the preeminent Indian diplomat of the era.

571 Important recent examples include Patel, *Naoroji*; Elena Valdameri, *Indian Liberalism between Nation and Empire: The Political Life of Gopal Krishna Gokhale* (London: Routledge, 2022); Visana, *Uncivil Liberalism*; Vineet Thakur, *V. S. Srinivasa Sastri: A Liberal Life* (London: Routledge, 2023).

572 Guha, *Dominance without Hegemony*, 174.

573 Keer, *Mahatma Jotirao Phooley*, 261–65.

574 *Times of India*, February 28, 1912, 10.

575 Guha, "The Absent Liberal", 4663, 4665; Bayly, "Empires and Indian Liberals", 74.

576 Rajendra Vora, "Two Strands of Indian Liberalism: The Ideas of Ranade and Phule", in Kenneth L. Deutsch and Thomas Pantham, eds., *Political Thought in Modern India* (Thousand Oaks, CA: Sage Publications, 1986), 96–97.

577 Jon E. Wilson, *The Domination of Strangers: Modern Governance in Eastern India, 1780–1835* (London: Palgrave Macmillan, 2008), 161–81; Jon Wilson, "Early Colonial India beyond Empire", *The Historical Journal*, Vol. 50, No. 4, December 2007, 969–70; Bayly, *Recovering Liberties*, 6; Rochana Bajpai, "Liberalisms in India", in Leigh K. Jenco, Murad Idris, and Megan C. Thomas, eds., *The Oxford Handbook of Comparative Political Theory* (Oxford: Oxford University Press, 2020), 500–501.

578 Macdonald, *The Awakening of India*, 20–22.

579 Y. R. Tamhane, ed., *Descriptive Catalogue of Papers Relating to Rajarshi Shahu Chhatrapati of Kolhapur*, Vol. 1 (Bombay: Government of Maharashtra, Department of Archives, 1979), i.

580 For instance, see "Letter from Poona Sarvajanik Sabha", January 13, 1880, The Gaekwar and His Ministers, Vol. 3, Section 6w, Daftar No. 71, Serial No. 352, Vol. 671, 1876–86 (Baroda Records Room); "The Installation of the Maharaja of Kolhapur", *Quarterly Journal of the Poona Sarvajanik Sabha*, Vol. 17, 1894, 2–6; "Visit of H.H. the Gaekwar of Baroda to the Poona Sarvajanik Sabha", Foreign Department (Political), Confidential-B, Internal Branch, Section-A, 1910, Nos. 7–8, 9 (British Library, IOR/R/1/1/1079); Y. R. Tamhane, ed., *Descriptive Catalogue of Papers Relating to Rajarshi Shah Chhatrapati of Kolhapur*, Vol. 2, 1982, 8 (Government of Maharashtra, Department of Archives).

581 "Report on the Education and Training of H.H. the Maharaja of Mysore", Mysore Residency Files, 41 (British Library, IOR/R/2/8/64); *Report on the General Administration of the Kolhapur State for the Year 1893–94* (Kolhapur: State Press, 1894), 171–72; Vilas Sangave and B. D. Khane, eds., *Rajarshi Shahu Chhatrapati Papers, 1894–1900*, Vol. 2 (Kolhapur: Shahu Research Institute, 1985), 36–37.

582 S. S. Bhosale, S. R. Chavan, and P. M. Bandivadekar, eds., *A Royal Philosopher Speaks* (Kolhapur: Kolhapur Zilla Parishad, 1975), 42–52.

583 Bhosale, Chavan, and Bandivadekar, *A Royal Philosopher Speaks*, 75–76.

584 Gail Omvedt, *Cultural Revolt in a Colonial Society: The Non Brahman Movement in Western India, 1873 to 1930* (Bombay: Scientific Socialist Education Trust,

1976), 129; S. M. Fraser, "Preface", in A. B. Latthe, *Memoirs of Shri Shahu Chhatrapati Maharaja of Kolhapur*, Vol. 1 (Bombay: Times Press, 1924), v, xi–xii; Dhananjay Keer, *Shahu Chhatrapati, A Royal Revolutionary* (Bombay: Popular Prakashan, 1976), 412.

585 Keer, *A Royal Revolutionary*, 300–302; A. B. Latthe, *Memoirs of Shri Shahu Chhatrapati Maharaja of Kolhapur*, Vol. 2 (Bombay: Times Press, 1924), 464, 489–90.

586 Andrew Sartori, *Liberalism in Empire: An Alternative History* (Berkeley: University of California Press, 2014), 4–5; Leigh K. Jenco and Jonathan Chappell, "Introduction: History from Between and the Global Circulations of the Past in Asia and Europe, 1600–1950", *Historical Journal*, Vol. 64, No. 1, 2021, 2–4; Sudipta Kaviraj, "Deparochializing Political Theory and Beyond", *Journal of World Philosophies*, Vol. 1, 2016, 166–67; Gurpreet Mahajan, *India: Political Ideas and the Making of a Democratic Discourse* (London: Zed Books, 2013), 6–8. This point was first made by S. P. Aiyar, "Some Aspects of the Study of Modern Political Thought", *Indian Journal of Political Science*, Vol. 33, No. 4, 1972, 403.

587 Shruti Kapila, "Global Intellectual History and the Indian Political", in Darrin M. McMohan and Samuel Moyn, eds., *Rethinking Modern European Intellectual History* (Oxford: Oxford University Press, 2014), 258.

588 Duncan Bell, "What Is Liberalism?", *Political Theory*, Vol. 42, No. 6, 2014, 682.

589 Alan Ryan, *The Making of Modern Liberalism* (Princeton, NJ: Princeton University Press, 2012), 28.

590 Bell, "What Is Liberalism?", 693.

591 William Selinger and Gregory Conti, "The Lost History of Political Liberalism", *History of European Ideas*, Vol. 46, No. 3, 2020, 354.

592 Michael Freeden, *The New Liberalism: An Ideology of Social Reform* (Oxford: Oxford University Press, 1986), 118–20.

593 Helena Rosenblatt, *The Lost History of Liberalism: From Ancient Rome to the Twenty-First Century* (Princeton, NJ: Princeton University Press, 2018), 226.

594 Vrajendra Raj Mehta, "T. H. Green and the Revision of English Liberal Theory", *Indian Journal of Political Science*, Vol. 35, No. 1, 1974, 37.

595 Richard Bellamy, "T. H. Green and the Morality of Victorian Liberalism", in Richard Bellamy, ed., *Victorian Liberalism: Nineteenth-Century Political Thought and Practice* (London: Routledge, 1990), 141.

596 Freeden, *The New Liberalism*, 150–51; Jonathan Parry, *The Rise and Fall of Liberal Government in Victorian Britain* (New Haven: Yale University Press, 1993), 249.

597 Sandra Den Otter, "Thinking in Communities: Late Nineteenth-Century Liberals, Idealists and the Retrieval of Community", *Parliamentary History*, Vol. 16, No. 1, 1997, 67.

598 D. Weinstein, "The New Liberalism and the Rejection of Utilitarianism", in A. Simhony and D. Weinstein, eds., *The New Liberalism: Reconciling Liberty and* Community (Cambridge: Cambridge University Press, 2010), 164, 176.

599 John Stuart Mill, *On Liberty* (London: John W. Parker, 1859), 13.
600 Mill, *On Liberty*, 17.
601 Krishna Rao, *The Growth of Indian Liberalism*, 19; Aiyar, "Some Aspects of the Study of Modern Political Thought", 404.
602 Melvin Richter, *The Politics of Conscience: T. H. Green and His Age* (London: Weidenfeld and Nicolson, 1964), 283–84.
603 Stefan Collini, *Liberalism and Sociology: L. T. Hobhouse and Political Argument in England 1880–1914* (Cambridge: Cambridge University Press, 1979), 29.
604 Isaiah Berlin, *Four Essays on Liberty* (Oxford: Oxford University Press, 2002),166–217.
605 Andrew Sartori, "C. A. Bayly and the Question of Indian Political Thought", *Modern Asian Studies*, Vol. 51, No. 3, May 2017, 875.
606 David Cameron, "Speech at Munich Security Conference", February 5, 2011 (www.gov.uk/government/speeches/pms-speech-at-munich-security-conference); Larry Siedentop, *Inventing the Individual: The Origins of Western Liberalism* (Cambridge, MA: Harvard University Press, 2014), 350; Pierre Manent, *Beyond Radical Secularism: How France and the Christian West Should Respond to the Islamic Challenge*, trans. Ralph C. Hancock (Indiana: St. Augustine's Press, 2016).
607 Alan Patten, *Equal Recognition: The Moral Foundations of Minority Rights* (Princeton, NJ: Princeton University Press, 2014), 29.
608 Bhikhu Parekh, *Rethinking Multiculturalism: Cultural Diversity and Political Theory* (London: Macmillan Press, 2000), 239.
609 Barry, *Culture and Equality*, 165; Chandran Kukathas, *The Liberal Archipelago: A Theory of Diversity and Freedom* (Oxford: Oxford University Press, 2003), 211–54.
610 Ayaan Hirsi Ali, *Infidel: My Life* (New York: Simon & Schuster, 2007), 285.
611 Clare Chambers, "All Must Have Prizes: The Liberal Case for Interference in Cultural Practices", in Paul Kelly, ed., *Multiculturalism Reconsidered: "Culture and Equality" and Its Critics* (Cambridge: Polity Press, 2002), 150, 159–63. For a general overview, see George Crowder, *Theories of Multiculturalism: An Introduction* (Cambridge: Polity Press, 2013), 71–75.
612 Thomas Hurka defines neutrality as follows: "According to this ideal, the state must not only not coerce citizens to make them better, it must never aim, coercively or otherwise, to promote one set of values over others. It must be neutral about the good, never having as its justification for acting that some ways of life are intrinsically preferable to other" (Thomas Hurka, "Perfectionism", in George Klosko, ed., *Perfectionism and Neutrality: Essays in Liberal Theory* (New York: Rowman & Littlefield Publishers, 2003), 131).
613 James Fitzjames Stephen, *Liberty, Equality, Fraternity* (New York: Holt & Williams, 1873), 15–16.
614 Stephen, *Liberty, Equality, Fraternity*, 56.
615 Stephen, *Liberty, Equality, Fraternity*, 53.
616 Stephen, *Liberty, Equality, Fraternity*, 56, 65–66.
617 Stephen, *Liberty, Equality, Fraternity*, 53.

A note on the text

This edition of *Letters to an Indian Raja* is based on the edition printed by the Tatva-Vivechaka Press in Bombay in 1891. It has been checked against copies held by the British Library in London and University of Illinois at Urbana-Champaign.[1] It has also been checked against the text published in the *Indian Spectator* in 1889 and 1890, copies of which are held on microfilm at the Center for Research Libraries in Chicago.[2] The original handwritten manuscript could not be traced.

The original text has been revised carefully. The only substantive change is that every letter has been given a heading, so as to make it easier for readers to grasp the theme. The other changes are stylistic. Because it was dictated to a notetaker, the original text had several imperfections: long sentences separated by semicolons, distracting typographical errors, and quotations that lacked citations. The first and second complaints have been addressed silently: Sentences have been broken up and printing errors have been remedied. In no instance has the meaning of the original text been altered. The third complaint has been resolved by tracking down and citing the various missing sources. In only a few instances has this proved impossible, and the absence of a citation has duly been noted.

The other significant stylistic change is with respect to spellings, which have been modernized. For instance, "subject-matter" is now rendered as "subject matter" and "non-descript" as "nondescript". A place name like "Jeypur" has been changed to the more recognizable Jaipur and "Brahmapootra" to Brahmaputra. The same has been done with respect to titles: "Bhagavad-gita" is now printed as Bhagavad Gita and "Mogul" as Mughal. Transliterations have been modernized too: "*gadi*" has been changed to

1 *Letters to an Indian Raja from a Political Recluse* (Bombay: Tatva-Vivechaka Press, 1891) (British Library, 8023.cc.28, T 36003; University of Illinois at Urbana-Champaign, 954.035 L569).

2 *Letters to an Indian Raja* (Bombay: Tatva-Vivechaka Press, 1891) (Center for Research Libraries, SAMP 82/61032).

gaddi, "*Nababs*" to *nawab*s, and so on. Such transliterated terms have been italicized except in cases where their usage is common. Thus, for example, Maharaja is not italicized, but *rawala* and *dharmshala* are. The extensive use of capitalization, which was characteristic of the era, has been reined in. Thus, "State" becomes "state" and "Ruler" becomes "ruler", and so on. Finally, to aid the contemporary reader, brief footnotes have been added to shed light on key characters or to explain transliterated terms. These definitions can also be found in the Glossary.

LETTERS TO AN INDIAN RAJA,

FROM

A POLITICAL RECLUSE:

REPRINTED AFTER REVISION FROM THE "INDIAN SPECTATOR."

PRINTED AT THE "TATVA-VIVECHAKA" PRESS,

BOMBAY.

1891.

Price one Rupee *or* two Shillings.

Title page of *Letters to an Indian Raja*, Bombay, Tatva-Vivechaka Press, 1891. British Library, 8023.cc.28 T 36003

DEDICATED

TO

THE RULING PRINCES AND CHIEFS OF INDIA;

WITH THE BEST WISHES

FOR

Their welfare, the integrity of their
power and the prosperity
of their states:

BY

Their humble and earnest well-wisher

THE AUTHOR

Notice

The Native States of India form an appreciable portion of the country and of its population, and enjoy complete protection against external aggression and internal troubles from the paramount power. If, in these circumstances, they were to imbibe at least the elements of a progressive spirit of which that Power furnishes abundant example, they would not only ensure their own welfare, but might react beneficially on British India in some important respects and thus serve to aid the general advancement of the country.

How this could be effected and what difficulties exist in its way is an important question, and it was to invite attention to that question that these *Letters* were primarily taken in hand. They have now been issued in a permanent form, because, when shown to a few friends eminently qualified to pass an opinion thereon, they elicited cordial approval. It was also reported to the writer from a reliable source that a very favourable opinion of the *Letters* had been pronounced in certain high quarters in Native Territory, and when informed of their intended republication, Sir W. W. Hunter, whose name carries such deserved weight and who has done so much to familiarise the British public with the more important of our popular movements, was good enough to furnish an Introduction which will speak for itself.

All the *Letters* have been carefully revised and improved since they first appeared in the *Indian Spectator* in the course of 1889–90, and Letter No. II, which was originally written under a disadvantage, has, besides, been largely added to, by expansion of the argument with the help of a friend who has made the subject his special study.

The author, mainly for personal reasons, withholds his name and leaves this little brochure to be judged on its own merits.

THE AUTHOR
October, 1891

Contents

Letter No. I[3]

On Counsel

MAHARAJA,

It is now some time since, by the grace of God, the king of kings, and by the kindness of the British government, the paramount power in the land, you have completed your minority and your education and ascended to the throne of your ancestors. You have already given proofs of becoming a capable ruler and virtuous prince, and, therefore, an ornament to your house and your class, a source of happiness to your state and its people, and of pleasure and satisfaction to the paramount British government. It is now the main business of your life to advance the welfare of your people and to maintain intact your engagements with the superior government.

These two objects happily are not inconsistent with each other; but the Native States of India are just now passing through a critical period of their existence – their present fortunes are as different from the past as the future promises or threatens to be from the present, and these will be a great deal determined by the conduct of their own rulers and administrators during this critical period. Their task, indeed, even in the case of an unbroken succession of capable princes on the *gaddi* and of worthy statesmen at the helm of affairs – a contingency which it is not possible to secure under any circumstances – is far from an easy one amidst their peculiar surroundings and the harassing difficulties of their situation, while in the case of a break in such succession, which is the rule as continuity is the exception, the difficulty of that task must often become phenomenal.

I need not stop to specify these difficulties, as indeed, I fancy, they already have commenced to offer themselves daily before your eyes in your dealings, on the one hand, with your hereditary nobility, the official hierarchy from the highest to the lowest, and the great body of your subjects; and, on the other, in your relations to the representative at your court of the British government which is enlightened, all-powerful and ever-progressive – characteristics which lead it, in dealing with ignorant, backward, and feeble races and administrations, sometimes to disregard (and indeed on occasions at least in view of larger interests it cannot help disregarding), the claims of right, and to prefer expediency to justice, as must happen with human agents exercising for the time power that is simply irresistible.

Under such circumstances I desire very much to communicate to your Highness a few suggestions which occur to me from my experience and observation of public life in Native States and in British India, and I shall

3 This letter originally appeared in the *Indian Spectator* on November 17, 1889.

be very glad if they should prove of the slightest service to you, and tend to any the smallest advantage or good to yourself or to your state. Before entering on the suggestions I have in view, however, I wish to answer one or two preliminary questions which will naturally occur to you, and a reply to which is essential to a clear comprehension of the object with which I am thus obtruding upon your Highness's attention, as also on your valuable time.

The first question then would perhaps be: Why do I address your Highness above all other Rajas and Nawabs in the country? Well, the reply is that you are the representative – and many circumstances have tended to make you a worthy and promising representative – of your class. To begin with, you not only have been generously endowed by your Maker with a sound mind and a feeling heart, but you have also received, through the kindness of the paramount power, a good education, such as falls to the lot of very few Rajas or sons of Rajas. What lends its special value to your education and to your natural gifts and graces is the salutary nature of your surroundings, *antecedent to your accession to your throne*, and consequently of the conditions under which the education for that exalted position was imparted to you. For, though an undoubtedly lineal and rightful offshoot of the ruling stock planted on the soil of Gujarat by the valour of Pilaji Gaekwad[4] and nourished by the courage and wisdom of Damaji Gaekwad,[5] you were born and bred up in early boyhood *as a subject*, and there is, for the purpose of my essay, a world of high moral significance in these three short words I have underlined, as you may easily realize by reflection and observation.

Being born outside the ruling branch of your house, you and your natural parents and brethren have known what it is to be a subject and a taxpayer, and now you have in the providential order of things attained to the high and onerous privilege of a spender of the taxes and a ruler of men, with power over their lives and fortunes. You are, therefore, better qualified to appreciate the sacred duties and responsibilities of that position than even pettier princes, born and brought up amidst enervating and demoralising influences and nourished in the intoxicating and dementing exercise of absolute and irresponsible power from their infancy within their small domains. You, in fact, occupy an enviable position which belonged to none of your predecessors, and which will not fall to the lot of any of your successors on the *gaddi*. Indeed, your position is unique. At a college examination

4 Pilaji Gaekwad ([?]–1732) was the founder of Baroda State, which he cobbled out of territories seized from the Mughals between 1721 and 1732.

5 Damaji Gaekwad ([?]–1768) succeeded Pilaji in 1732. His three-decade long reign stabilized and then expanded Baroda State, which he accomplished by expelling the Mughals from Gujarat.

in an advanced class there was once set this theme for an essay: "What measures would you adopt if you were made Governor-General in British India?" You may well imagine with what ardour the cleverest and most ambitious of the students reveled in dreams of a wise administration and philanthropic statesmanship, for the ambition of youth is naturally noble, and, when acted on by a sound education, coupled with a knowledge of the golden deeds and exemplars of history, delights in the contemplation of noble achievements. The students' opportunities and privileges, however, were imaginary and confined to pen and paper, and even with these substantial drawbacks they were limited to the few hours allotted for the composition, and, therefore, momentary, [whereas] yours are real and will end only with life.

Again, though the British Governor-General's field of work is vast, compared with an indigenous Raja's jurisdiction in India, what is wanted in extent by you is amply made up in depth. Moreover, wisdom and foresight, courage and resolution, tact and shrewdness, love of that which is good and great and true – and these are among the marks of the higher order of statesmanship – can be exhibited in a limited sphere of action as well as in an extensive one, and in fact it is easier to carry on and supervise with success the work of administration and any important measures of reform in a compact territory than is possible in an unwieldy empire. Further, your powers are more absolute and your field of work is new, and your task, too, is more arduous and less relieved by that ready cooperation and those steady helps which the Governor-General finds in the experience, knowledge, capacities, devotion to duty and similar other requisites of successful government in the uninterrupted succession and supply of his colleagues and lieutenants and in the established law and order of routine and precedent, while you, in your own sphere, unless you are content to continue the humdrum style of work, and go where things and times will lead you and your state, like dumb-driven cattle, will have yourself sometimes to originate, elaborate, and carry out, often to supervise but always to direct, almost every measure of state, and the advice and assistance you can command, circumstanced as the indigenous administrations are, will be uncertain, halting and half-hearted, and not always reliable. The consequence will be that, if you at all attempt anything like the work which morally devolves on you, and to specify a few particulars of which is the object why I am thrusting myself on your time and attention, your Highness will have to complain not of its smallness or lightness, but rather of its heavy and exacting nature. If, however, the task would be onerous, its successful performance, or even an honest endeavour to merit success would assuredly bring with it its inevitable reward, here and hereafter – within your bosom a noble feeling of satisfaction, "the purest allotted to man",[6] of having done your duty, name and fame abroad, happiness to your fellowmen, credit to your family and increase of its claims on the homage and gratitude of your subjects, and the continued respect, esteem, and confidence of the paramount power.

The second preliminary question which might be asked is: Why do I address your Highness thus publicly? I have, as you will see from the subscription, retired from the world, and am, therefore, prevented as much by the rules of such retirement as by my own inclinations from presenting myself at the precincts of palaces or *darbar*s (courts), or obtruding privately on any public personages. Nor can I be sure, even if I were to present myself at the door of your residence, whether I should be allowed to see you, or if I sent you a private communication that it would meet your eye; for, I do not know what the practice of your *darbar* in these matters is, while, on the other hand, I know there are Rajas and Nawabs who hear and see only what their functionaries permit to reach them. I am, therefore, doubtful what sort of reception your officials would be inclined to give to me or my views, if sought to be privately presented. And so I have thought that to write to you and to write thus openly is the surest means of placing these letters before you.

But in passing it would be as well to observe that those in attendance on great personages are given to shut out from them visitors or communications they may themselves not regard with favour, and they succeed in enforcing their wishes, because they themselves are the only media of intercourse and there is no means of penetrating the wall round their charges. The result is that men in power and position often find themselves cut off from the outside public and live in a world of their own without even suspecting it, while the public believes them to be wilful in their isolation. They must, therefore, take vigilant care that their accessibility to the general public is regulated according to their own views and wishes and satisfy themselves that their attendants do not intermeddle with it. Rulers of states and their chief ministers and advisers stand in need of such a precaution, because, to ensure an efficient discharge of their high functions, they of all others stand most in need to know what is thought and said of their work

6 These lines are adapted from Robert Hall's famous 1803 sermon "The Sentiments Proper to the Present Crisis" (*The Works of Robert Hall*, Vol. 1 (London: Henry G. Bohn, 1845), 191). The original reads:

> Should Providence determine otherwise, should you fail in this struggle, should the nation fall, you will have the satisfaction (the purest allotted to man) of having performed your part; virtue alone will atone for the outrages of fortune, by conducting you to immortality.

in spheres other than their own, but they will have no means of gaining such knowledge or a deep insight into human character, if they do not allow of their free and unrestricted approach to them. I will try to point out the full bearings of this question on the business of administration hereafter in its proper place. Here I only content myself with inviting your Highness's attention to it.

A third reason, however, for these letters being open is that, though directly addressed to you, they are designed equally for all those of your brethren – and there are many such – who are situated like yourself in regard to the advantages of education, and for all the Indian princes generally. They are intended no less for the attention of those native gentlemen who have received a liberal education and imbibed a liberal spirit, and who, though subjects themselves, are holding high and responsible offices in the Native States. They are or may, as they should, be actuated by a noble desire to exercise their opportunities and talents for statesmanship in the sphere of practical politics in which they are placed, to their own credit and to the advantage alike of their masters and their subjects, and who, therefore, may naturally be expected to take into consideration whatever may be found in these letters to be sensible and practicable within the states they are helping to rule.

And this explanation of the aim and scope of these letters will also supply an answer to the last preliminary question which may occur in regard to them, *viz.*, why they are not written in any of the vernaculars but are clothed in what for all purposes, political, administrative, and educational, is the *lingua franca* of the land.

Here, Maharaja, I close this first letter; and inviting you to reflect on its subject matter, I beg to be allowed to subscribe myself,

Your Highness's earnest well-wisher,
A POLITICAL RECLUSE

Letter No. II[7]

On Religion

MAHARAJA,

In my opening letter, I have indicated what special circumstances make your position among the Rajas of India exceptional, and invited you to bethink yourself of a higher task than the mere carrying out of the routine of the administration of your state as it exists. I may here add that [the] execution of that task will, as years roll on, be found more than ever to be necessary, to ensure the safety and permanence in a satisfactory form of the routine itself, amidst all changes of time and circumstances. Before specifying its features, however, I must draw your Highness's attention to certain conditions which are essential for its commencement and its continued success, as also for the permanent retention of its fruits, and these conditions must, therefore, be first attended to.

Now, these essentials are, above all things, moral in their nature, and, therefore, they are personal, and you must show them in your own person and family and surroundings – both as a ruler and man. It would be impossible to exaggerate the heavy responsibility which, in this respect, rests on you as the ruler of your state. There was a good deal of both practical and political wisdom when Frederick the Great said that "a king was but the first of his subjects",[8] by which maxim, I presume, he meant that a ruler of men was bound to exemplify in his own beliefs, opinions, and conduct, all those qualities of head and heart, all those principles and virtues, which he wished or ought to wish his subjects, in the interests of his state no less than for their own happiness, to possess and practice. The spirit of the maxim I have just quoted is not unknown in this country, where it has always been held and believed that "as the king is, so the subjects are".[9] This, then, points to the obligation which rests on the shoulders of a ruler to be the best exemplar to his own subjects.

7 This letter originally appeared in the *Indian Spectator* on December 1, 1889.

8 A famous line from Frederick the Great's *Essay on the Forms of Government and the Duties of Sovereigns* (1777). The original reads: "He is no more than the first servant of the state, obliged to act with probity, wisdom and disinterest, as if he had to give a report on the conduct of his administration to his citizens" (Avi Lifschitz, ed., *Frederick the Great's Philosophical Writings* (Princeton, NJ: Princeton University Press, 2021), xxxvi).

9 An allusion to the ancient Pali proverb "*Yata raja tata prajah*" (James Alwis, "On Buddhism", in T. W. Rhys Davids, ed., *Journal of the Pali Text Society* (London: Pali Text Society, 1883), 14).

And this grave moral responsibility attaches to you all the more, because you have received a high order of European education; but because of that very fact I hope and trust you have not imbibed with it the prevailing spirit of scepticism or materialism, which characterizes the ordinary educated Indian of the day. There are materialistic, empirical, or agnostic schools of philosophy, and there was a time when these, represented by John Stuart Mill, Alexander Bain, and Herbert Spencer, had an almost exclusive sway over the minds of educated Englishmen. They exercised a similar influence over our young men, and these embraced the materialism, scepticism, or agnosticism taught by the masters of those schools of philosophy. But there are other systems taught by minds as powerful, if not more so, and a reasonable person will not come to any conclusion on the momentous questions involved in a religious belief until he has carefully studied these systems also. Already in the universities of England, Mill, Bain, Spencer, and the rest have been dethroned and the study of the systems of the German philosophers, Kant and Hegel, is now pursued with vigour, and the Indian mind has during a long course of centuries been moving on lines so entirely removed from those pursued by the empirical philosophers, that it cannot for any length of time rest content with their doctrines. The immense progress that physical science has recently made, culminating, as it has done, in the theory of evolution is no doubt considered as unfavourable to a religious belief. Nothing, however, can be further from the truth, as has been pointed out by the deepest thinkers. The foundations of religion lie too deep in the intellectual and moral constitution of man to be shaken or even touched by theories such as these. Centuries ago, the founder of the study of this science wrote:

> I had rather believe all the fables in the Legend, and the Talmud, and the Koran, than that this universal frame is without a mind; and, therefore, God never wrought miracle to convince atheism, because his ordinary works convince it. It is true, that a little philosophy inclineth man's mind to atheism, but depth in philosophy bringeth men's minds about to religion; for, while the mind of man looketh upon second causes scattered, it may sometimes rest in them, and go no further; but when it beholdeth the chain of them confederate and linked together, it must needs fly to Providence and Deity: nay, even that school which is most accused of atheism doth most demonstrate religion: that is, the school of Leucippus, and Democritus, and Epicurus: for it is a thousand times more credible that four mutable elements, and one immutable fifth essence, duly and eternally placed, need no God, than that an army of infinite small portions, or seeds unplaced, should have produced this order and beauty without a divine marshal.[10]

10 Francis Bacon, "Of Atheism", in James Spedding, Robert Leslie Ellis, and Douglas Denon Heath, eds., *The Works of Francis Bacon*, Vol. 6 (London: Longman & Co., 1858), 413.

It is acknowledged that the evidence for the evolution theory is not complete, but supposing that it is, what the theory sets forth is that all the objects we see about us, including man with his intellectual and moral nature, have been developed by very slow and gradual changes out of dead matter which at one time was in the condition of vapour, and the theory of creation by God is erroneous. Now if the theory of divine creation supposes that for a long time there was nothing but God and that afterwards, by an effort of His will, all objects came into being ready made or possessed of the forms and natures which we find them to possess, the doctrine of evolution, no doubt, goes against it. But when in the early ages of humanity, men recognised the power of God in Nature, when for instance the ancient Rishis of India found Indra in the phenomena of rain and the lovely Ushas in the dawn, was such a theory of creation present before their minds? The mere occurrence of the several phenomena and the order which they observed in them all led them into the belief that they were caused by and were under the direction of wise and powerful beings.

Has the doctrine of evolution destroyed these phenomena and this order? If not, man will ever seek their efficient cause and will not be satisfied by being simply told that they were gradually developed out of other phenomena. The theory of evolution itself supposes a change at every step, though infinitesimal. And the human mind is so constituted as to look for a cause whenever there is a change. So that what this doctrine comes to is not that God did not create this universe; but that He did not create it all at once. The old theory of creation supposed Him to have done this and to have, as it were, retreated from His creation afterwards, leaving it to the mercy of certain laws which He had imposed upon it. But the doctrine of evolution represents Him to be ever present in all objects, giving them better and nobler forms; and it thus justifies the observation of the Upanishads and the Bhagavad Gita that God dwells in the heart of all things, the sun, the moon, the stars, the earth, the wind &c., and the soul of man and controls them and carries them through all their changes. It has thus served the cause of religion by rendering our idea of creation truer and grander.

But scientists tell us that it is force that does all this. The several forces known to us are but different forms in different conditions of the same force. When a ball in motion impinges against another and its motion is stopped, the force which caused that motion is not destroyed, but assumes the form of heat; for both the balls after the cessation of motion will be found to have risen in temperature. Heat assumes the form of light; light and heat are transformed into electricity, and electricity into magnetism. The process is also capable of inversion. The mere mechanical force, therefore, which causes motion, may under certain conditions appear as magnetism and perhaps also as vital force. Thus then, given matter and force, the whole world with its variety of vegetable and animal life is evolved out of them and there is again in all this no room for a creative mind. Still, somehow, we find order in the world and a beautiful adaptation of means to ends everywhere as if it was under the direction of a mind, a mind essentially of the same kind as ours, which apprehends that order and that adaptation.

Matter and force are the two great entities according to the scientist. He believes in a force, which works out certain visible results, and he speaks of the quantity of a force and of force as in store which has not yet spent itself. Matter in a certain condition, which we call effect, is traced to matter in another condition with a force existing in it; these, again, to matter in another condition still with force in another form, and so on until the scientist arrives at the ultimate molecules and still further at atoms with an ultimate force. This ultimate force cannot be traced further and must be accepted as a fact: What is the nature of force and whence do we derive our idea of it? The eye, the ear, and the other senses cannot give it to us, as force is something hidden from all our senses. Our first knowledge of a force must, therefore, be derived from our own conscious exertion of it. I *will* to raise my arm and I do it. Here I exert a force, the force of my will, and the effect is the raising up of my arm. This is the only way in which force becomes cognizable to us and the word can have any meaning for us. When, therefore, we in modern times account for changes in external nature by the supposition of a force and arrive at an ultimate force, what else can we mean by this force but a *will*? The ancients arrived at this *will* at once and believed all those changes to have been caused by the will of Indra, Varuna, and others; but we interpose many other phenomena between those changes and the will of a living being. And this is what Francis Bacon means when he speaks of second causes and the Deity as the ultimate cause.

All causation ultimately resolves itself into will. There alone our search for a cause ends. We cannot conceive dead, inanimate nature producing any change. Our demand for a cause in the external world is based on our direct experience of it within our personality. In the infancy of our race it was satisfied by our belief in a number of deities controlling the different phenomena of nature, and in our advanced condition by our faith in the ultimate will of a Supreme God, which will is called by the scientists the ultimate force to which all the other forces are reduced and which transforms itself into a variety of other forces. From these observations it will be seen that the fault of *regressio ad infinitum*[11] which some persons find in this argument has no basis in reality. If God is the cause of the world, God, they say, must have another cause, and that cause a third and so on *ad infinitum*. But the search for a cause means the search for a will that causes phenomena,

11 A Latin term for recursive arguments that create an infinite regress.

the only cause known to us being our will. We cannot and do not seek the cause of that will. All our search for a cause ends when we find the will; so that there cannot be a further search for the cause of the will. The question, therefore, who created God, is futile.

Further, the phenomena in connection with vegetable and animal life are such that they cannot be accounted for by a play of merely mechanical or inorganic forces, or looked upon as arising from a transformation of those forces. An animal is composed of parts, which form a system and each of which discharges a function which contributes to the growth of others and through it to its own growth. In giving itself up for others, it finds itself. If it ceases to perform its functions, not only are others destroyed but itself along with them. The bodies operated on by merely inorganic forces do not form such a system, have not such a common life, do not form such a unity. Their relations are merely external. One moving ball impinges on another and communicates its motion to it; but in doing so it simply loses and does not receive anything. Even the unity introduced in such a mechanism as that of a watch by the intelligence of man is quite external; the spring communicates its motion to the wheels, but the motion does not through their action return to the spring and keep the watch going without external force such as that of the muscles of the human hand. And the highest development of this organic unity is reached in the case of man, when the organism itself becomes conscious of its own unity in the mind of man. Again, the force which keeps vegetable and animal organisms going is a force that sets at naught the inorganic chemical affinity, inasmuch as it makes the elements enter into combination in proportions in which they ordinarily do not combine. In the case of animals, immediately after they are dead, decomposition sets in, that is, the elements, free from the control of the vital force which has now disappeared, disunite, and, the ordinary chemical affinity coming into play, enter into new combinations.

All this shows, therefore, that the nature and operation of the organic forces are so widely different from those of the inorganic forces and sometimes so subversive of them that the former cannot be evolved out of the latter. As the less in quantity cannot contain the greater, so the inferior force cannot in itself contain the superior force, or that out of which the superior force that overrides it is evolved. So that, if at the end of the process of gradual development the mind is evolved, it must be so because at the very first stage of the process the mind is present. If will is at the bottom of our conception of force, we can well understand how the mind whose attribute it is manifests itself in the lower forms of gravitation, heat, and other forces and gradually reveals itself more fully. But the reverse process of an inferior force, which is merely mechanical in its nature, developing itself into the highest organic force and ultimately into the mind, is unintelligible.

And independently of any theory of creation, the very aspect of the universe fills the mind of man with a sense of Divine presence. The earth with its mountains and caverns, its plains, its rivers and seas, its infinite variety of vegetable and animal life, its trees and flowers, and the canopy of the sky overhead with the sun shining by day and spreading its glories over all, and the stars glittering at night and the moon giving to everything a quiet, sweet, and lovely appearance, fill the mind of man with lofty thoughts and in the surrounding scene its sees beauty, grandeur, serenity, gladness, and joy, which inspire him with reverence and love. Grandeur, serenity, and joy can be the attributes only of a mind, and reverence and love can be felt only for a Being. The Great Spirit of the universe thus appeals through its aspects to the spirit of man, and the spirit of man responds in tones of worship, self-surrender, and prayer. In India the Rishis in the times of the Upanishads felt this influence very strongly and observed the *Paramatman* or Great Being everywhere and in everything, and were so overpowered by that perception that in comparison with it the pleasures of ordinary life became contemptible in their eyes, and the serenity, elevation, and joy consequent upon witnessing the Divine presence became the one object worthy of being pursued by man. And elsewhere, too, this visitation of God through the aspects of the Universe is represented similarly to have contributed in a large measure to prepare the great seers of mankind like Mahomed and others for the noble task which they undertook and fulfilled.

Again, the mind of man in the perception it has of right as distinct from wrong, a perception that carries with itself an uncompromising authority and claims obedience from us, bears in itself what has justly been called the voice of God. Various theories have been promulgated as to the nature of this distinction. Some have identified right and wrong with pleasure and pain, and others with the greatest happiness of the greatest number and its opposite, but all such theories fail to explain the sense of moral obligation, the authority which the perception of right evidently possesses to direct our will. Pity for a man in distress, or a diligent performance of the functions one has undertaken which involves the happiness or misery of thousands of human beings claims preference over a desire for personal ease, justice over selfishness, and respect for innocence over the fretful mood of an hour which sometimes leads even a mother to strike her inoffensive child. They claim preference, but, if left to ourselves, we would rather obey the inferior impulse, and, as a matter of fact, we often disregard the authority of the higher. But when we do so, we are punished, we are lowered in our own estimation and filled with a sense of shame.

Now, is the preference that is claimed, the authority that is asserted, consequent upon the superior pleasure arising from that impulse? If so, it would be a case of prudence, which is not obligatory on me, which has no inherent authority over me. My pleasure or my pain is solely my own concern, and I may, if I like, prefer a smaller pleasure to a greater. But I feel myself under an obligation, which I am not at liberty to violate, to obey the higher impulse; though, of course, I have the power of violating it and often exercise it. Neither can the consideration that the higher impulse will lead to the greatest good of the greatest number claim authority over me. In itself it constitutes no obligation. Why should I prefer other people's happiness to my own? What is the source of the obligation in that respect? If it is an obligation that is felt, you only refer the authority lying in our first higher impulse to another; and, in doing so, yield to us the point we seek to make out, but with reference to another impulse. But pleasure, whether of the individual or of the greatest number, is what follows from the impulses some of which claim preference over others; it does not determine the action, it is the fruit of an action; the action follows from the impulses alone without reference to its remote effects, and the preferential claim is asserted before the action and not after it.

When through our senses we perceive a body, we cannot conceive of its existence without space, and thus arises in us a knowledge of the existence of space outside as space in itself is something which we do not perceive by our senses. In the same manner, when both pity and selfishness or honour and perfidy urge our will, the right of the former to govern it in preference to the latter is felt – we feel a command to follow the one and not the other. If it is a command, it lies beyond our personality and must issue from a higher personality. And thus as our knowledge of a body leads to the knowledge of the existence of space outside, so the feeling of authority in one impulse as compared with another leads to a knowledge of the existence of a higher personality which envelops ours on all sides and issues its commands to us. When we disobey this command, a sense of ill desert hovers about us, we feel we deserve punishment from a higher power.

In an unsophisticated condition of society such as that represented to us in the Rigveda hymns, we find how this moral feeling naturally works itself out. The Rishis believed in a moral order as in a physical; the Adityas, the chief of whom is Varuna, identified often with the highest God, are the guardians of that order. They hate wrong, send out their spies to all quarters, keep watch on each transgressor, and witness the good and evil deeds of men. The mighty Varuna punishes the wrongdoer, he pursues him everywhere, there is no escape from him, except in his mercy; and this is implored in the most fervent prayers addressed to him by Vasishtha in particular, who on an occasion was overpowered with his sense of guilt. This was the interpretation which the Rishis in those simple times laid upon our moral intuitions, and what interpretation can be truer?

Again, man feels himself to be a dependent being, physically as well as morally, and this leads him to the conception of One on whom he depends. He believes himself to be a finite and limited being. He can have no conception of finiteness or limitation, unless he had an innate conception of the Infinite and the Unlimited. Though finite and limited, he ever seeks to transgress the limits within which he finds himself enclosed, to shake off the bondage. He is forever thirsting after knowledge and after goodness and is ever making greater and greater progress. This never-tiring thirst is impossible, unless there were hidden in his breast an ideal of the Greatest Knowledge or Omniscience and of the Highest Holiness. A belief in the real existence of such an ideal or of an Omniscient and Holy God alone can render the thirst active and fruitful. And the belief in a God with these attributes, which has come to prevail in India as elsewhere, is to be accounted for only in this way.

I have thus briefly endeavoured to show how the objections brought by evolutionists and scientists against a religious belief do not hold, and what it is in the nature of man that renders the belief as natural to him as that in the existence of an external world. I have also indicated how our ordinary human nature, intellectual, moral as well as aesthetical, worked itself out into that belief in this country in ancient times. It is impossible to do justice to the subject within the compass of a letter, long though it has become. Whole books have been written upon it. But it has been my object to show to you that this is a subject which does not deserve to be disposed of lightly, and to the consideration of which an educated man should bring all the seriousness, gravity, and depth, of which he is capable. Scientists, relying only on the practical operation of the intellect without inquiring into the basis of that operation, assert that that operation does not lead them to God and the truths of religion, and they depend on expediency as the sole source of morality and guide to human conduct. In addition, however, to the mistake just alluded to in the intellectual sphere, they discard from their investigations the workings of the moral and spiritual faculties of mankind and the knowledge and experience accruing therefrom. But we are bound to accept the teachings of all our faculties alike, that is, of scientists as well as religious thinkers, saints and devotees, so far as they conform to reason and the moral sense. The foregoing observations are, it will be seen, based on this wide principle; and to supplement them I will add in the words of an English Theistic writer:

> These modern Men of (merely physical) Science are so absorbed in their material researches that they have actually dropped out of sight all the moral and spiritual sciences together; and they go about in the footsteps of Mr.

> Darwin, endeavouring to gather the grapes of morality off the thorns of Physics and Zoology. No such fruit grows on such trees. Spiritual truths are spiritually discerned, and moral truths are morally discerned, and neither the one nor the other are to be got at through researches into things which are not spiritual and not moral. Is it any marvel that so it should be? If God be Himself the holy all-pervading SPIRIT of the universe, the impersonated Law of Righteousness ruling in all worlds forever, must it not be in the spirits of His rational children that He chiefly reveals Himself and His holy will? To imagine that He, our God and Father, never speaks in the "still small voice" of conscience, but does speak in the earthquake and the thunderstorm – this is the Baal-worship of modern days.[12]

We have then in our own constitution a guide and warranty for our behaviour in this world – for ennobling ourselves with knowledge acquired by the exercise of our intellects as well as by the attainment to moral excellence and spirituality. In other words, man's duties on earth flow from his nature taken as a whole, and the question of these duties is not affected by the mode of his creation. For, however made, man is man; "the Highest Being",[13] to quote the words of Thomas Carlyle, reveals itself in him, and his aspirations are higher and heavenward, not lower and bestial – and that is enough to vindicate and establish the fact of man's duties as inculcated by religion on earth.

Science, of course, is not to be despised or deprecated. On the contrary it is not less essential than religion for the development and progress of humanity, the two being, in the language of Spencer, "necessary correlatives"[14] of each other. The continued attempts of science to draw away the veil of nature are praiseworthy, and it has thereby not only invented many means for increasing the material comforts of man but has moreover led to a knowledge of her secrets that has destroyed many errors and superstitions. For all this service to truth and humanity in its own line, it is entitled to respect and attention, but it cannot on that account be held to destroy the basis or usurp the place of religion any more than religion can be justified in denying to science its own proper sphere. The one has no more right to rule a designing mind or moral government out of the universe than the other to declare that the sun moves round the earth, not the earth round the sun. The universe without a creator embarrasses one great philosopher, and the sense of responsibility within and the starry hosts above arrest

12 Frances Power Cobbe, "The New Morality", in *Pamphlets on Vivisection* (London: Office of the Society for Protection of Animals from Vivisection, 1882), 4.

13 Thomas Carlyle, *On Heroes, Hero-Worship, and the Heroic in History* (New York: John Wiley, 1859), 9.

14 Herbert Spencer, *First Principles* (London: Williams and Norgate, 1862), 107.

another, and neither was bound by any restraint on his judgement. Between sacerdotalism on the one hand and agnosticism on the other, therefore, religion may well remain "free, reverent, intelligent, unhampered by incredible ecclesiastical traditions, and unclouded by scepticism".[15]

Nor can men and women do without that morality, which is so intimately allied to religion, and derives its highest sanction from it, and it is well to remember as some proof of this necessity that the history of godless eras among men has led to the reflection that, if there were no God, it would be beneficent for mankind to invent one![16] This is so because the foundation of society is essentially bound up with man's religious belief. There can be no thirst after holiness, unless the moral command revealed in the heart is rightly interpreted as the command of Him who rules the universe and has filled it with beauty and joy. And there can be no striving after it, if there is no faith in His mercy and readiness to guide and help poor erring humanity. Religion is the source of comfort to the afflicted heart and of hope to the despondent spirit. Moral progress, again, is essential to all progress: there can be no advance in the provinces of politics, social organisation, and even commerce and industry, unless conscience has become keen and directs the actions of man in all these matters.

It is true there are philosophers and thinkers who doubt or deny the existence of God, but they, accepting a brotherhood of men without the common fatherhood of God, in place of Him worship the Good of Humanity. Their number is small, and as long as men are men it must ever remain so, while the foundation of their general morality, however estimably it may be observed by a few of its individual followers, is equally feeble, and under the denial of a creative basis for the universe. The negation of a spiritual living fountain-source of inspiration for man is well indicated by the passage: "Human society [according to Diderot] is not an organism but a machine ... Virtue and duty, justice and injustice, are mere matter of convention".[17] And if a higher ideal is conceived by the highest spirits among them, it is traceable indirectly to the lofty standard of duty and virtue set up by religion before men from the earliest times, when philanthropic secularism in the modern sense was unknown, just as the worship of Good has followed in the wake of the worship of God. The mass of mankind, therefore, with all their weaknesses and errors, will stick to their faith in a Creator and Moral Upholder. A religious paper well says:

15 "Mansfield College and Its Future", *Pall Mall Gazette*, October 15, 1889, 2.

16 A famous line in a letter that Voltaire wrote to Frederick II of Prussia (James Parton, *The Life of Voltaire*, Vol. 2 (Boston: Houghton, Mifflin, and Co., 1889), 554).

17 W. S. Lilly, "Right and Wrong", *The Fortnightly Review*, Vol. 49, January 1888, 66, 79.

> For the purpose of winning a noble character it is essential that the mind of man be under the all-controlling influence of some pure and lofty aim. Various have been the answers given to the question, "What motive, purpose, or principle is most beneficial for individual man to live under so that he may attain the true ends of life?" Religion gives the sanest and surest answer, as it goes to the centre of life and covers all that concerns it, while all other answers but deal with the surface of existence. The love of God, active trust in Him in all the affairs of life, is the most rational, satisfactory, and powerful influence that can act on the mind. Religion has always answered thus, whether it was spoken by the lips of ancient heathen philosophical devotees, Hebrew prophets, or Christian saints and sages.[18]

The same remark holds good of the teachings of the philosophical devotees, saints, sages and prophets of all religions, Hindu, Moslem, Zoroastrian, and others. It is the recognition of the essential truths contained in them all that is the characteristic of the liberal religion of the present age of the world, the basis of which was laid in this country by the first representative and interpreter of its modern dispensation, the great Raja Rammohan Roy, and which has nothing to fear from any advance of human knowledge in any department, for truth is all one and no one branch of it can contradict another in reality.

I shall finally observe that if there be any sense in the notion or phrase, "the divine right of kings to rule", it is that kings and rulers are vicegerents of God on earth, because of all other men they invested with authority over the lives and fortunes of his creatures, their own fellow men, and this authority surely must be used not only wisely but also righteously. This relationship to the King of kings was recognised by the wise Alfred, who laid the first foundation of England's greatness, when he prefixed the divine commandments to the laws he himself promulgated. The Ranas of Udaipur (Mewar) – the proudest ruling dynasty extant in India, which dates its beginning from the times of Saxon Heptarchy and traces its descent to the solar race of the Rajas Ram and Dasharatha of Ayodhya, and the annals of which present as bright a record of courage and virtue as anywhere can be found, combined with as much of order and good government as the indigenous system of rule could permit – have styled themselves as but the ministers of Eklinga, the deity they worshipped. I would ask you to note these and similar instances you would find in history, and to imitate a late brother ruler[19] of a mighty nation in Europe, of whom it has been said: "He possessed what makes every man a king in his own circle, what made him a king among king – the strongest sense of duty, and the most noble

18 The source of this passage could not be traced.
19 Kaiser Wilhelm I (1797–1888), the Emperor of Germany.

uprightness, and with that a trust in God – that is, a faith in triumph of good and right, which even defeats like Jena and Olmütz, and even ingratitude like that of 1840, could not shake."[20]

Thus trustful before God and exalted among men, you must go to your work, and your first aim, i.e., first in importance and not simply in time (for it is an object which never can safely be lost sight of) is to ensure a strong sense of duty and spirit of piety among those who form the pillars of your State, the members of your aristocracy, and the heads of your bureaucracy, and to discountenance all want of principle. You must bear in mind the truth conveyed in the wise laws: "kings are the religionisers of the people"[21] and "as is the king, so are the subjects".[22] I quote these maxims not to suggest that you are to coerce men's consciences, or encourage a simulation of views not really held or the suppression of opinions sincerely believed in, but to show the supreme value of salutary example and of the necessity of maintaining a high standard of public morality and ensuring sound moral progress among the people. You will not be causing hardship to anybody by exacting a high standard of duty from those about you when even sceptics and agnostics bow to view:

And because right is right, to follow right
Were wisdom in the scorn of consequence.[23]

The same sense is conveyed by another familiar saying of the day that "morality is the nature of things",[24] by which what is meant is that just as the world is ruled by certain physical laws, so it is also ruled by moral laws. Even freethinkers and atheists admit this; and the admission of this great truth seems to me to lead to the other great truth – which, however, they do not admit – that those laws have an intelligent source. But freethinkers will always be few and the believers many in all countries, especially in India. Your subjects, therefore, have a claim to something more than mere secular good government at your hands.

You are in a sense the head of the Church as well as of the State. You know that large sums of public money are spent in the name of charity, of

20 Friedrich Max Müller, "Memorial Oration, March 1888", *The Leisure Hour: An Illustrated Magazine for Home Reading*, Vol. 37, 1888.
21 The source of this phrase could not be traced.
22 An old Pali proverb, "*Yata raja tata prajah*" (Alwis, "On Buddhism", 14).
23 Alfred Tennyson, "Oenone", in *Poems* (London: Edward Moxon & Co., 1866), 104.
24 The quote is from John Morley, *On Compromise* (London: Champman and Hall, 1877), 21. The original is Joseph Butler, *Analogy of Religion: Natural and Revealed* (New York: Harper & Brothers, 1857), 311.

religion, and of religious observances. And it behoves an enlightened prince so to dispose of them as to bring permanent good out of this expenditure of money raised from toiling subjects. As India never formed one community politically, as it was always cut up into innumerable states, and even the villages and towns composing a state were held together by but a loose bond of unity, and there never was a strong secular government that could weld the people into one nation, so in like manner there never was a strong church government or church organisation that could introduce unity into the religious faith of the people. And the result is that side by side with the elevated religious ideas of the Upanishads and the Bhagavad Gita we have a most irrational, complicated, and grotesque ritual, and even the fetishism and demonology of savages. Oftentimes beliefs and practices characteristic of the different stages of human progress are found illogically associated in the same mind, and it may even be questioned whether the higher religious thought of the country exercises at present any practical influence over the people. To this result the principle of exclusiveness that has always been at work in Indian society has no doubt materially contributed.

What the circumstances of the country now demand is that its higher religious thought should be brought once more into prominence, and what is inconsistent with it and characteristic of a rude and semi-civilised condition of society should be swept off, not through religious intolerance but by the introduction of a system of religious instruction, by means of books, lessons, lectures, and discourses. Culture and assiduous attention together with status and character are necessary for the maintenance and advancement of knowledge and proficiency in all lines of secular work. Yet in the highest subject of human concern and for purposes of spiritual ministration they are held of no account here at present! Is it a wonder that religion should lose its hold and efficacy on the public mind? In this state of things who but an educated and enlightened prince like your Highness can be expected to rescue it from its unmerited reproach? For religion has been brought into discredit far less by the advance of scientific knowledge than by its own practical surrender of its spiritual functions, replacing them by dead and senseless ceremonials conducted mechanically and performed by priests more ignorant and less advanced than many of the laity, and thus rendered capable of imparting to them little or no moral strength and no intelligent and elevating support amidst their sufferings or trials in their struggle with the world. To educate the former then and to raise their status so as to fit them to command the homage and reverence of the latter and carry out their exalted functions – and people of all faiths among the taxpayers have a claim in proportion to their numbers to state grants-in-aid of voluntary efforts, especially where there are no endowments in support of the cause

– is an important item in the scheme of religious education just mentioned and it is one of the means by which a high tone of morality and a love of righteousness is to be maintained among the people.

"Righteousness exalteth a nation",[25] so if a state is to be elevated among nations, its first ambition ought to be to aim at its own moral elevation. "The moral law", says one of the greatest of the living historians of the day, summing up the lessons, "is written on the tablets of Eternity. Justice and Truth alone endure and live. Injustice and Falsehood may be long-lived, but doomsday comes at last to them in French Revolutions and other terrible ways."[26] The same truth is differently expressed by another writer in these words:

> The philosophy of history teaches us that the law of retribution and eternal truth reigns in the world in spite of temporary violation on it. Nemesis never closes her eyes. She observes the actions and watches the fate of nations and "every guilty action is avenged in this world", according to the expression of the immortal Goethe.[27]

The law works with nations as it does with men, but it is not evident to a superficial examination. It is only by moral elevation in either case that its forfeit can be avoided. This moral elevation, however, is not practicable unless the state recognises the truth that men and their rulers are not the sports of chance, but are ruled by certain *moral laws*, the existence of which imply a lawgiver, and which, therefore, are not to be regarded as mere mechanical rules to be adopted for utilitarian convenience but constitute, so to say, an organic scheme connecting men with the Highest Being and directly concerning their progress and welfare here and hereafter. Without religion man is but the creature of a moment; with it he is the child of eternity. Without the moral strength and guidance which religion imparts, government would be a curse, society would be on the road to ruin, the arts and amenities of life, which add to happiness or mitigate suffering, sweeten fellow feeling and ennoble our nature in spite of its many aberrations under misguided influences or views of religion, would cease to exist; while without the consolations and aspirations it holds forth, even the most exalted among men will find his earthly existence to be not only a vanity of vanities but also a dreadful dream. If this terrific picture is not ordinarily realised here below, it is because human nature and its institutions are too much embedded in religion to admit of it, even though its dictates are so often

25 *The Holy Bible* (Cambridge: John W. Parker, 1844), Proverbs 14:34.

26 James Anthony Froude, *Short Studies on Great Subjects* (London: Longmans, Green & Co., 1868), 18.

27 C. J. Cooke, "Is the Fall of England Near?", *United Service Magazine*, Vol. 173, August 1889, 416.

disregarded by frail humanity; for it is the spirit of religion which tends to keep up what is proverbially recognised as "the salt of the earth".[28] Such is the supreme importance of the subject; and that is my excuse for dwelling on it at this great length.

Yours &c.,
A POLITICAL RECLUSE

28 *The Holy Bible*, Matthew 5:13.

Letter No. III[29]

On Education

MAHARAJA,

In my last, I have dwelt at some length on the basis of religious truth in general and pointed out the necessity and importance of example in moral principles in the ruler of a state to its good government and to the welfare and happiness of its people, which is identical with his own.

Now, before proceeding to the consideration of the next question, I think it as well to refer to one feature of his family arrangement which always has an important bearing on his own peace of mind and domestic felicity, and which often though invisibly thwarts the course of the administration, and sometimes results even in danger to the interests of the state. I here allude to the many evils resulting from the existence of a plurality of wives and sons born of different mothers. The desire of offspring is a natural instinct in man and is the source of pleasure and joy in early age, and of strength and support in declining years. It has, however, its drawback in jealousy, disputes, and enmities which are peculiarly developed under polygamy, and these evils show themselves virulently under circumstances which are calculated to produce alienations of feeling, and in which natural affection and love are replaced by bitterness, ill will, and inextinguishable rivalries tending to destroy all harmony and neutralise and mar what to distant spectators might appear to be enviable and unfailing means of happiness. These disturbing causes are particularly associated with the possession of wealth and power which cannot be equally divided among the rivals, and can, therefore, be possessed only by one individual at a time, and their force, therefore, is in direct ratio to the magnitude of the heritage.

Now this heritage is an apple of discord even among full brothers – i.e., sons by the same mother and father, but its power of producing dissension is greatly enhanced when they happen to be half-brothers, i.e., sons by different mothers, especially when the latter are all living at the same time, and are, as is generally the case, ever busy with poisoning the minds of their children against their brothers and sometimes even against their parents, and imbuing them with the spirit of their own feminine jealousies and fratricidal ideas of ambition and their relative rights and claims. The strife and heart-burnings, the plans and intrigues, and plots and counterplots, with which the very atmosphere of such a household must always be surcharged often make

29 This letter originally appeared in the *Indian Spectator* on December 8, 1889.

"lie uneasy the head that wears a crown";[30] and not only do they distract the powers and energies which should be given to the government, but, as already observed, they sometimes prove injurious to the interests, and even the existence, of the state itself. Nor are the causes of anxiety confined to the progeny alone. The mothers themselves, whether they have children or no and before or after they are born, occasion no little worry on their account. "Polygamy", truly observes the historian of Rajasthan,

> is the fertile source of evil, moral as well as physical, in the East. It is a relic of barbarism and primeval necessity, affording a proof that ancient Asia is still young in knowledge. The desire of each wife that her offspring should wear the crown is natural; but they do not always wait the course of nature for the attainment of their wishes, and the love of power too often furnishes instruments for any deed, however base.[31]

And the turmoil resulting from such a situation is intensified by the occasional presence of a smart and ambitious handmaid or two in the *zenana*.[32] The historian's contention may then be admitted at once that "the prince who can govern such a household, and maintain equal rights, when claims to pre-eminence must be perpetually asserted, possesses no little tact. The government of the kingdom is but an amusement compared with such a task, for it is within the *rawala*[33] that intrigue is enthroned."[34]

Against these domestic troubles and dangers, which defy the resources and darken the days of even a strong mind, the one sovereign remedy is strict monogamy, and I invite your Highness to set an example in this important respect too. Nor is this negative expediency its only recommendation. Monogamy is nature's own sacred law, and, therefore, its violation is invariably visited with distressing evils as its consequences. A holy and undivided partnership in mutual trust and love is possible only in monogamy which disassociates from the sacred union that marriage in the real sense of the term implies, all idea of sensuality, banishes jealousy and distraction from the family, and produces instead a heathy moral tone in the household and tends to the preservation of the mental and bodily vigour so much needed for a due discharge of the public duties. What nobler ideal, indeed, can a modern Indian Raja follow in this respect than that of Raja Ramchandra of ancient Ayodhya?

30 William Shakespeare, "King Henry IV", in *The Plays and Poems of William Shakespeare*, Vol. 17 (London: J. Rivington, 1821), 107.

31 James Tod, *Annals and Antiquities of Rajasthan*, Vol. 1 (Madras: Higginbotham & Co., 1873), 258.

32 A Persian term referring to the quarters in which women were secluded.

33 A Rajasthani term for the *zenana* or the secluded quarters for women.

34 Tod, *Annals and Antiquities of Rajasthan*, 258.

The old law no doubt sanctions a second wife where the first is found incapable of bearing children, particularly sons. The old conditions, however, are so completely changed that there is hardly need to regard the sanction in any other than a permissive light. Still in the present state of things I freely admit that this is a matter for each individual to decide for himself. All I say is that, speaking generally from the public point of view I do not think there is an absolute necessity for acting on it. In the first place, natural offspring is not quite so necessary to the personal help or happiness of the possessors of kingdoms, states, and large estates as to men in private life. In fact, as already observed, children born to inherit power and greatness generally, where they exist, are occupied more with the schemes and chances or exercise of their own power and position than with concern for their parents during their declining days. Indeed, instances are not wanting in which they wish for or compass their removal by death. Again, princes do not stand so much in need of the help and support of sons in their old age as men in humbler and less responsible conditions of life. Moreover, the devouring application of the doctrine of lapse has ceased to exist, and the state, like the family, can now, as it was before the days of the prevalence of that doctrine, be continued by adoption as well as by a male heir; and adoption offers a choice of a son and successor based on the possession of mental and moral qualities, which is denied to birth.

I am far, indeed, from deprecating the natural desire for offspring of one's own body even in rulers. I am only saying that where Providence denies its satisfaction, a plurality of wives cannot be indulged in without serious drawbacks; that strict monogamy accompanied by childlessness need not be considered a grave misfortune by rulers of states when men with enlightened minds and generous feelings, similarly situated in private life, are found to adopt and endow the public in place of the family; that the situation in question has its moral advantages; and that the absence of an heir can be made good by adoption. I must add that the rejection by the more enlightened among Indian rulers of the custom of polygamy and their adherence to the principle of monogamy is calculated to exert a healthy moral and social influence among their own brethren, their aristocracy, and their people, and through them on Indian society generally all over the land.

The next object to be attended to immediately is the training and education of your own children and of those who have in times past been and, if they choose, can under the present altered circumstances still remain the pillars of your state. "Nothing can possibly be said in favour of an uneducated class of rulers,"[35] says a distinguished ornament of the British aristocracy,

35 Lord Reay, "Twenty-Eighth Convocation", in K. Subba Rao, ed., *Convocation Addresses of the Universities of Bombay and Madras* (Madras: Lawrence Asylum Press, 1892), 226.

who is an eminent scholar himself and has proved a capable ruler among the governors of British India. But an uneducated class of rulers and an ignorant aristocracy have been, unfortunately, the rule rather than an exception in Indian society – not as an accident, as it appears to have been elsewhere, but as the inevitable result of the social polity which has ruled the destinies of this country for centuries past, and owing to which not only have ignorance and want of culture and absence of love or appreciation of knowledge characterised its kings and nobles as a class, but come to be looked upon even as their privilege, and the same feeling or fashion has descended to all men of wealth and position. This evil of a society which made knowledge the right and the occupation of an exclusive class has been aggravated by temporal tyranny and the consequent absence of any field for the exercise of genuine public spirit or incentive to any public virtue among the people at large. But now that a different dispensation has dawned on the land and knowledge has ceased to exist as the monopoly of a special cultus or caste, in their own interests it is needful that

> the highest representatives of the Indian nobility should not rely on the privileges of birth alone. First among their countrymen, they should now be first among them in the pursuit of knowledge.[36] Their duties are manifold, and they cannot be discharged properly unless they themselves rise to the highest level.[37]

Princes and nobles and men of position and means, therefore who have in the past relied only on their birth, and thus made the dreary history of that past, must turn a new leaf. The future cannot admit of their continuing ignorant and uneducated as before. Even for self-preservation they must add education to their birth and position, and you may well imitate Alfred the Great of Old England, who under somewhat similar circumstances not only founded schools and colleges for the instruction of the people but passed a law enforcing on the nobles the education of their children. But that education must be – and this is the point to which I wish here to draw your Highness's special attention – not the sickly and dry acquisition of the

36 *Original footnote*: Parenthetically, I might here mention that it was a keen perception of the absence of men of substance among the pursuers of knowledge that moved an observant European professor of an important Indian college, many years ago, to recommend either that these men should be invited to be educated, or the educated classes be substantially raised, but no change worth speaking of has occurred in the situation, and the representatives of the nobility have not yet, as a body, joined the pursuit of knowledge and learning. Nor have the classes which have been educated commenced to exemplify a disinterested love of knowledge or produced instances of a passionate devotion to its pursuit for its own sake and to the exclusion of any other aim or object of life, such as would impress the inheritors of wealth and position with the idea that liberal education can serve higher purpose than as a means of earning a livelihood and thus remove their indifference to it.

37 Lord Reay, "Twenty-Eighth Convocation", 226.

elements of knowledge gathered within their own homes with the aid of obsequious teachers who have to wait on their pleasures and whims, and amidst pandering parasites who ever humour and spoil their wards with adulation and make them wayward and capricious from early age. Under such influences the young rulers grow up wilful and are fed on the notion that no man ever speaks the truth except when it suits his own ends. Their moral nature is thereby destroyed and replaced by a general distrust of all truth and by faith in falsehood as a guiding principle of conduct. It is a serious thing, however, thus to poison the stream of life at its very source and great care ought to be taken to prevent it, especially as men generally are more prone to evil than to good, and impressions received in childhood are enduring. It is, therefore, a duty on the part of the parents so to arrange their surroundings that these impressions shall be of the best.

On this point there is a beautiful passage in Sir T. Martin's *Life* of the late Prince Albert the Good, consort of Her Majesty Queen Victoria, which might be appropriately quoted here. Of no duty was the Prince more careful than that of training his children and on this as in regard to many other subjects he constantly corresponded with his countryman friend and preceptor, Baron Stockmar.[38] It was a saying of this thoughtful preceptor that "a man's education begins the first day of his life".[39] Those who know how powerfully children are influenced by their surroundings cannot fail to be struck by the shrewdness of this remark or its special importance to persons on whose training, temper, and character depend the welfare or misery of numberless human beings.

> "Good education", the Baron wrote in a memorandum on the education of the Royal children so early as the 6th of March 1842, "cannot begin too soon." "To neglect beginnings", says Locke, "is the fundamental error into which most parents fall." In the child affections and feelings develop themselves at an earlier period than the reasoning or intellectual faculties. The beginning of education must, therefore, be directed to the regulation of the child's natural instincts, to give them the right direction and above all to keep the mind pure. "This", continues he, "is only to be effected by placing about children only those who are good and pure, who will teach not only by precept but by living example, for children are close observers and prone to imitate whatever they see or hear, whether good or evil."[40]

38 Christian Friedrich, titled Baron von Stockmar, was Secretary to King Leopold I of Belgium. He helped arrange the historic marriage between Leopold's nephew (Prince Albert of Saxe-Coburg-Gotha) and Leopold's niece (Queen Victoria). He then became a leading member of the Royal Court and advisor to both Victoria and Albert.

39 Theodore Martin, *The Life of His Royal Highness the Prince Consort*, Vol. 1 (London: Smith, Elder & Co., 1875), 97.

40 Theodore Martin, *The Life of His Royal Highness the Prince Consort*, Vol. 2 (London: Smith, Elder & Co., 1876), 175.

Equally instructive is the following extract from a letter of the Baron's to His Royal Highness:

> Continue, dear Prince, to insist upon honour, integrity, and order in your household. This inspires respect and gives a good example and warning to others. Believe me, a character and disposition like yours must be surrounded by none but the good, the loyal, and the well-disposed. At your present time of life you must have nothing to say to churlish, commonplace, repellent, or unconscientious people. Such characters, as indeed you say yourself, will only dwarf and drag you down. You must be fostered, developed and strengthened, for a time at least, by love and attachment, by unselfish and warm sympathy.[41]

This language pleasurably reminds one of the stories of ancient times in this country which relate that its Rajas used to place their sons for education not under commonplace or worldly-minded instructors but under men of talents and accomplishments, austere virtue, much learning, plain living and high thinking. But no one nowadays thinks of reviving either in form or spirit good old practices, which though long subverted by untoward circumstances, involuntarily command approbation. Everybody is a slave to existing custom and the highest wisdom and patriotism is held to consist in paying homage to this custom, even though it may be clearly injurious and unsuited to the requirements of the times.

However, I have said enough to indicate with clearness the kind of influences which should surround young princes and nobles at home or outside. Their general education must be a manly and vigorous prosecution of studies carried on in the classrooms of public schools and colleges, in competition with the intellect of the commonalty, under teachers inspired by a lofty regard for right and truth and in consequence commanding respect and homage from all who come under their influence and inspiring in them a love of high principles. The system under which they are trained, to quote for the third time the terse language of the scholar and statesman referred to above, must "not admit of dividing lines in educational institutions which are not the natural result of brain power, and all aristocracies are the better for a common struggle with those whose studies must be taken up in good earnest".[42]

Power and wealth, if rightly used, can conduce to great blessings, but if abused, they are the parents of equally great curses. Those, therefore, who are born to power and wealth must be taught to feel in the impressionable years of their life that those advantages have serious responsibilities attached to them, and the best mode of inspiring them with that feeling and that conviction is to educate them under conditions which would imperceptibly

41 Martin, *The Life of His Royal Highness the Prince Consort*, Vol. 1, 96.
42 Lord Reay, "Twenty-Eighth Convocation", 226.

lead them to compare themselves with the sons of the middle classes as men, and to feel that their true worth must depend on their mental and moral attributes which the accident of birth, wealth, and position cannot create but which are calculated to adorn and enhance it. In short, their education must tend to effect by a system what has happened to yourself by accident – they must be taught to feel that moral and intellectual excellence have greater claim to respect than mere rank and station and to realise that outside their homes they are no better than ordinary men, and that it is their behaviour as such that alone can reflect lustre or shame on their birth or their fortunes. To this end their education and treatment must be so conducted as to counteract the enfeebling and demoralizing or seductive effects of the position to which they are born. "The annals of Mewar", their chronicler observes,

> seldom exhibit those unnatural contentions for power from which no other Hindu State was exempt; this was owing to the wholesome regulation of not investing the princes of the blood with any political authority; and establishing as a counterpoise to natural advantages as artificial degradation of their rank, which placed them beneath the sixteen chief nobles of the State, which, while it exalted these in their own estimation, lessened the national humiliation when the heirs apparent were compelled to lead their quota in the *arrière-ban*[43] of the [Mughal] Empire.[44]

When a rule that is apparently so obnoxious to the self-love and dignity of absolute sovereigns finds acceptance in the proud and punctilious Rajput, there must surely be not a little virtue in it and therefore the principle which underlies it deserves to be noted.

Of no less significance and of even wider applicability is the lesson conveyed by the following incident concerning the commencement of the school education of the present Emperor of Germany when his grandfather ruled and his father was Crown Prince. Young William, says the report,

> was duly entered as a scholar at the public Grammar School of Kassel. Imitating the practice usually observed in the country, his parents took him to the Head Master, and like ordinary citizens had him examined in their presence. Before leaving, the Crown Prince stipulated that his son was not to be addressed as Royal Highness, but to be known only under the name of Prince William and treated in all respects like other boys.[45]

This little anecdote is full of much serious import, and every ruler, great or small (and indeed every nobleman and man of wealth and position) who

43 A medieval-era French term for the vassals summoned to undertake military service for their king.

44 Tod, *Annals and Antiquities of Rajasthan*, 335.

45 "The Heir to the German Throne", *Manchester Courier*, October 2, 1874, 3.

consults his own happiness and the true welfare of his family and his state, ought to treasure it as a precious counsel in the training of his children in their best interests; and I commend it to your Highness's attention.

When the princes, their nobles, and the classes from which their ministers and other officers of the higher grades are generally drawn, are thus educated to a right appreciation of the responsibilities of their positions, and begin to be, as it were, instinctively inspired by noble ambition to turn their talents, their opportunities, and their energies to achievements calculated to advance the public good, a most important factor of successful government may be said to have been secured. But, of course, you need not wait to begin your work till such education has taken deep root in your own state, for the seats of learning long ago planed by the British government in the different parts of the country are rearing educated men in numbers, from amongst whom you can find by careful selection competent persons ready to hand. The employment of qualified outsiders in preference to uncultivated men belonging to the state itself must act as an incentive to the latter to fit themselves for work and functions which are their birthright, but which in the true interests of the state as a whole it is found necessary to entrust to the former because of the latter's want of fitness for them. I have here spoken only of the education of higher orders; popular education will come in for consideration in its proper place hereafter.

Yours &c.,
A POLITICAL RECLUSE

Letter No. IV[46]

On Prudence

MAHARAJA,

I have, in my last, quoted a weighty declaration from the views of a cultured and wise statesman, that "nothing can possibly be said in favour of an uneducated class of rulers", and that "their duties are manifold, and they cannot be discharged properly unless they themselves rise to the highest level of knowledge".[47] A ruler's education, however, should be such as to fit him for the duties of his high office, and therefore, his general culture must be supplemented by specific studies bearing on the problems of government. "Lifelore is better than booklore":[48] It is greater and more fruitful to be learned in life than in books, and as rulers have to do with life and deal with men on a very extensive scale and with every variety and shade of character and condition, much more than any subject can individually have to do, they must study life more than books, or rather study books which open to view the springs of men's conduct in life. As to learning arts and acquiring accomplishments, rulers must aim at appreciating and encouraging them in others and not trying to excel in them themselves. Any undue attempt at the latter would not only present a pedantic example of misdirected ambition and culpable waste of energy, but might also lead to an equally culpable neglect of the work which constitutes their first and foremost duty. They, however, need not forego reading or intellectual engagements. Like all men of sound culture, they may have their favourite subjects of study to which they may devote their leisure, and for which they will be all the better able to stand the demands of their ordinary work and the strain of onerous duties and cares of state. Nor, further, can they neglect knowledge which bears even collaterally on that work or is calculated to advance its quality or success.

These lines of study will suggest themselves in the usual course. The one to which I wish here to invite your particular attention is rather of a character which will, along with your general education, serve as an incentive to your future task. I understand you have taken to reading *The Prince*.[49] Well, of course, it is a good book in its own way, if it is understood in the right spirit, but there is a general tendency to interpret it in a manner which has served to make the name of its author a synonym for low statecraft and

46 This letter originally appeared in the *Indian Spectator* on December 15, 1889.
47 Lord Reay, "Twenty-Eighth Convocation", 226.
48 The source of this phrase could not be traced.
49 Niccolò Machiavelli, *The Prince* (London: J. M. Dent, 1908).

unscrupulous cunning rather than far-seeing statesmanship and exalted wisdom. What I wish you to do is to study the lives of distinguished monarchs, wise statesmen, and philanthropic politicians or public men who have been inspired by constructive genius and a desire not so much to indulge in the exercise of their authority and parade their power and personality before the world as to devote their gifts and opportunities to the permanent good of their own countries, and have, by helping to advance the cause of human progress and to repress human wrongs, contributed also to the lasting benefit of mankind – such, for instance, as Alfred the Great, Albert the Good, Queen Elizabeth and Queen Victoria, Peter the Great and Frederick the Great, Akbar and Ahilya Bai Holkar, George Washington, Dr. Benjamin Franklin, Abraham Lincoln, Camillo Benso di Cavour, Jacques Turgot, William Pitt, Baron von Stein, Otto Bismarck, William Wilberforce, Richard Cobden, John Bright, and others. I may also suggest, as being worth your attention, the life of Shivaji, so far as it was reflected in his construction of the civil government and influenced by the spiritual teachings of Ramdas[50] and Tukaram,[51] as well as the career of Raja Sawai Jai Singh of Jaipur of scientific fame, founder of the modern city of Jaipur in Rajputana, which of late years has in education and some other matters shown a commendably liberal spirit and promises to take among the Rajput states in the future the place of precedence occupied by Mewar in the past; and also that of Zalim Singh[52] of Kota.

How can you find or make time for all these studies along with your public duties, private affairs, and personal concerns? Well, much would be practicable with regularity and method, by the adoption of which the great Akbar, who had to conduct the military and civil affairs of a vast empire, found leisure to preside over religious and philosophical discussions and even to attempt the elaboration of a new faith. For this purpose you may well adopt the truly royal rule of Alfred the Great who divided the night and day into three equal parts and out of them assigned eight hours to sleep, meal, and exercise, eight to public business, and eight to reading, writing, and devotion. You will then have time for everything and everything will have its proper time. I cannot resist the temptation to quote here as an

50 Samarth Ramdas (1608–81) was a poet and wandering ascetic whose works are renowned for their patriotic sentiments and their admiration for Chhatrapati Shivaji, the contemporaneous founder of the Maratha Empire.

51 Tukaram (1608–50[?]) was a poet and ascetic whose devotional songs and poems espousing egalitarianism have had profound influence on Maharashtrian culture and identity.

52 Zalim Singh (1740–1824) had been Regent and *dewan* of Kota from 1771 until 1824. A shrewd but honorable diplomat, under his command Kota prospered even as the rest of Rajputana was devastated by unending war.

illustration of the great fruitfulness of this methodical use of time the following description of the varied activities displayed by the late Prince Consort:

> His comprehensive gaze ranged to and fro between the base and the summit of society, and examined the interior forces by which it is kept at once in balance and in motion. In his well-ordered life there seemed to be room for all things – for every manly exercise, for the study and practice of art, for the exacting cares of a splendid Court, for minute attention to every domestic and paternal duty, for advice and aid towards the discharge of public business in its innumerable forms, and for meeting the voluntary calls of an active philanthropy: one day in considering the best form for the dwellings of the people; another day in bringing his just and gentle influence to bear on the relations of master and domestic servant; another in suggesting and supplying the means of culture for the most numerous classes; another in some good work of almsgiving or religion. Nor was it a merely external activity which he displayed. His mind, it is evident, was too deeply earnest to be satisfied in anything, smaller or greater, with resting on the surface. With a strong grasp on practical life in all its forms, he united a habit of thought eminently philosophic; ever referring facts to their causes, and pursuing action to its consequences. Gone though he be from among us, he, like other worthies of mankind who have preceded him, is not altogether gone; for, in the words of the poet:
>
> Your heads must come
> To the cold tomb;
> Only the actions of the just
> Smell sweet and blossom in their dust.
>
> So he has left for all men, in all classes, many a useful lesson, to be learnt from the record of his life and character.[53]

His Royal Highness was not a ruling sovereign himself but only the consort of one, and occupied a somewhat delicate position in the state, and consequently his political services to the country were indirect in form. Yet the work he did was equal in amount and importance to the public interests to any which falls to the lot of many a ruling sovereign, and therefore his life is as much worthy of study and imitation as that of any sovereign ruler, statesman, or philanthropist.

Now you might well enquire what I mean by recommending the perusal and study of the lives mainly of kings and warriors and statesmen, who have distinguished themselves on the battlefield and taken part in political revolutions and carving out kingdoms, to an Indian Raja who finds himself stripped by the British paramount power of all field for the display of similar ambition, who cannot even communicate with his brethren except through

53 William E. Gladstone, *Gleanings of Past Years, Vol. I: The Throne, and the Prince Consort; The Cabinet, and Constitution* (London: John Murray, 1879), 4–5.

its watchful agents, whose privileges of making wars and treaties have been taken away and lodged with that power within folds of solemn engagements, and who has in the very commencement of this series of letters been enjoined a strict fidelity to those engagements among his first public duties.

My reply is short and simple. It is true you are not now an independent ruler, like your forefathers, at liberty to open and conclude hostilities with whom you please, and that all your activity must be confined to peaceful operations within your own dominions. But, Maharaja, it must be remembered that peace has its victories as well as war, that the victories of peace are nobler and more beneficent to humanity, if less glittering or less bloody than those of the battlefield, and that it is the very dispensation which has deprived you of the opportunity of achieving the latter that renders it possible for, and even incumbent on, you and your brother princes to pursue the former. What is it, then, that you have to do? It is, to my mind, nothing short of *founding a state*. Your ancestors, [Pilaji] and [Damaji], as I have already observed, by their valour and wisdom founded a dynasty and carved out an estate. It is now yours to construct out of these materials a *state*.

But, it may again be asked, why should you disturb the present easy style of administration and go to the trouble of a change which on the face of it would be no easy task? I might reply, briefly, that on the one hand it is the highest fulfilment and wisest, and, therefore, the most beneficial discharge of an onerous duty which, however much it may be paltered with, cannot be got rid of; and, on the other, it is demanded by the spirit and the circumstances of the times which cannot be resisted with impunity, and, therefore, duty and interest alike demand at any rate an earnest attempt at its performance.

It is an old Indian saying that the possession of earthly rule is followed by the relegation of the soul of the possessor to the dark regions after death. And, to say the truth, all human government generally, and absolute rule especially, whether carried on by individual or corporate authority, partly from the fallibility of man's judgement but more from his self-seeking and other moral faults of one kind or another, leads so much to failure or denial of justice, to abuse of power, to oppression over human beings, and violation of their rights and of God's law, that its natural consequences to those on whose heads that load of the sins of omission and commission rests, may well be accepted as embodied in the popular maxim. And it is to avoid this fate after death that ideal kings of old are represented, towards the declining days of their lives, as making over the care and burden of the rule to their youthful heirs, and themselves retiring into private life so as to be able to devote their old age to penance and devotion. But it is better surely for a ruler as it is to a private individual in relation to his sphere of work to deprive power of its sting of abuse so far as it is practicable, and to exercise it for the good of his subjects for the whole of his life or as much of it as he chooses, than to divide that life into two periods – one of which is given up to its guilty use and the other to penitential retirement.

This, however, is only by the way. We are not directly concerned here with the next world, and it is more to my purpose to observe that the inconveniences of absolute rule even in this life are not few nor small. An absolute ruler – and a dynasty is only a succession of rulers, and so what holds good of the link applies equally to the whole chain that is made up of such links – knows not the human happiness which the humblest private individual enjoys. His subjects look up on him as an enemy; his servants as a game; his relations as a rival – the nearer the relationship, the greater the envy and hatred; he cannot be sure that his food, his medicine, and even his drinking water – albeit served in golden goblets – will be free from deadly poison! And yet, strange to say, while everyone about him is on the alert to get for himself or for his clique what benefit he can out of him or his possessions, none but the ruler alone can feel anxious for or interested in the safety or the prosperity of those possessions! Such a spectacle ought then to be suggestive of a lesson, if not a warning. "Lucky Prince of Wales! Poor Czar of all the Russias!"[54] exclaims an observant French writer, and the exclamation hardly needs to be explained to an oriental reader, and yet there is a great difference even from this point of view between absolute rule generally in Europe and in Asia, all in favour of the former. For, however despotic a European sovereign may be, he is subject to restraints of public opinion, ministerial counsel, and constitutional usages, which have obtained nowhere in Asia, except to some extent in China, though the Chinese government is popularly considered to be as unmitigated a despotism as any in the East.

There is another drawback on this species of rule, which might also be alluded to here, and that is, its enervating effect on the mental and moral vigour of the ruler personally, and through him on the welfare of his charge. A late able Anglo-Indian statesman is reported to have made this significant remark when he heard someone speak about the wrong-headedness manifested by an African despot:

> He is probably more or less mad. Men sitting up in solitary grandeur with despotic powers generally become so. You can observe it with our Indian Viceroys after a few years of Supreme Government. They get their heads turned: they cannot help it.[55]

If this observation be correct, to however small an extent, it would supply abundant reason for the Government of India in their Foreign Office and

54 Max O'Rell, *John Bull and His Island* (New York: Charles Scribner's Sons, 1889), 182.

55 *Pall Mall Gazette*, December 4, 1888, 4. The remark was made by Henry Bartle Frere, the former Governor of Bombay, with respect to the "intractability" of Yohannes IV of Abyssinia.

for its political officers accredited to native princes to treat the aberrations of the latter with some sympathy while helping them out of their evil ways, as it should teach the wiser of the princes themselves to set well-defined but safe limits to the exercise of their power. For, the Viceroy, though highly educated and fitted by talent and general experience for the post he holds, is after all a subject himself, liable to be called to account at every step. He is bound by rules and responsible to higher authority, and he holds office only for a *lustrum*,[56] while the Rajas subject to his control have very little education and training, they rule for life and inherit irresponsible power and authority. That in spite of these and similar other disadvantages, the native princes of India possess the mental stamina they do, speaks much for the innate capacities of the race, and affords a reasonable hope that with a few well-considered changes of method and a considerate and sympathetic treatment and help, their administration of their territories may be advanced to the requisite standard in the not distant future.

But to return to the point in hand. It is not domestic enemies alone, however, that an absolute ruler has to dread. Neighbours, powerful or ambitious, are even more to be feared, because, while the former only aim at supplanting him on the *gaddi*, the latter would subvert the *gaddi* itself. It is true the paramount power in the country now has guaranteed the permanent maintenance of the existing Native States against internal and external foes. But while the conditions of protection against the latter are defined and clear, the nature of their obligations in respect of security against the former and, therefore, indirectly against itself, are vague and indefinite, and might be inferred from one of the grounds assigned for annexations in the past *viz.*, the existence of misrule. The dominions annexed were regarded as the estates of the ruling families and not as states in which the rulers and the ruled by an explicit – I say *explicit* because in all governments, however despotic or backward, all relations are *implied* – reciprocation of powers and privileges, rights and obligations, formed so many organic societies, the heads of which could not be injured – much less removed – without their respective bodies politic feeling the shock. The internal protection of the states, with all their powers, privileges, and dignity, therefore, is far from unconditional, though the conditions may not be expressed clearly and definitely or in detail in the treaties. A late Viceroy, speaking at a dinner given by one of the leading princes of India, is reported to have said:

> Indeed, I do not know in the world a more enviable position than that of the Princes of India, enjoying as they do under the aegis of the British *imperium* an absolute immunity from those anxieties by which chiefly European States are perpetually exercised; namely, dangers threatening them without, and the fear of revolution within. They are able to give their whole time and attention

56 Latin term for a public sacrifice conducted every five years in ancient Rome.

> to the most interesting and the noblest task which can occupy the human mind – the advancement of their States along the road of progress, and the increase in material welfare and happiness of the millions who are entrusted to their charge. Such a field as this is amply sufficient to satisfy the widest ambition or the most soaring aspiration that ever entered the heart of man; and not only so, but they have the additional satisfaction of knowing that her Majesty and her Government have but one desire; that is, to extend to them, on all occasions, the heartiest sympathy and assistance, to do everything in their power to augment their prestige, support their authority, and enhance their personal consideration. *In return we ask them for nothing but that they should administer their States wisely and beneficently in accordance with their lights and the local requirements of their situation*; for the long years of traditional and unswerving loyalty, exhibited through many generations on their part, renders even the mention of such a requirement as fidelity to their Sovereign unnecessary.[57]

I have italicised the clause which, for my purpose, is the most important, but I am free to confess that this eloquent passage, which was spoken, as it were, demi-officially and, in a sense, impersonally at a festive gathering, is defective inasmuch as, while indicating clearly the duties of the Indian princes and their felicities, it ignores entirely obvious considerations on the other side of the question. For instance, it does not even remotely allude to the one source of anxiety which mars the happiness of the princes and often makes them feel the lot of the humblest *subjects* of the British government to be enviable compared to that of its feudatory *allies*. For, it is a very common remark, which finds utterance from every mouth wherever an illustration of the truth occurs, that while the former have the privilege of an open trial and protection of the law even when charged with the worst of crimes, the latter do not share its benefit even in cases of suspected misbehaviour. This feeling of course will not find expression on conventional occasions or in formal communications, but to anyone who is acquainted with the undercurrents of thought and feeling it is as clear as his own existence. Nor does the extract made above allude to the internal difficulties of the princes in the matter of administrative reform or even good government on existing lines. I must, however, reserve the consideration of both these points for my next; and mean time, Maharaja, I remain,

Yours &c.,
A POLITICAL RECLUSE

57 Frederick Temple Blackwood, "Banquet at Hyderabad", in *Speeches Delivered in India: 1884–8* (London: John Murray, 1890), 138.

Letter No. V[58]

On Relations with British India

MAHARAJA,

The nature of the relations existing between the British government and the Native States has a very important bearing on the aim and object of these letters, and the present number, therefore, must be devoted to the consideration of that question.

Under the treaties and engagements, which exist between the two parties, every Indian prince is afforded by the paramount power complete protection against danger from without or revolution from within. But that power in dealing with the princes has practically to rely on the reports and views of its own officers who act the part of their censors and critics more generally than of friends or even unprejudiced judges. The result of this arrangement is that the very existence of the prince as a ruler depends too often on the opinion of a single individual and he, too, an alien in race, language, religion, sentiment, and habits of thought. The mischief arising from this divergency is further increased by the fact that the latter is immeasurably superior to the former in education and culture, and possesses, in his own individual training, experiences and aptitudes for business, and still more in the system of graded authority and constitution of the government he serves and represents, immense advantages over his diplomatic or political charge in the conduct of every official transaction and especially in every dispute between them.

This serious drawback in the position of the Indian princes, as I have already remarked, is not noticed in the passage from the Viceroy's speech I have quoted in my last letter. The passage in question merely describes the principle of interference, or more correctly the condition of non-interference, in general terms and therefore reads easy and smooth, but the difficulty which it covers is felt and perceived whenever it has to be applied to specific cases – and this difficulty arises from the very nature of the situation. For, you, Maharaja, and your brethren, are not now independent sovereigns so that the paramount power could have no concern with, or nothing to say to, the manner of your internal administration, nor are you its official subordinates to be dictated by it, in detail, regarding it. You are in *subordinate alliance* with it and herein lie the advantages as well as the difficulties of your situation; for, if you have not to defend yourselves against foreign or domestic foes, you have to perform the not very easy task of keeping a distant arbiter of your fate pleased through his agents, whose

58 This letter originally appeared in the *Indian Spectator* on December 22, 1889.

judgements, though dictated by pure motives and good intentions, are liable to be influenced not only by your real faults and shortcomings, but may also be unconsciously misled or warped by their varying temperaments, their personal opinions or prejudices, or by the workings of adverse parties or cliques, and even by a concern for the interests of the paramount power itself whether as they are in reality, or as its representatives may conceive them to be.

Hence it was, I take it, that the Viceroy,[59] in whom genial frankness and instinctive love of fair play were united to other qualifications for that high office and who, from a sympathetic personal intercourse with your brethren, perceived the injurious effects of these causes on the relations between them and his own government, styled the Political Agents, "dangerous officials".[60] But it is plain that it is the system or rather the anomalous position in which they are placed at the courts of native princes that makes "dangerous officials" of gentlemen who, outside that system or position, make more safe and efficient administrators and officers. This evil, however, is not new and the root of it is thus noticed in Col. Tod's[61] *Annals and Antiquities of Rajasthan*,

> With our present system of alliances, so pregnant with evil from their origin, this fatal consequence (far from desired by the legislative authorities at home) must inevitably ensue. If the wit of man had been taxed to devise a series of treaties with a view to an ultimate rupture, these would be entitled to applause as specimens of diplomacy.
>
> There is a perpetual variation between the spirit and the letter of every treaty; and while the internal independence of each State is the groundwork, it is frittered away and nullified by successive stipulations, and these positive and negative qualities continue mutually repelling each other, until it is apparent that independence cannot exist under such conditions. Where discipline is lax, as with these feudal associations, and where each subordinate vassal is master of his own retainers, the article of military contingents alone would prove a source of contention. By leading to interference with each individual chieftain, it would render such aid worse than useless. But this is a minor consideration to the tributary pecuniary stipulation, which, unsettled and undetermined, leaves a door open to the system of espionage into their revenue accounts – a system not only disgusting but contrary to treaty, which leaves "internal administration" sacred. These openings to dispute and the general laxity of

59 Richard Bourke (1822–72) had served as Chief Secretary for Ireland and then as Viceroy from 1869 until 1872. Better known as Lord Mayo, he was highly regarded by Indians, especially the aristocracy of the Native States.

60 *Subodh Patrika*, December 6, 1885.

61 James Tod (1782–1835) served in the Bengal Army in the Anglo-Maratha Wars and then was Political Agent in Rajputana. A celebrated Orientalist, he is best remembered for his *Annals and Antiquities of Rajasthan* (1829).

> their governments coming in contact with our regular system present dangerous handles for ambition: and who so blind as not to know that ambition to be distinguished must influence every vicegerent in the East? While deeds in arms and acquisition of territory outweigh the meek *éclat* of civil virtue, the periodical visitation to these kingdoms will ever be like the comet's – *foreboding change to princes.*
>
> Our position in the East has been, and continues to be, one in which conquest forces herself upon us. We have yet the power, however late, to halt, and not anticipate her further orders to march. A contest for mud-bank has carried our arms to the Aurea Chersonesus, the limit of Ptolemy's geography. With the Indus on the left, the Brahmapootra to the right, the Himalayan barrier towering like a giant to guard the Tatarian ascent, the ocean and our ships at our back, such is our colossal attitude! But if misdirected ambition halts not at the Brahmapootra, but plunges in to gather laurels from the teak forest of Arracan, what surety have we for these Hindu States placed by treaty within the grasp of our control?
>
> But the hope is cherished, that the same generosity which formed those ties that snatched the Rajputs from degradation and impending destruction will maintain the pledge given in the fever of success, "that their independence should be sacred"; that it will palliate faults we may not overlook, and perpetuate this oasis of ancient rule, in the desert of destructive revolution, of races whose virtues are their own, and whose vices are the grafts of tyranny, conquest, and religious intolerance.[62]

Much of the grave catastrophe dreaded and also the fond hope cherished by the historian have been simultaneously realised. For the reflections quoted above were published in 1829 since which date gigantic changes have taken place, and the torrent of British power on the Indian continent has overflowed all its natural boundaries and is still showing a tendency to run further east, north, and west. It has swallowed the whole of Burma and is threatening Afghanistan and trying to scale even the giant barrier of the Himalayas. And yet, strange to say – this is undoubtedly, like the rest of the occurrences, a providential event – many of the Native States within those borders, and especially those respecting the independence of which the gallant writer so pathetically pleaded, have remained intact and safe. This political miracle was due to the moral crisis created by the Mutinies of 1857–58 which put an end to the existence of the East India Company. That Corporation had risen to political dominion from the smallest beginnings and, though it had at last attained the position of a superior to all the native potentates, its relations with them were not free from the jealousies and suspicions of a rival in power. But this situation changed when the Company was superseded by, and the native rulers came face to face with, the British Crown, and

62 Tod, *Annals and Antiquities of Rajasthan*, 111.

being reduced formally to the status of feudatories, were guaranteed permanent safety with the concession of the right to adoption.

This change in the position of the Native States, however, has not deprived their relations with the paramount power of the objectionable features ascribed to them by Colonel Tod. It has only changed their mode of operation, and thus it is that the Residents or Political Agents have become, or rather continue to be, even in the altered circumstances of the case, "dangerous officials" to the Native States, instead of being, as they are supposed and fitted to be, their best friends and safest guides. For, these states have now no fear of being conquered or annexed, but they are more liable to the danger of a disintegration and supersession of their authority by that of the British government within their own limits. Even sixty years ago Colonel Tod saw reason to remark, "That our alliances have this tendency cannot be disputed. By their very nature, they transfer the respect of every class of subjects from their immediate sovereign to the paramount authority and its subordinate agents."[63] The truth is that the institution of Residents and Political Agents is suitable and can work fairly and satisfactorily only when it is natural, or, in other words, subsisting between governments and states with reciprocal obligations and privileges. For these representatives in that case serve not only to watch the interests of their own governments, but also to explain and remove misunderstandings, to ensure equal and fair dealing and thereby to preserve peace and amity between them and the powers they are accredited to.

But here the arrangement is practically all one-sided. It is true the British Political Agents are placed in Native States not only to guard the interests of the paramount power, but also to aid and advise the native princes, and not to annoy or injure them. It is undeniable, however, that their main function after the care of the interests of their own government is the check and criticism of the conduct of their charge. This circumstance, joined to the many causes of the divergence between them and the princes already mentioned, often tends to make them unsympathetic critics and "dangerous officials", to whose vanity or love of power are ascribed measures of interference which their government may adopt towards the princes, but which being looked upon as acts of highhandedness, procure for the authors or supporters of misrule, the public sympathy that is due to its victims. This state of things is, in the end, baneful in its effects on the trustful and cordial relations which ought to exist between the paramount power and the feudatory states, but it must continue as long as constitutional remedies are not adopted.

Now, what should these remedies be? I cannot undertake to answer this question with any confidence, but there is little doubt that the result to be

63 Tod, *Annals and Antiquities of Rajasthan*, 113.

aimed at is that on the one side individual political officers must be deprived of the powers they now possess virtually of deciding the fates of ruling houses and their thousands of subjects, and on the other the forces which are inherently arrayed against the cause of good government in the states themselves must be overcome. How is this double reform to be secured? It has been remarked by someone that the political officers are intended to be the mentors of the native princes, but that the system is also calculated sometimes to make them their tormentors, and such a situation cannot but tend to weaken and demoralise the latter out of that energy and honourable ambition which the extract from the Viceregal speech quoted in my last letter appeals to and invites them to put forth. Self-respect is "the cornerstone of every virtue with States as with individuals",[64] and it cannot flourish in a ruler whose public repute or position as a ruler and even peace of mind are dependent entirely on the opinion, if not the breath, of an individual political officer who is practically both his accuser and judge.

A radical change must, therefore, be made in the position of the Political Agent, and the best mode of effecting the change seems to me, after giving the question all the thought I can, to be that he, the political officer, should be held responsible *along with the Raja* for the good government of the state to whose court he is attached. And should he, in his discharge of that or any other duty, be dissatisfied with the conduct of the latter and bring forward any accusation against him, the function of deciding on the merits of the charges or questions which may be raised must be left not to the Foreign Department of the Government of India to which the political officer is a subordinate and under the direct instructions of which he acts at every step in each case, but to a special tribunal composed of the peers of the accused and the representatives of any of the other interests which may be concerned, and presided over by a British jurist – a tribunal the finding of which could be trusted to be free from bias or influences calculated in any way to be prejudicial to justice. A satisfactory solution of this problem might well be urged on the attention of the Viceroy personally by the Indian Rajas on suitable opportunities, for of course it is a very delicate question and it would be impossible for them to deal with it in any formal manner, but this very circumstance renders the existing position of things all the more unsatisfactory. Indeed, almost any other arrangement, even leaving the states to their own devices, would be preferable to the present under which the Viceroy with the Foreign Department and its subordinates virtually are accusers, jury, and judge; and His Excellency, while in that capacity practically deposing a Raja, has, as head of the entire government, almost with the same pen, to address the condemned ruler as "My Honoured and

64 Tod, *Annals and Antiquities of Rajasthan*, 111.

Valued Friend"! This is, of course, a diplomatic necessity of the situation, but it sounds to common sense as morally grotesque, and what is morally grotesque can hardly be politically wise or even expedient in the long run.

A proper adjustment of the relations between the Government of India or rather its Political Agents and the rulers of the Native States is, therefore, urgently needed, and so long as this question is not fairly settled, I venture to think it unsafe to assume that these rulers have the satisfaction of knowing, in the words of the Viceregal utterance quoted in my last, that "Her Majesty and Her Government have but one desire; that is, to extend to them, on all occasions, the heartiest sympathy and assistance, to do everything in their power to augment their prestige, support their authority and enhance their personal consideration".[65] This conviction, however, is to be ascribed not to any disbelief in the sincerity of the kindly intentions or declarations of that government but must naturally result from the unsatisfactory character of the arrangements by which its relations with them are maintained. A modification of those arrangements, therefore, as already explained, is clearly called for, and this change, as has been hinted at above, must be calculated to overcome the difficulties which naturally beset the position of native princes in regard to good government in their territories.

The native princes being absolute rulers, they appear at first sight to be the sole source of all obstacles to any change, but a nearer acquaintance will show that view to be not quite correct. As a body they are undoubtedly intelligent; they are not all equally devoid of a love for their subjects or the desire to govern them well; yet the general complaint is that their rule is oppressive. How is this to be accounted for? The fact is the princes are after all individuals and are not only subject to the unwholesome influences of their early training but in the absence of any system are helplessly in the hands of their surroundings. Now, these surroundings consist of vested interests of all sorts in whose eyes the one merit on which the existence of the state rests is indiscriminate charity to idlers of sorts and indulgence to the privileged and official classes, and the one sin is strictness in the expenditure of the taxes or justice to the toiling *ryot*. In such a situation zeal for reform or love of economy cannot be expected to flourish; nor can any reforms, if introduced by a strong-willed ruler, be trusted to be safely carried out for any time or continued by a successor. Is it then a wonder that they should let well alone? Here is an illustration which relates to a time not a decade old. A very shrewd, intelligent, and energetic prince was interviewed by a disinterested visitor, who urged on him the advisability of his spending money on the comforts and conveniences of his people. In reply he was addressed thus, when the two were alone:

65 Blackwood, "Banquet at Hyderabad", 138.

> Brother, what use setting apart lakhs of rupees in a lump for Public Works? Do you think we need prompting in such a case? I should like very much to have reservoirs for my people, and roads and gardens. If I could, I would gladly build a railway, too. You ask why I don't, and you are disappointed. My heart may not be as warm as yours – when you are poor, you can afford to be extremely liberal. But, brother, will you enjoy parting with your lakhs even for charity, when you cannot be sure that an account will be rendered to you? When I give a lakh, and find a work done for forty thousand, and when I am snubbed in private or even officially insulted if I ask to be shown the details of construction, what, do you think will be my feelings? I know I am not to carry my wealth with me; let me reserve it for my heirs who may be better able than myself to have sixteen annas worth for a rupee.

Now this standard of return for money is perhaps too patriarchal to be secured in any public expenditure even when hedged in by a system of checks and counterchecks, but situated as the native administrations are, without the help of any reliable agency or system or even the sympathy and support of a strong public opinion, is it impossible to sympathise with them in their difficulties?

I may cite another instance of a Raja equally intelligent, who, when asked to raise the salaries of his officials to prevent them from levying exactions from his people, answered: "What would be the use? They will get the increased salaries and continue the exactions all the same." Here was a confession of helplessness even in an absolute ruler, to which I have already referred. This same prince had employed an educated gentleman and put him in charge of the judicial work. In a case coming up from the districts his officer issued an order which was sent for execution in due course. In a few days, however, one of the parties came back loudly complaining that the order had not been executed and the delay was hurtful to his interests. The explanation was this. There was an able and experienced courtier of the old school, a native of the place, who had filled the highest posts in the state, but who, though not in the service any longer (in fact he had been debarred from office for some misbehaviour at the instance of the British government), because of his knowledge of state affairs and his large following possessed influence with the *darbar* and in consequence was resorted to by all disappointed suitors to gain their ends. The party dissatisfied with the decision in the case referred to obtained through his influence secret instructions to the district official to suspend execution of the judicial order. When this interference with the course of justice was resented by the highest judicial officer, the old gentleman remarked in all sincerity that, if all things were to be managed straight in native as in British territory, what should constitute a *Rajwada* or a Native State? It is some twenty years since the two incidents just related occurred, and during this interval people in power even in the Native States have learnt the advantages secured by liberal professions and love of progressive *forms* of administration, and so an honest avowal like that of the old courtier will not be easy to obtain in these days, yet I doubt if the old obstacles to reform are less powerful now.

How, then, is reform to be introduced and maintained in the face of those obstacles? It has been already shown that, though a ruler is inclined to introduce measures of reform, the inertia of his surroundings and the vested interests arrayed against the change would thwart their successful execution even during his own lifetime and the chances after him would be still more uncertain unless there was continuous extraneous help against which such obstacles would be powerless. This help would be effectually forthcoming if the Political Agent were to share with the Raja his responsibility for efficient administration. In that case, the political officer will be able to realise the difficulties in the way of the prince better than he now can, and then, but not till then, will his authority and influence be truly utilized in the promotion of good government in the state. The anomaly of the present system is that the Rajas are backward and, even if they are educated, their surroundings rivet them to that condition. To enable them to rise above it, which the British government not unreasonably expects of them, it is bound to give them the needful aid especially when it can do it without inconvenience or sacrifice. And this, I submit, it can do by holding its political officers formally responsible along with the native rulers for the character of their administrations. Then truly can the native rulers be made sincere friends and friendly allies "leaning on the dominant power by seeking its counsel and following its example";[66] and thus the same measure which improves the character of the relations of the British government with the native princes will also tend powerfully to advance their administrations in the wished-for direction.

It is time, I submit, this question received earnest consideration. But how is it to be secured? The position of the princes themselves as already observed is too delicate to permit of their moving in the matter. The subject would seem properly to fall within the province of the Government of India which has to initiate as well as carry out measures of policy for the Indian empire. But none the less does it require to be urged on the attention of that authority as well as on that of the government in England by the general public, which is interested in a just, safe, and sound imperial policy and in the permanency of the relations between India and England. I take it for granted that the existence of well-managed and friendly Native States presided over by trusted and trusting rulers would be a far greater advantage to British

66 F. A. H. Elliot, *The Rulers of Baroda* (Bombay: Education Society's Press, 1879), 247.

India than their total absence. To the government it would be a source of moral strength as it is an element in its political greatness; to the people, of social and economic benefits; but their present relations with the British government are not calculated to produce the greatest good the situation is capable of yielding.

The British government further is morally bound to cherish the Native States at their highest, because, in the first place, after a century of scrupulous observance of engagements, an English historian could truthfully declare that "English valour and English intelligence have done less to extend and to preserve our Oriental Empire than English veracity";[67] and secondly, the English nation through their sovereign has solemnly proclaimed to India, that "while we will permit no aggression upon our dominions or our rights to be attempted with impunity, we shall sanction no encroachment on those of others. We will respect the rights, dignity and honour of native princes as our own."[68] This declaration was made in 1858 when it was acknowledged that the Native States had acted as breakers to the storm which had immediately preceded that year.

In the third place, the burden of governing British India itself is proving heavy and a desire to share it with the Indian princes has begun to find expression from the lips of its governors, and offers of cooperation in one important department, the military, have already been sought or welcomed. But this cooperation cannot be so hearty or successful as it should be nor can it react so beneficially on the conduct of affairs in Native States as it ought unless the same spirit is extended to the political relations between the two parties, and naturally the military or administrative rapprochement must proceed from the political as its basis.

Then, again, this Indian dominion, the major portion of which willingly allowed itself to pass into English hands and was not strictly speaking "conquered by the sword", has been ruled not on the principles of force and repression but on those of an enlightened and liberal policy. Still, partly from the nature of the situation and partly from other causes which cannot be entered into here, it will, I imagine, be long before the political aspirations of the people can find full scope under British rule, or any large share of real power and initiative will be placed in their possession. On the other hand, I believe all sober statesmen hold that a fifth of the human race cannot always be governed under leading strings without the risk of a natural revulsion in some shape or other and sooner or later, and that it is both

67 Thomas Babington Macaulay, "Lord Clive", in Hannah Trevelyan, ed., *The Works of Lord Macaulay*, Vol. VI (London: Longmans, Green & Co., 1866), 419.

68 Proclamation by the Queen in Council to the Princes, Chiefs and People of India, November 1, 1858, 1 (British Library, IOR/L/PS/18/D154).

wise and just to leave it a fair and unrestricted field for autonomy in all lines of public life and national existence. The need and the utility of such field for the exercise of indigenous talent is evident from the fact that this talent which would remain without scope in British territory finds employment in the highest posts in Native States without reference to race, creed, or locality. It is thus that, irrespective of the place or province from which they may happen to hail, Muslim ministers serve Hindu Rajas, and Hindu *dewan*s (ministers) act under Mahomedan *nawab*s, while Parsi *karbhari*s (administrators) are patronised by both classes of potentates. From this point of view, it would behoove the British government to create and maintain Native States if there were none. It, therefore, goes without saying that those which already exist should be cherished at their best. Their existence might further be useful to the growth of a healthy type of civilisation under foreign influences which are directly at work in British India, and indirectly in native territory.

For all these and other reasons,[69] then, I believe we shall have Native States in India, but they must also be well managed and progressive, and to secure this end the British government must give them its guidance and help, and still more protection against itself or, more correctly speaking, against its agents, either in some such manner as is indicated above or any other which may be deemed meet. This will settle one half, and by no means the less important half, of the problem before us. The other half, Maharaja, will rest with you and your brethren. But it is time to close this letter.

Yours &c.,
A POLITICAL RECLUSE

69 *Original footnote*: Since the observations in the text were first published, the East India Association adopted the following Resolution at a meeting held on the 5th of December 1889 which is quite in conformity with them: "That this Meeting considers that the maintenance of the rights, status and privileges of the Native Princes of India is essential to the prestige of the British Government, and to the public interests and welfare of the inhabitants of India generally."

Letter No. VI[70]

On Constitutional Rule

MAHARAJA,

In my last I have discussed, with tolerable fullness I hope, the question of the relations between the British government and the Native States in India as they are, and observed that a reform in those relations is urgently called for in the interests alike of justice, good government, and good policy. The nominal position of the states at present is that of internal independence, but the British Political Agents are and from their position must always be, busy in accumulating black marks against their rulers, and when its Foreign Office considers the score sufficiently heavy, or when a disturbance occurs in a state, the paramount government considers a wholesale interference including a supersession or deposition of the individual ruler justifiable. It is true that these agents also report the good conduct of the princes and the supreme government reward it with honours and titles, but this circumstance for reasons already explained can hardly touch the fringe of the administrative problem, which, therefore, remains to be solved.

The only method which at present is available is the one of violent interference from without. But that method acts in a spasmodic manner and, if anything, tends rather to create among the people at large sympathy for the author of the misrule sought to be remedied. Now, if it [is] right [to] violently cure the evil, it ought to be equally right, and it is certainly better, to prevent it or rather to induce, help on, and sustain in its place a gradual growth of reform from within. Probably no better means of bringing about such a result or disposition of things could be devised than to hold the Political Agents responsible for the proper administration of the Native States equally with their actual rulers, and if they in their efforts to fulfil that function have any complaints to urge against the latter, these complaints ought to be heard and decided by an independent tribunal, and not by the head of the executive department of which the accuser is a direct subordinate and which happens, generally speaking, to be already identified with his action because that action is shaped by its own orders. The Foreign Department of the Government of India is virtually bound to look to all matters and questions its agent submits more or less through the colour of his spectacles, as it cannot stultify itself or discredit him without undermining his authority and endangering the working of the entire system. This arrangement, as I have already remarked, is fair neither to the political officers nor to the princes to whose courts they are attached and who, while thus dependent

70 This letter originally appeared in the *Indian Spectator* on December 29, 1889.

for their very existence on the judgement or even the caprices or errors of individual officers, cannot be inspired by that feeling of self-respect and moral strength which are so essential to the conduct of all efficient rule.

Accordingly, the present relations between the political officers and the princes ought to be so modified as to place all the influence wielded by the former, which means in reality the influence and authority of the supreme government, at the disposal of the latter for purposes of good government without detracting from the personal prestige or dignity and the position of the princes. This, to my mind, is the direction which the reform of the relations between the British government and the Native States must take, and as an additional justification for this view it is well to remember that in every case in which the native system of administration has been reformed the chief motive force has been the influence and authority of the Political Agent and of the Government of India either directly exercised on occasions of minority or supersession of the ruler or indirectly supporting the administrator who has brought about the change.

What I propose then really amounts to nothing more than the systematic application of this method shorn of its violence and possible injustice to individual rulers, and retaining all its beneficent consequences. For, circumstanced as the native princes at present are, they are not only generally powerless to adopt or carry out reforms, but their true position is often incapable of being properly represented and thus in one sense it may be said that their version of a dispute is rarely heard. All these difficulties and anomalies would disappear under the change of system herein proposed, and when it is effected, it will have disposed of one-half the problem now facing both the native princes and the British government, and it is only then that the former can really feel that the latter have (to use once more the terse language of the Viceroy already quoted) "but one desire, that is to extend to them on all occasions the heartiest sympathy and assistance, to do everything in their power to augment their prestige, support their authority and enhance their personal consideration".[71]

The settlement of the other half of that problem which will then be rendered comparatively easy rests, as already observed, with the princes themselves, *viz.*, to reform the administration of their territories so as to be able to rule them "wisely and beneficently in accordance with their lights and the local requirements of their situation",[72] and thus render themselves invulnerable on the only side on which they are open to attack. Their loyalty to the Crown of England even under the trying circumstances of their position has become traditional like its recognition by the *suzerain*. Loyalty

71 Blackwood, "Banquet at Hyderabad", 138.
72 Blackwood, "Banquet at Hyderabad", 139.

alone, however, will not save them – they must advance administratively and maintain their position, or gradually cease to exist. Of overt and sudden annexation in defiance of the obligations of treaties and of Her Majesty the Queen's solemn promises of 1858, which I have referred to in my last, there need be no fear. The English nation will not consciously commit or sanction such a gross violation of right, but the princes must know that they cannot count on its forbearance without taking note of two forces – official and non-official, which go to shape public opinion – the former of which is formed by the daily note-taking and communications of the political officers, and the latter by a variety of private, irresponsible, and nondescript agencies working through the public press.

No cause and no body, however innocent, that does not stand well with these two factors of the public opinion which rules the English government and nation, need expect either justice or mercy from either. This remark will, perhaps, put you in mind of how some really good people have suffered by neglecting, and bad men flourished and made a name by wisely taking in hand, some of the elements which go to constitute these forces. But I do not think that that undignified course lasts or remains undetected long or entails in the end less cost and humiliation, and neither the princes nor their ministers have any right to sacrifice the dignity or the resources of the state simply to secure immunity from personal trouble or escape from an irksome position at the expense of the commonwealth which they are bound to conserve. Such conduct is as much a commission of wrong as despoiling a neighbour.

Therefore I hold that without doubt the straightest, surest, wisest, and worthiest course – one which combines duty with interest, and honour with policy – is for you and your brethren to turn their principalities into *states*, as I have already suggested, and thereby formally to create that identity of interests, or rather remove that apparent absence of such identity between yourselves and your subjects, which is the main, indeed the only excuse for the paramount power for interfering with the affairs of the Native States. The policy of annexation solemnly abandoned thirty-three years ago is now condemned on all hands, but that condemnation is calculated all the more to give force to the policy of interference which has succeeded to it, and against which all that has to be said concerns only the mode of carrying it out. Peace and order are essential to the security of government and subject alike, and the more civilised the government, the greater is the care it takes of them. The British government, which fosters so much the arts of peace, naturally cares, above all, for the maintenance of that peace and order throughout the territories subject to its rule and influence. The protection it affords to the native rulers of India against their own subjects is rightly considered to deprive the latter of their old and usual method – rebellion

– of seeking redress against oppression or wrong. Hence arises the moral obligation of the British government to put down such oppression, and hence the excuse for its interference. If you and your brethren wish to obviate it, do adopt such constitutions as will place in the hands of your subjects peaceful and efficient remedies for all administrative wrongs they may be liable to or may think they are suffering. When this is done to the extent that is possible under the circumstances, the British government will cease to concern itself with your internal affairs, because it will have no ground or excuse for it. [It] will see that then it will be acting in opposition not to the Rajas *as against their own subjects*, but against the entire states, their Rajas *and subjects together*, and for such interference not only will it have no motive, but it will be contrary to its professions, its self-interest, its policy. These causes together with its sense of righteousness and justice will always dissuade it from that course: in fact, in such a situation the interests or rather the attitude of the two parties will be identical. Then indeed the Indian princes can fight with the British government for their rights and interests on equal ground, the essential condition of which in the authoritative words already quoted is "that they administer their States wisely and beneficently in accordance with their lights and the local requirements of their situations".[73]

Now, it seems to me that to carry out this object and ensure its permanence it is necessary to adopt principally the following measures:

1. The separation of the *khangi* or private purse from the state treasury.
2. A written code of laws.
3. The separation of the judicial from the executive offices.
4. The creation of an audit department as a check on all expenditure of the administration.
5. A systematic employment of qualified official agency, its retention during good behaviour and efficiency, and provision for superannuation or invalid pension.
6. Delegation of powers and distribution of responsibility.
7. An elastic system of district administration.
8. The constitution of (a) a general or cabinet council to regulate and (b) a Privy Council to supervise the whole administration under the presidency of the ruling authority.
9. Subsidiary measures like education, promotion of arts, institution of orders of merit, &c.
10. A consultative popular assembly, and publication of annual accounts and report of the administration.

73 Blackwood, "Banquet at Hyderabad", 139.

Of these measures, the first three were originally laid down more than twenty years ago by the late lamented Major Evans Bell,[74] whose knowledge of the position and requirements of Native States was equalled only by his heartfelt sympathy with and earnest desire for their permanence.[75] The rest might suggest themselves to any ordinary observer of the administrative system of British India as being subsidiary helps, to carry out in practice the three main constitutional principles laid down by the intelligent student of their history and the sincere friend and advocate of their welfare, for the purpose of removing the radical defects of indigenous rule in India and thus making it the means of happiness and progress among the people subject to it. They, therefore, deserve the most serious and earnest attention of the heads of the Native States themselves and of all those who desire to see them happy and prosperous in themselves and enabled to contribute their appropriate share to the general progress alongside and under the influence of the British government in India. The general bearing of these measures on the object aimed at here is so plain that I will only make a few notes on each of the heads mentioned above.

The separation of the khangi or private purse from the state treasury. A *khangi* treasury exists in most, if not all, states, but in many it exists only in name, and in none is it really separated or divided from the public or state treasury in the sense used by Major Bell and intended to be conveyed here. To effect, such separation, the demands of the ruler's family for all their ordinary private expenses, and of the ruler himself for his own personal and public charges on the yearly revenue, must be fixed. The rest of the *fiscus* (treasury) must be regarded as the assets of the general administration. The amount of the former charges may assume the form of a *proportion* of the entire revenue or a lump sum fixed on a liberal estimate of the various items it has to cover. The former mode would be preferable to the latter and would, as it should, make the Raja a sharer in the fortunes of the Raj and its people. The settlement must lay down a scale of allowances for non-ruling members of the family, and it may be over and above its *watan*s (land grants), *inam*s (land leases), lands and other private demesnes. Extraordinary emergencies and rare occasions, too, must be provided for in the constitution, on a scale suited to the means and dignity of the state and the nature of the occasions. But it is not needful here to go into any of these details.

74 Evans Bell (1825–87) was a retired Company officer and administrator. Opposed to annexation, he produced important essays detailing and defending the rights of Native States, especially Nagpur and Mysore.

75 Thomas Evans Bell, *Our Great Vassal Empire* (London: Trubner & Co., 1870), 114.

All I wish to insist on is a recognition and adoption of the principle of separation between the two departments of the treasury, and limit to the demand on the state revenues for the private or personal needs and purposes of the ruler and his family. The Raja and his house have, indeed, a clear claim on the income of the Raj, because the former is necessary for the existence of the latter, even to greater degree than the latter is for that of the former. But that claim ought not to be exclusive or forgetful of justice to the taxpayer, or else the very *raison d'etre* of the thing ceases to have force, and the king is thus both the master and the servant of the people. The two claims, therefore, must balance each other in fairness; for the true interests of the people and of the rulers are identical, and a sense of justice and regard to mutual wants and circumstances must underlie their relations. This principle then is one of the two main supports of good government and a happy state. The other is the supremacy of law over all individual will and power, which leads to a consideration of the second head mentioned above.

A written code of laws is, indeed, a plain necessity in the management of any territory deserving to be called a state. Rules and instructions are required even in the conduct of any private business or property which has to be managed through agents; a state or kingdom, therefore, must have a written code of laws above all things. We have now in some of the states such a code, and in others its rudimentary substitute called by the names of *Rasam*s or *Sadamat Shirasta*s or standing customs, but as laws are sought to be twisted to their ends by parties to a suit, so the precise meaning or even existence of the customs is often called in question. It would therefore be well to have the true import of these customs ascertained by a commission irrespective of application to any individual cases or dispute, and systematised. They would, then, form a good basis of legislation which could be amended and improved with adaptations from the *shastraic* institutes of old and from the laws of British India, so as to supplement what is wanting, and modify what is defective, and refine what is crude and barbarous in the existing arrangements.

But great care is necessary to avoid, as far as possible, the niceties and technicalities of the present British Indian codes which are demoralising its people, and under cover of which lying and dishonesty flourish in luxuriance, and insolvency itself is often used as a cover for living in ease, and litigation nourished to the injury of social peace and of the morals and means of the subjects. Wise legislation ought to aim at discouraging this tendency in human nature as much as possible. An advanced state of society and complicated transactions of trade and business, no doubt, create a necessity for complicated laws, and inevitably lead to the evils referred to. But Native States ought to guard against them as much as they can and their position permits them to do, and I think this may be effected to a great extent by having a plain and simple code of laws – like the old Elphinstone Code[76] – for all ordinary cases, and leaving questions which could not be decided under it to be settled by a resort to *panchayat*s and arbitrators nominated from amongst the business men and experts concerned in each case, and also by reserving power to decide all such cases involving any great principle to a supreme appellate authority which should be created after the manner of the Judicial Committee of the British Privy Council.[77] A remedy like this is likely to keep down vexatious litigation, whereas elaborate technical legislation is sure to act as oil to the burning wick.

But the making of laws is not half so important as the observance of them, and to secure this end no one, however highly placed, must be exempted from their operation. The king himself must not be above the law, though he is the first and chief agent for framing and carrying it out. And when a necessity for action arises, which is not provided for legislatively, a law must be made for it and thus the reign of law must be perpetuated and people taught practically to feel that no one is above the law.

Yours &c.,
A POLITICAL RECLUSE

76 The Elphinstone Code served as the basis of the judicial system in the Bombay Presidency in the Company era. It was celebrated for its brevity and clarity as it distilled extant laws and usages into a few equitable regulations.

77 The Judicial Committee served as the final court of civil and criminal appeal for members of the British Empire.

Letter No. VII[78]

On Public Administration

MAHARAJA,

The next measure for consideration is the *separation of the judicial from the executive office*. A combination of these functions in the same hands is naturally dangerous to the purity of justice and to the liberty of the subject and must often interfere with timely dispatch of work in some direction or other. The power to prosecute, decide, and execute, when centered in one and the same individual officer, virtually results in making a local despot of him by reducing the checks on or increasing the temptation to his abuse of authority. Individual powers and energy too are limited, and where a multiplicity of functions is combined in one person, he has to use deputies, and thus, though the power rests in that one person nominally, a division of labour is inevitable except in very small areas of local administration. To avoid both these evils it is a wiser course to separate the offices than to divide the work in amount and retain them in the same hands, while enough work for an officer might be provided by an extension of his jurisdiction in regard to his own special duties. Again, a man who has only one set of duties to perform gets a facility for their performance and does them better and quicker than if he has a multiplicity of functions to carry out. The example of the administration of British India in all its varied branches affords such a clear illustration of this principle that it is needless to dwell longer on it.

I must not, however, be understood to advocate the extension of this principle all over the areas of administration from top to bottom. In the case of the higher jurisdictions, civil and criminal, it is necessary to carry it out. But in the small rural areas and in the villages elementary magisterial powers may still be vested in the head of the local executive of the government. This might especially be advisable in the Native States, where the administrative organisation is either imperfect or backward or both, and where, owing to the immemorial existence of despotic rule and absence of recognition of rights in the subject on the part of the rulers, the people are inclined to regard their own interests as always hostile to those of the state, and being ever accustomed to labour for the latter under compulsion, may mistake liberty as a justification for indifference or neglect or even obstruction hurtful to the public service and general welfare. The performance of casual and unimportant but very essential local public business is in such a case likely to suffer or entail a very great amount of public expenditure. This

78 This letter originally appeared in the *Indian Spectator* on January 19, 1890.

latter must, indeed, mean an additional tax on the people themselves, but they cannot be expected to act on such an analysis anywhere, much less in Native States. A certain degree of discretion may, therefore, be allowed in this matter, and any change must be made cautiously and tentatively. Further the heads of the local executive should be paid so as to be ordinarily above temptation and their work must be constantly under supervision of higher authority, and subject to moral checks and departmental control, though not liable to technical appeal in all cases. I have here roughly, yet I hope sufficiently, indicated the extent of the exception which may be safely made to the general rule of a separation of the judicial from the executive offices.

An audit department as a check on all unauthorised expenditure is necessary in the interests of the state itself. Nothing favours peculation and misappropriation of the public money so much as entrusting one and the same department with the power of collecting taxes, sanctioning or incurring expenditure, and keeping accounts. Therefore, this function of keeping accounts, and of seeing that no department, however important, and no officer, however exalted, incurs the smallest expenditure that has not been previously sanctioned, must be vested in a special department, which shall have no hand or part in any branch of the work of administration, and the head of which is subordinate only to the ruling authority. The wisdom of this policy of separation of these different functions carried on by different departments acting in cordial cooperation with each other and loyal subordination to all constituted authority and to the head of the management, is demonstrated by the British system of administration and is among the most important lessons taught to India by it. It cannot therefore be too early or too faithfully followed, not only in the government of Native States, but also in the conduct of all corporate functions, and all private enterprises and joint undertakings whatsoever. For, it hardly needs to be pointed out that it is this system that enables not only the government to carry on its work but also private companies successfully to undertake large commercial, agricultural, and manufacturing enterprises from headquarters thousands of miles away and with the help mainly of paid agency. Of course, the moral character of the men constituting that agency – their sense of duty and trustworthiness generally – is an important element in the case, but it is equally true that without the help of a proper system even they would not be able to achieve the success they do.

Qualified agency for Public Service, its tenure of office, &c. The necessity of qualification in the public services is self-evident, because there is no business, even of a private character, which can be well done by any man who has not acquired some sort of training to enable him to perform it. But what we have to learn from our English friends is the wisdom of their policy in securing along with efficiency the maintenance of a general sense of responsibility and fidelity in the discharge of duties in the members of the public services. And these, so far as administrative means are concerned – for, the ultimate basis of success and strength is high-toned public morality combined with public spirit – are generally insured by the two conditions of (1) a certainty of tenure during good behaviour and capacity for work, and (2) a prospect of pension during the period of superannuation as a provision for old age and infirmity. It is these two conditions which attracted thousands upon thousands of the Indian people of all classes and grades to the service, alike in military and in civil departments, of alien rulers, even at a time when physical contact with them was regarded as contamination, and enabled the latter to acquire, and still helps them to govern their vast dominions from a base more than four thousand miles away. The working of this principle well illustrates the remark made by one of their eloquent and thoughtful historians, which I have already quoted, to the effect that English valour and English intelligence have done less to extend and to preserve their Oriental empire than English veracity, and that no oath, hostage, or fastness imparts that security which is enjoyed by one who is armed with the British guarantee.[79] The remark, it is true, was made directly with reference to politics, but in reality what is said therein about the moral effect of the trust reposed in fidelity to engagements in the political, extended to undertakings in all departments of the state, and the confidence which is thereby created, secured, and still continues to secure, faithfulness in the discharge of public duty of every kind and in every line of work. This is the reason why even higher paid posts in Native States are not readily accepted unless they are either temporary exchanges for the British service or are in some form or other guaranteed by the British government.

It is an essential part of this system, however, that while efficiency and good behaviour are always allowed their dues, all proved breach of trust and wilful dereliction of duty and commission of wrong are promptly and adequately punished, so that fear of punishment plays therein at least as great a part as the love of reward. This is an old truth. Manu[80] in his chapter "On Government" says:

79 Macaulay, "Lord Clive", 419. The original reads:

> No oath which superstition can devise, no hostage however precious, inspires a hundredth part of the confidence which is produced by the "yea, yea," and "nay, nay," of a British envoy. No fastness, however strong by art or nature, gives to its inmates a security like that enjoyed by the chief who, passing through the territories of powerful and deadly enemies, is armed with the British guarantee.

80 The ancient lawgiver customarily deemed the author of the *Manusmriti* (or *Manava Dharmashastra*), a foundational text of Hindu law.

> Punishment is an active ruler; he is the true manager of public affairs; he is the dispenser of laws. ...
>
> Punishment governs all mankind; punishment alone preserves them; punishment wakes, while their guards are asleep; the wise consider punishment as the perfection of justice.
>
> When rightly and considerately inflicted, it makes all the people happy; but, inflicted, without full consideration, it wholly destroys them all.
>
> If the king were not, without indolence, to punish the guilty, the stronger would roast the weaker like fish on a spit.
>
> The whole race of men is kept in order by punishment; for a guiltless man is hard to be found; through fear of punishment, indeed, this universe is enabled to enjoy its blessings.[81]

Let it not, therefore, be supposed that it is all a trick of administrative skill and policy that effects such a wonder. No, it is the systematic maintenance by means of appropriate rewards and punishments of the claims of right and justice, which the strict observance of official promises implies, that forms the real basis of the strength and success of British rule. It will be found that, in the long run, power waits on moral attributes and far-sighted wisdom and that similarly it decays with the decay of virtue in its possessors. The popular belief, therefore, that a rule betokens the beginning of its end when its representatives, in the hauteur and pride of their physical might, begin to despise and trample right and truth under foot because the aggrieved are too weak to exact justice, is well founded. And by none does this truth need to be more constantly borne in mind than the politicians and rulers of Native States, because the prevalence and success of intrigue or high-handedness or both combined, from above and below, with which they are so unfortunately familiar, and of which they happen to be both victims and authors in turn, are sadly calculated to blind them to it, and the temptation to disregard its stern lesson and to make a shortsighted and easy expediency the rule of conduct is in their case strong and almost irresistible. But I am digressing, and to resume the subject I must pass on to the question of [delegation].

A delegation of powers. Along with certainty of tenure and remuneration, it is equally necessary that every office and post from that of the *dewan* or minister to the smallest functionary should have its precise power and responsibility defined. For it is only then that responsibility can be properly exacted, as it ought to be, and the possession of responsible authority, and

81 *Institutes of Hindu Law or the Ordinances of Menu*, trans. William Jones (London: W. H. Allen & Co., 1869), Book VII, 17–22, 127–28.

the certain knowledge that it will have to be promptly and duly exercised, help to secure a faithful discharge of trust and continued efficiency. In many Native States, however, this defect alone is enough to account for a great deal of the looseness which characterises their conduct of affairs. For, in the absence of defined powers and responsibilities, the biggest official sometimes has to abstain from exercising the smallest power, and as a consequence almost everybody shirks the performance of any duty for which, should it not prove agreeable to the powers that be, he is not sure he may not be taken to task, and yet the performance of which may be essential to the public welfare.

Another advantage of the gradation of power and responsibility is that the mistakes to which men are liable in work of the first instance can be rectified by those above them, and that in due course it becomes the prerogative and the privilege of the supreme ruler to eliminate, as far as is given to human agents honestly exercising power to eliminate, all error and injustice and oppression from the administration, and thus make for good government and righteous rule. Officers, however, who are to be entrusted with power must be selected with care. The rank and file must, as a rule, belong to the state, and their nomination be subject to regular tests. But in making selections for the higher and responsible offices it is necessary to guard against two sorts of people: (1) those who from their position and circumstances would supply an illustration of the phrase that the nose ring is heavier than the nose,[82] and (2) those likely, from the same influences, to be tempted to make hay while the sun shines. Of course, this is only a general observation, and personal antecedents, character, principles, and temperament, which go to counteract the natural inclinations of a class, must not be overlooked, especially as it will be long before you can dispense with the necessity of employing in important offices others than your own subjects, and, indeed, in some cases it would be even wise and beneficial to keep up that practice.

It is now time to consider what should be the system of district administration which you ought to adopt, for it is here that the real merits of a rule are manifested, and its characteristic fruits developed and displayed; but the consideration of this question must stand over for the next.

Yours &c.,
A POLITICAL RECLUSE

82 An old Marathi proverb, "*naka peksa moti jad*", that warns against excess or living beyond one's means.

Letter No. VIII[83]

On District Administration

MAHARAJA,

We have now, in the course of this discussion, arrived at the stage where it is necessary to consider what should be the system of district administration to be adopted. This is a matter of the utmost importance, because, as I have remarked at the close of my last letter, it is the nature of its district administration more than anything else that indicates the true character of a rule and determines the condition of its subjects. Urban populations, living usually in compact masses, following independent lines of occupation and possessing worldly means, are surrounded by conditions favourable for the development of intelligence, culture, and public spirit, which may tend to modify within their own limits the legitimate results of the action of a government ruling over them. But these results show themselves in their true colours in the villages in which all the world over the people live scattered, poor, ignorant, and depending for their weal or woe mainly, if not entirely, on the conduct and policy of their rulers. Hence the solicitude of every wise and enlightened government ought to be specially devoted to its district administration, which is also the chief basis of its strength.

It is, then, hardly necessary to observe that for the Native States in these times anything having the least approach or semblance to the old custom of farming any portion of the work of administration is out of date and out of the question. The administration must be all departmental, after the model of British India. Authority in native territory generally is often feebly and irregularly enforced, and wherever or whenever it is exerted with persevering strength or energy, it is not from the best or wisest of motives. But in British India it is exercised with uniform strictness, which is necessary to secure efficiency and respect for the law. The law itself may be mild or mildly administered from principle, but there must be no paltering with its execution. Hence the necessity of adopting a machinery which might be depended upon duly to carry out orders and to ensure the maintenance of peace. This virtue the centralised system possesses, because under it even the smallest official feels that he has the strength of the whole government at his back, and therefore it is that the management of the country by the British succeeded even at a time when their ideas and principles of government differed so much from those of the people they were called upon to rule and they were themselves individually few in number compared with the masses of the latter.

83 This letter originally appeared in the *Indian Spectator* on February 16, 1890.

But the system has this inherent drawback that it places much power in the hands of subordinates by whom it is liable to be misused. Centralisation, according to the thoughtful author of *The Original*, has these two vices, that "it must necessarily create a tribe of subordinate traders in government, who, with whatever English feelings they might set out, must, from the nature of things, they or their successors, become arbitrary, vexatious and selfish", and that it deprives "the citizens of the invigorating moral exercise of managing their common affairs".[84] Now, if this be true to any extent of Englishmen and of England, the children and the home of liberty, how much more must it be so in India, where, according to immemorial usage, check on the use or abuse of power proceeds only from the goodness of him who wields it and not because of the existence of rights in the subject or of the restriction proceeding from that principle?

The subordinates therefore have here special opportunities to misbehave. But as there is no system which is not open to some objection or other, wisdom consists in adopting the one which contains the greatest good, providing remedies against the abuse to which it is liable. Even in the management of private business, constant care has to be taken to prevent misconduct or breach of trust. Much more effort, therefore, is needed to watch over the concerns of a people and the affairs of a government. Superior officers must look after the conduct of their subordinates, while, on the other hand, the people themselves must be no less watchful of their own interests, remembering that violence to the rights of the smallest member of society, if tolerated and acquiesced in for any time, must sooner or later result in the invasion of the rights of or injury to the whole. Solon, the famous Greek lawgiver and wise man, summed up the whole principle of liberty in one small sentence, when, being asked how men could be most effectually deterred from committing injustice, replied: "If those who are not injured feel as much indignation as those who are."[85] Hence, "freedom like health can only be preserved by exercise",[86] "eternal vigilance is the price of liberty"[87] – these are among the maxims which are avowed by and guide the daily conduct of people who are anxious to protect themselves from official oppression or wrong, and those who wish to reap the fruits

84 William A. Guy, ed., *The Original by Thomas Walker* (London: Henry Renshaw, 1885), 136.

85 Diogenes Laertius, "Life of Solon", in *The Lives and Opinions of Eminent Philosophers*, trans. C. D. Yonge (London: Henry G. Bohn, 1853), 28.

86 Guy, *The Original by Thomas Walker*, 136.

87 Popularly attributed to Thomas Jefferson or Wendell Phillips, this quote appears to have actually originated with John Philpot Curran (see Suzy Platt, ed., *Respectfully Quoted: A Dictionary of Quotations* (Washington, DC: Library of Congress, 1993), 200).

of such wise maxims must follow their example. The task devolves primarily on the men of means and leisure, intelligence and public spirit, but to be successful in their efforts they must have the countenance and support of the community generally.

You must then adopt the departmental system, because it is the only efficient method of carrying on the work of administration, but at the same time you must guard against the evil to which it is characteristically prone and for checking which the Native States possess some facilities which are wanting in British India. For instance, their areas are small and can, therefore, be supervised more easily. Again, in British India the ruling class are separated from the ruled by a wide social gulf, in consequence of which matters which are fully talked about and believed in among the latter are unknown to the former and even when they are reported to them in some shape they do not find easy credence. Whereas, in spite of all their differences of creeds and castes, there is no social chasm nor much diversity of language between the rulers of Native States and their subjects and in this fact they possess an advantage which can be utilised for the purpose referred to. There the humblest subject can speak to the highest authority with a confidence and a certainty of being understood or at any rate of not being misunderstood. This, I believe, is the probable explanation of the spirited bearing which the Prince of Wales is said, during his tour in India in 1875–76, to have observed in the people of the Native States as contrasted with those of British India. For, being unconscious of the existence of any social distance or separation between themselves and their rulers, the subjects of the former would naturally feel more self-possessed than those of the latter. On the other hand, British India enjoys a constitutional government and safeguards of liberty to which the meanest can appeal for protection against the most exalted personage but which the Native States totally lack. Under the shelter, however, of the great advantage of social solidarity with their subjects which the native princes possess, it would be possible for them to remove the chief defect of their rule and construct a system of local administration tolerably free from the drawback attaching to centralised authority.

The essential features of such a system must be, on the one hand, a close and constant supervision of the subordinates from above. There should be no judicial ignorance of, or neglect to inquire into, wrongful practices which give clear indications of their existence, and anybody found guilty of corrupt or oppressive behaviour must be sternly dealt with and made an example of. On the other hand, as much of the administration as is possible with safety to all interests must be placed under the influence of the people themselves. To indicate what might be the general character of the arrangement, I quote from the authority cited in my second letter the following brief but clear description of the English system:

> In England we have self-government without autonomy – Acts of Parliament rule and overrule every detail of the administration, but the administration is not carried out by a bureaucracy; it is left to a variety of local bodies to carry out the laws. These local bodies, however, have no legislative functions. In England, we have the maximum of legislative centralisation with a minimum of bureaucratic centralisation and of autonomy. The administration is carried on by the people themselves, but it is carried on without autonomy on lines laid down by the central legislature. There are no inferior legislative bodies with independent powers. A strong legislative centralisation is quite compatible with delegation of administrative powers to local bodies, subject to carry out what the law prescribes, and unable to follow their own inclinations or to wander outside a strictly defined legal sphere. The results of this system are general respect for the law based on general understanding of law, as all classes of the community are called upon to join in its execution, absence of conflict between the central law and the laws promulgated by other legislative units, absence of bureaucracy except for the highest Imperial concerns.[88]

Put in for "Acts of Parliament" your own laws and regulations, such as they are or might be made, and also substitute the word "state" for "imperial" in the above passage, and you have in a small compass a pretty clear idea of what sort of a system the Native States might aim at constructing for carrying on the district administration of their territories. Even then of course, the passage quoted must be taken to indicate the general lines and not to lay down the details of the plan to be adopted; the principles it explains have to be applied, as far as possible, to the circumstances and requirements of each state and the capacities of its people.

Now, it might perhaps be thought that the model thus set forth is British and not British Indian, but I recommend it not in any spirit of imitation, because I am not for imitating any form which does not bring with it the substance. Nor am I one of those who hate every custom or institution because it is foreign and admire or seem to love it simply because it is indigenous. It is not such prejudices, but the soundness and justice or otherwise of the principles involved and their suitability to times and circumstances, that ought to be held to decide in such cases. The Native States, being under home rule, to that extent resemble England rather than British India, and, therefore, I think they might conduct their local affairs *so far as may be practicable* on the English model.

Again, in recommending such a course, it might be similarly remarked, that I was treating with unmerited neglect a more efficacious basis in our ancient village system, which it is often asserted contained the true germ of

88 Reay, "Twenty-Eighth Convocation", 215.

local self-government or representative institutions.[89] I, however, humbly think on the contrary that this village system has been overpraised and credited with virtues that did not belong to it, and held guiltless of evils which are clearly traceable to its influence. Indeed, so far from proving the germ of local self-government, that time-honoured system did not even pave the way for the introduction of the present municipal institutions which had to be gradually forced on the people by the British government, as a glance at the course of its legislation on the subject will show. The truth is the village system is not an exclusively Indian institution. For, in the absence of a generally settled order of things, and of a stable and all-pervading government, to which men must look up for justice and protection – and this condition was universal in the old world, and even now it is not extinct – some arrangement like the village system could not but spring into existence if any society which had passed beyond the primitive stage was to hold together at all, and accordingly village communities managing their local affairs have existed in all countries, in the East and West, but not necessarily as elective or representative institutions. Indeed, even Russia, barbarous and despotic as she has been held to be, had and still has in its *Mir*[90] a complete village organisation, which must be considered to be superior to the Indian village society, inasmuch as the former is said, unlike the latter, to afford the freest scope to individual liberty of action to its members. I, therefore, do not think much of the inherent merits of the village system as generating or even encouraging the spirit of self-government, although in times of old it may have proved an efficient instrument in the management of local public affairs. The learned author of *Ancient Law*, whose researches into the subject are well known, observes, in his *Village Communities in the East and West*:

> India has nothing answering to the assembly of adult males which is so remarkable a feature of the ancient Teutonic groups, except the council of village elders. It is not universally found. Villages frequently occur in which the affairs of the community are managed, its customs interpreted and the disputes of its members decided by a single Headman whose office is sometimes admittedly hereditary, but is sometimes described as elective; the choice being generally, however, in the last case confined in practice to the members of one particular family, with a strong preference for the eldest male of the kindred,

89 Richard Temple, "Effect of Religious Thoughts among Indian Natives", in *Oriental Experience: A Selection of Essays and Addresses Delivered on Various Occasions* (London: John Murray, 1883), 166.

90 The term for the council in a self-governing peasant commune in nineteenth-century Russia.

> if he be not specially disqualified. But I have good authority for saying, that, in those parts of India in which the village community is most perfect and in which there are the clearest signs of an original proprietary, equality between all the families composing the group, the authority exercised elsewhere by the Headman is lodged with the village Council. It is always viewed as a representative body, and not as a body possessing inherent authority, and whatever be its real number it always bears a name which recalls its ancient constitution of five persons.
>
> I shall have hereafter to explain that, though there are strong general resemblances between the Indian village communities wherever they are found in anything like completeness, they prove on close inspection, to be not simple but composite bodies, including a number of classes with very various rights and claims. One singular proof of this variety of interests, and at the same time of the essentially representative character of the village Council, is constantly furnished. I am told, by a peculiar difficulty of the Anglo-Indian functionary when engaged in 'settling' a province in which the native condition of society has been but little broken up. The village Council, if too numerous, is sure to be unmanageable; but there is great pressure from all sections of the community to be represented in it, and it is practically hard to keep its numbers down. The evidence of the cultivators as to custom does not point, I am told, to any uniform mode of representation; but there appears to be a general admission that the members of the Council should be elderly men. No example of village or of district government recalling the Teutonic assembly of free adult males has been brought to my notice. While I do not affect to give any complete explanation of this, it may be proper to remember that, though no country was so perpetually scourged with war as India before the establishment of the Pax Britannica, the people of India were never a military people. Nothing is told of them resembling that arming of an entire society which was the earliest, as it is the latest, phase of Teutonic history. No rule can be laid down of so vast a population without exceptions. The Mahratta brigands when they first rose against the Mahometans were a Hindu hill tribe armed to a man; and before the province of Oudh was annexed, extreme oppression had given an universally military character to a naturally peaceful population. But for the most part, the Indian village communities have always submitted without resistance to monarchs surrounded by mercenary armies. The causes, therefore, which in primitive societies give importance to young men in the village assembly were wanting. The soldiers of the community had gone abroad for mercenary service, and nothing was required of the council but experience and civil wisdom.[91]

This, I believe, is a brief but pretty exhaustive description of the nature of the Indian village system, and is the utmost that can be urged in favour

91 Henry Sumner Maine, *Village-Communities in the East and West* (London: John Murray, 1872), 124.

of it. The absence of a general arming of the population, in spite of the perpetual scourge of war afflicting the land, and the submission of the village communities to tyranny practiced by kings surrounded by mercenary troops, at which the author justly expresses surprise, because the country has always teemed with population are, however, explained by the fact that the caste system through its sharp division of labour made fighting the occupation of one section of the people alone and reduced the rest to a helpless, indeed to an abject, condition. The exceptions to this rule noticed in the extract were due to the necessity for mere self-preservation, when it was endangered by extreme persecution or oppression as in the case of the Sikhs, the Marathas, and the people of Oudh. These exceptions were individual in their nature, and consequently they were temporary and local. Beyond this most indirect reflection, however, there is no mention made here of any other demerit of the institution. On this point I have to add a remark or two which must stand over for my next.

Yours &c.,
A POLITICAL RECLUSE

Letter No. IX[92]

On the Village System

MAHARAJA,

I have said in my last that the Indian village system has been held up to praises it did not deserve, and that its serious defects have been little recognised. The alleged merits of the system could not probably be expressed with greater force than in this eloquent language of Sir C. T. Metcalfe:

> The village communities are little republics; having nearly everything they can want within themselves, and almost independent of any foreign relations. They seem to last where nothing else lasts. Dynasty after dynasty tumbles down; revolution succeeds to revolution; Hindu, Pathan, Mogul, Mahratta, Sikh, English, are all masters in turn; but the village community remains the same. In times of trouble they arm and fortify themselves: an hostile army passes through the country: the village community collect their cattle within their walls, and let the enemy pass unprovoked. If plunder and devastation be directed against themselves and the force employed be irresistible, they flee to friendly villagers at a distance; but, when the storm has passed over, they return and resume their occupations. If a country remain for a series of years the scene of continued pillage and massacre, so that the villages cannot be inhabited, the scattered villagers, nevertheless, return whenever the power of peaceable possession revives. A generation may pass away, but the succeeding generation will return. The sons will take the places of their fathers; the same site for the village, the same position for the houses, the same lands will be re-occupied by the descendants of those who were driven out when the village was depopulated; and it is not a trifling matter that will drive them out, for they will often maintain their post through times of disturbance and convulsion, and acquire strength sufficient to resist pillage and oppression with success. This union of the village communities, each one forming a separate little state in itself, has, I conceive, contributed more than any other cause to the preservation of the people of India, through all the revolutions and changes which they have suffered, and is in a high degree conducive to their happiness and to the enjoyment of a great portion of freedom and independence.[93]

And this is the view generally held, but with all deference to the great authority on which it rests, I cannot help feeling that it is not a correct one. In fact, it seems to me to reverse the position of cause and effect. If it be true indeed that the village system of India contributed to the preservation

92 This letter originally appeared in the *Indian Spectator* on February 23, 1890.

93 "Minute of Sir C. T. Metcalfe, 7 November 1830", in *Minutes of Evidence Taken Before the Select Committee on the Affairs of the East India Company*, Vol. 3 (London: House of Commons, 1832), Appendix No. 84, 332.

of its people amidst the succession of wars and revolutions through which the country has passed, it must be remembered that at the same time it equally tended to expose them to those calamities with all their disastrous consequences. For, it is because of the peculiarly isolating influence of this institution and of their strict division into unchangeable castes and occupations that the people became indifferent and apathetic to all but their village affairs, devoid of any public spirit or concern for public as distinguished from purely parochial interests, and consequently incapable of conceiving public duties or forming defensive combinations or organisations on an extended scale to which their own vast numbers so well invited them. Thus was any fear or possibility of a general rising or arming of the population against a foreign invader effectually prevented, and thus was drawn towards it conqueror after conqueror and revolution followed revolution. The villages, so long as they themselves individually were safe, cared not for what the invaders or his foreign or domestic enemies did with him who was their sovereign for the time being or with the rest of the country, and they even supplied him with mercenaries to serve as the instruments of his despotism while he was in possession of power. The Indian village system, therefore, while it enabled the people to live amidst wars and revolutions, also stood in the way of those obstacles against these dire occurrences which the country as a whole prompted by the natural love of independence might otherwise have put forth. This serious demerit of the institution is thus noticed by G. R. Gleig in his *History of India*:

> A striking and, to a certain extent at least, a mischievous effect of the village system of Hindustan was to stifle altogether that love of country which we are accustomed to dignify with the appellation of patriotism. Leave him in possession of the farm which his forefathers owned and preserve entirely the institutions to which he had from infancy been accustomed and the simple Hindu would give himself no concern whatever as to the intrigues and cabals which took place at the capital. Dynasties might displace one another; revolutions might occur; and the persons of his sovereign might change every day; but so long as his own little society remained undisturbed, all other contingencies were to him subjects scarcely of speculation. To this, indeed, more than to any other cause, is to be ascribed the facility with which one conqueror after another has overrun different parts of India; which submitted, not so much because its inhabitants were wanting in courage, as because to the great majority among them it signified nothing by whom the reins of the supreme government were held.[94]

This, I think, must be allowed to be a sounder view to take of the subject. It was thus the Indian area of patriotism came to be confined, at first, to

94 George Robert Gleig, *The History of the British Empire in India*, Vol. 1 (London: John Murray, 1830), 47–48.

one's village, and, then, to one's family, and through strict heredity of occupation and interdiction on intermarriage, to one's caste; and these two institutions would appear to have contributed to the destruction of anything like public spirit among the people to a greater degree than any other cause or causes put together. The effect could not escape the observation of intelligent strangers. Ninety years ago, Colonel Arthur Wellesley and Major Thomas Munro who were serving in India, though not yet known to their future fame, were corresponding with each other on the desirability of extending British dominion in this country, and the former writing to the latter on the subject said: "As for the wishes of the people, particularly in this country, I put them out of the question. They are the only philosophers about their governors that ever I met with – if indifference constitutes that character."[95]

Thirty years later, Mountstuart Elphinstone, who accepts Metcalfe's view of our village system, however, in his account of the Indian character, makes this remark: "The villagers are everywhere amiable and affectionate to their families, kind to their neighbours and towards all *but the Government*, honest and sincere."[96] I underline those three words. An institution which leads a people to look upon the character of the government that rules over their destinies with indifference and apathy, if not with dislike or hatred, without at the same time moving them even in their dreams to oppose or correct any of its evil ways, cannot but be considered inherently vicious. How noble by contrast with this teaching appears the motto of William Penn that "a man should make it part of his religion to see that his country is well governed"?[97] The villages thus destroyed the country and could realise no public interests beyond their immediate concerns within their own respective limits, and what genuine fellow feeling and public life could have been cultivated within these limits would appear to have been prevented by the rules of caste, which obliged men to withhold their sympathies from their next-door neighbours and reserve them for distant people with whom alone they could associate or intermarry. Is it a wonder that a people nurtured under such influences should not be remarkable for a pervading sense of public duty, a regard for political rights or the value of official integrity, and concern or readiness of self-sacrifice for the general good?

95 John Gurwood, ed., *The Dispatches of Field Marshal the Duke of Wellington*, Vol. 1 (London: John Murray, 1837), 209–10.

96 Mountstuart Elphinstone, *The History of India: The Hindu and Mahometan Periods* (London: John Murray, 1889), 218.

97 William Penn, "Preface to the Frame of Government, 1682", in Philip B. Kurland and Ralph Lerner, eds., *The Founders' Constitution*, Vol. 1 (Indianapolis: Liberty Fund, 2001), Chapter 17, Document 4, 613.

Equal with the political, if not still greater, has been the injury done to the country socially and morally by this village system. For it combined in itself all the blighting elements of temporal tyranny and sacerdotal despotism, and embodied their essence in the baneful maxim so eminently calculated to repress all originality of thought, of moral vigour and independence and force of character, to arrest progress, and to pave the way to national weakness and degradation. The maxim is *yadyapi sudham lokaviruddham nákaraniyam nācharaniyam*, which, of course, means that even if correct in itself, a course which is opposed to the popular view should never be accepted or followed. Enforcing this fatal precept with the remorseless instrument of civil death, [the village system] effectually crushed out all life, and produced in the name of order the stillness of dormancy, if not death, in which the country has long stagnated – a result to which the modern system of caste has silently contributed its due share, as it is, while tolerating abuses, still checking all conscious and real progress. Truth itself must be powerless before such a deadly combination. For, nowhere can the popular mind be enlightened all at once on any subject, and in such a case error must be simply long lived.

A very trite example will suffice. Astronomy was early cultivated in this country, and centuries ago the true cause of the eclipses was discovered. But the genius who made the discovery with very indifferent helps, when only remonstrated with on his heresy by his priestly brethren, so far from insisting on the assertion of his precious truth, yielded at once to their ignorant superstition and freely avowed that *their* monsters, *Rahu* and *Ketu*,[98] became for the moment the shadows in the sky which *he* found to cause the phenomena. Under this subtle timidity the discovery was buried as soon as it was made, and to this day not only the multitudes of ignorant men and women, but even the educated fraternity from the humble schoolboy to the exalted legislator or scholar who can in the classrooms and public halls demonstrate the scientific causes of the eclipses, fast and bathe on the occasions, as if they thought, like some ignorant savages, that unearthly beings were trying to swallow up the orb of day or night and casting gloom and impurity on mankind below! Of course, the excuse is that it is the uneducated women and priests who compel this sorry observance against clear convictions of the natural truth. But what should keep such precious members as the women and priests of a cultured society in a mental condition on a par with their menial servants but obedience to the great maxim already quoted? How could any progress or reform be expected to make head where

98 In the Puranas, solar and lunar eclipses are ascribed to *Rahu* and *Ketu*, monsters who devour the sun and moon (W. J. Wilkins, *Hindu Mythology: Vedic and Puranic* (Calcutta: Thacker, Spink & Co., 1882), 363).

every innovator was sure to be smothered like the struggling fly within the spider's net?

British rule with its liberty of action checked this repressive force to some extent and the salutary impulse derived from English education led a few great spirits to start new movements which have been followed more or less feebly by a comparatively small number of congenial minds. But the great majority even now receive them with a logic in which assumption does duty for fact, prejudice for argument, and passion for appeal. Thus, in spite of progressive education and enlightenment, are perpetuated hurtful errors, degrading superstitions, and baneful customs and institutions, and yet their vitality is assumed to follow from their sound basis and regarded as a matter of congratulation. Of submission to the inevitable, especially when associated with worldly advantages, even when opposed to the aforesaid maxim or some other belief, there is not much lack, and the resulting sense of violated conviction is satisfied with some sort of easy penance. But such submission is far from a virtue and brings on weakness and degeneracy of spirit instead of strength. Indeed, the general want of manliness and backbone among the people which is now and then brought out may not incorrectly be ascribed to this national habit of paltering with principle.

There is still another evil which also appears to be traceable to the same cause, and that is what in France is called the "one man power".[99] Under the village order of things, the *patel* (manager) or the *mukhi* (headman) is the king – the only cock on the dunghill – who can brook no rival near the throne, though everyone would aspire to the place which must descend to his son and in a few years become a bone of contention amongst many heirs. The village system was but an assemblage of diverse hereditary functionaries, who carried on their respective duties in accordance with standing usages or the decision of the headman or council of elders in case of dispute, and, therefore, there was little room in it for intelligent subordination or loyal cooperation. So ingrained and general has been the love of personal rule produced by this ancient "germ of representative institutions" that it did not, as was observed in my last, create a demand even for *municipal* self-government, but on the other hand it seems to have effectually banished from the popular mind all idea of co-ordinate or corporate action, and substituted for it an inordinate love of authority. The result is that, even among those who have received an English education and are imbued with a love of the free political institutions of Europe, the strange spectacle is seen of every one wishing to rule and none inclined to obey – everyone laying down plans and none executing them – as also of mutual jealousy and desire for superiority over others on almost all occasions. And yet strangely enough,

99 A reference to despotism as embodied by Napoleon in particular.

with all this impatience of outward restraint, they are unable to shake off the degrading bondage of senseless or baneful customs and practices, although their numbers in each caste are now so large that they could act up to their convictions even without any violence to that institution. But everybody waits for everybody else to begin, and only discounts the examples which happen to be already set as an excuse for doing nothing himself.[100]

Such, in my humble judgement, are among the evil legacies of the village system and they promise little or no aid to self-government or to any joint work at all. If, in these circumstances, I suggest to you, Maharaja, the advisability of framing your district administration on popular lines, it is not because any hopes can be based on the development of the old village system, but because of the moral basis of the institution of *panchayat* which depends for its general acceptance on the agency of personal character and qualification more than mere birth or hereditary position in the performance of civic business carried on under the eye, as it were, of the local public of each place, and therefore within the ken of all interested in its proper and honest execution. Disinterested public services of this kind must be encouraged and rewarded with social honours and personal distinctions.

This, then, is the principle – and the basis of it lies in human nature more than in any local custom or institution – which must be made use of in constructing local organisations for the management of local affairs. Responsibility for the state dues, management of the local police, and liability to make good losses caused by thefts occurring within local limits; award of punishment for petty offences, decision of civil disputes by arbitration in the first instance and even absolutely in cases where possible; provision of means with the help of the state for carrying out schemes of local utility and local purposes, such as sanitation in all branches, construction and repairs of wells and temples, charities, ceremonies, amusements &c. – may, as of old be the objects, but some departure must be made in the mode of their local administration. The institution and encouragement of such local organisations are to be desired not for the fashion of the thing, but because they conduce to beneficial ends. They practically educate and interest the people in public business and range them on the side of peace, law and order, and thus attach them to the central authority – the government – in due relation. They save a great deal of expense and trouble to the latter which, in other words, means the people themselves. Lastly, they serve to bring out facts of first instance in as little official antagonism as possible,

100 *Original footnote*: An analysis into deeper causes of this phenomenon does not appertain to the subject in hand and will not therefore be attempted here, but such an inquiry ought to prove very instructive to all friends of genuine progress among the people in all lines of national life.

and leave to the central government the easier task of deciding only the application of law and principle to all disputes. The last is not the least advantage, as it reduces all friction to a minimum, and must together with the rest be productive of public benefit and content to a far greater extent than any other course is calculated to lead to.

How to construct the requisite system is a problem for each state to solve for itself. But some hints of possible use as to both principle and detail might be obtained by a study of similar institutions in other countries. I will here reproduce a suggestive passage or two from *The Original* which has been cited in my last:

> The machinery, by which alone this desirable end can be accomplished, must consist of local governments so ordered that those who are most successful in the honourable conduct of their own concerns, would be selected, and being selected, would be willing to give up time sufficient to superintend the affairs of their respective communities. Now this can only be permanently effected by making government a social and convivial affair – a point of interesting union to the men most deserving the confidence of their fellow citizens.
>
> Under such circumstances, the expense of government might be greater than at present, but the expense of want of government would assuredly be more than proportionately less, and the state of society would be healthy and constantly improving.
>
> It is by the principles alone of self-government by small communities that a nation can be brought to enjoy a vigorous moral health, and its consequence – real prosperity. It is by the same principle alone that the social feelings can be duly called into action, and that men, taken in the mass, can be noble, generous, intelligent, and free.[101]

Of equal importance is the nature of the relations which should subsist between the central government and the local bodies, and on this point I will adduce a few general remarks from *Local Government* by Mr. M. D. Chalmers. Regarding the necessity of a guiding and controlling central authority – which everywhere is as a matter of course superior in intelligence and knowledge to the rural localities, but the total absence of which was the great defect of the Indian village system – the author quotes this dictum as laid down in the Report of the Royal Sanitary Commission of 1869:

> However local the administration of affairs, a central authority will nevertheless be always necessary in order to keep the local executive everywhere in action – to aid it when higher skill or information is needed, and to carry out numerous functions of central superintendence.
>
> There should be one recognised and sufficiently powerful minister not to centralise administration, but, on the contrary, to set local life in motion a

101 Guy, *The Original by Thomas Walker*, 144, 148.

> real motive power, and an authority to be referred to for guidance and assistance by all the sanitary authorities for local government throughout the country. Great is the *vis inertia*[102] to be overcome; the repugnance to self-taxation; the practical distrust of science; and the number of persons interested in offending against sanitary laws, even amongst those who must constitute chiefly the local authorities to enforce them.[103]

The book concludes with these observations:

> "Power", says Mr. J. S. Mill, "may be localised but knowledge to be most useful must be centralised. There must be somewhere a focus at which all its scattered rays are collected, that the broken and coloured lights which exist elsewhere may find there what is necessary to complete and purify them. The Central Authority ought to keep open a perpetual communication with the localities, informing itself by their experience, and them by its own, giving advice freely when asked and volunteering it when it seems to be required." At any rate until our rural system of local government is better organised, the ratepayers will be grateful for the central audit; but the extent of the administrative control that the Central Government should exercise is a most difficult problem. Obedience to the general laws which the Legislature has laid down for the preservation of private and individual rights and the limitation of the power of local authorities, can be enforced by the courts of law; but how far ought local bodies to be allowed to mismanage their own affairs? If they are superintended by an intelligent and conscientious central department, armed with large executive powers, it is apt to err on the side of undue interference. When it sees things going wrong it steps in with a high hand to set them right. Yet it is only by a succession of tumbles that a child can learn to walk. A local authority in leading strings is not likely to learn aright the lesson of self-government. If local autonomy possesses the political value its admirers assert for it, it may be well worthwhile to make some temporary sacrifices to develop and strengthen it. In local matters "that which is best administered" may not be "best" in the long run. The tendency to regard all England as a suburb of London is certainly not a healthy one. Anything that can give vigour and colour to local life should be encouraged. In the case of local bodies, as in the case of individuals, it may be better and healthier to be too little governed than to be too much governed, even though the government be good. "The difficulty is to promulgate only the necessary laws; to remain ever faithful to the truly constitutional principle of society, to put oneself on guard against the fury of the Governor, the most fatal malady of modern Governments."[104]

102 Formally, the Latin term for inertial force, but more often used metaphorically to refer to inactivity.

103 M. D. Chalmers, *Local Government* (London: Macmillan & Co., 1883), 149.

104 Chalmers, *Local Government*, 159. The closing quotation is from Honoré-Gabriel Riqueti Mirabeau, *Discours de Monsieur Mirabeau l'Ainé, sur l'Education Nationale* (Paris: Vue Lejay, 1791), 74.

It will probably be long before the conditions dwelt on in this passage will be fully realised in Native States or even in British India, but the passage ought to prove very suggestive as to what should be done, and what avoided. No mere paper constitution will serve any useful purpose, and I do not at all suggest one. What you must do is to take up each village and township, and wherever the necessary material exists, give to each the necessary local powers fully covered by local responsibility, [and] leave the rest to the supervision of a properly constituted central office. But where there is no desire or intelligence on the part of the people to undertake the duty, leave your official agency to carry on both the local work and the supervision, with the prospect of a transfer of the former to local hands whenever a desire for it among the people themselves clearly manifests itself. Thus the work may go on quietly and by calling up the powers of the people tend to progressiveness. This is all that a Raja need or can do to give a healthy shape to the district administration of his state, for thereby he would be just to his subjects and just to himself, and give to the former good government and at the same time provide for their advancement in local self-management which is alike beneficial to them and to him, and therefore to the entire state.

Yours &c.,
A POLITICAL RECLUSE

Letter No. X[105]

On the Council and Assembly

MAHARAJA,

[Even] the most elementary scheme of administration of a state must have a central authority to direct and regulate its course, remove its difficulties, remedy its defects, and settle ever-recurring questions, whether of a general or individual character, and thus ensure the successful working of the entire machinery. Much more, therefore, must such a need arise in the case of the system contemplated herein, with its laws and regulations, separation of offices, delegation of powers, and other measures previously described. Now, this central authority must take the form of a body which might be well called the Cabinet Council, composed of the heads of all departments with the Raja as its president and the *dewan* or the premier and head of the executive as vice-president. In all executive matters a final appeal must lie to the Raja and all measures of general applicability passed by the council must be submitted for his confirmation before they are permitted to take effect.

To this council solely, in the present state of things, must appertain the function of making laws and regulations, but, as has been observed in a previous letter, over-legislation must be carefully avoided and no law or enactment made unless its necessity is clearly perceived. Further, in any case of a proposed law, objections and suggestions which may be urged by the people through their representatives in the public assembly (to be presently mentioned) must be duly heard and taken into consideration. The same course must be followed with regard to the levy of any new tax or taxes, and every tax, law, or measure passed by the council must, as already intimated, receive your confirmation and assent before it comes into operation. This giving of formal assent is a prerogative of the ruling authority, without whose sanction no law should be brought into force, but the form, too, is not without its use and significance even where the executive authority itself proposed the measure or is otherwise concerned in passing it. It indicates that the sovereign is the source of all legislation and thus serves as a recognition of that principle, and moreover it is useful as a reminder to the sovereign that he is responsible for all laws. Again, every measure should be carefully considered from all points of view and made as unexceptionable as it can be *before* it comes into force. But it is not always possible to anticipate every objection, and occasionally some serious defect or flaw may be discovered immediately after it has passed through the final stage. In such

105 This letter originally appeared in the *Indian Spectator* on April 27, 1890.

cases the assent is withheld and the law returned for amendment, and thus what is usually a mere formality serves to obviate a practical difficulty.

While on this subject I may in passing observe that, in view of the demands of an improved system of administration and of the necessity for the advancement of education, of arts and industries and other measures for promoting the welfare and happiness of the people, no taxation should be lightly remitted unless it be found by its very nature to be harassing in its mode of assessment and collection, or really injurious in its economic effects on the condition of the subjects. Purity of the public service, and through it of the public administration too, demands that it be adequately remunerated. High salaries alone, it is true, will not suffice to keep any set of officials free from corruption. I have in a previous letter mentioned that an intelligent Raja, when he was asked to increase the scale of pay of his public servants as a means of keeping them above temptation and thus prevent their oppression of his subjects, replied that it was no use his doing so as they would receive the higher rates of pay from him and carry on their exactions from the *ryot*s all the same. And he was right in his view, because no other reform was suggested to him along with enhanced remuneration of the services, but this last is one essential means along with others for ensuring the purity of the public administration, and it must cost money. Then, again, there are many other public needs and measures of public usefulness, which must also entail heavy charge on the public treasury. Now, it must not be forgotten that the people who would welcome these boons would by no means always welcome the imposition of taxes which alone could supply the necessary funds. Therefore, no existing source of income should be given up except for the two reasons already mentioned, and they should be clearly ascertained.

Paternal consideration, also, may well be shown to the *ryot* in the assessment and realisation of the public dues generally, and especially on occasions of difficulties created by natural causes, so as to avoid unequal pressure and rigour. For, after all, the people's wealth and prosperity are the ultimate assets of the government and the state, and any measure which tends to their preservation or increase must add to its resources and serve also to create and maintain for it a reserve to fall back upon in case of emergencies. But for administrative reasons the abandonment of a tax must be considered as serious a measure as the levy of one, and neither step ought to be taken lightly and without the most careful consideration of all circumstances connected with it and all its probable consequences. Large and permanent public works of a reproductive nature, however, ought not to be constructed out of current taxation alone and it should be largely supplemented by public loans, so that the cost of the undertakings may be spread over a long period and recouped in light instalments from the many generations who are to enjoy their benefits in the future. But borrowing is a device for raising money which from its apparent ease almost always leads to waste and extravagance and must therefore be resorted to with caution and as a rule only in the case of reproductive works.

Here, though not quite in the order originally indicated, may be noticed the subject of *finance* and the *annual report*. Finance indeed is the backbone of a state and no difficulties it may have to encounter can be compared with the troubles and dangers which have their root in disordered finances. This fact has been so well established by experience both here and elsewhere that little need be said in favour of their sound and careful management. The two great helps to such management are accurate accounts of past years and a tolerably reliable forecast of the income and liabilities of the coming twelve months, in the absence of which the ablest ruler can only grope in the dark and unconsciously tread on pitfalls except of course where the efficiency of the public administration is held to be a matter of little or no consequence. With the audit and other departments in fair working order no difficulty whatever ought to be experienced in securing these helps. A summary of the figures together with the leading facts of the administration should be published in an annual report, which should inform both the people and those who rule over them in what direction and manner the vessel of state is steering, what are its needs and requirements, and how they may best be met. The regularity, punctuality, and correctness with which these results of the year's working of the administrative machinery can be furnished to the public will afford no small proof of the efficiency of the different departments which compose it and of the satisfaction they are capable of giving to the subjects, and this is a point which should always be kept in view by the supervising authorities.

The last and the highest form of the central authority must be a Privy Council to review and supervise the work of the administration from the standpoint of the highest knowledge, wisdom, statesmanship, and breadth and liberality of view, which the resources of the state can command. The Privy Council ought, therefore, to be composed of the wisest and best men available in the state, and even outside it, for I see not only no harm but much social and moral benefit in the Indian Rajas offering to men of light and leading, of moral and social weight and position in British territory, honourable seats on their Privy Councils. Such appointments seem to me to be not ill calculated to bring about a fusion of the sentiments, ideas, and practices obtaining in the two sets of administration, which cannot but react beneficially, in however small a degree, on both and favour the cause of progress. The whole Privy Council which would include the cabinet members will attend in response to a summons whenever some question of exceptional importance has to be considered and its advice thereon is desired. But ordinarily only the official portion of it will work and for that purpose it must be divided into as many committees as the nature of the work of final appeal and supervision it will have to do will require. It will, however, suffice for all practical purposes to have a judicial and a general committee, the former of which will decide questions of law and justice, and the latter attend to a review and supervision of all the rest of the field of administration and the issue of orders and instructions for the correction of abuses or the introduction of reform wherever they may be called for.

With the aid of arrangements like these, Maharaja, you ought to be able to raise yourself above the details of the administration, and at the same time to improve its tone and strengthen your own control over it by adding to the thoroughness and the beneficial character of your supervision. Freedom from the worry of administrative details is, indeed, a privilege of the highest ruler, as a comprehensive supervision and an inspiring direction of the machinery of government is his duty, but while many a Raja freely avails himself of this *privilege* of his position, very few are alive to their *responsibility* which they think is well discharged vicariously by a *dewan* or full power minister and his subordinates acting as best they can or will, except where the master may feel personally interested in interfering. One cause of the prevalence of this unfortunate condition of things undoubtedly is the absence of all constitutional arrangements and reliable helps, so that a Raja who may really wish not to shirk his duty is obliged to work very hard, to attend to every measure at every stage, see everything with his own eyes, and thus sacrifice his health and comfort, whereas under even a tolerable system, the task of administration would wear a much less repulsive or harassing aspect and bring the higher powers and the nobler side of the ambition of the ruler into honourable and beneficent play. You, Maharaja, must therefore so arrange your administration that you could always stand aloof from its details and reserve your governance for the higher purpose of direction and supervision, and to this end, in the words of a wise counsellor, "preserve the rights of inferior place and think it more honor to direct in chief than to be busy in all".[106]

This course would conduce not only to practical convenience and to economy of precious time and of still more precious health and energy but serve also to further still higher purpose. All work of first instance – such is human weakness – is almost always liable to mistakes and errors, even when performed by men free from carelessness or corrupt motives, and these mistakes and errors are more discernible to an onlooker. Hence arises

106 Francis Bacon, "Of Great Place", in James Spedding, Robert Leslie Ellis, and Douglas Denon Heath, eds., *Collected Works of Francis Bacon*, Vol. 12 (Boston: Brown and Taggard, 1860), 114.

the necessity and also the value of the provision for appeals. Now, the king being the highest court of appeal in the state, it is his privilege and his prerogative to detect and remove all errors and faults in its government, and thus advance the cause of right and justice and keep up the purity of the administration. To ensure that result, therefore, you must on all occasions and in all cases, which call for the exercise of that exalted prerogative, provide yourself with the most efficient helps available and be surrounded by the best influences, and carefully guard against any sinister or misleading factors entering into your deliberation, or contributing to its results at any time.

But, under a constituted order of things like the one suggested above, would not the Raja's occupation, like Othello's, be gone or his prestige and authority weakened? I believe, on the contrary, that, if, as an old and shrewdly conceived maxim has it, *obedience is the essence of rule*,[107] they will both be strengthened, and, therefore, the most ardent lover of the exercise of power among your brethren need entertain no misgiving on that point excepting of course indulgence in mere caprices, but as such indulgence in the end benefits no more its author than its victims, the exception hardly needs to be considered. Further, let us look at a typical case on the other side. The government of England is a limited monarchy, and the authority of its sovereign is so hedged in by laws and restrictions of the popular will and opinion as to make him appear to people generally a mere ornamental figurehead with the least power of any ruler on earth. Yet one of its most eminent prime ministers, with more than half a century's practical experience of political life, thus describes the position of that sovereign:

> Although the admirable arrangements of the Constitution have now completely shielded the Sovereign from personal responsibility, they have left ample scope for the exercise of a direct and personal influence in the whole work of government. The amount of that influence must vary greatly, according to character, to capacity, to experience in affairs, to tact in the application of a pressure which never is to be carried to extremes, to patience in keeping up the continuity of a multitudinous supervision, and, lastly, to close presence at the seat of government; for, in many of its necessary operations, time is the most essential of all elements, and the most scarce. Subject to the range of these variations, the Sovereign, as compared with his Ministers, has, because he is the Sovereign, the advantages of long experience, wide survey, elevated position, and entire disconnection from the bias of party.
>
> Little are they who gaze from without upon long trains of splendid equipages rolling towards a palace conscious of the meaning and the force that live in

107 A dictum cited by Edward Coke, *obedientia est legis essentia* (obedience is the essence of the law). On this, see *The Reports of Sir Edward Coke* (London: Joseph Butterworth and Son, 1826), 11:100.

> the forms of a Monarchy, probably the most ancient, and certainly the most solid and the most revered, in all Europe. The acts, the wishes, the example, of the Sovereign in this country are a real power. An immense reverence and a tender affection await upon the person of the one permanent and ever faithful guardian of the fundamental conditions of the Constitution. He is the symbol of law; he is by law, and setting apart the metaphysics, and the abnormal incidents, of revolution, the source of power. Parliaments and Ministries pass, but he abides in life-long duty; and he is to them as the oak in the forest is to the annual harvest in the field. When the august functions of the Crown are irradiated by intelligence and virtue, they are transformed into a higher dignity than words can fully convey, or Acts of Parliament can confer; and traditional loyalty, with a generous people, acquires the force (as Mr. Burke says) of a passion, and the warmth of personal attachment. But by those to whom we are attached, we are ready and prone to be, nay, we are already, influenced.[108]

This description refers chiefly to the social position and influence of the head of the state and makes no mention of his prerogatives such as the power of appointing and dismissing ministers, dissolving parliaments, giving or withholding assent to laws, pardoning crimes, or abating punishment, not to speak of the right of initiative in foreign politics which is out of place here. But what follows is still more to my point as it relates to the right of exercise of his power by the monarch directly over the *government of the country itself*:

> He is entitled, on all subjects coming before the Ministry, to knowledge and opportunities of discussion, unlimited save by the iron necessities of business. Though decisions must ultimately conform to the sense of those who are to be responsible for them, yet their business is to inform and persuade the Sovereign, not to overrule him. Were it possible for him within the limits of human time and strength, to enter actively into all public transactions, he would be fully entitled to do so. What is actually submitted is supposed to be the most fruitful and important part, the cream of affairs. In the discussion of them, the monarch has more than one advantage over his advisers. He is permanent, they are fugitive; he speaks from the vantage ground of a station unapproachably higher; he takes a calm and leisurely survey, while they are worried with the preparatory stages, and their force is often impaired by the pressure of countless detail. He may be, therefore, a weighty factor in all deliberations of State. Every discovery of a blot that the studies of a sovereign in the domain of business enable him to make, strengthens his hands and enhances his authority. It is plain, then, that there is abundant scope for mental activity to be at work under the gorgeous robes of Royalty.[109]

108 Gladstone, *Gleanings of Past Years*, 41, 43.
109 Gladstone, *Gleanings of Past Years*, 232.

If this is the case with the head of the government of England, which, as already observed, is a limited monarchy almost bordering on a republic, in which the chief power is in the hands of the people, it is evident the widest constitution that an Indian Raja can give to his state must, from the very nature of the case, leave his autocracy untouched, except to a very small extent, and that extent will prove beneficial to himself and his house as much as to the people. While, on the other hand, a systematisation of the administration will ensure for his power or authority a degree of unfeigned respect and implicit obedience, which do not now characterise native rule generally in the absence of all system. In fact the Raja will, for a long time to come, have to be his own king and parliament, ruler, supervisor, and critic, all in one, as also the sole source of the motive power which is to keep up the machinery of the administration going on steadily like time, tide, and public life which wait for no man. For this purpose he must have special officers charged with the responsibility of taking care that no function gets into abeyance and no department goes to sleep over any portion of its duty. In the discharge of the higher task of supervision he must, to the utmost of his power and judgement, gather about himself "men whose conduct is invariably regulated by private honour and public interest, and in whom the enthusiasm in the pursuit of national objects which seizes other men by fits and starts is constant and uniform".[110] It should ever be borne in mind that the selection of proper agents is one great secret of successful administration.

This completes what may be called the official side of the constitution which is herein proposed, and it would be very desirable to supplement it by an outside or popular element which, under existing circumstances with any advantage to anybody and, indeed, with safety to the working of the public administration, can take the form only of a Consultative Assembly composed of the leading representatives of all the different interests and classes throughout each district or division of the state, moderate in numbers and meeting once a year at the capital on a fixed suitable day. Its functions should be to submit to the government of the state any well-grounded representations it may wish to make on behalf of the people in regard to:

1. Any law which it may be proposed to enact;
2. Any new tax which it may be proposed to be levied;
3. Any items of revenue or expenditure of the state as entered in the estimates of the next year;

110 Alexander J. Arbuthnot, *Major-General Sir Thomas Munro, Governor of Madras: A Memoir* (London: Kegan Paul, Trench & Co., 1889), 22.

4. Any inconvenience which may have been occasioned, or believed to be caused, to the people by the working of any law or department of the state during the preceding year;
5. Any general grievance or evil they may have suffered from or been subjected to during that period, or may apprehend in the next twelve months; and
6. Any other suggestion which they may wish to make in regard to the public good.

And the government, which must give to the deputies of the people sufficient time to frame their representations, must accord to them their attentive consideration and either accept, modify, or reject the said representations and suggestions in whole or in part and assign reasons for their orders which, however, may be considered as final.

Some such plan as this would enable the people to take as much interest and part in the administration of the state as is demanded by their own welfare, and at the same time is consistent with its safety, and put upon their rulers as much sense of responsibility as is immediately necessary for the benefit of the commonwealth. More it is not feasible or wise to aim at just now lest the work of the administration should come to a deadlock. Further progress in that direction, therefore, will be possible only when the people are capable of realising the higher responsibilities of government and ready and able to share in its labours, and that time is so distant that we need not trouble ourselves with a consideration of its requirements. It is indeed, at all times well for the rulers and the ruled alike that as much of the detail of the administrative work, not only in the villages but even in the larger areas of the districts, should be carried on by and through the people themselves. For it would serve to reduce to a minimum all friction and differences between the people and the officials as to facts of the first instance, simplify and facilitate the application of general principles and laws, and economise the expenditure of the public time, talent, and money, on the public business which, with every advance from autocratic simplicity, always has a tendency to an enormous increase and leads to overwork and delays and often under such pressure to perfunctory performance. But before even such a task can be transferred to them, the people must establish their fitness and evince their desire for it by a successful and satisfactory discharge of their local and municipal functions in the villages and towns, a reference to which has already been made in Letter VII.

Self-government to any extent or degree is no easy task, especially for a people disunited by race and caste, creed and tradition. These differences naturally tend to produce alienation of feelings and narrowness of views, and, as few public measures can affect or benefit all alike so as to obviate sectional jealousies and rivalries, there is always the fear of a conflict of opinions, prejudices, and interests proving inimical to the common cause. The main requisite of successful self-government (in the words of Lord Lansdowne[111] who is reported to have used them as a friendly warning in his parting address as Viceroy of the Dominion of Canada, which is composed of a European population divided by race as well as by creed) is "a patriotic spirit strong enough not only to inspire men's tongues with patriotic utterances, and their minds with vague aspirations after national greatness, but strong enough to extinguish local jealousies, to efface the rivalries of race, of party, and of creed – strong enough to secure the subordination of sectional interests whenever the sacrifice is demanded in the interests of the nation – strong enough to enable the people to bear prosperity without intoxication and adversity with dignity and patience".[112] This spirit must be evinced instinctively as a settled principle of action and a deep-seated conviction of the public mind on each occasion calling for its exercise. It is only when thus moved that a community can efficiently manage its local affairs or profitably cooperate with the government.

In the case in hand, as one means of enabling the people to qualify themselves for rendering such cooperation, and for realising successfully even the small advance sketched out in these letters, education and enlightenment must be spread among them both broadcast and deep. Men will then only learn to regard their own welfare as bound up with that of the state, they will then only rise above and superior to their petty selves, narrow views, or class prejudices, and try to prove useful and loyal citizens, when they are educated and enlightened and thereby enabled to realise that each of them is a citizen and that as such he must sacrifice something for the public good. It is by awakening the mental and moral capacities of your subjects by means of a general diffusion of knowledge and of culture that you will be able to rouse the idea of true patriotism in your subjects so as to fit them for a proper exercise of their rights and a just discharge of their duties as the members of a commonwealth. This is a duty which primarily devolves on the state, though its full development depends on the leaders and instructors of society. The moral aspect of this important question has been dwelt on in my second letter; the secular will be discussed in the next.

Yours &c.,
A POLITICAL RECLUSE

111 Henry Petty-Fitzmaurice (1845–1927) was a prominent British aristocrat and Whig politician who served as the Governor-General of Canada from 1883 to 1888 and then as Viceroy of India until 1894.

112 "Speech of His Excellency the Marquis of Landsdowne at the Toronto Club, 10th January, 1884", in Henry James Morgan, ed., *The Dominion Annual Register and Review for 1884* (Toronto: Hunter, Rose & Co., 1885), Appendix No. 4, 427.

Letter No. XI[113]

On Popular Instruction

MAHARAJA,

In the course of my third letter, I have pointed out the importance and necessity of the princes and nobles, and the higher orders generally, being brought up on a sound system of education so as to be enabled suitably to discharge the public duties of their high stations in life, and I reserved the question of popular instruction for future consideration. It is now time to address ourselves to the latter subject.

Ignorance is a curse and enlightenment a blessing in every rank and condition of life and of society. Hence the government of a state, which wields its resources and shapes its destinies, is bound to provide for the enlightenment of its subjects by means of education. From a remote period, however, as observed in the letter referred to above, all knowledge and enlightenment were in this country held to be the exclusive privilege of a small class, and ignorance happened to be the portion of the multitude. But, as was also remarked in the same place, a very different order of things now obtains in the land, and it not only permits but even demands as an essential for very existence a spread of education through all classes of the people. An exponent of the spirit of this new dispensation, an eminent member of one of the prominent British universities, observes:

> It would be of little avail to the peace and happiness of society, if the great truths of the material world were confined to the educated and the wise. The organization of science thus limited would cease to be a blessing. Knowledge secular, and knowledge divine, the double current of the intellectual lifeblood of man, must not merely descend through the great arteries of the social frame, it must be taken up by the minutest capillaries before it can nourish and purify society. Knowledge is at once the manna and the medicine of our moral being. Where crime is the bane, knowledge is the antidote. Society may escape from the pestilence and may survive the famine; but the demon of ignorance, with his grim adjutants of vice and riot, will pursue her into her most peaceful haunts, destroying our institutions, and converting into a wilderness the paradise of social and domestic life. The State has, therefore, a great duty to perform. As it punishes crime, it is bound to prevent it. As it subjects us to laws, it must teach us to read them; and while it thus teaches, it must teach also the ennobling truths which display the power and the wisdom of the great Lawgiver, thus diffusing knowledge, while it is extending education; and thus making men

113 This letter originally appeared in the *Indian Spectator* on June 1, 1890.

> contented, and happy, and humble, while it makes them quiet and obedient subjects.[114]

Popular education, therefore, must be taken in hand at the same time that the instruction of the higher classes is attended to, and it must be based on a compulsory system of primary education among the masses. For, if compulsory education has been found to be desirable or necessary for the general welfare in Europe and America, where the bulk of the people are so far advanced in knowledge, how much more is it not needed in this land of darkness where the unlettered and ignorant among the population including almost the whole of the female sex reckon at ninety-five in every hundred, and entire classes present a total blank in intellectual enlightenment?

Nor, I do believe, would there be any great difficulty experienced in introducing such a measure, for the generality of the people, though kept out of the reach of the light of knowledge, have always had a regard for the elements of learning and, if placed in the way, would welcome it as a boon for their children. There is only one condition which must be observed, and that is *to offer it free of cost*. Let free schools for primary education, therefore, be established in every town and village, and let them be thrown open to all, and attendance made compulsory on every male child of school-going age of the settled population, while periodic schools, similarly exempt from any charge, are opened for the children of *bona fide* cultivators who cannot spare them from their work during their busy season. The fees in secondary schools, attendance at which may not be compulsory, should be of a very moderate character, so as to suit the means of even the poorest classes, and after this stage has been reached, that is, in high schools and collegiate institutions established and maintained by the state for imparting higher general, professional, and technical education, the fees levied may have reference to the public expenditure incurred thereon. Mr. T. N. Mukherji of the Indian Economic Museum, evinces a keen perception of the situation when, in addressing himself to the economical problem in British India, he suggests as the first step towards its solution the institution of

> a mass education of a preliminary character just sufficient to prepare the way to dispel the darkness of the mind and to give it the power of sight to see the knowledge of the world; a technical education by which bread can be earned in humble life; and a higher education by which the intellect can press the modern sciences to the work of producing wealth on a large scale. Nothing is more important to the welfare of the country than primary education among

114 "Address of Sir David Brewster before the Twentieth Meeting of the British Association at Edinburgh, July 31, 1850", *The American Journal of Science*, Vol. 10, No. 30, November 1850, 319.

> the masses. It will break the present pride of education and will prevent the severance of the educated from the plough and the chisel. It will bring better skill, greater thrift, more independence and the power of a higher combination in the production of wealth. It will make them observe facts and phenomena which nature every day presents before their eyes, to put them together, to draw inferences from them, and to utilise them. What a vast field is this country to observe nature's phenomena with the light of modern knowledge, from the growth of a tiny plant to the brewing of a mighty storm, from her soft pleasing moods to her sulky caprices, to those mighty outbursts of her power which have ever brought mankind down upon its knees, to pray with clasped hands to the god of the firmament, the god of the wind, the god of the sun and the god of the sea. It will make our people better understand the teachings of the modern sciences, which at present they will fling away if not attended with immediate and palpable profit. Mass education is, therefore, the foundation on which to base all our work for the improvement of the condition of our people.[115]

These remarks are of equal applicability to all parts of the country, and on this basis of the primary education of the masses must be raised the edifice of higher education in all branches of knowledge, theoretical and practical, through the vernacular and English languages. It is not needful to go into any details regarding any scheme of this higher education for the Native States, as everybody is familiar with them from the institutions of British India and even from a few of their own. But in addition to the usual arrangements for imparting instruction, some provision should be made, and here private benefaction may well cooperate with the state, for carrying on original research and investigation into the physical and moral sciences in their application to this country. The necessity for such provision is indeed self-evident. Without original researches and investigations, all education must remain more or less a mechanical process, all knowledge, ancient or modern, inherited or acquired, a dead possession, unable to influence the national life materially, morally, or socially below the surface or make any advance over what is taught and learnt at schools and colleges.

Nor, lastly, must the sacred cause of female education be neglected. Free schools for the primary and secondary instruction of girls should be opened, and though attendance on their part may not be made compulsory as in the case of the boys, much might be effected by rewards and encouragement, and the very creation of well-paid posts of female teachers throughout the state will act as a stimulus to its spread. Beyond this degree of progress, however, the development of higher education among women must be

115 Trailokya Nath Mukherjee (1847–1919) was a civil servant in the Revenue Department in Bengal and a famed curator of Indian manufactures. The original source of this passage could not be traced.

influenced from above, that is, in other words, here you yourself and your higher classes must lead the way. Indeed, in this, as in all other questions connected with the social and moral condition of the people, Indian rulers have an immense advantage over the governors of British India, because they can directly lead Indian society, and mould its sentiments which the latter from the very fact of their being aliens are incapacitated from doing. This advantage can, when the former are equal to their position and become alive to their duties, be utilised to set to British India that example in female culture, and refinement and in social progress generally, which has heretofore been presented by it to the Native States chiefly in regard to the intellectual training of the men. National life must remain incomplete and at a low and unprogressive level where the females from want of education, a recognised position, or from any other cause, are incapable of sharing in the views or cooperating with the aims and objects of the males, and family life is a one-sided assortment in which highly cultivated and liberally educated men are joined in wedlock with ignorant and superstitious women, who, however good and affectionate they may be, can never command from their spouses that innate and continued respect and regard which one cultured mind inevitably feels for another and which is essential to complete the union of hearts.

Not only so, but in such circumstances even the knowledge and education which obtain among men will remain stationary or barren and incapable of creating an intellectual atmosphere. As has been well said, to educate a boy is only to bring up an individual, but to educate a girl is to train a whole family. When with the aid of knowledge and experience gathered in the past, the mothers of each generation begin to instruct their children from infancy, education in a community must improve rapidly in quality and extent, and with a progressive spirit of training and increasing knowledge society must advance in all other respects. Childhood is the most impressionable period of a man's life and during that period the mother constitutes to him not only the whole world but also his sole and infallible guide. The father's attentions are and ever will be momentary and superficial, and the importance of this function of the mother to the child's future cannot be over-estimated. For under her tender care and loving guidance his faculties can be awakened, principles and manners impressed, and impulses aroused – and all this imperceptibly and unconsciously accomplished – with an efficaciousness which the deftest and most sympathetic pedagogue, philosopher, or friend can never hope to bring about in after life. And it is thus that where women are educated and fitted (in the absence of education however only a very few souls who happen to be rarely gifted by nature can be fit) for the performance of this precious duty, in the case of almost every man who has achieved something great or good in the world, the inspiration is traced to the mother's guidance during childhood, while the sympathy and cooperation of the wife is not less valuable.

Female education and culture, therefore, are essential not only for the elevation of the sex and the felicity of domestic life but also for the proper training of children and the enlightenment and progress of society itself. The educated men of the day however, as a body, seem somehow disinclined to accept or act on this truth. I think here there is much need of a superior lead and example but, situated as things are, the want can be supplied only by the native princes and rulers. The only exception to the general disregard and distrust of female education is found in the case of that small section of the educated class which aspires after a higher ideal of religious, moral, and social life not unknown in the past and that ideal necessarily implies the enlightenment of the female mind. But on the whole, it is to be feared, it will be long before this important desideratum among the essential elements of progress and advancement in India will be supplied.

I have said above that the whole cost of the primary instruction and the greater portion of that of secondary education of the males should be borne by the state, and that after that stage things should be left to take the usual course. An exception, for some time to come, must, however, be made in favour of what may correctly be called the backward classes, that is, classes who have remained ignorant and outside the pale of knowledge and enlightenment, not of their own accord or owing to any fault of theirs, but because of their compulsory exclusion from those advantages. These classes must, then, be helped and encouraged to emerge out of their condition of darkness and ignorance, and the wisest and fairest means of effecting the object would be to select the most promising of the boys belonging to those classes from each grade of schools for special rewards if they are well to do, and support them entirely at the public expense if they are poor, to prosecute their further studies in the lines most suited to their talents and natural bent of mind and thereby enable them to attain to an equality of opportunity and so to compete, as far as practicable, on equal terms with the rest of their brethren. No objection can, I think, be reasonably taken to such temporary help being given to the deserving children of the classes who are the producers of the wealth of the land, but who have been arbitrarily debarred from all access to culture and enlightenment exclusively enjoyed by those who live on the fruits of their labours. But it cannot be too emphatically stated that after they have been furnished with the requisite general knowledge, no specific line should be selected for them without any regard to their tastes and capacities but that they should be trained to that for which nature has endowed them with the best aptitude. It is only then that they will be able to do themselves and to society at large the good they are capable of.

No small loss has been incurred and no little advantage foregone because of the failure to put to their appropriate uses talents and capacities with which nature is seen more or less indifferently to endow individuals among the different classes of a nation, and the natural fruitfulness of which therefore is sadly marred by "a monotony and monopoly of occupation"[116] artificially inflicted on their possessors from generation to generation. If any boy inherits a precious trade secret or capacity for his father's occupation, or at any rate has no special liking or aptitude for any other, by all means let him keep to it and make the best of his advantages. But it will be found all the world over that it is natural talent and aptitude which have served to advance human arts, and these special talents and aptitudes are not always or universally hereditary. What seems to be like it in many cases is the result of early training and association, but when their object is not in unison with the natural bent of mind, its valuable power is wasted, and this is what happens under the custom of hereditary occupation blindly followed. If arts in India once attained to a great excellence, it is not shown that it was due more to heredity of occupation than to natural genius. The reverse seems proved by general experience. It is undoubted that arts were cultivated in this country at an astonishingly early period, but at that time members of the same family appear to have followed different pursuits and neither caste nor occupation was hereditary. The greatest advance again was made during the prevalence of Buddhism which put a scant value on the rules of caste or of descent in any line of life. On the other hand, the arts, instead of reaching perfection as they should have under the alleged virtue of heredity, have been stagnant if not retrogressive during the long succeeding centuries which have been characterised by an unmitigated supremacy of caste division and of exclusively hereditary occupation.

Further, the social isolation which is the direct and natural offspring of these twin institutions has also in more recent times contributed powerfully to their decay by greatly facilitating the course of foreign competition. That decay is now the subject of general complaint and almost of pathetic lament as being the effect of the policy of a foreign government. But surely the destruction was not brought about in a day and fully to manifest itself it took well-nigh a hundred years of British supremacy. It may, then, be asked where during all this time was all the desire and the enthusiasm to keep up the indigenous arts which now find such expression, and why no effort was made to improve and support local industries so as to have enabled them to some extent at least to hold their own against foreign competition. Native society was surely wealthy and powerful and native rule extended over wide area enough to take care of native industries if they cared for them. But the

116 The source of this phrase could not be traced.

truth is the artisans formed so distinct a community by themselves and had so little to do with the higher and governing classes that they might as well have lived in another country if not in another continent. Nor were their own faculties enlightened or views expanded by education to enable them to perceive their danger or prepare to resist it. When, therefore, foreign fabrics were brought into the country they were readily purchased to the exclusion of home manufactures by the cultured and consuming classes because of their comparative cheapness, and this process went on without let or hindrance and the condition of the indigenous artisan proportionately deteriorated without its being much noticed. There was no sort of communion or sympathy between the manufacturing and consuming classes and thus the growing miseries of the former in no way affected or attracted the attention of the bulk of the latter because they were not connected by any social or family ties. Even now when the industrial collapse has been nearly complete and its economic effects on the general condition become so palpable, this state of things cannot be said to have *practically* altered.

I will cite an anecdote or two in illustration. When some twenty years ago popular feeling on the subject was first excited and shops for the sale of locally made fabrics were opened, a middle-class acquaintance was asked whether he was prepared to purchase from them in preference to any other. What object, said he enthusiastically, could be dearer than patronising goods made in one's own country. But when he was told he would have to pay a little dearer for them, he quietly added – "Ah! In that case it is a matter for consideration". Much more recently, a gentleman of means, position, and culture was declaiming against the policy of the government which had ruined indigenous arts and manufactures and pleading before a company for their revival. One of the hearers however was curious to know how much of locally made wares and manufactures the speaker himself was consuming. But on scanning his dress from head to foot, from turban to shoe, it was found that every article was of foreign manufacture with the exception of the sacred thread he wore which probably cost two annas a year! This was the magnificent extent of his patronage of local industries for the revival of which he vehemently pleaded. Was he then so silly or insincere in his profession? No. He said and did what everyone else was saying and doing, i.e. speaking from sentiment that did not reach home to him and hence the absence of serious or sustained practical effort in the matter. This is the natural result of the existing social and industrial arrangements.

I am aware of the fact that the action of the government in England was in the past directly hurtful and even now is not very friendly to Indian industries. Nor am I here pleading for the policy of protection or against the right of every man or country to buy in the cheapest market. I am only showing how subtle and far-reaching is the effect of the isolation produced by caste and hereditary occupation but for which the once flourishing industries of India could have been helped to maintain themselves even against foreign competition at least to some extent by calling up the resources and talents which have lain dormant. The fact is a certain social solidarity, and unity of interests is essential for a successful development of national industries as of all other sources of prosperity and greatness and to secure this development, talent, and aptitude of all kinds wherever and in whomsoever they may be found to exist should be given a free scope instead of being thwarted or misdirected by artificial restrictions and checks on their exercise. For, other conditions being equal, they are the most potent factors of progress, and the cases of other countries of the world, from conservative China to radical America, prove clearly that not only in arts and manufactures, but in all lines of life natural talent and aptitude do more for human advancement and prosperity than heredity of occupation.

Therefore, if arts and industries are to be developed – and that they must be developed is one of the urgent needs of the times – natural talent must be utilised and improved by the best training which can be given on the spot or obtained in foreign countries where it is at its highest. The knowledge and skill thus acquired must be applied to the development of the resources of the state, whether agricultural, mineral, manufacturing, or artistic, and they must be directed towards the production of articles of such quality and at such cost that they shall be enabled to hold their own against outside competition. But your court and your administration must set the example of extending their patronage to them. Under such an impulse, the old arts and industries ought not only to preserve their special characteristics, but also to be able by comparison with foreign models even to strike out new styles of work and ornament, and thus add to their excellence and reputation.

In the case of entirely new lines of business, however, the state, in the present want of knowledge and enterprise among its people, must also, cautiously and under well-considered conditions, take some share of the initial risk. In these and in similar other ways must technical education and industrial enterprise be made fruitful of good and a source of prosperity to the people and to the state. Of course, all these measures will require money, and money must be found for them, even if as a prudential investment in behalf of the commonwealth. This is why, among other reasons, no existing tax should be lightly given up. For it is from the taxes that the money which the state has to expend on these objects must come, and next to the preservation of the public peace and the maintenance of an efficient administration, the taxes cannot be applied to a more important purpose than in bringing about a development of its resources in all directions, material as well as moral, progress in both of which, indeed, must go together.

The educational efforts of a state, then, ought not to end with schools and colleges, but they must run through other measures and institutions calculated to exert an educative and inspiring influence on the mass of its people generally, and stimulate their intelligence and industry. Museums, in which are gathered together for the inspection and edification, even of the untravelled, the distant products of skill and industry, might be established in suitable centres. Exhibitions and shows [may be] held periodically at which the people would be able to realise how far their near and remote competitors fell short of or surpassed them in the production of superior goods and stock, and stimulated to attain facility and excellence therein. Special prizes might be offered and patents given for the introduction of new workmanship and industries, or for improvements in the methods of the old. These and other means, which ought to be adopted for unfolding the material side of the resources of the state, are well known from their success among Europeans and need not be dwelt upon here.

I attach, however, still greater importance to what may be called the cultivation of the moral resources, that is giving a free scope and full encouragement to the development of the mental and moral capacities of man himself, because it is the unfolding of those capacities which forms man's crown on earth, which constitutes the real greatness of a people, and which is intimately connected even with material progress. Of this, too, we have examples in European countries, but here I will refer to one nearer home – China. A mention of the name of that country in this connection will probably appear startling to some people, but I believe that a close and unprejudiced study of its institutions will discover much of order and constitution and sound social arrangements which certainly no other country in Asia is capable of showing and owing to which alone the celestial empire with its swarming population, its civilization, its laws, its literature, its science, its arts, its industries has steadily outlived its contemporaries of hoary antiquity, and though approached and occasionally menaced by powerful rivals and neighbours from land and sea, [it] not only betrays no sign of decadence but on the contrary gives a promise that it means to turn its contact with the advanced West to its own advantage and strength, and European critics even regard it as the great power of the future.

I think then that in spite of some of its barbarous customs and foolish prejudices including its contempt for the outside world (the knowledge and skill of which, however, with its wise instinct it has been slowly absorbing), it seems to me from the wise and liberal character of some of its political and social institutions, and still more its educational and industrial activity, to be, for the dormant and despotic East, a very advanced country. Its government is, no doubt, absolute in form and patriarchal in its executive methods but not, as generally held, quite arbitrary in practice. For, though the emperor is the sole interpreter of the decrees of Heaven, that august function is in truth sustained with the assistance of the sons of men, for His Majesty is helped by a cabinet council and boards and departmental committees, which are presided over by the ablest and most experienced officers who are originally selected for the state service from among the youths of the empire by open competition, and which are the depositories of knowledge of all laws, and customs, and precedents and it is on these that the imperial behests and commands ultimately rest.

Moreover, unlike any other Asiatic country, it has a public opinion expressed through printed placards and newsletters by a section of the educated middle class known as the "literary and gentry" who stand midway between a vast body of interested officials on the one hand, and the mass of the people on the other. This middle class consists of those who have been admitted to a government examination, but who have not succeeded in being of the select number to whom degrees are granted. "They exercise a salutary and, within limits, a powerful influence." Archdeacon Gray, from whose *History of the Laws, Manners, and Customs of China* I am quoting, adduces the following testimony of an American consular officer regarding the position and functions of the class referred to:

> "They act", writes Mr. Low from the United States Legation at Pekin, in an official letter (January 1871) to his Government, "as advisers to the lower classes, and their good offices are sought by the governing class in the management of local concerns. By their superior intelligence they are enabled to control most of the property and yet few acquire such wealth as would enable them to oppress the people were they so disposed. This class create the public opinion of the country, which exercises a controlling influence over the officials, and is usually powerful enough to thwart the intentions and nullify the action of the officers, from the Emperor down, whenever popular rights are in danger of being invaded or the people unduly oppressed. So powerful is the influence of the literati that all officials endeavor to conform their action to the popular will, and in this view the Government of China is essentially democratic in practice."[117]

This compliment coming from the representative of a pronounced republic of the West must be considered significant and is doubtless deserved. Indeed, the Chinese constitution may well be regarded as liberal since the emperor has the right to select a competent outsider to succeed him, if there should be no member of his family qualified to rule. This right is, of course, scarcely ever exercised, but the provision shows much regard for the claims of the subjects to good government. Again, His Majesty is regarded as the child

117 John Henry Gray, *China: A History of the Laws, Manners, and Customs of the People*, Vol. 1 (London: Macmillan & Co., 1878), 182.

of the Sun, but he does not seek his domestic alliances among other children of the sun or the moon, but selects even his empress, the sharer of his exalted position, from among the marriageable daughters of his subjects on account of their personal qualities, and attractions without reference to their families and positions. There are no distinctions of caste among the people; titles of honour and degrees of nobility are not permanent but limited to certain generations proportioned to the degree of the founder's merit; and even the imperial blood is distantly absorbed into the body politic. Education is universal among men, and general among women; humane institutions, like asylums for the blind, the leper, the infirm, the foundling, &c., are not wanting; but I need not go into these details regarding the celestials.

I have made this brief allusion to the general character of the political and social institutions of the country only to show there is an example of some sort of impersonal order and constitution even in Asia. My chief object here, however, is to draw attention to the means which the state among that conservative people uses to draw out the intellectual and moral capacities of the nation. The public service, for instance, is recruited by free competition from among all classes without restriction, and Carlyle, who was chary of bestowing praise where not much was deserved, thus descants on this particular measure:

> By far most interesting fact I hear about the Chinese is one on which we cannot arrive at clearness, but which excites endless curiosity even in the dim state: this namely, that they do attempt to make their Men of Letters their Governors. It would be rash to say, one understood how this was done, or with what degree of success it was done. All such things must be very unsuccessful; yet a small degree of success is precious; the very attempt how precious! There does seem to be, all over China, a more or less active search everywhere to discover the men of talent that grow up in the young generation. Schools there are for everyone: a foolish sort of training, yet still a sort. The youths who distinguish themselves in the lower school are promoted into favourable stations in the higher, that they may still more distinguish themselves, forward and forward: it appears to be out of these that the Official Persons, and incipient Governors, are taken. These are they whom they try first, whether they can govern or not. And surely with the best hope: for they are the men that have already shown intellect. Try them: they have not governed or administered as yet; perhaps they cannot; but there is no doubt they have some understanding – without which no man can! Neither is Understanding a tool, as we are too apt to figure, "it is a hand which can handle any tool". Try these men: they are of all others the best worth trying. Surely there is no kind of government, constitution, revolution, social apparatus or arrangement, that I know of in this world, so promising to one's scientific curiosity as this. The man of intellect at the top of affairs: this is the aim of all constitutions and revolutions if they have any aim. For the man of true intellect, as I assert

> and believe always, is the noble hearted man withal, the true, just, humane and valiant man. Get him for governor, all is got; fail to get him, though you had Constitutions plentiful as blackberries, and a Parliament in every village, there is nothing yet got![118]

This one institution alone cannot but prove a mighty stimulus to national education and enlightenment, and the historian accordingly observes that there is perhaps no country in the world "in which education – up to a certain point – is more generally diffused among the male population".[119] I am tempted here to quote, as an illustration of the manner in which it is calculated to work on the public mind, the following account from Mr. Gray's book of the treatment of graduates passing the highest test of knowledge and capacity:

> The examination for the degree of Han-lin or LL. D. is conducted in the Imperial Palace at Pekin by the Emperor himself. The test is a written answer to any question which the Emperor may propose. The successful candidates are divided into four classes. Those of the first class have the degree conferred on them and are reserved for important vacancies. Graduates of the second class become members of the inner council; those of the third class obtain situations in the six boards, and those of the fourth become district rulers. The newly made Han-lins are entertained at dinner by the Emperor, and, as a mark of great honour, each guest sits at a separate table, upon which the most reçherche viands are spread. The graduate at the head of the list is called Chwan-yuen, and his reputation extends to all parts of the empire. Wandering heralds carry his name to remote villages as well as populous towns, and both high and low make a point of becoming acquainted with some particulars of his family and early training. When he travels, the keepers of the various hostelries at which he lodges consider themselves highly honoured by the presence of so distinguished a visitor. In 1872, Canton had the honour of Chwang-yuen, and the most distinguished of the Han-lins for that year entered the city in state. The Han-lin Hall, in which the degree of Doctor of Laws is conferred, is in the form of a parallelogram, and on each of the four sides there is a cloister. Against the walls of the cloisters are placed marble slabs on which are inscribed the original text of Confucius. In the centre, under a pavilion, is the throne on which the Emperor sits when called upon, in the discharge of his imperial duties, to explain the doctrines of Confucius to his ministers. When the degree of Doctor of Laws is conferred, the approved candidates arrange themselves round the throne, and as the name of each candidate is called, the Emperor makes a mark against it with his vermilion pencil in a list which he has before him.[120]

118 Carlyle, *On Heroes, Hero-Worship, and the Heroic in History*, 152.
119 Gray, *China: A History of the Laws, Manners, and Customs of the People*, 166.
120 Gray, *China: A History of the Laws, Manners, and Customs of the People*, 177.

And yet the young scholars thus honoured and advanced may be the humblest in birth and position among their countrymen. Then again, the state marks with the stamp of its approval a high proficiency in knowledge and bestows social distinctions on its possessors at any stage and in any condition of life, and men of sixty appear at examinations for degrees as eagerly as any youth. Similarly are rewarded distinguished public services and uncommon degrees of virtue exhibited both in public and private, including instances of exceptional filial devotion and even the attainment to a very old age! How much sound sense and philosophy is there in this last ordinance! For a green old age is, as a rule, only the result of a virtuously spent youth and manhood and a public sentiment which regards such a life and such old age as in themselves worthy of respect cannot but prove salutary in its effect on the national mind and morals.

Now, all this is intended to lead to the suggestion that you should institute orders of distinction within your own dominions for the public recognition of worth and the reward of merit among your own subjects. The love of honour and distinction in the eyes of our fellow men is strong in the human breast, and it is wise and just to gratify it when deserved through exemplary behaviour. The individual, indeed, must pursue right and duty for their own sake, but the state cannot be doing wrong in putting its own value on such a pursuit, and thus using it as a means for raising the moral tone and promoting the happiness of the community – nay, it is its duty not to neglect those means which have been placed at its disposal to that end.

There should, then, be established orders to distinguish all kinds of public services and personal merits and virtues throughout the state. Exceptional fidelity to trust in the presence of great temptation, originality in literature and science, inventiveness in art or manufacture, courage and intrepidity in saving human life, self-sacrificing exertions in relieving human suffering, munificence and liberality directed to the advancement of the general welfare, disinterested devotion to and pursuit of the public good – signal examples of these and similar other virtues and also extraordinary examples of devotion to duty and tenderness shown even in humble private life under trying conditions and circumstances should be formally recognised by the state and honoured with suitable distinctions according to their degrees of merit, from rewards and titles to mere mentions with approbation in the state *Gazette*, which, when judiciously and impartially bestowed, cannot fail to be appreciated and prized.

The holders of these distinctions will then go to form a veritable Legion of Honor; they would constitute the true nobility of nature and the aristocracy of intellect among the people and vying with the men of birth, wealth, and position, would imperceptibly contribute to the elevation and advancement of society. Of course the Raja must be the head and patron of all the orders, because he is the representative of the state and as such the fountain source of all honour and authority proceeding from it, and from this double position duly sustained it must follow that your court will be the cherished home of those beneficent agencies and influences appertaining to times past and to times present which make for the improvement of man's condition in this world and fit him for a better – a source of pride and hope to your people and of envy and example to your neighbours.

I believe, Maharaja, you will now perhaps realise the full force of the observation which has been previously made to the effect that the reforms I have recommended in the constitution and in the administration of your state are calculated not to diminish but rather to strengthen and enhance your power and dignity. I have yet one more letter to address you before I shall have done.

Yours &c.,
A POLITICAL RECLUSE

Letter No. XII[121]

On Good Government

MAHARAJA,

You are now placed, under the scheme developed in these letters, at the head of a constitutionalised government and at the top of a society endowed with two of the essential elements of progress, *viz.*, education or the means of attaining knowledge and enlightenment, and freedom or full scope for the development of its genius and its resources. I think you will find, as remarked at the close of my last letter, that this new position, so far from detracting from your authority and prestige, as compared with the old precarious order of things, will only add to them, and very justly too, because it imposes on you strenuous duties and weighty functions, the fulfilment of which necessarily constitutes moral force; and it is moral force which, on a large view of things, will be found to prevail in and rule the world.

There is yet one more of these duties and functions which is as essential as the rest that have been already described, but it is by no means as onerous as most of them, *viz.*, the duty, in one word of keeping complete touch with the country. You must be "a man of your time accessible to ideas, well aware of what goes on in spheres very unlike his own". To sustain this position you must on occasions travel out of your state privately and, if possible, even *incognito*, in which case you will be not only spared the time and trouble spent in formalities but also be able intimately to know the land through which you pass and the real sentiments of its people. It is, however, with reference to your own state that this duty has an especial claim on your attention.

A personal acquaintance with the different portions of his dominions and a correct insight into the character, condition, and the wants and wishes of the people are essential in a ruler for success in his work. Not to speak of any higher object, it will enable him quickly to comprehend and correctly to appreciate whatever official papers and information will come before him for disposal in the course of business. So, to acquire such acquaintance and insight into your own state, you must make periodic tours through your territories. These tours, entered upon with no larger retinue than is absolutely necessary so as to involve no heavy expense and also to make the smallest possible demand on local resources, may be undertaken at convenient times and seasons, but they must be so regulated that no part

121 This letter originally appeared in the *Indian Spectator* in two parts, on December 14 and December 21, 1890.

of the state, however humble or remote from your headquarters may remain unvisited for any very long interval, while special occasions might require special visits to particular localities.

This duty would be far from unpleasant. Change of scene and climate is always agreeable, and it often becomes necessary for the restoration of health and energy to an over-worked constitution. Indeed, Nature, who is a teacher and a nurse herself, suggests this idea of change and through her wondrous succession of seasons kindly furnishes it even to those who remain rooted to one spot. An occasional peep into the simplicity of village life, the quietude of rural existence and the stillness, grandeur, and sublimity of Nature may, therefore, pleasurably alternate with the splendour of palaces and the crowds, the din and the business of capital cities and towns, and tend to increased zest for work and enjoyment just as the tamarind fruit or mango pickle occasionally tasted restores the relish of one satiated with indulgence in sweetmeats. An ancient European poet has, perhaps with a touch of envy, put the same truth in this form:

> Sometimes 'tis grateful to the rich to try,
> A short vicissitude, and fit of poverty.
> A savoury dish, a homely treat,
> Where all is plain, where all is neat,
> Without the stately spacious room,
> The Persian carpet or the Tyrian loom,
> Clear up the cloudy foreheads of the great.[122]

Now this renovation of strength is not a small gain to be derived from tours in the country. The places visited, too, will not be without a reciprocal benefit. Their denizens will naturally feel honoured and welcome you with preparations which would incidentally effect the removal of some local discomforts, e.g., a broken road. While your presence among them might well encourage them with your aid to provide some public want, a tank, a schoolhouse, a *dharmshala*, and so forth, and thus these visits would leave beneficent mementoes behind them. But, of course, their main purpose is for you to know the country and to be known by it, to acquire a living knowledge of the people, their condition, sentiments, and feelings, which must be obtained by a free intercourse with them and by an interchange of thoughts and of hospitalities. A short converse with a plain villager or an unsophisticated rustic casually met, too, will often prove more instructive for the purpose in hand than a formal interview with a professedly representative man.

122 Lord Ravensworth, trans., *The Odes of Horace* (London: Upham and Beet, 1858), XXIX, 378.

While, however, you thus freely mix socially with the people, you must guard against being officially inaccessible to those who would seek you on business. To this point I have briefly alluded in my opening letter, and I must say a few words here in explanation of it. Accessibility is a characteristic virtue of personal rule and must not be abandoned where the administration is systematised, but it must be judiciously utilised to test its working, and, where possible, to supplement its defects or shortcomings. You have probably heard of the emperor Akbar's bell-court, i.e., a chamber attached to the palace in which there hung a bell. Any subject, who wished to relate the story of his grievance to His Majesty in secret, had only to ring this bell and the emperor stood before him alone ready to listen. This contrivance, it is said, inspired the imperial officials with a wholesome fear of their responsibility, and the people ceased to suffer from any oppression.

The story is popularly related and, whether true or not historically, it conveys a moral which is worth bearing in mind though, no doubt, secret methods of this kind are from their very nature almost certain to lead to demoralisation on both sides and should therefore be resorted to only in special cases. [Therefore] you must be accessible in a business-like manner, and for this purpose what I would suggest is that whenever you are on a visit to a place, you must set apart some time, and, while in the capital, a fixed day in the month, when any subject might freely call on and lay before you a personal or general grievance for which no remedy has been provided, and you may take such action thereon as may seem to be called for. Of course, such cases ought to be very few because they are not to include matters which have been decided by duly constituted judicial or executive authority and by yourself in appeal, and people who are once found to make a frivolous use of the privilege may be deprived of it altogether.

Limited by these conditions, your personal accessibility to your subjects will, I believe, be free from objection or embarrassment of any kind. It may, on the contrary, serve to bring to your notice exceptional cases and interesting incidents such as you could come across only if you were yourself moving among them in disguise, and it seems well calculated not only to remove all reasonable ground of complaint but even to produce a feeling of confidence and general satisfaction among the people at large. With a mind thus kept awake by personal intercourse and instructed by official information, you will be able to "survey society and the administration from top to bottom, and examine the interior forces by which they are kept at once in balance and in motion".[123] From your vantage ground you will be able to detect and remove any danger to the public interests; find out and redress individual wrongs or injustice; and alleviate distress and suffering

123 Gladstone, *Gleanings of Past Years*, 4.

which might otherwise afflict their victims in hopeless despair. In some cases, a mere word of explanation, sympathy, or encouragement would be enough to soothe heart-burnings; in others official inquiry and action might be called for or an exercise of your prerogative necessary to heal a wound otherwise irremediable; and in others still the judicious bestowal of a little "secret service money" – it would really deserve to be styled "sacred service money" and should yearly find a place as discretionary allowance among the heads of the state budget – would remove some unmerited privation, hardship, or suffering.

Through continued ministrations of this kind you will be able to diffuse happiness and contentment throughout the state, and be justly regarded as, in the best sense of the expression, the father of your people; creating a noble tradition in your family; supplying worthy precedents for the guidance of your successors; affording, a bright example to your brother rulers; furnishing material for many a tale and panegyric to be handed down from generation to generation of your subjects; and thus bringing vividly to men's minds a felicitous combination of the poet's ideal of the king in the East:

> Here reigned a king who walked in Virtue's path,
> Who ruled his country only for his God.
> His people's good he deemed his only care,
> Their sorrows were his sorrows, and their joys
> He counted as his own; such was the king
> Whose daily prayers went up to Him on high
> For wisdom and for strength to rule his men
> Aright, and guard the land from foreign foes[124]

with that of him in the West:

> We see him as he moved,
> How modest, kindly, all-accomplished, wise,
> With what sublime repression of himself
> And in what limits, and how tenderly;
> Not swaying to this faction or to that;
> Not making his high place the lawless perch
> Of wing'd ambitions, nor a vantage-ground
> For pleasure; but thro' all this tract of years
> Wearing the white flower of a blameless life,
> Before a thousand peering littlenesses,
> In that fierce light which beats upon a throne,
> And blackens every blot.[125]

124 T. Ramakrishna Pillai, *Life in an Indian Village* (London: T. Fisher Unwin, 1891), 112.

125 Alfred Tennyson, "Idyls of the King", in *The Complete Works of Alfred, Lord Tennyson, Poet Laureate* (New York: Harper and Brothers, 1884), 148.

Here my task may be said to end; but just as I began, so do I wish to conclude these letters with answering a few questions.

And the first question which occurs is: Why should you impose on yourself the troublesome task of reform and innovation when an indolent continuance of the existing order of things is possible? I have already made an answer to this question before, but it will well bear a little variation. Every man and every enlightened man who recognises the dignity of his nature must regard it as his duty and his privilege humbly to strive his best in the sphere in which he is placed to leave the world better than he found it. For a ruler, especially one who is gifted and enlightened, this conception of his position opens out no end of reform and improvement in the administration on which depend the happiness and welfare of millions of human beings and of generations yet unborn, and hence the more permanent the seeds of reform the greater is the value and fruitfulness of the achievement.

There is, besides, a very old precept or precedent for the kind of reform herein urged. The idea of the will of a sovereign being limited by the dictates of right and wrong, and controlled and guided by the advice and experience of responsible ministers, spiritual and temporal, as also influenced by the voice of representatives of the people, appertains to very ancient times in this land, but it has become quite obsolete by the later prevalence of absolute despotism, under which the king [knows] no law but his will. Even then, however, an ideal monarch is universally held to be he who personally goes about, often in disguise, to find out the wrongs of his people and afford instant redress. It is thus that the names of Vikramaditya and Bhoja among Hindus, and of Harun al-Rashid and al-Ma'mun among the Mahomedans, have become famous and typical of good sovereigns, and their successors are esteemed only in proportion to the degree to which they follow their example.

But an individual ruler, whatever his energy and intelligence, is not ubiquitous, nor possessed of the faculty of perceiving what is not immediately before his eyes or within his hearing. What is thus impossible to the individual, however, is rendered feasible by systematic or constitutional government, which may be likened to a net of feelers conveying to the centre knowledge of things remote as well as near. Again, despotic rule, which is injurious to the interests of the subject, is no more favourable to the steady fortunes of the state nor of the reigning dynasty. It is a historical truth that under such rule the state rises or falls both in reputation and prosperity according to the personal character of the ruler, and personal character is not only uncertain but more often than not falls short of the requisite standard. Therefore it is that Col. Tod, in recounting with the fullest sympathy the results of the best type of indigenous rule India presented in the stirring story of Rajputana in general, and of Mewar, its premier state, in particular, in which etiquette, custom, and observance approached the dignity but fell far short of the substance of a constitution, is obliged to exclaim, "Happy the country where the sovereignty is in the laws, and where the monarch is but the chief magistrate of the State unsubjected to those vicissitudes, which make the scepter in Asia unstable as a pendulum, kept in perpetual oscillation by the individual passions of her princes; where the virtues of one will exalt her to the summit of prosperity as the vices of a successor will plunge her into the abyss of degradation."[126] This is a brief but suggestive observation and it holds good of all states in all conditions and circumstances.

Now, I conceive that, to aspire after such a model, the Native States in India are or ought to be powerfully propelled from three different directions at the present time. In days gone by, they had to hold their own in war or diplomacy against encroaching neighbours, and this condition kept up their energies, though in a rude form. But protection being now ensured by the British government, the resulting repose and security is calculated to lead to degeneracy of spirit and body, unless a higher responsibility is created in the conduct of their internal affairs to which they are now confined. This can only be secured by the adoption of constitutional methods of administration which bring out mental powers and moral vigour and keep them in salutary play, while they serve to advance and safeguard good government.

Again, every day the intercourse between British India and native territory is developing, and as the reign of law and rights of citizenship ripen in the former, its people will be impelled to cry out against a continuance of patriarchal rule in the latter and invoke the interference of the paramount power to force reform on it. Fortunately for you and your brethren, however, educated British India is not in a hurry to march socially and morally to the requisite standard. If anything it shows signs of being quite restive, if not reactionary, in regard to those vital questions and evinces a desire to cherish rather than reform or correct a state of society that is based on or favourable to abuses and wrongs and penetrated with baneful influences in itself as much as it is inconsistent with the growth or existence of citizenship or national progress in any direction whatever. If, meanwhile, the Native States choose to act voluntarily, they have the means not only of marching alongside British India, but even going ahead of it in some important respects and furnishing an example to it.

Lastly, there is the huge car of the Government of India itself treading heavily onwards with its wheels within wheels and its many and diverse conductors, all cooperating with each other, no one thwarting another, and turning even their mistakes to its own aggrandisement. In these circumstances

126 Tod, *Annals and Antiquities of Rajasthan*, 272.

woe to the state which throws itself in its path, or rather does not keep itself out of its way.

All these, then, are powerful motives for the Indian princes not only to put their existing administrations on their best behaviour, but also to improve the very system, so as to ensure continued good government for the future amidst all individual changes.

And this remark leads to the next question which might occur: Is the course herein recommended practicable? I cannot see why it should not be. I do not suggest the promulgation of a complex constitution which could not without difficulty be carried out in practice and may only prove bewildering to the people. What has to be done is that, with the aid of proper instruments carefully chosen and all wilful obstruction sternly repressed, the requisite measures be taken in hand one after another in the order of their importance and urgency, and set agoing, and there is little doubt that if this is done the outlines of a system will have been laid out in a few years. This is what was done and is still being done in India by the British Government itself, and there is no reason why what they find practicable over a large extent of territory and among diverse masses of people varying in race, custom, creed, and intelligence, should not be feasible in the small areas and comparatively homogeneous populations of the Native States – with earnestness of purpose, with intelligence, and vigilant supervision.

Again, will it be acceptable to the subjects? There can be no question on that head, too. No one likes to be arbitrarily governed, and all would welcome right and liberty. The only question may be whether, so long accustomed to despotic sway, they would have the courage and public spirit to assert their rights as against local hierarchies. But in this they only differ from the subjects of British India in degree, and, indeed, have some advantages over the latter as has been explained in the letters on district administration. In both alike the supervising authorities have need, in order to help their subjects in the realisation of their boons, to be ever watchful and to allow no judicial ignorance to prevent their inquiring into abuses known to exist. In China, it is said this duty is assigned to a special board – not a bad idea.

But, once again and for the last time, it may be asked – Can the system thus commenced be expected to flourish in safety? May it not be thwarted, if not upset, by inimical cabals or influences or by a successor who may be differently inclined? This is not very likely. The moral force of public opinion generally would be opposed to such a retrogression and the paramount power may be expected to throw in its weight on the side of that opinion, but I confess a really reliable guarantee would be furnished only by the Political Agents of the British government at the native courts being held answerable for their good administration along with the princes themselves.

At present, these able officers, besides watching the interests of their own government, have mainly to perform the duties, as it were, of surveillance and to make reports, which at the critical stage cannot be considered as other than one-sided, on the faults and failings of the princes. But such a modification in their position as that suggested [previously] would render their services far more prolific of good to the Native States and to the British government. A quarter of a century ago, the then Secretary of State for India ordered an inquiry into the relative merits of English and Native rule in this country, and a leading London critic noticing the subject held it proved that England had "pressed out all vital energies from the Native States".[127] That was as inevitable as it was true, for the states used to spend their energies more on fighting with their neighbours and rivals, including the British power, than on their own affairs, and peace was uncertain in that condition of things. But now from rivals they have become subordinate and protected allies. Therefore, the same far-sighted policy, which then neutralised their energy, now demands that it be restored and sustained for work within their own bounds.

This can only be compassed by altering the relations of the Political Officers to the Native States as already indicated. The change would be just and beneficial to the states and would not be without some direct gain even to the British government itself. It would for one thing remove all cause of distrust or anxiety on either side and all feeling of irritation and friction between them, and this by itself would not be a small advantage. But there is yet another no less important: the British empire in Asia has become unwieldy and is still growing. Its government has already invited or welcomed offers of military aid and cooperation from the Indian princes in the external defence of that empire, and its responsible rulers declare the burden of governing it to be heavy, indeed, and would gladly share it with Native potentates. There is no reason to doubt the sincerity of that declaration, for the task of governing a fifth of the human race, aliens in blood, language, creed, and thought, and that too from a base 5,000 miles away cannot be an easy one. But on the ordinary ground of human nature it strikes me that so long as their present unsound political relations exist, or, in other words, so long as the fate of a prince practically rests in the hands of a single Political Officer, i.e., is decided in accordance with his report – and the Government of India and the Secretary of State as his immediate official superiors are too much identified with him and with the general tenor of his official acts not to accept or act on his views in any dispute between

127 *Homeward Mail*, January 4, 1868.

the two parties – no cooperation between them can be ungrudging and salutary in its consequences, though it may be rendered by the weaker merely because withholding it would displease the stronger side.

All this would change if the Indian princes could feel that the responsibility of the Political Officers towards the good government of their territories lay actively and formally on the same side with their own, and that in case of any serious differences between them they would be judged by an independent and impartial tribunal. No other course seems so well calculated to inspire them with a sense of security for their position and with self-respect, self-possession, and courage to undertake a difficult and onerous task, and yet this attitude of the mind is essential to enable them to deal with the standing obstacles and vested interests in the way of all reform and change and to their efficiency as rulers of their own territories and also as friends of the British government in any matter in which their help and counsel might be sought or be useful.

I have referred to this point once more, because, as I have observed in speaking of it in its proper place before, to my mind it covers more than half the problem in hand, and without a satisfactory settlement of the former the solution of the latter would be extremely difficult, if not impossible. If any proof of this view be wanted, it is abundantly supplied by the fact that almost[128] all instances in which any reform or system has been adopted in

128 *Original footnote*: An exception must be made in justice to the memory of a very interesting and singular character, the late Anandashram Swami. He was an educated and intelligent Bengali gentleman, who having entered the *sanyasi* order betook, as required by its rules, to travel away from the province of his birth, and passing through Northern and Central India about a quarter of a century ago reached one of the leading states of Kathiawar. Here he saw instances of misrule and exposed them in newsletters to a paper published in Bombay. Their appearance attracted attention and produced excitement and curiosity in the state as it was not easy in those days to find in so remote a quarter a man who knew and could write English. The author, however, was soon found out and taken before the Raja who remonstrated with him on his conduct, but the *swami* persisted and when threatened with the jail – for he was too sacred a person to be given any violent punishment – he declared that as he had given up home and family, the jail to him was as good a place of residence as any other and that so long as he saw oppression practised on the people he would continue exposing it, whatever the consequences to him personally. This exhibition of disinterestedness melted the heart of the old Rajput ruler of the state and he offered the *swami* the post of his *dewan* that he might manage things as he thought best. The latter however pointed to his cloth as forbidding his re-entrance into worldly occupation but undertook to procure a competent man for the office, and an educated gentleman from Bombay was induced by the *swami* to accept it. The new regime introduced reforms in the judicial system and began the practice of passing decisions in the chief judicial court irrespective of frowns and favours from persons in authority and unbiassed by other personal considerations. It also

any of the Native States have occurred through the British government intervening, whether on account of the minority of their rulers or from any other cause and either directly administering their possessions or lending their full support to the ministers by whom the changes in question were introduced.

I have done. I have only to add that I do not claim to have said in these letters anything that is very deep or new. As I have confessed at the outset, the reforms herein urged were either suggested by others or are such as might occur to anybody who would care to think on the matter: I have only brought them together in a convenient shape. Some of them, too, have already been adopted more or less completely in some of the states, including your own, and others in some others; but I believe in no state have all of them been carried out, and there are many in which little or nothing of this kind has been done. I, therefore, sincerely trust that these letters will prove of interest to many in and out of Native States, and I earnestly pray that any effort which you or anyone else should be inclined to make to give effect to any of the suggestions they contain may be crowned with success.

influenced reforms in departments other than the judicial and partially though indirectly helped on the abolition of the farming system which was a source of much abuse. These arrangements gave satisfaction to the people and the name and fame of the *swami* spread throughout the province. The anti-reform party in the state however could not brook the new order of things and after incessant intrigue and misrepresentations succeeded in undermining his influence and procuring the dismissal of his nominee. But though the men were changed, the reforms they had introduced not only remained intact but were gradually adopted by the other states in the province. Neither did the old party regain the uninterrupted lease of power it had enjoyed before nor the same degree of it. Now this case is an exception to the rule mentioned in the text as the specific reforms referred to were brought about solely by the exertions of the *swami* and in no way were prompted or helped by the British government or its Political Agent. Of course their influence always works on the side of improved administration and it was so working even at this time in the province generally, but in the particular case here mentioned the Political Agent so far from seconding the *swami* for a time even looked upon him with some suspicion because it was unusual to find a man who put on the yellow garb of the orthodox hermit and conformed to orthodox ways of life and yet read and spoke English and concerned himself with politics and the worldly welfare of his fellowmen. Hence the *swami* received from the Agency officials the soubriquet of "A Political Sanyasi". His, I believe, has been the only instance of its kind. However, it shows that it is possible to find even an Indian Raja willing to reform his administration in the interests of his subjects but that as in the case of despotic rulers all the world over he must be surrounded always with favourable influences. But what influence could be more favourable for this purpose and what more permanent than that of the Political Agent if he be held responsible conjointly with his charge for good government.

Finally, esteemed Maharaja, I wish you God's choicest blessings, health and longevity, success and prosperity, and, hoping that you may deserve the name and fame of a model ruler and an exemplary prince, I beg to take my leave of you and ever to remain,

Your Highness' earnest well-wisher,
A POLITICAL RECLUSE

Appendices

ENGLISH AND NATIVE RULE

IN INDIA.

Bombay:

Printed and published by Rámchandra A. Udás,

at the NATIVE OPINION Press.

1868.

Price 8 *annas*.

Title page of *English and Native Rule in India*, Bombay, Native Opinion Press, 1868. British Library, Tr.958(n)

I

English and Native Rule in India (1868)[1]

I. Introductory[2]

Lord Cranborne's[3] official connection with this country, short-lived as it unluckily was, has proved, and will doubtless continue to prove, a great gain to its administration. For his Lordship not only evinces a uniform interest in the subject, but brings to bear on it a tolerable amount of information, keen powers of perception and reasoning, a rectitude of judgement, and a ready eloquence. And these qualities are accompanied by a shrewd imagination – a faculty which does not, as in the case of many cursed with the power of fancy, serve to lead his Lordship astray, but only helps him to add vividness to the notions his intellect correctly forms, even of distant objects. Thus it is that during the Parliamentary debate on the Orissa famine, he unmistakably divined the want of sympathy on the Anglo-Indian community towards the children of the soil, and it is in the same manner that, while the question of the restoration of Mysore was being discussed before the same assembly, his Lordship remarked, anent[4] the working of the English and Native rule in India, that

> he was not of course for a moment denying that our mission in India was to produce order, to civilise, and to develop a system of native government, but he certainly demurred to the wholesale condemnation of that native system which, though it would be perfectly intolerable on our own soil, having grown up among the people subjected to it, had a fitness and geniality which we

1 [Narayan Mahadev Parmanand,] *English and Native Rule in India* (Bombay: Native Opinion Press, 1868). This text is based on the only surviving copy, which is held by the British Library.
2 Originally published in *Native Opinion*, January 19, 1868.
3 Robert Cecil (1830–1903), later the Marquess of Salisbury, had served as Secretary of State for India in 1866–67. He would later go on to lead the Conservative Party and serve three times as Prime Minister.
4 An archaic term for about or with respect to.

indeed could not realise, but which compensated in some degree for the material evils which its rudeness often induced.[5]

This cautious and easily tenable position of Lord Cranborne has been confounded by the Government of India into a doubt, whether the system of British administration in India possessed, in the estimation of the natives, any superiority over the method of government pursued in the Native States. And His Excellency the Viceroy, considering the occasion a good opportunity to concentrate statistics in order to refute the supposed meaning of Lord Cranborne, has invited the opinions of various political officers in all parts of the country, by a circular which thus begins with the statement of Sir John Lawrence's[6] own personal conviction:

> In any attempt to gauge the inclinations of the people, large allowance must of course be made for the principle of nationality. None of the various conquerors of India have been so alien to the population in colour, religion, and every other characteristic as ourselves. It would be unreasonable for us therefore to expect the same measure of popularity as would spontaneously accrue to a good Native Ruler, or even to a Chief whose administrative merits should not rise above an absence of great vices. Moreover, for one class of men – the clever, the bold and the ambitious – the prospect, which every Native State, however ill-administered, has to offer, of a "career open to talents", must invest that form of government with attractions superior to any which our system has to offer. Indeed, our system, with the monotonous and machine-like play of its centralised power, has much about it that is repellent, especially to the upper classes. Another circumstance not to be overlooked is, that under the influence of the tendency which all persons have to exaggerate the advantages of the "good old times", and to feel a present inconvenience more keenly that the recollection of a past misery, those who have been the longest under British rules are, of all natives, the least conscious of its benefits, the most alive to its petty annoyances, and the foremost to forget their previous sufferings from despots of their own race.
>
> All these points the Viceroy freely admits. But His Excellency, nevertheless, is of opinion that the masses of the people are incontestably more prosperous and (*sua si bona norint*[7]) far more happy in British territory than they are under Native rulers: and he considers that the present would be a good opportunity for proving this belief by a concentration of statistics from different parts of India.

5 *Observations*, Vol. 187, May 24 (London: Hansard, 1867), Col. 1074.

6 John Lawrence (1811–79) was the serving Viceroy. Prior to his appointment in 1864, he had served on the Council of India, and before that he had served as Chief Commissioner of the Punjab from 1853 to 1858.

7 A Latin phrase, originally from Virgil's *Georgics II*, which means "if only they knew it".

> Therefore, under His Excellency's orders, I am to request that you will be good as to favour me with any statements on this subject which your experience may enable you to furnish. ... In case circumstances should prevent your submitting a detailed report, a simple indication of the record from which you know data to be obtainable will not be without its value.[8]

The volume of replies thus sought from subordinate officials has been exposed to several very evident remarks. In the first place, it is an attempt at refuting an assertion which has not been made by anybody. Secondly, the intrinsic merits of the replies are diminished at least to some extent, by the circumstance that they were furnished by subordinates, at the instance of a superior authority who had a declared opinion to maintain, and they may therefore naturally partake of pleadings for supporting a foregone conclusion. The third remark is that since the inquiry relates to the value of the British and indigenous systems of rule *in the estimation of the natives*, it is strange that not a single native of any rank, position, or acquirements has been asked to say what his or his own countrymen's views on the matter are. We do not perceive however that this omission could be easily supplied, and so under the circumstances it does seem to us that the case is best argued out as it is, i.e., *ex parte*.

Owing to the wrong direction imparted to the inquiry at the very fountain source, the official replies are almost all of them defences of a position which nobody doubts, *viz.*, the superiority of the British administration in India over the system (or rather the absence of it) pursued in Native States. Any ordinarily intelligent person must admit, and certainly every native, even the most orthodox, who is at all acquainted with the subject, does admit the great advantages which the first has over the second in organisation and good intentions, but the real question ought to be whether under the former the people are so very much happier than the subjects of the latter, as the vast difference between the two systems leads one to expect. If such were the case, the people of the Native State ought to emigrate into British territory en masse, leaving their sovereigns surrounded by their fiddlers and perhaps their large landowners. But no such thing has taken place anywhere.

Look at our neighbouring Native State of Baroda. It is certainly not the best governed spot in India; its administration has the repute of being one of the worst. There is no end to exactions and disorders, and it is a mere misnomer, judged by the British standard, to call its management a government. Nay more, the bulk of its subjects are of a different nationality from the rulers and they follow the pursuit of trade or agriculture. Now this state

8 "Correspondence Regarding the Comparative Merits of British and Native Administration in India" (Calcutta: Office of the Superintendent of Printing, 1867), 1–2 (British Library, IOR/L/PS/20/H44).

is not only surrounded by British territory but is connected with the metropolis of the Presidency by a railroad. Intercommunication between the two jurisdictions is thus incessant, and many residents within the one have relations living under the other. Here then is everything calculated to cause daily or even hourly emigration. Nor can the people's love of their natal spot be solely able to prevent a result toward which so many forces apparently tend; for the distance to which many of the Gaekwad's[9] subjects would be required to retire in order to pass from tyranny, oppression, and misery to freedom, happiness, and prosperity must be in many cases very short indeed. But we have not heard of any such emigrations. Why is this? It is absurd to say that the people are totally incapable of judging for themselves in the matter. Are there then any circumstances which modify the defects of the one or mar the excellence of the other system and thus serve to lessen the practical differences between them, at least to some extent? Only a few of the officers consulted by the Viceroy have addressed themselves to this question. The majority have simply confined themselves to pointing out instances of wrongdoing in Native States and getting angry with the untravelled Lord Cranborne for suspecting that such wretchedly bungled tracts as the Native States could even in any single respect be compared with the heaven administered by themselves and their brethren.

II. Genuine characteristics of native rule[10]

If we seriously set ourselves to the task of estimating the relative merits of English and Native rule in this country, or even if we busy ourselves with pointing out the defects of the former and the excellences of the latter, it is surely not because we can, even for a moment, entertain the idea of exchanging the one system of government for the other. For, not only have we ourselves been brought up with tastes and ideas which cannot but make us like the rule we live under in preference to every other, even though indigenous, but the blessing of education we have received has taught us to set a peculiar value on England's supremacy over our country – a value that in our opinion is fully justified by the expectation of great national ends which the connection is calculated to serve, and of which signs may be perceived by any man that chooses to look about him and reflect. But the firmer this conviction, the more anxious ought we to be to see the system of government we cherish so much free from defects and shortcomings which practically detract from

9 The dynastic title of the rulers of Baroda.
10 Originally published in *Native Opinion*, January 26, 1868.

its merits and prevent the full amount of good it is calculated to produce. We therefore make no ceremony in entering into the present discussion and instituting any comparisons between English and native rule in India, which appear to us reasonable and sustained by facts.

To begin, then, we admit that there is an essential difference between the theories of government in the East and West: the one is patriarchal the other more or less democratical; the first is stationary and the other progressive. No native Raja or Raj in India has advanced during the last two thousand years an inch over the days of Vikram,[11] in the theory or practice of government. But even a cursory glance at the history of European and particularly the English rule shows great progress in the conception of its duties and responsibilities. Perhaps one cause of this state of things is the very perfection to which the theory of patriarchal rule, the only form of government which has shown itself in Asia, could be and was carried. The king being the father and protector of his people, the *sarkar* (government) was to look after every public object, from the apprehending of a thief and the erection of a *dharmshala* (rest house) to the repelling of an invasion and the construction of the grandest public work. Of course, such a system would require a succession of sovereigns like the "five good emperors"[12] to produce the fullest benefit it is capable of yielding. This requirement, however, can never be fulfilled, and power unchecked is in the long run sure to be abused. Asiatic governments therefore have, as a rule, been what despotisms may be expected to be. But it would be unfair to call them anarchies where neither life nor property is secure. These governments have for centuries declared wars and made peace, collected revenue, and administered laws amidst wealthy and civilised communities. There has thus been an accumulation of precedents and formalities which every tolerably good ruler is required by the *shastra*s (classical treatises) and the public opinion of the state to follow. These precedents of course occupy the place of usage and cannot claim the privileges of *law*. But exactly in this lies the merit as well as the demerit of the native system of rule. The usage may be violated for evil as well as for good. It is set aside as well in summarily proscribing the vice of drinking or relieving popular distress, as in disregarding the rules of strict justice, in remitting a revenue in times of difficulty, as well as in imposing

11 A reference to Vikramaditya, the semi-historical monarch celebrated for millennia in India as an emblem of righteous kingly rule (A. N. D. Haksar, *Simhasana Dvatrimsika* (Delhi: Penguin, 1998), 1).

12 A reference to the successive rule of Nerva (96–98 AD), Trajan (98–117 AD), Hadrian (117–38 AD), Antoninus Pius (138–61 AD), and Marcus Aurelius (161–80 AD) under whom the Roman Empire reached its zenith.

an additional impost in times of plenty. This is in reality what Lord Cranborne called the "rough and ready means"[13] of native governments and Sir Richard Temple styles their "virtues of patience and mildness [and it should be added their parental kindness] in dealing with their subjects".[14]

There is another circumstance which has tended to curb the sting of despotism in this country – it is the existence of municipal self-government among people. The very name of native government has so long been connected with nothing but fiddling and a centralised system of oppression and exaction, owing to the prevalence of the literature and opinions of the annexationist school,[15] that this statement may sound strange to some ears. But there is nothing new in it to those conversant with the subject. The village system of India is known even to the general reader to have acted as a sheet anchor to the people during the storms of anarchy and disorder. Within the walls of their respective little domains, the village *panchayats*[16] settled their affairs and paid taxes to the ruling powers like tributes. We have no cause to be very thankful to this institution; for we believe it is that which, by affording a tolerable refuge to the subject's hearth and home, made him indifferent to the fate of his country. But there can be no doubt that it actually counterbalanced the effects of the prevailing despotism. Nor is it only in India that the germs and the spirit of a local self-government have existed. We have the authority of Mr. T. C. Anstey[17] – who certainly cannot be accused of believing anything good of Asiatics without sufficient evidence – that the institution exists in China as well as in India, where, doubtless, it serves the same end.

Then, again, the local officers could not be so entirely free from control as the nature of the whole government might lead one to suppose. They had on one hand to please the superior authorities, and on the other to keep the people in content; for in case of a breaking out of popular discontent, supposing the sovereign was inclined to enforce responsibility (which certainly was not a unique step), they could not shelter themselves behind any excuse

13 *Observations*, Vol. 187, May 24, Col. 1074.

14 "Correspondence Regarding the Comparative Merits of British and Native Administration in India", 105.

15 A reference to Anglo-Indians that favored expanding British India by annexing the Native States, a view most associated with James Ramsay, the Marquess of Dalhousie, who was Governor-General from 1848 to 1856.

16 The term for a council traditionally employed to arbitrate disputes between members of a community, and to voice or represent the considered view of the community to authorities outside of it.

17 Thomas Chisholm Anstey (1816–73) was the senior-most advocate in the Bombay Bar. A former member of parliament from Ireland and Attorney General of Hong Kong, he was infamous for mocking educated natives.

under colour of obstructive laws or boards. And as access to the royal person was not difficult, such a contingency could not be overlooked. This security against maladministration, precarious though it was, is admitted to have existed in former times.

Thus, then, under the native system of government there were circumstances which tended to check the extreme of personal despotism, and thus it was that a tolerable state of things was the result.

III. How far these characteristics hold in the case of the existing Native States[18]

In our last article on this subject, we have pointed out certain accompaniments characteristic of native rule, which not only take away the sting of its despotism, but, joined to its "flexibility" and the fact of its being an indigenous institution, having grown up amidst the people, commend it to their approval. A really good ruler under this system draws down on it and on himself the blessings of mankind; a tolerable one works it to ordinary satisfaction; but even a very bad one, though incurring the execrations of his subjects, is prevented from inflicting on them the full measure of his badness, for, to quote Sir Richard Temple's words once more, he "is seldom strong enough to annihilate by his stroke, and there is always a chance of parrying or avoiding the blow; thus the worst native governments sometimes possess the virtues of patience and mildness in dealing with their subjects."[19]

An additional safeguard against the personal tyranny of the sovereign is the mediation of the minister who in many cases, especially if he is an exemplary ruler, as it were by general consent, virtually supplants the sovereign. Indeed, according to the Hindu political philosophy, the minister is the sole eye of the king, and it has generally happened that the master and the servant have made up for each other's failings – an incapable or vicious sovereign has often found a competent minister on whom to devolve the cares of government, and who like a faithful agent has been always found true to the trust; while a virtuous and able sovereign has supplied the want of vigorous ministers. Thus, upon the whole, though of course, constitutional checks or restraints on despotism there could be none, and arbitrary conduct towards individuals for good or for evil could be met with in particular instances, a considerable amount of good government, it cannot be denied, was obtained under native rule.

18 Originally published in *Native Opinion*, February 16, 1868.

19 "Correspondence Regarding the Comparative Merits of British and Native Administration in India", 105.

But it may be asked – and this is the question most pertinent to the point – whether and how far these softening influences are found at work in the present existing Native States in India, and in what degree they affect or favour the cause of good government. Here it is that the one-sided character of the disquisitions evoked by the Viceroy shows itself most. For, while we have on the one side, clever, educated, observant, and experienced English political officers, naturally influenced in favour of their own and not without some tinge of prejudice against the native governments, to point out the virtues and excellence of the one and the vices and shortcomings of the other, we have absolutely nobody to represent the other side. That good office is left to the stray chance of a well-informed and fair-minded advocate of the opposite party. Thus we have described at length in the correspondence before us, numerous instances of oppressions, exactions, and denial of justice perpetrated in Native States, but we do not know what those charged with their commission may have to say on the subject. To illustrate our meaning further, we see, for instance, Colonel Daly,[20] officiating Political Agent at Gwalior, relates many a case in which the Maharaja Sindhia[21] is represented as arbitrarily thwarting the administration of the law and denying justice to suitors in his Court. And the number of such instances of oppression occurring in the state of Gwalior was such, the Colonel was informed, that he could not help exclaiming, even after fully stating a good many instances, that "the subject bursts with fullness".[22]

Now we have ourselves nothing to advance regarding these assertions. They have been made in the most perfect good faith and there is some probability of their truth. But all we say is that the discussion is altogether one-sided, that with respect to the particular instances, the opposite party may from its own point of view have some explanation to offer in the matter, and that an officer similarly situated to Colonel Daly on the side of the native rule probably would, to improve his case, point to similar instances of failure of justice at the hands of British officials, owing to an unfair exercise of power to the prejudice of the rights and interests of suitors and subjects. Indeed, if we may speak out freely the opinion of our people, an unlimited amount of scandal of this sort attaches to every Political Agency,

20 Henry Daly (1821–95) was a decorated military officer who had recently taken charge of the Residency in Gwalior. He would go on to be appointed Agent to the Governor General for Central India in 1870.

21 Jayajirao Sindhia (1835–86) was the Maharaja of Gwalior. His reign had begun in 1854 and had been marked by important land and fiscal reforms undertaken by his famous *dewan* Dinkar Rao.

22 "Correspondence Regarding the Comparative Merits of British and Native Administration in India", 117.

and there is no act of *khatpat*[23] which stinks so much in the nostrils of all honest men but of which the central figure is not some political officer and the aim of which, the good graces of the *meherban* or *bahadur*.[24] We leave it to the reader to judge whether this opinion could be so general as it is among us, without some solid foundation of fact for it. But we can assure him that the subject literally "bursts with fullness", and therefore we cannot stop here to particularise.

Then again, if only half the oppression which is described as rampant in every Native State be real, the emigration from them ought not to be confined to the exceptional instances recorded in the correspondence. Indeed, we heartily wish that this summary, but the fairest and most effectual method of teaching the native princes their duties as rulers, were adopted by their subjects en masse or at all events in any striking manner. But, fortunately or unfortunately, such is not the fact. It is absurd to say that the people cannot judge for themselves or are unable to distinguish between a state of happiness and prosperity on the one side and a pining misery on the other. We must also have some proof of the assertion that emigration is prevented by coercive measures adopted by the native sovereigns of discontented subjects.

To revert to the instance of Baroda alluded to in our opening article on this subject, this state, as we then observed, has had the repute of being one of the worst governed among its sort. The late Gaekwad was immersed in drinking and debauchery, the former of which was his acquisition during his visit to Bombay. The administration of the state then was certainly very bad. The present Maharaja is free from the particular vices of his brother and predecessor, but he is surrounded by flatterers and coarse buffoons on whom he lavishes his money and whose base flattery and servility to His Highness's whims and weaknesses is not the less injurious because of its finding its way in newspapers owned and managed by the parasites themselves. The subjects of the state therefore are always laid under contribution to support their ruler's extravagance and the avarice of his flatterers. Add to this that the majority of them are not of the same nationality with him and so can have no personal attachment to such a tyrant; and that the country they inhabit is now entirely surrounded by British territory that at all points except the centre, it might be drained of its population by a thorough emigration. Has such a result been prevented solely by the ignorance of the people

23 A colloquial term for the practice of bribing officials to secure or fix a favorable outcome.

24 These honorifics – the kind and the brave – were traditionally accorded to high officials in the *darbar*. Here they are being sarcastically accorded to native assistants and peons that controlled access to the Political Agent.

of the administrative bliss awaiting them beyond their border or by the coercive measures of the native government? If it were so, we ought to hear something more of it than the mere allusion made to it by Mr. Hope[25] in his long spun out contribution of a few facts to this correspondence. On the other hand, we have this testimony from Sir Richard Temple on the subject: "In 1864 I passed through the Baroda territory; certainly that district, the valley of the Mahi is in external prosperity hardly surpassed by any British district that I have ever seen at least."[26] The Resident of Baroda also reports favourably of the management of the state and the Bombay government voluntarily make a present of their right of veto to the nomination of *dewan* to the Gaekwad and thus withdraw one of the chief safeguards of good government and the only check on His Highness raising in a moment of caprice or weakness an illiterate noodle or an unprincipled sycophant to the power and position of his minister. Either then native governments are not so bad as they are generally represented, or their shortcomings are shared by British authorities to a greater extent than is commonly believed. And probably there is truth in both.

We are, however, far from wishing to maintain that the Native States are models of perfect rule. Of the inherent vice and weakness of the native system of government and of its tendency to tyranny, we have already spoken. The present existing Native States must of course be subject to this defect and produce their fair amount of administrative evil. But they have been subject to another weakening cause. None of the native governments in India were in their normal condition when they came in contact with the Europeans, but this contact, we believe, has had an evil influence on their moral and political condition, which we will consider in our next.

IV. The character and condition of native rule as it exists at present[27]

We have to consider today the character and condition of native rule as it exists at present, its defects and their probable causes and remedies. According to the account which is generally placed before the European public, whose opinion alone has hitherto guided political action in this country, every

25 T. C. Hope (1831–1916) was the Collector of Surat. A civil servant of ability, he would go on to become Finance Secretary and Revenue Secretary, and eventually serve on the Viceregal Council.

26 "Correspondence Regarding the Comparative Merits of British and Native Administration in India", 100.

27 Originally published in *Native Opinion*, February 23, 1868.

Native State is a species of purgatory on earth, where the subjects are employed as drudges to supply means for the bestial pleasure of their rulers, who therefore deserve to be improved off the surface of the globe. This, however, is the extreme and irresponsible view of European journalists blinded by prejudice, passion, and interest and incapacitated from judging correctly for other reasons. It has a counterpoise in the few honourable exceptions who conscientiously try their best to represent the subject in fair colours. Still, as we have already shown, there can be only one side to it for the present, and it is exhibited on the whole in an unexceptional spirit in the official correspondence. But even according to this authority, oppression and mismanagement is the rule, and good government the exception, in Native States. Our own impression is that even in those states which are reputed to be misgoverned, whatever the intellectual or moral tone of the courts, exhibition of luxury and vice at the capitals, and in spite of occasional acts of oppression against individuals, the great mass of the subjects drives a pretty even tenor of life.

But, as intimated in our last, we are far from maintaining the native rule of today as the model of good government. On the contrary, we believe that where special causes are not at work to prevent the evil and convert it into an opposite good, there is apparent a general deterioration in its vigour and quality. We have already observed that one cause of this state of things may be found in the inherent proneness of all despotic rule to degeneracy. But this is not enough to account for the entire phenomenon. For despotism has been as old as the oldest mountain in this country, and yet it cannot be denied that good government has existed among us. We may quote the latest instance from the testimony of Sir Richard Temple:

> Further, in justice to Native rule, it should be said that, within the century of our supremacy there have not only been good sovereigns, who are too well known to require mention here, but also good Ministers, really capital administrators who have adorned the service to which they belong, such are Purnaiah of Mysore and Tantia Jog of Indore, in the past, and Sir Salar Jung of Hyderabad, Sir Dinkar Rao of Gwalior, Sir T. Madhava Rao of Travancore, in the present.[28]

Now in the direction of the observation which Sir Richard makes in a footnote that "both Sir Salar Jung and Sir T. Madhava Rao owe much to the training they received from British officers", we believe, lies the future remedy of the evil. But so far as the immediate past and the present are concerned, there is little doubt that the growing deterioration in the vigour

28 "Correspondence Regarding the Comparative Merits of British and Native Administration in India", 101.

and quality of native rule is, so far as it is a fact, due to the indirect influence of British supremacy.

That supremacy has worked in a way very different from that of the Mughal domination. It has in fact imperceptibly acted like a spider's web which covers and controls every limb of the animal involved in its folds. This must follow from the very reason of the thing. The Mughal supremacy was a moral acknowledgement of political superiority embodied only in the payment of tribute. For every other purpose, the tributary was and felt itself as independent as the paramount power. British suzerainty on the other hand has had its basis in Lord Wellesley's[29] system of the subsidiary alliances. Under this policy the British government has commanded a vast military force maintained at the expense of the Native States. So long as the allied sovereigns were obsequious to the wishes of the British government, the military contingents were ready to uphold them against every foe, but the moment they exhibited signs of an independent will in any matter whatever, the same force was equally ready to be turned against themselves. The combined action of this military threat joined to diplomatic tact or wiles (as our own people would say) has wrought such a marvellous change in the mutual relations of the two parties that, at the end of less than half a century, the one has been enabled not only fearlessly to dictate treaties to the other, but even arrogantly to interpret them as it likes, or set them aside if it should choose to do so, as may be seen from the whole history of the question of adoption, and the discussions on the case of Mysore. A disregard of moral obligations may bring on a natural retribution in an unexpected shape as the Mutinies,[30] but this does not affect the question before us. It is, however, in no captious spirit that we write thus of Lord Wellesley's policy. For, besides answering its immediate purpose, *viz.*, the strengthening of the British power, it has also given the country the blessings of a general peace. But while it has done this good, it has also had its evil effects. By its insidious working, it has, to borrow the terse expression of the *Homeward Mail*, "pressed out all real vital energy from the decaying body of native rule", and weakened the stimulus to vigorous native government.[31] For, if a sovereign cannot of his own will raise a single soldier or address a neighbouring brother sovereign, unless under a surveillance, he must soon be tamed indeed and his powers of carrying out great administrative measures must grow dormant. Opportunities make men and a continued

29 Richard Wellesley (1761–1842) served as Governor-General between 1797 and 1805. He greatly expanded British control over India by subordinating the Native States of the Deccan, especially Hyderabad and Mysore.

30 A reference to the insurrections that occurred intermittently in the nineteenth century when natives rose up against British encroachment, the most notable example being the 1857 Mutiny.

31 *Homeward Mail*, January 4, 1868; *Times of India*, February 13, 1868.

dullness must give rise to mediocrity, unless a refined education keeps the mind at a proper tension. It is all very well then to say that our princes having no enemies to contend against, must devote their heart and soul to the work of internal administration, but the stimulus and energy demanded by a successful discharge of the latter task cannot be easily found in men who are not educated to the requirement and whose natural powers have remained dormant for want of stimulus, opportunity, and exercise. It is surely not to be inferred from this that we wish our princes had possessed the will and the power to inflict the curse of continual wars on the country. But it is evident that the means which have been employed to disarm them (certainly not in their interests) have left their evil behind, and that it is unfair to charge it to its victims.

Hence, it is monstrous in the British authorities to be affected into annexing Native States because of the oppression practised by their rulers on their subjects, and this for two reasons: first, because, to quote the English journal named above, even "supposing that we could incontestably demonstrate that the people will be happier under our rule, we should not, therefore, be justified in appropriating a Native State in defiance of the faith of treaties, or of the general promises made to the people to respect their religious and social usages".[32] For on this principle, in the words of the *Pall Mall Gazette*, "one-half of the world would have to give up the superintendence of their affairs to better managers than themselves; and strong men with good opinions of their own administrative capacity would be continually possessing themselves of the bank books and strong boxes of their weaker neighbours, and sweeping the balances into their own hands".[33] But secondly, as our government is responsible for whatever misrule may prevail in Native States over and above that which their subjects voluntarily put up with, it is bound to cure it, in compensation, not by violent annexation but by persuasion and advice and the recommendation of well-educated and honourable native officers for employment at native courts. The system adopted by Travancore, the Council of Administration instituted at Jaipur, the regularisation of his administration by the Maharaja Holkar,[34] and the reforms introduced at Khetri and in the states of Gwalior and Hyderabad show that native princes are fully amenable to the influence of wise precept and example when only brought to bear on them. These efforts require to be guided by a disinterested and sympathetic agency until they culminate in Major Bell's[35] three guarantees of good government: (1) a separation of the judicial from the executive

32 *Homeward Mail*, January 4, 1868; *Times of India*, February 13, 1868.

33 *Pall Mall Gazette*, Vol. VII, No. 910, January 10, 1868, 4–5.

34 Tukoji Rao Holkar II (1835–86) was the Maharaja of Indore.

35 Thomas Evans Bell (1825–87) was a former East India Company officer. A defender of the Native States, he wrote extensively on questions relating to their rights. The reference here is to *Our Great Vassal Empire* (1870).

functionaries; (2) a code of laws; and (3) a limit to the sovereign's personal demand on the state revenue. The first two are being adopted generally, the last has been acted on by Travancore for the last few years. It is for our government to see that its political officers are – which at present they generally are not – men who would zealously, disinterestedly, and patiently bring about this consummation. No other course towards the Native States would command the sympathy of good men, while if this cannot be done, no stretch of the conception of the right can justify any interference with those states. But it is time for us to retire into British territory.

V. The alien character of English rule not in itself a great drawback[36]

Having in the previous numbers dwelt on the causes which tend to counterbalance the evils which are the natural and usual effects of native rule, as it once obtained in this country and as it still prevails in Native States, it now remains for us to consider the circumstances which detract from the merits and hinder a complete realisation of all the benefits and advantages that, in the nature of things, ought to follow from such a well-organised, well-intentioned, and altogether superior *system* of administration as the government of the British Indian territories, and to point out the moral suggested by the official correspondence.

The natives of India and England are opposed to each other in almost every national and social particular: in their manners and customs, religion and language, habits and ideas, their past achievements and future aspirations. Hence, the most obvious shortcoming in the government of the one country and people by the other would appear to be the fact of its being alien. And certainly to a government which sincerely wishes and earnestly tries its best to benefit its subjects according to its own enlightenment and well-meaning views, no mortification or difficulty is greater or more discouraging than its being considered by them in the heart of their hearts an *alien* government, alien in its origin and character, and in its aims and endeavours – alien in the worst sense. For, it will not be denied, we suppose, that the Hindus (and whatever is true of these people is more or less true of the Mussulmans and other natives of this country) can make such a distinction, or contended that they are not dead to all sense of a nationality and national feelings. For they are no savages with a mere animal existence about them. They are a people who have had a national and political existence, a language and a religion, literature and science of their own, who have made wars and

36 Originally published in *Native Opinion*, March 22, 1868.

peace, and founded kingdoms and exercised power over men, and cultivated and practised the arts of social and settled life. It is no wonder therefore that people with such traditions and recollections should, as a body, not relish a foreign rule for its own sake. It is no wonder that their patriotism should at times and under circumstances clash with their allegiance to it. But however true as this may be, we do not think that it really affects the present question. A Hindu's patriotism has never been marked by that narrow yet fierce political grain which characterises some nations or tribes. It has rather shown itself in a fond attachment to the natal spot, an interest in the local affairs of the village, and a sentimental attachment to the religion and the manners of his ancestors. These principles indeed in a way constitute patriotism and exercise on the mind of the people an influence akin to it. But still, they are not the same as that ardent love of a definite "country" and "nationality" which burns fiercely in the veins of the European for instance, which would make him jealously guard (in however narrow a spirit) every national interest, and which would make him scorn the offer of any advantages in return for his national independence. Whatever the causes of this peculiarity – and among them appear to us to be the unworldly spirit of Hindu institutions and the undeniable mildness of the Hindu character, joined to the Mussulman's distracted notion of country or nationality – there can be no doubt of its existence or its results. When the use of Indian cotton cloths, for instance, began to grow familiar in England, a great outcry was raised by the people about the trade injuring the domestic manufactures, and even violent measures for its suppression were resorted, but when the reverse process took place and English piece goods began to drive the Indian loom out of the field, the native population after a few ephemeral murmurs about the painful result, began freely to patronise the fabric because of its comparative cheapness, in spite of a lurking superstition against the foreign article and of well-founded apprehensions about its inferiority in strength and durability.

Again, the rapid rise of the British power in India amidst many rivals and enemies is another and striking instance of the same truth. Whatever may the bumptious Britons of today, either from griffinish[37] ignorance or natural self-complacency or from both causes together, advance to the contrary, we believe a careful and impartial reader of the history of the British power in India cannot fail to come to the conclusion that its rise was due as much to the passive acquiescence and approbation and active help rendered by the people as to the valour of the few English troops that could be brought

37 A colloquial Anglo-Indian term for a newcomer ignorant of the norms and personages of British India (Walter Roper Lawrence, *The India We Served* (London: Cassell and Company, 1928), 20).

over to this country or the skill and vigour of English diplomacy. The English appeared on the political stage of India at a particularly exceptional time. The venerable fabric of the Mughal Empire having nearly crumbled to pieces and the adventurers who swarmed to build their greatness on the splendid ruins, possessing few of the virtues of princes and sovereigns, the country was reduced to confusion and lawlessness. It was at this juncture that the British appeared on the scene, possessing the attributes both of honest traders and diligent rulers who strictly observed their engagements and attentively cared for the rights and well-being of their friends. The country perceiving the difference certainly sympathised with the "stranger a friend" and contemned the "countryman a tyrant".[38] The readiness and the public approbation with which what might be called the native yeomanry enlisted under the banners of the former professedly to be led against the latter – the result of the contest does not need to be told – is surely some indication of the popular feeling. Nor was sympathy from higher circles altogether wanting. The revolution consequently was rapid. It commenced in the east, in Bengal whose bankers and other leading men conspired with Clive[39] to depose the tyrannical Siraj-ud-Daulah;[40] it culminated in Western India where the Deccan *sardar*s played a similar part to be rid of the detested son of *peshwa* Raghunath Rao.[41] It would have been a wonder, perhaps a miracle, if the British power had risen to its present position in this country, had it shared nothing but that hatred and detestation with which some Anglo-Indian writers of the hour credit the people of India.

Upon the whole then we believe the mere fact of our government being foreign does not *per se* prejudice it in the eyes of the people, at least not to any appreciable extent. Those who willingly accepted it for its possession of certain virtues will not repudiate it, unless in their eyes the virtues have in the course of time been neutralised by defects or drawbacks. Whether there are any such, and if any, what they are, must be left for future consideration.

38 An adaptation of a haunting line in William Drennan's 1795 famous poem "Erin" (Edward Hayes, ed., *The Ballads of Ireland, Vol. 1* (Boston: Patrick Donahoe, 1857), 279). The original reads:

> When the int'rest of state wrought the general woe,
> The stranger a friend, and the native a foe.

39 Robert Clive (1725–74) transformed the East India Company into a territorial power by expelling the Mughals from Bengal and Bihar. He went on to serve two terms as Governor of Bengal.

40 Siraj-ud-Daulah (1729–57) became the Nawab of Bengal in 1756. His reign was terminated in 1757 following his defeat to Robert Clive in the Battle of Plassey.

41 Raghunath Rao (1734–83) was *peshwa* (prime minister) of the Maratha Empire in 1773–74. The machinations of his son, Baji Rao II (1775–1851), who became *peshwa* in 1796, helped the British subvert the Maratha Empire.

VI. The costliness of the English rule its great drawback[42]

We have now prepared the ground for considering the drawbacks on the excellence of the British system of administration and the causes which prevent a realisation of the benefits it is potentially capable of producing. The first of these appears to us to be its great costliness. Not only is every branch of the entire machinery far more costly than the costliest institution under native rule, but the machinery itself is complicated, vast and capable of indefinite extension or improvement, which, as it is actually brought into practice, entails proportionate additional expenditure and brings continued taxation in its train. The British Indian government has been very significantly and very aptly styled an enlightened despotism. As such it knows no end of the most worthy objects to patronise and look after, and in its expense has been guided more by the calls on its purse than the means of replenishing it. While its good intentions may to some extent justify this tendency to extravagance, its power and position has exempted its disbursement of the public funds from all check arising from the taxpayer's impatience or any feeling of its own helplessness. The result, in spite of a growing revenue, has been the well-known impecuniosity of the exchequer and a dread of increasing taxation among the people. It might perhaps be urged that this is more or less the case with nearly every government, but there are circumstances which in our case aggravate the evil and render the drawback we are considering, very serious. In the first place, the natural costliness of the administrative machinery is enhanced by the absence of a sense of responsibility or obligation to rigid economy in those charged with its conduct. Under the present constitution of our government, motives to public economy cannot exist or rather everything is calculated to produce extravagance and unthrift. The vast majority of those who have to propose and carry out expenditure know nothing about or have little to do with raising the revenue, while it is their interest to spend during their short tenure of office as much money as possible in order to show results and add to their official reputation, and this temptation is the more importunate as few can count on any certainty of remaining at the same post for any number of years. Thus the personal sense of responsibility vanishes with every fresh officer and each one considers himself by no means amenable to his superiors for the failures of his predecessors.

Another cause of our fiscal pressure must be sought in the origin and history of the government itself. The British Indian Empire is as "exceptional" in its origin as in some of its characteristics. It was not founded by a nation or an adventurer who conquers a country with his sword and settles in it

42 Originally published in *Native Opinion*, April 19, 1868.

or rules over it as a tributary from afar. The Company of Merchants, who began their humble enterprise centuries ago, neither would nor could act such a role. Like rigid men of business, therefore, they had to evolve their whole future greatness out of their small stock in trade. The people of India, therefore, have had not only to pay taxes to their English rulers after they had become their subjects, but they had also to recoup them for their outlay in the struggles which ended in the change of rule. In short, they themselves became the stock in trade of their trading masters who, whether they paid a dividend on their original capital, built an India Office in London for the transaction of their business, a depot for lodging their recruits or a Haileybury for training their younger sons and nephews for writerships[43] in this country, whether they created a navy for the safety of commerce, held the port of Aden for the security of the overland passage or St. Helena for this or that purpose, established communication with China, opened up the trade of Japan, or were required by the ministry to uphold the national prestige on either side of the Indian Ocean – whatever they did they had no other resource to fall back upon except the fiscal proceeds of their stock, the empire. These and such other charges on India, adding to the innate costliness of its system of administration still exist and are paid out of Indian revenues. Thus has this country had to meet not only the strict cost of its own government but a great many other items which are no essential parts of any administration, however unavoidable they have been in their origin in the present case.

A third cause which aggravates the pecuniary situation of India is the abstraction of capital that takes place through its governing population. The European, whether official or non-official, contributes little to the revenue of the state, but profits most under the regime. He monopolises every species of the best-paid posts in the country, occupies the foremost ranks in all the lucrative lines of independent life. But though he this earns much, he spends very little on or in the country. His credibility, industry, and energy in making money is matched by his equally commendable prudence in saving it in order to secure his early withdrawal from the heat and dust of the tropics to the coolness and comforts of his native home. All this is very natural and very proper in him from his own point of view; but the economic effects of the arrangement on this country are not less injurious or real on that account. They may differ in their origin, but they are the same in their nature as those of a huge absenteeism. The fact may be scientifically explained or accounted for, but its existence is undoubted and is one of the most dreaded results of the introduction of English rule. The security of property

43 The starting rung of employment in the East India Company. A writer was equivalent to a clerk.

afforded by that rule is freely admitted. Under it one might travel over to Benares, it is observed, with his gold attached to the very end of his walking stick, but it is immediately added, that unluckily the gold itself has been fast disappearing.

Equally proverbial is the thorough belief in the insatiable avarice of the *angrez sarkar* (English government) whose chief object is the collection of money from the people and its transmission to *vilayat* (abroad). There is no measure which the government undertakes but which is not ascribed to this motive, if it has the slightest connection with pecuniary transactions. Of course this belief is entertained only by the ignorant or the orthodox classes of the people, but its general prevalence, joined to the fact that it is especially strong in those who have known the exactions of native rulers, can only be accounted for by the abstraction of capital which takes place under British rule and which is naturally unknown under a native regime. In truth, then, there is little real difference between this complaint of the ignorant and orthodox Hindu and that of enlightened Englishmen like Major Wingate[44] or educated natives like Mr. Dadabhai Naoroji,[45] who dwell on the injurious effects on the economic condition of a country, when taxes raised in it are spent beyond its limits. They both refer to the same result but only account for it in different ways.

In point of costliness, then, English rule must stand at a disadvantage in comparison with native rule. And it is no wonder the difference should be felt. For with all her proverbial riches, her classic pearl and gold and precious stone, India is not a wealthy country. Its resources have not been developed and the material standard of life of its people, of their comforts and luxuries, has not been very high. The English system of government therefore (unlike the cheap and simple though "rough and ready" native rule) cannot but be felt as costly by such a country and people. And were it not that the peace and security it affords tends indirectly to foster industry and productiveness, the cost would have proved crushing in a very short time indeed. The only effectual counterpoise to this evil of British rule would be a thorough development of the country's resources. But in this direction, little has yet been done. What has been effected is due rather to accidental causes such as the Russian or American wars which have stimulated particular industries. It is only when the government will venture on a bold policy of investment and the country will be overrun by broad canals placing the means of irrigation

44 George Wingate (1812–79) served in the Bombay Engineers. After acting as Revenue Survey Commissioner in Bombay, he published a much-noticed work, *A Few Words on Our Financial Relations with India* (1859).

45 Dadabhai Naoroji (1825–1917) had taught at Elphinstone and University College London and founded the East India Association. A critic of imperialism, he had recently charged Britain with "draining" wealth from India.

at the disposal of every *ryot* (cultivator) in the plains and doubling and trebling the extent of his fields by increasing the number of his crops, that real compensation will have been made to India for that abstraction of capital which is unavoidable under the circumstances.

VII. Costly justice another drawback of English rule[46]

Against the great costliness which we have mentioned in our last as one of the greatest drawbacks on the excellence of the English system of administration, it might be urged perhaps that the land tax, the chief item of Indian taxation, is not levied in such heavy proportion as was or is done under native rule. But in the first place, the lightness of its incidence is counterbalanced (as observed in our last) by the circumstances of the taxes being spent out of the country; and secondly, it is more than made up by the levy of a variety of cesses, tolls, and other imposts. The most important and objectionable of these imposts, however, is the tax on justice. Nor is this the sole price the people have to pay for that article under English rule. The full charge is made up not only of the various amounts of stamp duty, which are required to be paid at each step in the progress of a suit towards its final stage, but includes also the lawyer's fees and perquisites under diverse names, crowned over by the vexatious delays and glorious uncertainties of the law. This is indeed a great defect in the British system and one in respect to which it contrasts unfavourably with native rule. We are far from saying that there is no failure of justice under the latter; but clearly the settlement of a claim does not cost three times its value in good money, nor is a man required to spend eighty thousand rupees simply to know that the court to which he takes his case has no jurisdiction in the matter. The native system is rough and ready, but it does not cost much in time or money and is easily accessible; the British is costly and cumbrous and tardy and interposes many a middleman between the suitor and the judge, and yet withal it is hard to say whether on the whole this difference between the natures and the cost of the two systems is justified by that between their respective fruits – whether, in brief, the one dispenses substantial justice more unerringly than the other.

This then is another drawback on the excellence of English rule. We are aware of the difficult situation of the British government in this particular. It was bound to see justice administered to its subjects, and being an enlightened government it was anxious to do its duty. But as it was at the same time foreign, it could not perhaps be much censured for wishing to

46 Originally published in *Native Opinion*, April 26, 1868.

adopt the method it had most confidence in or for not trusting too much to the indigenous agency in vogue, especially as the latter was not in its best state at the time it came in contact with the new order of things. But if this much may be said on behalf of the government, it must also be observed in vindication of the people that they have not had justice done them. Indeed, they have in this matter been doubly wronged: on the one hand, they have had thrust on them a machinery for the settlement of their disputes, which, while it costs more time, trouble, and money, cannot guarantee substantial justice more than their cheap and simple method; and on the other, though thus suffering from the shortcomings of the new system, they have themselves been held responsible for its faults and made to expiate this responsibility by having to undergo additional pains and penalties on its account. Because business has flocked to the courts and because the system of administering them has necessarily created a class of men of questionable integrity (certainly not unknown in England itself), the natives of this country, the respectable classes among whom have been known to have a great aversion to enter the precincts of the courts, have been branded as a nation of perjurers and forgers and stigmatised as drawing their very life from litigation, and the last allegation has been authoritatively adduced by the hon'ble Mr. Maine[47] to defend an increase to the taxation already levied on justice!

But even supposing these charges are well founded – for it is yet to be proved by comparative facts and figures that other countries similarly situated do not similarly offend – is no portion of the blame due to the exemption enjoyed by the lying which flourishes in the courts under the shadow of English law? Is none of the incessant appealing that goes on from court to court due to the great uncertainty of results which characterises their adjudications? Would people resort to appeals if they were tolerably certain of the consequences? Would a European readily give up the opportunity of appealing against an adverse decision if he were not quite uncertain that what has proved a bad case in the one court might prove the reverse in another? The germs of all vices and virtues lie in every nation; their development depends on conditions. But we have dwelt enough on the subject. The English system of judicial administration is already firmly established, and all our efforts must be directed to show in what way it might be best simplified and assimilated to the wants of the country and how some of its evils at least might be obviated.

47 Henry Maine (1822–88) was a prominent legal scholar from Cambridge. He had been appointed to the Viceregal Council in 1861, where he was leading the codification of law in British India.

VIII. Defects in the executive administration of the English system[48]

From the mode of the dispensation of justice to the general executive administration is but a natural step. We have already mentioned the defects to which, under British rule, the former is liable. Let us now consider those which attach to and obstruct a smooth working of the latter.

The excellence of the British system or constitution of government is an axiomatic truth admitted by everyone, but it is in the practical execution of it that difference of opinion arises. It is a well-known observation that the worst system of government, properly administered, is capable of producing greater present benefits than the best if it is indifferently or rather imperfectly carried out. This remark may to a certain extent and in some sense be applied to native and English rule in India. There is no systematic good in the one except what arises from the fact of its indigenous character, but there is also much systematic (if not inherent) evil in the other. The spirit of the former government demands from the ruler the exercise of a ubiquitous intelligence joined to conscientious benevolence which must detect and remedy the grievances and the woes of the subject. The genius of the latter, on the other hand, consists – and this arrangement is doubtless more in consonance with human nature and consequently fails less than the other – in devolving on the subject the protection of his own interests and enabling him to vindicate his rights. But, as yet, we have made little progress towards an attainment of this true privilege of British citizenship. The wealth and intelligence and freedom and prosperity of the Presidency towns is indeed the most favourable illustration of the good effects of English rule, though even here the good is only partially effected. But this state of things, such as it is, is reversed beyond the limits of these towns. There the official nod has been the law not in theory but in fact, and under its shadow a great deal of subordinate mischief and oppression has been worked. Both in the Revenue and Police departments not a little high-handed oppression and extortion is practised on the humble *ryot*. The European reader will probably be surprised to learn that impressment and exaction are still systematically practised by the underlings of office during the tours of high functionaries in the districts. It was but the other day that public attention was drawn to a most illegal and oppressive measure taken by a revenue subordinate in the Ratnagiri districts in order to coerce unwilling subjects to the official wishes or crotchets. The matter happily attracted the attention of government and the officer in charge of the district on being called upon submitted an explanation that the conduct of his subordinate

48 Originally published in *Native Opinion*, May 3, 1868.

was legal[49] but unauthorised and that the measure complained of would be countermanded. Now, this particular matter found its way to public prints because of its particular importance at the time, and so it was righted. But for every such exposure and redress of a grievance, who knows how many go unnoticed and unattended to?

The case with the police is even worse. In that department there is much more scope for abuse of power and exercise of tyranny, and if but one half of what falls on our ears and on those of every well-informed person in native society about its doings in that line be true, our assertion would be fully borne out. A correspondent of the *Englishman* of 21st September last, evidently an Anglo-Indian officer on furlough, well acquainted with the subject, thus contrasts the police administration of this country with that of France:

> It is not too much to say that when a theft of any magnitude less than a dacoity takes place in Lower Bengal, not one in fifty of the villagers has the least hope of the depredator being discovered by the regular action of the police, and not even that confiding individual in fifty, entertains any hope of the stolen property being recovered. In rural France no one has any fear of his property being plundered in the first place, and in the second, if it be plundered, he feels certain that the thief will be caught, and even hopeful that the missing articles may be restored. This in itself is some comfort, but it is by no means the only or indeed the chief benefit of exact administration. The cruel feature of our present inaccurate system of rural government is not so much the want of detective ability, as the sanction it gives to official violence and fraud. It is not so much that the authorities are not a terror to evildoers, but that they are a terror to those who do well. An army of badly disciplined armed policemen is let loose upon a peaceful people, with what result native public opinion explicitly shows. With just sufficient of the soldier in him to make him a thing of form and routine, and to drive out any little spark of original talent that might have been developed into detective skill, the Bengal policeman is to the French one what an Italian Brigand is to a scout attached to a legitimate army. The common gendarme of a French village or railway station is indeed a man of drill and formality, but he is only a lay figure in the police establishment. He represents peace and order, and to that purpose wears white gloves, a toy sword and a cocked hat, but he is not expected to do much more. The detective ability of the French police keeps indoors. It wears easy clothes, and knows nothing of the goosestep, but it descends like a flash of lightning on the scene of a recent crime and seldom misses its prey. This is one of the benefits of exact administration. A sufficient body of able subordinates exists to do the work rapidly and well, and the chiefs are numerous enough to be able to see that each individual piece of work is so done. In Bengal not only are the chiefs less numerous, but the police from beginning to end is purely mechanical, the lower ranks are sham sepoys, the upper ones

49 The original text printed this incorrectly as “illegal”.

> consist of gallant, but we cannot help adding, misemployed military men; and an amount of detective ability which would with difficulty procure an inspectorship in rural France is rewarded in Bengal by the appointment of Deputy Inspector General.[50]

It is hardly needful to observe that though the above is related of Bengal, it is equally true of this side of the country. The writer, however, does not confine himself to the subject of police. He observes, regarding the general administration:

> The point in which French Departmental government differs most widely from our *mofussil*[51] administration is with respect to its knowledge of what is going on among the non-criminal classes. Until a Bengali commits an offence, or fails to pay a tax, he is of no interest whatever to the government. A village or city may think as it pleases, its population may increase or fall away, new markets and manufactures may spring up, old ones may decline or altogether disappear, harvest may be superabundant or insufficient, but until the individual is guilty of some overt offence, or the district is on the verge of famine, neither the district nor the individual are considered fit subjects for attention or inquiry on the part of government.[52]

Nay, more, it not unoften happens that the local officials govern the people, as it were, with a vengeance. A high judicial officer in this Presidency was notoriously known to inflict the most cruel persecutions on prisoners in the jail under his charge, simply because of their religious scruples with regard to eating and drinking, and this practice he carried on for years without receiving any check or reprimand. One recent and by no means anti-native ex-Governor, it is said, used to affirm the degree of unpopularity of a public servant to be an index of his efficiency, and only such as could succeed in raising a popular outcry against themselves could count on receiving certain promotion.

The most significant example of the existence of this official trait is furnished by the famine in Orissa,[53] the local officers of which province not only did not know the real condition or feelings of the people, or put any trust in their declarations, but actually based a policy of abstract political economy and inactivity on the supposition that the *mahajans*[54] were villainously concealing grain in order to command high prices, while in reality their customers, the *ryots* (peasants), on whose existence alone

50 The original source of this extract could not be traced.
51 A colloquial term for the countryside.
52 The original source of this extract could not be traced.
53 The Orissa Famine of 1866 had claimed more than a million lives (or about one third of the region's populace).
54 A term used interchangeably for traders, merchants, and moneylenders.

depended their own wealth and profits, were dying by hundreds of mere starvation! Thus does the official mind consider itself possessed of innate wisdom and *a priori* knowledge, and thus despising the native subject and his belongings, conceives it can best preserve the state prestige in the eyes of the people by bringing it home to their business and their bosoms, that its delegates can govern them in defiance of their wishes and their remonstrances. And the repressive influence which the higher functionaries exercise in their well-meaning loftiness is imitated by the lower and ill-paid ones from baser motives, and whoever dares to oppose either party is immediately crushed down with the weight of official displeasure, which also means the active though covert hostility of the circle in and about which the little magnate moves. This sort of thing is not unknown even in the Presidency towns with all their publicity, freedom, and Europeanisation, and it is no wonder therefore that it should be rampant in the close and far *mofussil* devoid of these salutary influences.

Thus then upon the whole, although there are guarantees for personal rights under English rule such as have never existed under any native regime, they are not as yet possessed or enjoyed in that unhampered manner that might be supposed by a superficial observer. Indeed, the taxpayer in India is as yet nobody and his relative position to the public servant is the very reverse of that which it is in England, for instance. We will not surely be told in reply that this is the people's own fault. Patience of wrong is indeed a fault with them, but at present the odds are great against them. Even wealth and intelligence together find it hard to hold their own against bureaucracy and its rebuffs. It is therefore no wonder that they singly or their opposites should be helpless and that a single *pattawala*[55] or a *sahib*'s butler should set a whole village in terror. With time however even this evil may be expected to go out under the progressive English rule, but there can be no doubt that it has existed and does still exist and therefore ought not to be lost sight of in considering the subject under discussion.

IX. Social and political relations between the English government and the people[56]

We now come to the question of official patronage, and of the political and social relations between the governors and the governed. These are the respects in which foreign government, however good, must, from the very nature of the case, present a very unfavourable contrast with native

55 A uniformed peon.
56 Originally published in *Native Opinion*, May 10, 1868.

rule, however bad or imperfect. In a state governed by its own people, the question of patronage has no place except as between one individual and another of the same race. The pressure of taxation is neutralised by the circumstance of the proceeds being spent within the country and amongst the people themselves, whilst social and religious communion and festivities, enjoyed and participated in common by the ruler and the subject alike, reduce the evils of despotic administration to a minimum and take away its sting, making the people feel, as it were by one national touch of nature,[57] that they all form one body politic. Thus it is that there exists a considerable amount of wealth and contentment among the people of Native States as the last Administration Report of the Rajputana Political Agency testifies.[58]

Much of this, however, if not all, is changed in the case of a state or country subject to exotic sway. Foreign rule must bring on its subjects exclusion from places of trust and emolument, a denial of opportunities for acquiring honour and distinction, and a general diminution of their social, religious, and political importance in their own and their neighbours' eyes. But this evil, which is commonly incidental to the condition of a subject people, is aggravated by the very system and almost mechanical symmetry which characterise the constitution of our government. The Mussulman ruler, though perhaps scarcely less alien to the Hindus than his European successor, and without much kindness in him, did not hesitate to raise them to the highest military command or civil post, even when at war with sections of their nation. But the most fatherly of our Governors or Governors-General cannot raise the most deserving native in all India an inch above the grade fixed for the subject people. The army is indeed a sealed department except in its menial ranks to which no native who wishes to serve the state for a higher reward or distinction than the wages of a day labourer need think of aspiring. The same may be said of almost all the other departments except the civil service in its various divisions, which is removed from them but by a single step. The civil posts which are exclusively given to natives are such as Europeans neither can nor will accept. The middle grades are shared in by both classes, with ease by the European and with difficulty by the native, while the highest have been the exclusive heritage of the ruling race. With the help of the Appendix C attached to the Civil Service Memorial

57 An adaptation of a famous line in William Shakespeare's *Troilus and Cressida*: "One touch of nature makes the whole world kin" (Alexander Grant, *The Ethics of Aristotle*, Vol. 1 (London: Longmans, 1866), 256).

58 *Report on the Political Administration of Rajpootana for the Years 1865–6 and 1866–7*, Part I (Calcutta: Foreign Department Press, 1867), 10.

of the Bombay Association to the Secretary of State, we are enabled to give the approximate figures.[59] Excluding the head of government, we find the civil service posts with the salaries attached to them thus distributed between Europeans and natives in the Bombay Presidency:

Distribution of covenanted civil service posts between Europeans and natives

Covenanted			
Number of posts	Monthly salary total aggregate	Value of 115 posts held by Europeans	Value of 1 post held by a native
116	Rs. 1,66,050	Rs. 1,65,350	Rs. 700

Distribution of uncovenanted civil service posts between Europeans and natives

Uncovenanted			
Number of posts	Monthly salary total aggregate	Value of 140 posts held exclusively by Europeans	Value of 673 posts held by both classes
813	Rs. 2,83,420	Rs. 1,37,500	Rs. 1,45,920

It will thus appear that of about four and a half lakhs of rupees debited as salary to government servants in the civil department, only about three quarters of a lakh, i.e., half the value of the appointments which alone natives are allowed to share, goes to them. To this inequality of patronage between the two races we have to add, first, that the list given above is exclusive of the Medical, Political, Military, Ecclesiastical, Marine, Naval, Public Works, Telegraph and Engineering Departments (where natives are but sparsely employed) and, second, that out of the small residue of the uncovenanted civil service, Europeans enjoy a monopoly of most of the better paid appointments. Is it then any exaggeration to say that the share enjoyed by the people in the administration of their country is but as the

59 Bombay Association, *Memorial for Affording Facilities for the Free Admission of the Natives of India into the Covenanted Civil and Medical Services of India* (Bombay: Duftur Ashkara Press, 1868).

crumb that falls from a sumptuous table? And how far is this fact calculated either to flatter the feelings of the people or act as a counterpoise against the foreign character of the administration? Thus, then, in the words of Mr. Davies,[60] Chief Commissioner of Awadh: "There is no greater administrative evil in our system than the manner in which many native officers of ability are, at an early period of life, shorn of all incentive to exertion by the bar set to their promotion."[61] The case is different in Native States in spite of caste exclusivism to which the Official correspondence alludes. We would adduce the following testimony from the Hon'ble Mountstuart Elphinstone:[62]

> Under a Native government, independent of the mutual adaptation of the institutions and the people, there is a connected chain throughout the society, and a free communication between the different parts. Notwithstanding the distinctions of caste, there is no country where men rise with more ease from the lowest rank to the highest. The first Nawab of Awadh was a petty merchant, the first *Peshwa* a village accountant. The ancestors of Holkar were goatherds, and those of Sindhia slaves. All these and many other instances took place within the last century. Promotions from among the common people to all the ranks of civil and military employment short of sovereignty, are of daily occurrence under Native States; and this keeps up the spirit of the people, and in that respect, partially supplies the place of popular institutions. The free intercourse of different ranks also keeps up a sort of circulation and diffusion of such knowledge and such sentiment as exist in the society. Under us, on the contrary, the community is divided into two perfectly distinct and definite bodies, of which the one is torpid and inactive, while all the power seems concentrated in the other.[63]

The amount of this evil, great as it is, is however, matched or shall we say overmatched, by its rank quality. It is bad enough that but a very small share of public employment falls to the lot of the natives compared with the portion of the European, but the comparative terms on which that small

60 Henry Davies (1824–1902) was the Chief Commissioner of Awadh from 1865 to 1871. He would go on to be appointed Lieutenant Governor of the Punjab in 1871.

61 "Correspondence Regarding the Comparative Merits of British and Native Administration in India", 149.

62 Mountstuart Elphinstone (1779–1859) was the diplomat and statesman responsible for subduing and then pacifying the principalities of the Maratha Empire. He served as Governor of Bombay from 1819 to 1827.

63 "Mountstuart Elphinstone to Thomas Hyde Villiers, August 5, 1832", in *Appendix to the Report from the Select Committee of the House of Commons on the Affairs of the East-India Company* (London: J. L. Cox, 1833), 43.

share is obtained or held is even worse. The European has a greater facility in getting an appointment, is fully paid for the work he does, is treated with indulgence, and considers his place, when once obtained, as a rightful possession which no one can or will deprive him of except for the clearest reasons. The case with the native is very different. In the first place, a native aspirant after public honours obtains a situation with difficultly and as a great favour. In the second, the scale of remuneration is reduced even if the work he does should be the same as that performed by a European. Thirdly, he holds office on mere sufferance and his tenure hangs chiefly on the breath of his European superior. However long or faithful his services or whatever his past character and conduct, he is liable to be dismissed, degraded, and disgraced if but an "impression" unfavourable to him creeps into his superior's head – whether it is sound or not, for who dares to examine into what passes in the profound depths of consciousness of great officials. Whatever the moral responsibility of the higher and European officers to government, they hold their subordinates responsible to themselves in a far greater degree, and almost the whole work of administration in the first instance is done by and through the natives. This in itself is a matter for rejoicing though one of necessity, and we would even wish our countrymen in all ranks would perform their tasks, however humble, with alacrity. But in order to secure this result the status of the native public servant stands in need of improvement and recognition, not perhaps in theory but certainly in practice, at least in the majority of instances. There are very few, we believe, who have not had occasion one time or other of their career to feel that they were after all working for mere hire under no sympathetic masters, and that their feelings or their concerns were not of the slightest interest to those above them.

But the evil we complain of is not confined to the limits of the bureau or to strictly official relations of superior and subordinate. It pervades the entire political and social intercourse between the governors and the governed. Of course, a species of equality is supposed to direct this intercourse, but freedom and frankness are conspicuous by their absence, except of course where the parties have a personal esteem for each other. Nothing is supposed to be so acceptable to a European official as the genuine opinion and wishes of the native on every subject that may concern them both or the public at large, and yet when that opinion happens to be disagreeable or opposed to that of the inquirer, its expression is always repressed. We will give an illustration that recently occurred at Poona. A distinguished and highly cultivated European (not a civilian) officer had a friendly visit from the editor of a respectable local native journal. Our contemporary was condescendingly asked what he thought of the address given to Sir Bartle

Frere[64] by the people of Poona (i.e., the officials of the place among whom this one would appear privately to have taken a prominent part). He replied that he approved of it as a whole but thought the tone rather too adulatory.[65] What was the foolish editor's reward for his pains? Why, his host was in an instant flame and fury and told the guest a bit of his mind, hurling a taunt at his nation in some such words as "I knew it before – you natives would always think so – nothing would satisfy you". And the honoured guest was politely ordered away.

This was perhaps too violent an exhibition of the reality but it correctly portrays the actual state of things (under whatever colour it may be commonly veiled) as it obtains on all occasions of political, social, or civic intercourse, whether at the municipal or council boards or any other place or occasion. The people ought to do nothing beyond seconding and adopting the views of the officials as their own and to pay for them in the bargain. If they differ, their fate is unenviable. Of course, there is the great safety valve of appeal – but there is also the stereotyped reply to it. The newspaper press is indeed coming into existence, but the causes already mentioned serve to keep its conductors in dread, and their vaticinations have no great chance of attracting the attention of the official class, unless they partake of the libellous. Owing to the prestige of the ruling race and their belongings, the non-official European is free from these annoyances and is scarcely aware of their existence. Thus has native society an existence and views and feelings and joys and sorrows of its own to which the European is an utter stranger, though it passes for "the public" of British India.

All these causes act and are acted on by the tone of European society generally, and joined to the contempt and jealousy of the native by the independent European, serve to keep open that social gulf which already exists between the two races. Wherever he comes in contact with the European, whether in the public service or out of it, whether as a member of a civic or political body, whether travelling by the railway or the steamship, and even associated with the Christian missionary in teaching or preaching, the position of disadvantage, danger, and disgrace belongs to the native who is thus forcibly reminded of his subject position. Against all this bitter teaching of experience, there is to the ordinary subject little to weigh except the

64 Henry Bartle Frere (1815–84) started as a writer in 1834, rose to be Commissioner of Sindh in 1850 and then member of the Viceregal Council in 1859, before serving as Governor of Bombay from 1861 to 1867.

65 "Farewell Address on Behalf of the Chiefs and Sirdars of the Deccan" commemorated Frere's services to the Presidency (Balkrishna N. Pitale, ed., *The Speeches and Addresses of Sir H. B. E. Frere* (Bombay: n.p., 1870), 375–77).

general security of person and property and the theoretic fairness of professed law. Is this enough?

X. Conclusion[66]

It is time to conclude. The series has been intended, as it must have been easily perceived, to supplement the official correspondence from a native point of view. We are aware our sketch has been very deficient and meagre, but we believe that we have sufficiently indicated the direction in which the supplemental inquiry should be made, if it be made at all, in order to arrive at a fair balancing of the two sides of the question. We have shown what there is to be said for native rule, and also what might be put to the debit side of the British administration of the country. The defects of the former can be easily seen and pointed out because of the simple state of society and organisation that obtains under it; those of the latter are buried within the folds of system and repressed under the weight of bureaucracy. In the one case, the local officers are in sole charge of their districts without the aid or interference of systems and departments, and consequently the content or discontent of the people immediately under them becomes a sure test of their management, and *vox populi* more or less *vox Dei*,[67] unless the central authority is exceptionally bad or careless. In the other, a fact – whether for good or for evil – must be admitted by the central head of a department before it can be called such, and it has to suffer distortions through the medium it passes through according to the tone and temper of the latter, meanwhile the official thoughts, under the shadow of regulations, accusing or excusing each other. The first requires systematisation, the second popularisation. An inquiry into the comparative merits of the two indeed is of no direct use – unless the conclusion is to be acted on; unless the whole country is to be made over to that rule the merits of which might preponderate over the other; unless in short – which is the only alternative that can be believed as possible if not probable under the circumstances – the British policy of annexation is to be justified. Such a sly aim is actually hinted at as a possible intention on the part of the Government of India towards Mysore by Mr. Smollett[68] in his Parliamentary speech on the subject of the

66 Originally published in *Native Opinion*, May 17, 1868.

67 An adaptation of the Latin proverb "*vox populi, vox Dei*" (the voice of the people is the voice of God).

68 Patrick Boyle Smollett (1804–95) was the Conservative member of parliament for Dumbartonshire. He had previously served for three decades in the Madras Presidency, retiring in 1857 as the Collector of Vizagapatam.

official correspondence.[69] But of course, no one seriously believes it and neither do we.

We have not the least doubt that Sir John Lawrence conscientiously believed that the official inquiry would confirm his personal conviction that under British rule, the people of India are very happy. The replies from his own subordinates and the public criticism on them have shown how far the Viceroy was wrong. The theory of unconscious happiness especially is most liable to objection. Few people are satisfied with so little and fewer so grateful for it, as the natives of this country, and we believe we have shown that no mere sentiment of nationality has prevented them from recognising whatever good has come to the Hindus from their foreign rulers. If, therefore, this recognition is not proportioned to the efforts put forth on their behalf or the good intentions which may have prompted them, it is time to inquire how far these efforts have been ill-directed, and whether or not there are any drawbacks on the excellence of the British system, which prevents it from carrying to the door of the humblest *ryot* that administrative bliss it is potentially capable of yielding.

When the official correspondence was published and the subject was being discussed, we inquired of a Parsi friend how it was that, with the advantage of good government, friends and relations in Bombay, and everything else calculated to induce them to emigrate into British territory, his co-religionists in the Gaekwad's dominions put up with the tyranny of the "barbarian of Baroda".[70] He replied that there were no doubt evils to be endured under the native rule, but that the British rule also had its disadvantages, which were felt by those who lived under it, and that therefore passing from the one under the other was not probably so unmixed a good as might at first sight appear. It is not therefore enough for our government to say that the masses of its subjects, *sui si bona norint* (i.e., as Mr. Smollett somewhat humorously but quite correctly renders it, unless they are "great jackasses") are incontestably happier than they have ever been under native

69 *Observations*, Vol. 191, March 27 (London: Hansard, 1868). In his speech, Smollett speculated:

> The Viceroy wanted to have in that compilation of papers, a concentration of opinion on which he might on some future occasion found an appeal to the English people: he wished to have a lever by which he might be enabled to say to them, "If you desire to govern the people of India on the true Benthamite principle of the greatest happiness for the greatest number, the only way in which you can do this is by seizing all the Native States and annexing them to your territory, and by subduing those that are really independent."

70 *The Bombay Gazette*, June 17, 1868, 2. The phrase was originally coined by Dinshah Ardeshir Taleyarkhan, the verbose editor of the *Gujarat Mitra*.

rule, but to make them feel so.[71] There must be a very serious defect indeed in the constitution of the native Indian mind or in that of the British Indian government, when the latter thinks it can make the former incontestably happy and yet the happiness escapes the very subject in whom and for whom it dwells. It is evident then the people must, to some extent at least, go along with the government instead of the latter doing everything for them according to its own judgement.

But how are the people's wishes and views to be arrived at when no social intercourse exists between the rulers and the ruled? We believe the government, by its generous policy of education, has created a certain means to effect this most desirable purpose. The opinion of the average educated native, when uninfluenced by hope or fear, we believe to be as correct an index of the views and the wishes of the people as a thermometer is of atmospheric heat. He, the educated native, is by means of his education in a position to look at things from a European point of view, while the fact of his birth and social relations and the sympathetic hold the country's traditions naturally have on his mind, enable him to conceive and feel how it strikes his own countrymen. In short, he is sufficiently Europeanised to be free from the most worthless prejudices of the natives, while he is enough of a native to resist exceptionable exotic influences. When therefore he is not bigotedly wedded to any given creed or theory, his utterances may fairly be taken to represent the views of his countrymen at large. It is thus constituted that we have here spoken and always do profess to speak. Of English rule in this country, let us then repeat what we have said at the commencement of the subject, *viz.*, that

> not only have we ourselves been brought up with tastes and ideas which cannot but make us like the rule we live under in preference to every other, even though indigenous, but the blessing of education we have received has taught us to set a peculiar value on England's supremacy over our country – a value that in our opinion is fully justified by the expectation of great national ends which the connection is calculated to serve, and of which signs may be perceived by any man that chooses to look about him and reflect. But the firmer this conviction, the more anxious ought we to be to see the system of government we cherish so much, free from defects and shortcomings which practically detract from its merits and prevent the full amount of good it is calculated to produce.

What these defects and shortcomings are, we have attempted to show. They are in brief: a most costly administration, vexatious, uncertain and dear purchased justice, caste exclusivism of the ruling race, and a close and

71 *Observations*, Vol. 191, March 27.

high-handed official bureaucracy. It is a mistake to call these "little annoyances":[72] if they are little in the eyes of great men, they are great to little ones who count by the million. It is our firm conviction that in the course of time, even these will disappear. The English rule is an eminently growing institution. The connection began with the very humble and sordid motive of monetary gain. War and negotiation followed. But as soon as they were conscious of possessing a territory and subjects, our Leadenhall Street[73] rulers felt and expressed anxiety for their enlightenment and welfare. And now that they are what they once eagerly longed to be – "a nation in India"[74] – they equal and surpass any set of rulers in their good intentions and liberality towards the subject people. They may not be generous by fits and starts or from the merest instinct, but their calculating regularity makes us certain of whatever steps we may have gained. The most friendly of their Governors may not be able to raise any of us an inch higher than the grade fixed by law – but it is equally true that the most unfriendly one cannot easily depress us below the regulation level.

Of all their gifts, however, we value most two, *viz.*, a liberal and enlightened system of education and a free press. With the aid of these possessions – we had almost said blessings – we are enabled not only to distinguish between what is good and what is bad in our government (instead of ignorantly disliking, as otherwise we should perhaps have done, everything appertaining to it), but also to take and even demand an intelligent and loyal share in the administration of our country's affairs. And it is with their aid that everything else needful for the regeneration of the country will be effected. It is through the enlightened agencies created and set to work by the British government itself that England will be enabled to avoid the common fates of governing nations and to discharge her trust to her own glory and to our welfare and satisfaction. As to native rule in India at the present day, it is enough to observe that it must be what the direct and indirect influences of the British government itself would tend to make it; of the past it is not needful to speak.

72 "Correspondence Regarding the Comparative Merits of British and Native Administration in India", 1. The original memorandum has it as "petty annoyances".

73 A reference to East India House, the headquarters of the East India Company, which was located at Leadenhall Street in London.

74 A reference to the famous 1689 missive from the Directors of the East India Company directing their officers to acquire dominion in India (James Mill, *The History of British India*, Vol. 1 (London: Baldwin, 1820), 108).

II

Introduction to the first edition (1891)

I read with interest the series of "Letters to an Indian Raja", by A Political Recluse, as they appeared from week to week in the *Indian Spectator*, and I have now much pleasure in writing a few words by way of introduction to them in their collected form. It is not necessary that I should express my entire concurrence with the author upon all the important questions with which he deals. It is sufficient for me to state my belief that they form a valuable contribution to Indian political knowledge, and that they will be read with profit not only by the feudatory Rajas, to whom they were addressed, but by all serious thinkers in British India on the great subjects of which they treat.

The writer is, I regret to say, personally unknown to me. He is, I believe, exactly what he signs himself, a political recluse, who after a life of practical acquaintance with the problems with which he deals, has now devoted a strict retirement to recording the conclusions at which he has arrived. His views are the result of actual experience in the administration of a Native State. That practical experience has led him to take up a position halfway between the old school of Indian thinkers, who would let things rest as they are, and the new school who would like to see everything changed within a single generation. I confess that his attitude of moderation strongly commends itself to my mind, and it is because I believe this attitude is the wisest one for Indian reformers at the present moment, that (without endorsing all their views) I commend the following "Letters" to the perusal of thoughtful men, alike in India and England.

The Political Recluse brings to his task a knowledge of administration, obtained both in the British and Native territories, such as few men now possess. As an educational officer in the Western Presidency, and for some years in the Secretariat, he had the opportunity of thoroughly studying our British departmental methods. To this he joins reminiscences in early life of indigenous rule in a small principality, and experience as a judicial officer, in a position of trust, in an important Native State. His political views may possibly be found tinged with a spirit of pessimism, consequent on the grave defects in administration which have come under his notice, and with a certain despondency, arising out of the inconsistent lines pursued by some of his countrymen with regard to political and social progress. The religious views expressed in these "Letters" have also a deep interest for those who desire to gain insight into the inner spiritual life of a cultivated Indian thinker of the present day.

To the feudatory chiefs of India, these "Letters", addressed to a typical Maharaja, ought to prove of great value. The writer advises them in the capacity of a candid friend: but as a friend who is sensitive for their honour, and who earnestly desires to uphold the integrity of their power. If his counsels in regard to the internal administration of a Native State and with reference to the relations which should be maintained by a Native State with neighbouring feudatory princes and with the British power, are laid to heart by any young Maharaja, that Maharaja might make his territories a model state in India. Not the least valuable section of his work is directed to the establishment of a sounder connection between the *darbar* of such a state and the accredited Agents of the Government of India. Here, too, the writer speaks from personal knowledge; and his views, whether accepted in their entirety or not, are worthy of careful attention by our own Political Department, not less than by the feudatory chiefs.

I need only add that in their present permanent form, the "Letters" could not be more appropriately dedicated than to the princes and chiefs of India. The editor and proprietor of the *Indian Spectator*, the journal in which they originally appeared, has won for himself a unique position of usefulness, standing as he does between the peoples and princes of India on the one hand, and between the more conservative and the more advanced political schools of native thought on the other. Mr. Malabari's visit to England last year, made independently of any Congress or other organisation, but simply in the interests of Indian social reform, has proved in a conspicuous manner how great may be the results of one man's self-devotion to a righteous cause. It is no small advantage to these "Letters" that they go forth under such auspices.

W. W. HUNTER

III

Preface to the second edition (1919)

These *Letters to an Indian Raja* were from the pen of the late Mr. Narayan Mahadev Parmanand. They originally appeared as from "A Political Recluse" in the columns of the *Indian Spectator*, edited by the late Mr. Behramji M. Malabari, and attracted considerable attention. After the series had been completed in those columns, Mr. Malabari and several other friends and admirers of the author – among them Sir William Wedderburn – induced him to publish them in a book form. Sir William Hunter, well known for his scholarship and as editor of the *Imperial Gazetteer of India*, who, after a distinguished career as a member of the Indian Civil Service, retired to England and contributed every week till his death his brilliant letters on Indian affairs to the *Times* in London, wrote for the publication an appreciative Introduction. The author of the *Letters*, however, chose to remain anonymous, because he disliked publicity.

The present is the second edition of the *Letters*, which deserve to be read with particular interest at this stage in the history of India, when the question of progressive and popular changes in the constitution of British India and the government of Indian states has engaged the serious attention of both the official and non-official public, both in this country and in England, and reform in the administration on more or less democratic lines is about to become an accomplished fact.

I have been asked by the present publisher of these *Letters* to write a few words by way of preface to this publication, because I had not only the privilege of intimate acquaintance with the author and almost daily sitting at his feet and learning, but each of these letters was, after composition, read out to me by the author before it was sent to the *Indian Spectator* for publication.

Mr. Narayan Mahadev Parmanand was born on the 3rd of July 1838 at Mangaon in the Sawantwadi State. He came to Bombay in 1848 and received his education first in the Elphinstone Institution and afterwards in the Elphinstone College, where he had as his fellow students the late Mr. Justice Ranade and Sir Ramkrishna Bhandarkar. His literary talents, especially his proficiency in English, attracted the notice of the late Mr. J. P. Hughlings, who was then professor of English Literature in the Elphinstone College. After completing his college education and serving for a short time in the Educational Department, Mr. Parmanand became the first editor of the English columns of *Indu Prakash*, an Anglo-Marathi weekly, started by the late Mr. Vishnu Parashram Shastri, the champion of widow marriage. Mr. Parmanand's able conduct of the English columns of the *Indu Prakash* led to his selection as the editor of the *Native Opinion*, another English weekly of the time, by its proprietor and general editor, the late Honourable Rao Saheb Vishwanath Narayan Mandalik. For nearly four years Mr. Parmanand edited *Native Opinion* with striking ability and vigour. Sir Bartle Frere, who was then Governor of Bombay, was one of the most careful readers of the paper.

In 1868, when Mr. Parmanand had made his mark as one of the sober, trenchant, and constructive critics of the [Bombay] administration, he was offered a post by one of the chiefs of Kathiawar. That offer came to him under the following circumstances. In a footnote to Letter No. XII the author has referred to a highly educated Bengali who had become a *sanyasi* (ascetic) and taken the name of Anandashrama Swami as a member of his religious order. It is stated in that footnote that the said *swami*, "a very interesting and singular character", travelled through Northern and Central India and at last "reached one of the leading states of Kathiawar. Here he saw instances of misrule and exposed them in newsletters to a paper published in Bombay" – that was *Native Opinion*, edited by Mr. Parmanand. "Their appearance attracted attention and produced excitement and curiosity in the state." The writer of the newsletters having been discovered, the *swami* (preceptor) was taken before the chief, who threatened to send him to jail if he should persist in writing against the administration of the state. The chief, impressed by the courage and candour of the *swami*, as well as by his ability, offered him the post of *dewan* in the state. The *swami* declined the offer on the ground that the rules of his order prohibited him from holding any secular office, and recommended the chief to employ a competent man. The chief agreed and the *swami* was requested to make a selection. His choice fell on the author of these notes, whose upright character and ability had struck him when the *swami* had been in Bombay. Mr. Parmanand was accordingly appointed by the chief to a high judicial post in his state. But after having held that appointment for about a year and done his duty fearlessly, he found his position intolerable on account of intrigue, a frequent and common experience in Native States. He returned to Bombay in 1869.

Sir William Wedderburn, who had known Mr. Parmanand by his writings in the *Native Opinion* and who was then Registrar of the Bombay High

Court, appointed him to a well-paid post in that court. When Sir William became Judicial Secretary to the Government of Bombay in 1872, he took Mr. Parmanand into the Secretariat. He served there till 1883, when illness compelled him first to take long leave and at last to retire on pension. For ten years after 1883 – i.e. till September 1893 when he breathed his last – he was an invalid, but his mind was active to the day of his death. During that period he contributed frequently to the papers, and interested himself in all public questions.

One of the ablest, most intellectual and, above all, spiritual Indians of his time, Mr. Parmanand spent himself in the service of his country. By nature simple, quiet, and unassuming, he avoided publicity and preferred to work silently and unostentatiously. There was not a single question of public moment, political, religious, or social, in which he did not interest himself and which he did not seek to help. The late Mr. Justice Ranade, the late Mr. Justice Telang, the late Mr. Sorabjee Shapurjee Bengalee, and Sir Ramkrishna Bhandarkar were among his most ardent admirers and frequently met him at his residence, which became a sort of club for the discussion of public questions. Saintly in his character, he was loved by all who came in contact with him and his counsel was respected as that of a political sage. So great was the respect paid to him that he used to be called "Uncle Parmanand" by all who knew him more or less intimately. Sir William Wedderburn was to the last one of his admirers.

When Sir William was a district officer, on almost every occasion when he visited Bombay he would see Mr. Parmanand and exchange views. When Sir William acted in 1884–85 as a Judge of the High Court at Bombay, he made it a point to visit Mr. Parmanand almost every Friday evening and consult him on Indian questions. The late Mr. Sorabjee Shapurjee Bengalee, who is remembered to this day as the Lord Shaftesbury of India for the factory laws enacted in this country upon his initiative and his fight for redress of the hardships of labourers in the Indian mills, was brought into contact with Mr. Parmanand in 1871, when the abuses in the municipal administration of Bombay led to great excitement, and there were crowded public meetings of all classes of citizens in the Town Hall to demand a radical reform by legislation in the Municipal constitution of this City. Mr. Bengalee was one of the leaders of the movement for Municipal reform, and was instrumental with others in starting a Bombay Ratepayers' Association, which rendered yeoman's service to the cause until Bombay obtained from the Legislature a reformed and popular Municipal Constitution in 1873. The representations addressed to the Government by the Association were nearly all drafted by Mr. Parmanand, who, I was informed by Mr. Bengalee, assisted the Association with his advice and suggestions and contributed by his silent labours to the success of its mission. The late Honorable Mr.

Morarjee Goculdas, one of the leading public men and merchants of Bombay during the regime of Sir Richard Temple as Governor of this Presidency, was another admirer of Mr. Parmanand. Mr. Morarjee started in 1877 a Famine Relief Fund to relieve the famine-stricken in the Deccan and in almost all his plans and measures he consulted Mr. Parmanand. Mr. Parmanand was one of the most active workers of the late Bombay Association; he was one of the founders of the Theistic Church in Bombay known as the Prarthana Samaj; he among others assisted in the widow marriage movement led by the late Vishnu Parshram Shastri. The two greatest social reformers this Presidency has produced – the late Mr. Karsandas Mulji and the late Mr. Madhavdas Raghunathdas–were among his best friends and turned to him constantly for guidance and counsel in their sorest moment of trial and persecution.

What most appealed to all who came in contact with Mr. Parmanand and earned him their affection was the simple piety of his godly life. To religious reform he attached the greatest importance and, soberly practical as he was as a politician – the late Mr. Justice Telang used in his moments of well-meant humour to call him "the silent politician" – he held firmly to his creed that all political reform must have for its root and basis "the moral strength and guidance which religion imparts". He makes that the forefront of his counsel to Indian Rajas in these *Letters*, which he almost begins with the pregnant remark that "without religion man is but the creature of a moment; with it he is the child of eternity", and that, "without the consolations and aspirations" which faith in the Supreme Lawgiver and Love alone gives and ennobles, "government would be a curse, society would be on the road to ruin".

Mr. Parmanand's whole life was regulated by his abiding sense of that faith. He was one of the leading members of the Prarthana Samaj and its interests were his prime care. Though it has been the practice in the Samaj since its foundation in 1867 for its leading members to preach from its pulpit at its weekly and other services, Mr. Parmanand never appeared in the pulpit and never delivered any sermon, because he was of too retiring a disposition to court publicity of any character in any sphere of life. But his life was itself a sermon and no member of the Samaj was respected so highly for his holiness as he was. Humble, loving all, loved by all, ready and regular in the performance of even the most trivial duties which he thought he owed to his fellow beings, he carried about him the edifying example of a man, who in all the walks of life lived in communion with God and so held to his fellowship with men. Though he was by no means blessed with the riches of the world, he never spared of his humble means to help the poor and distressed, especially afflicted and starving Hindu widows and orphans.

Such was the man, whose *Letters to an Indian Raja* are now republished. In writing them the author had in his mind one of the leading of our Indian princes, who had a few years previously completed his minority and education and been installed on the *gaddi* of his ancestors. The Indian prince referred to in the first of these letters has since their first publication proved one of the enlightened and progressive of the rulers of our Native States. He had great respect for and confidence in the author of these letters, and he sought several times Mr. Parmanand's views on questions that related to the government of his state.

The problems of administration in Native States, which are dealt with by Mr. Parmanand in these letters, are still the same in substance and in point of principle and practice that they were when those letters appeared originally in the columns of the *Indian Spectator* nearly thirty years ago. Whether our Native States have advanced materially in the improvement of their administration on the lines of constitutional government and popular rights; whether secrecy of rule, intrigue, and the eyewash of office have disappeared substantially and smoothed the path of well-ordered, regular, and industrious rule – these are questions which have become of pressing importance in these days when autocracy stands condemned and bureaucracy is severely criticised. Some of these states have on the whole a good account to give of the progressive character of their administrations. But though something has been done, much remains to do. Native States can no longer be in the *purdah* (veil) in which they were wont to live years ago. Some of our Indian princes, enlightened and aspiring nobly, have expressed themselves in public in clear terms with dignified patriotism as being in warm sympathy with the legitimate political aspirations of the people in British India. That is a healthy and promising sign of the times. At such a momentous and hopeful juncture in the history of India's forward movement to take her place as one of the leading nations of the world, under the guidance and inspiration of England, our Indian princes are sure to find in these *Letters to an Indian Raja* much that is highly suggestive and inspiring for them to follow.

N. G. CHANDAVARKAR
Bombay
November 8th, 1918

IV

Obituary in the *Indian Spectator* (1893)[1]

Another worker in the field of *Aryavarta*[2] gone to his rest! This time it is Narayan Mahadev Parmanand, held in respect verging on reverence by select circles in Maharashtra, Gujarat, Kathiawar, and Sindh, who delighted to address him as Mama. A selfless being has been absorbed in the Universal self of the Upanishads – our Parmanand has reached the source and centre of supreme Happiness, implied by his earthly designation. How wise, how tender and yet how courageous this Hindu of Hindus was always: above prejudice in things small and great; the same to all men, in all things, at all times. In early manhood he seems to have been associated with almost all progressive movements in Bombay. And although stricken down before his day and condemned to a bed of pain, he yet remained the same to his friends a trusty guide, adviser, referee, arbiter; a sort of buffer between the too aggressive and the too timid of his race.

I met him first, a few years ago, when Mama was only a name, a tradition. But how kindly he took to me! In a very short time he came to be the best contributor to the columns of the *Indian Spectator.* I could trust him entirely, whether in town or out of it. With all his increasing ailments Mama continued to write so long as he could hold his pen. He then took to scribbling in pencil; gave that up for dictating; and when voice and hand both failed, he resorted to pencil jottings. Very valuable were his hints to me; but for hints or paragraphs or articles it was always a struggle to get him to disclose his ownership or to accept a modest honorarium. Well could such a man afford to be poor and obscure! In this respect I have learnt not a little from N. M. Parmanand.

As a publicist Mama was a whole man. To him political progress was not the be-all and end-all of our existence. Politics claimed only a part of

1 Originally published in the *Indian Spectator*, September 17, 1893. The author was Behramji Malabari.

2 An allusion to the Indian landmass. Literally, the term means the land (*varta*) of the nobles (*Aryas*).

his homage. And yet, which of our exclusive politicians surpassed Parmanand in sagacity and force of character? He had a firmer grain than Telang, probably a shrewder sense of the fitness of things than Nulkar, and decidedly more tolerance than that veteran, Vishvanath Mandalik. Of late, he began to be puzzled and bewildered at the one-sided activity of his countrymen, and he deplored their want of courage to recognise and eradicate the inherent defects of society. On this subject, Nulkar, Bhandarkar, Parmanand, and Telang seemed to be of one mind. Each of them remonstrated with the more eager of our English friends; Parmanand was perhaps the most outspoken in taunting them with the results of one-sided advocacy and foretelling still more deplorable results.

I was much with him during his last illness. His bodily sufferings were at times insupportable; it seemed as if the imprisoned spirit wanted to escape by a violent effort. At such times his mind used to wander. I tried to catch him at these troubled intervals, to see how much a man would look and talk with his body on the rack and his mind unhinged. A scene of martyrdom like this has somewhat of a fascination for me. But, curiously I never found Mama other than he had been to me – tender and true in personal matters, lucid and logical in discussing public questions. He talked in faint whispers and was easily tired. But for me his intellect remained unclouded to the end. Only the day before his death, after hours of unconsciousness, succeeded by incoherent speech, he recognised me instantly, asked me to put my ear close to his lips and went through the pros and cons of a successful Viceroyalty. "I care not two straws", he whispered, after going over the familiar ground, "who comes out as Viceroy. He can do little unless India is secured a right measure of financial justice in regard to all imperial enterprises at and beyond her frontiers." He urged me – never to let go my hold on that subject. It was practically his last message to India; whom this noble invalid loved with a burning, consuming love – "Oh if I had a little strength" – he used to cry out when thinking of her wrongs, self-inflicted and inflicted by others, and this message he committed to me with perhaps his last breath. After a sip of water he recovered strength only to add – "Now I must say goodbye to you – I say it with infinite regret." I whispered a promise to look in again at which he smiled wistfully. That was the last I saw and spoke with Mama alive; and around him, the dear ones who had given up everything to minister to his wants, wondered how he could be so clear, so collected with me, who, a few minutes before, had been so lazy and incoherent, and would be so again a few minutes after.

Next time I went to Girgaon, it was with a serious misgiving, and my worst fears were confirmed before I reached the station. I found Mama already gone to the rest he had so longed for and which he so needed, with the loving children and the devoted wife, now a *sati* (widow) in the original sense, busy with the last sad rites due to the head of the house. Friends came in one after another, as I stood there gazing at his placid features. The funeral service, or rather the farewell prayer, given by Dr. Bhandarkar, was simple but impressive to a degree. It was said in Marathi, so that all might follow it. Everything was quiet and orderly till within a minute of the removal. What a contrast this to some other funerals I have attended, with the heartless tittle-tattle and the hollow jargon muttered by hirelings, paid for so much by the hour! I accompanied the mourners up to Sonapur Lane, where I left the eminent "Political Recluse", whose death causes a void not likely to be filled by any twenty of his better-known, more pushing countrymen. In many respects, N. M. Parmanand was one of the wisest and bravest of the Hindus I have known.

Index